The Path of the Worshipful Servants
to the Garden of the Lord of All the Worlds

[Minhāj al-ʿĀbidīn ilā Jannati Rabbi 'l-ʿĀlamīn]

The Path of the Worshipful Servants
to the Garden of the Lord of All the Worlds

[Minhāj al-ʿĀbidīn ilā Jannati Rabbi 'l-ʿĀlamīn]

IMĀM ABŪ ḤĀMID AL-GHAZĀLĪ
TRANSLATED FROM THE ARABIC BY MUHTAR HOLLAND

AL-BAZ PUBLISHING, INC.
FT. LAUDERDALE, FLORIDA

Surā al-Ikhlāṣ - Q.112

Cover photography: Robin Roslund - www.photofl.com
Cover Design: Dryden Design, Houston, Texas
C over Preparation: DesignbyIndigo.com, Fort Lauderdale, Florida

Body text set in Ghazali and Jilani fonts by Al-Baz Publishing, Inc.

Printed on acid-free paper

Library of Congress
Catalog Card Number: 2011921727

First Edition February 2011

ISBN: 978-1-882216-26-0

Published by:

Al-Baz Publishing, Inc.
1516 NE 38th Street
Oakland Park, FL 33334, U.S.A.
(425) 891-5444
E-mail: albaz@bellsouth.net

Printed and bound in the United States of America by Sheridan Books, Inc.

Contents

Acknowledgments

All praise is due to Allāh, the Beneficent, the Merciful!

We bear witness that there is no god except Allāh, and that Muḥammad is the Messenger of Allāh!

Our Lord, thank You for giving us this wholesome task!

Grateful thanks to Muhtar Holland for devoting years of his life to translating these works; may Allāh bless him! Thanks also to the many who have helped make this publication possible, among them the following:

Nadeem Syed and his group of friends, may Allāh reward them.

Rashid and Mahomed Raidhan

Audria Gardner for the cover preparation

Hani Nimr for the plate from Jerusalem with the Surā

Translator's Introduction

First and foremost, I wish to pay personal tribute to Imām al-Ghazālī (mayAllāh be well pleased with him). As a non-Muslim university student and then lecturer in the field of Islāmic studies, I had acquired a superficial knowledge of the Imām's life and work, but it was only in the mid-to-late 1960's that I really "discovered" *Ihyā' 'Ulūm ad-Dīn* [Revival of the Religious Sciences], his *magnum opus*. At that stage in my life, I would express my view of religion by saying: "If I ever embraced a religion outwardly, it would be Islām, for I am inwardly convinced that Almighty God is One and that Muḥummad is His Messenger." For a variety of reasons, I resisted a growing urge to profess my Islāmic faith openly, but those reasons gradually ceased to prevail. One very important factor in dispelling my resistance was undoubtedly the wise influence of Imām al-Ghazālī (may Allāh be well pleased with him), and I feel sure that his spiritual presence was there among the living witnesses to my public testimony of faith in 1969.

Shortly after declaring myself a Muslim, I felt moved to translate *Duties of Brotherhood*, part of Book 15 of Imām al-Ghazālī's *Ihyā' 'Ulūm ad-Dīn*. My translation was eventually published in 1975, and so began my career as a translator. I often say with a smile: "The author of *Duties of Brotherhood* has come to be my Elder Brother, guiding me from one part of the world to another, and helping me survive on translation work as a full-time profession!"

However sincere, my own appreciation of the venerable Imām may seem rather modest. Let me therefore assure the reader that his inestimable worth has been extolled in far more glowing terms. As reported by Aflākī, for instance, Jalāl ad-Dīn Rūmī (may Allah sanctify his spirit) once said: "Imām Muḥammad al-Ghazālī has purified the ocean of science in the world of the angels. He has raised its standard high. He has become the guide of the universe and the sage of mortal beings."[1]

[1] See: J. S. Trimingham. *The Sufi Orders in Islam*. Oxford University Press, London, 1971, p.52.

For a lengthy account of the many works by Imām al-Ghazālī, the subjects covered in those works, and a selection of books and articles devoted to his biography and his literary compositions, I recommend the article by D. B. Macdonald in Encyclopaedia of Islam.[2]
As for the work entitled *Minhāj al-Ābidīn ilā Jannati Rabbi 'l-Ālamīn* [The Path of the Worshipful Servants to the Garden of the Lord of All the Worlds], it is the very last book composed by Imām al-Ghazālī. The author was under no illusion as to the nature of this path:

> It is indeed a rugged path and a hard road, fraught with many obstacles, serious hardships, remote distances, enormous difficulties, frequent hindrances and impediments. It is beset with deadly perils and interruptions, abounding in enemies and highway robbers, and offering very few companions and followers. This is exactly how it needs to be, since it is the path to the Garden of Paradise....

He regretted that his earlier works had proved "too abstruse for the understanding of the common folk, who consequently found fault with them, and wallowed in what they did not comprehend about them." He obviously felt an urgent need to bequeath one very special handbook for the spiritual traveller, containing concise yet comprehensive guidance in the clearest possible manner. As he tells us:

> I therefore made humble supplication to the One who holds in His hand the creation and the commandment, beseeching Him to make it possible for me to compose a book—one that would meet with unanimous approval, and the reading of which would result in positive benefit.
>
> That request of mine was granted by the One who responds to the distressed when he calls unto Him. He made me privy, by His gracious favour, to the mysteries involved, and He inspired me with a marvellous arrangement, the like of which I did not recall in any of the previous compositions dealing with the secrets of religious practices. This is the arrangement I am applying to the present work, so I must say: "Enabling grace comes only through Allāh [*bi'llahi 't-tawfīq*]!"

This English translation is based on the Arabic text presented in a recently printed edition, under the title:

Sirāj at-Ṭālibīn [The Lamp of the Seekers] by Shaikh Daḥlān al-Kadīrī, commentary on *Minhāj al-ʿĀbidīn* [The Path of the Worshipful Servants]

2 Also published in *Shorter Encyclopaedia of Islam*. E. J. Brill, Leiden, Netherlands, 1961: art. AL-GHAZALI.

by Imām al-Ghazālī, 2 vols., Dār al-Fikr, Beirut, Lebanon, A.H. 1416/1996 C.E.

Shaikh Daḥlān's extensive commentary (almost a thousand pages long) is indeed a useful "lamp," a most helpful of light for the translator. May Allāh reward him for his valuable labour. May Allāh reward all those worshipful servants of His who have assisted me in this work of translation, which I regard as a very special privilege.

Muhtar Holland
October 2000

Concerning the Author

Abū Ḥāmid Muḥammad ibn Muḥammad ibn Muḥammad ibn Aḥmad aṭ-Ṭūsī al-Ghazālī was born in A.H. 405/1058 C.E., and his earthly life ended in A.H. 505/1111 C.E. As the surname "aṭ-Ṭūsī" indicates, his birthplace was the Iranian town of Ṭūs.

For the Western reader, it may be helpful to note that al-Ghazālī was a small boy in 1066 C.E., the famous date of the Battle of Hastings. The Norman conquest of England would hardly have caused a stir in Ṭūs, but it did contribute to a shift in the balance of power between Christian Europe and the Islāmic world. It was during al-Ghazālī's lifetime that the First Crusade was launched, and Jerusalem was captured from the Muslims in 1099 C.E.

At the time of al-Ghazālī's birth, the Seljuq Turks had assumed a leading role in the Islāmic world. As well as defending Islām against the infidels from without, they were in conflict with powerful and dangerous schismatics, notably the Fāṭimid Shī'a of Egypt. The Shī'a saw in their leader something far more autocratic than a custodian of the Law who was himself governed by it. For them, the leader was himself the Law, since he was in receipt of infallible divine guidance. Their doctrines undermined the whole traditional basis of the main Islāmic community.

In response to the Fāṭimid challenge, the Seljuqs initiated an ambitious educational program. A vizier called Niẓām al-Mulk founded colleges in the major cities of the Seljuq domain, including Nishāpūr, where al-Ghazālī became a student. He proved a brilliant scholar in Islāmic jurisprudence *[fiqh]* and theology *[kalām]*, and was eventually appointed professor at the celebrated Niẓāmiyya University in Baghdād. As a powerful weapon in the ideological warfare with the Fāṭimids, he enjoyed favor in the highest circles.

The Crusaders and the Shī'a were not the only enemies of traditional Islām. Another threat came from the philosophers, with their tendency to put human reason above the belief in divine revelation, on which the Islāmic community was founded. After making a profound study of philosophy, Imām al-Ghazālī delivered a fatal blow to its practitioners, in a work entitled *The Incoherence of the Philosophers*.

Despite his glittering success, Imām al-Ghazālī was inwardly dissatisfied, so he abandoned his career for the life of hardship, abstinence and devotion to worship. During ten years of wandering, he experienced a spiritual transformation, in which the Truth came to him at last, as something received rather than acquired. Blessed with an inner certainty, he then applied his outstanding faculties and vast learning to the task of revitalizing the whole Islāmic tradition. Through his direct personal contacts, and through his many writings, he showed how every element in that tradition could and should be turned to its true purpose. That purpose was to help the believer to live a life devoted to the service of Allāh, the One Almighty God, in constant remembrance of Him, and in preparation for the Life Hereafter.

Like most Muslims of his time, Imām al-Ghazālī wrote mainly in classical Arabic, though some of his books were written in the Persian language. His *magnum opus* is aptly entitled "The Revival of the Religious Sciences *[Iḥyā᾿ ʿUlūm ad-Dīn]*." In its four volumes, the author deals with every aspect of the outer and inner life of the Muslim. The first volume covers the Islāmic forms of worship: ritual prayers, fasting, pilgrimage and so on. The second considers the behavior of the Muslim as member of a community of believers. The third treats of the perils of the soul, and the fourth is devoted to the means of salvation. Largely because of this monumental work, he came to be known as *Ḥujjat al-Islām*, "the Proof of Islām."

May Allāh bestow His mercy upon him!

The Path of the Worshipful Servants
to the Garden of the Lord of All the Worlds

[Minhāj al-ʿĀbidīn ilā Jannati Rabbi ʾl-ʿĀlamīn]

Preface

In the Name of Allāh, the All-Merciful, the All-Compassionate
[*Bismi'llāhi 'r-Raḥmāni 'r-Raḥīm*]

It was the righteous and ascetic jurist [*faqīh*], Shaikh ʿAbd al-Malik (may Allāh grant him forgiveness) who said:

"This concise book was dictated to me by my most splendid Shaikh, the ascetic, fortunate and successful Imām, the Proof of Islām [*Ḥujjat al-Islām*], the Adornment of the Religion [*Zain ad-Dīn*], the Honour of the Community [*Sharaf al-Umma*], Abū Ḥāmid Muḥammad ibn Muḥammad ibn Muḥammad al-Ghazālī aṭ-Ṭūsī (may Allāh sanctify his spirit, and may Allāh exalt his degree in the Garden of Paradise).

"It is the very last book that he composed, and none received it from him by way of dictation, except the special élite of his companions."

Author's Introduction

Praise be to Allāh, the Sovereign [*al-Malik*], the Wise [*Ḥakīm*], the Generous [*al-Jawād*], the Noble [*al-Karīm*], the Glorious [*al-ʿAzīz*], the All-Compassionate [*ar-Raḥīm*], the One who created the human being in the fairest stature,[1] and created the heavens and the earth with His Power, and arranged all matters in the two abodes [of this world and the Hereafter] with His Wisdom, and did not create the jinn and humankind except for His worshipful service.[2] The path toward Him is evident to the aspiring travellers, and the signpost to Him is clearly visible to those who look, but Allāh causes whom He will to go astray, and guides aright whomever He will,

> and He knows best the rightly guided.
> *wa Huwa Aʿlamu bi'l-muhtadīn.* (6:117)

May His blessing be upon the Chieftain of the Messengers [*Sayyid al-Mursalīn*], and on the righteous, good and pure members of his family, and may He grant them peace and honour until the Day of Judgment.

You must realize, O my brethren (may Allāh favour you and me with His good pleasure), that worshipful service [*ʿibāda*] is the fruit of knowledge [*ʿilm*], the benefit of life [*ʿumr*], the income of strong servants, the stock-in-trade of the saints [*awliyāʾ*], the path of the truly devout, the allotted portion of the mighty, the goal of those endowed with aspiration, the emblem of the noble, the vocation of real men, and

[1] An allusion to the verse [*āya*] of the Qurʾān:

> Surely We created the human being in the fairest stature.
> *la-qad khalqna 'l-insāna fī aḥsani taqwīm.* (95:4)

[2] An allusion to the verse [*āya*] of the Qurʾān:

> I did not create jinn and mankind except to worship Me.
> *wa mā khalaqtu 'l-jinna wa 'l-insa illā li-yaʿbudū-n.* (51:56)

the choice of those with faculties of vision. It is the way of good fortune and the path [*minhāj*] of the Garden of Paradise.

Allāh (Exalted is He) has told us:

> And I am your Lord, so worship Me.
> *wa Ana Rabbu-kum fa-'ʿbudū-n.* (21:92)

He has also said (Exalted is He):

> Behold, this is a reward for you.
> *inna hādhā kāna la-kum jaẓā'an*
> Your endeavour has found acceptance.
> *wa kāna saʿyu-kum mashkūrā.* (76:22)

We therefore looked into the subject of worshipful service, and made a careful study of its path, from its beginnings to its destinations, which are the desired goals of its travellers. It is indeed a rugged path and a hard road, fraught with many obstacles, serious hardships, remote distances, enormous difficulties, frequent hindrances and impediments. It is beset with deadly perils and interruptions, abounding in enemies and highway robbers, and offering very few companions and followers. This is exactly how it needs to be, since it is the path of the Garden of Paradise, and this represents a confirmation of the saying of the Prophet (Allāh bless him and give him peace):

> The Garden of Paradise is indeed surrounded by things that are repugnant [*makārih*], while the Fire of Hell is surrounded by objects of lustful desire [*shahawāt*].

He also said (Allāh bless him and give him peace):

> The Garden of Paradise is indeed a rugged ground on a hill, while the Fire of Hell is indeed a smooth ground in a sheltered courtyard.

Then, in addition to all of that, the servant [of the Lord] is weak, the time is difficult, and religious commitment is subject to retrogression. There is little leisure and much preoccupation. Life is short, and there is incapacity in work. The critic is perceptive, and the appointed term is near. The journey is long, and worshipful obedience [*ṭāʿa*] is the necessary provision, but it is transitory, so there is no replacement for it. If someone succeeds in obtaining it, he has triumphed, and he will enjoy good fortune for the eternity of those who are eternal [*abada 'l-ābidīn*] and for the endless duration of those who are everlasting [*dahra 'd-dāhirīn*]. If someone misses that, however, he will suffer loss together with the losers, and perish together with those who perish.

This therefore becomes, by Allāh, a highly problematic affair, and the danger involved is enormous. That is why those who set out on this path are very few and far between. Then rare are those travellers who reach the destination and obtain the object sought. Then rarest of all are those who are chosen by Allāh (Almighty and Glorious is He) to receive His intimate knowledge [*maʿrifa*] and His love [*maḥabba*], and whom He guides with His enabling grace [*tawfīq*] and His protection [*ʿiṣma*], then causes them, by His gracious favour, to attain to His good pleasure [*riḍwān*] and His Garden of Paradise.

We therefore beg Him (Glorious is His remembrance) to include all of you, and us, among those who are triumphantly successful through His mercy.

Yes, indeed. Once we had discovered this path, and found that it matched the above description, we focused our attention on the manner in which it could be traversed. We tried to determine what the servant [of the Lord] would need, in the way of preparation, equipment, instruments and skills, in terms of both knowledge and practice, so that he might traverse the path in safety, with the benefit of Allāh's enabling grace [*tawfīq*], and not be trapped in its perilous obstacles, so that he would perish along with those who are doomed to perdition. The only sure refuge is with Allāh [*wa 'l-ʿiyādhu bi'llāh*]!

We therefore composed several books on the subject of traversing and travelling this path, such as *Iḥyāʾ ʿUlūm ad-Dīn* [The Revival of the Religious Sciences], *al-Qurba ila 'llāhi (taʿāla)* [The Approach to Allāh (Exalted is He)], and others besides. These works dealt with subtle aspects of the sciences, too abstruse for the understanding of the common folk, who consequently found fault with them, and wallowed in what they did not comprehend about them. Ah well, what speech is more eloquent than the speech of the Lord of All the Worlds? Yet they dismissed it as: "Mere fables of the men of old [*asāṭīru 'l-awwalīn*]."[3]

Have you not heard the words of Zain al-ʿĀbidīn ʿAlī, the son of al-Ḥusain, the son of Alī, the son of Abū Ṭālib (may Allāh's good pleasure be upon them all)? It was he who said:

[3] Q. 6: 24, 8:31, 16:24, 23:83, 25:5, 27:68, 46:17 and 68:15.

I will surely conceal the jewels of my knowledge,
lest the ignorant should see them and act misguidedly.

innī la-aktumu min ʿilmī jawāhira-hu
kai-lā yarā dhāka dhū jahlin fa-yaftatinā

In this respect, the father of Ḥasan has preceded
al-Ḥusain, and has given good advice before him.

wa qad taqaddama fī hādhā Abū *Ḥasanin*
ila 'l-Ḥusaini wa waṣṣā qabla-hu 'l-ḥasanā

Oh, many a jewel of knowledge, if I should disclose it,
I would be told: "You are one of those who worship idols!"

yā rubba jawhari ʿilmin law abūḥu bi-hi
la-qīla lī anta mim-man yaʿbudu 'l-wathanā

Muslim men would consider it lawful to shed my blood,
regarding the ugliest deed they commit as something good.

wa la-'staḥalla rijālun muslimūna damī
yarawna aqbaḥa mā yaʾtūna-hu ḥasanā.

In the opinion of those devoted to religion [*dīn*], they being the noblest of Allāh's creatures (Exalted is He), the matter called for sympathetic consideration of all the creatures of Allāh, and for the abandonment of contentious dispute. I therefore made humble supplication to the One who holds in His hand the creation and the commandment, beseeching Him to make it possible for me to compose a book—one that would meet with unanimous approval, and the reading of which would result in positive benefit.

That request of mine was granted by the One who responds to the distressed when he calls unto Him.[4] He made me privy, by His gracious favour, to the mysteries involved, and He inspired me with a marvellous arrangement, the like of which I did not recall in any of the previous compositions dealing with the secrets of religious practices. This is the arrangement I am applying to the present work, so I must say: "Enabling grace comes only through Allāh [*bi'llāhi 't-tawfīq*]!"

[4] An allusion to the verse [*āya*] of the Qurʾān:

> Is it not He who answers the distressed, when he calls unto Him,
> *am-man yujību 'l-muḍṭarra idhā daʿā-hu*
> and removes the evil, and has made you viceroys of the earth?
> *wa yakhshifu 's-sūʾa wa yajʿalu-kum khulafāʾa 'l-arḍ :*
> Is there any God beside Allāh? Little do you reflect!
> *a-ilāhun maʿa 'llāh : qalīlan mā tadhakkarūn.* (27:62)

When the servant [of the Lord] is first awakened to worshipful service [*ʿibāda*], and devotes himself exclusively to travelling its path, he is motivated by a heavenly vibration from Allāh, and a special enabling grace of Divine origin [*tawfīq khāṣṣ Ilāhī*]. This is what is signified by His words (Glory be to Him):

> Is he whose breast Allāh has expanded to receive Islām,
> *a-fa-man sharaḥa 'llāhu ṣadra-hu li'l-Islāmi*
> so that he is guided by a light from his Lord...?
> *fa-huwa ʿalā nūrin min Rabbi-h.* (39:22)

It has also been indicated by the Master of the Sacred Law [*Ṣāḥib ash-Sharʿ*] (may the blessings and peace of Allāh be upon him), for he said:

> When the light enters the inner feeling, it expands and opens up.
> *inna 'n-nūra idhā dakhala 'l-qalba 'nfasaḥa wa 'nsharaḥ.*

This prompted someone to ask: "O Messenger of Allāh, is there any obvious sign by which that can be recognized?" He replied:

> The shunning of the abode of illusion, turning in repentance to the abode of eternity, and being prepared for death before the advent of death.
> *at-tajāfī ʿan dāri 'l-ghurūr—wa 'l-inābatu ilā dāri 'l-khuld—wa 'l-istiʿdādu li'l-mawti qabla nuzūli 'l-mawt.*

Suppose this occurs to the heart of the servant, first of all:

"I find myself endowed with various kinds of benefits, such as life, power, intelligence, speech, and other noble faculties and pleasures, while all kinds of disadvantages and afflictions are averted from me. There must be a Benefactor [*Munʿim*] who bestows these benefits, and who requires me to respond by thanking and serving Him. If I neglect to do so, He will remove His gracious favour from me, and make me taste His harshness and His retribution.

"He has sent me a Messenger [*Rasūl*], whom He has confirmed with miracles [*muʿjizāt*], disrupting the customary patterns of nature and exceeding the capability of the ordinary human being. He has informed me that I have a Lord (Glorious is His remembrance) All-Powerful [*Qādir*], All-Knowing [*ʿĀlim*], Ever-Living [*Ḥayy*], Purposive [*Murīd*], a Speaker [*Mutakallim*], One who commands and forbids, One who is Capable of punishing if I disobey Him and of rewarding if I obey Him, Aware of my secrets and of what pervades my thoughts. He has promised and He has threatened, and He has ordained compliance with the rules of the Sacred Law [*Sharʿ*]."

—It then occurs to his heart that it must be possible, since there is no absurdity in that concept, as initially conceived by the mind. He therefore fears for himself and feels alarmed. It is this experience of alarm that alerts the servant and obliges him to produce convincing evidence. It deprives him of any excuse and urges him to investigate and seek proof. The servant is agitated and perturbed by this, so he examines the means of salvation and the acquisition of safety from what has impressed his heart, or what he has heard with his ears. He finds no alternative to using his mind to investigate the evidential signs, and to draw conclusions about the Creator from the creation. He may thus obtain the knowledge of certainty concerning that which is concealed, and realize that he has a Lord who has charged him with obligations, commandments and prohibitions.

The hurdle of knowledge [*ʿilm*] and insight [*maʿrifa*].

This is the first hurdle to be confronted on the path of worshipful service [*ʿibāda*], and it is the hurdle of knowledge [*ʿilm*] and insight [*maʿrifa*], so that progress can be made with sharp discernment [*baṣīra*]. In order to surmount it, the seeker must inevitably engage in thorough investigation of the evidential signs, in abundant contemplation and study, and in consulting the scholars of the Hereafter, the guides of the spiritual path, the lanterns of the Islāmic community and the chiefs of the leaders. Useful advice must be sought from them, as well as their righteous supplication [*duʿāʾ*] for enablement and support, so the seeker may surmount the hurdle with the gracious help of Allāh (Glory be to Him). He may thus obtain the knowledge of certainty concerning the Unseen, meaning that he has One God, without any partner, that He is the One who created him and bestowed all these blessings upon him, that He has charged him with gratitude to Him, commanded him to serve Him and obey Him with both his outer and his inner being, warned him against unbelief [*kufr*] and the commission of sinful acts of disobedience, decreed everlasting reward for him if He obeys Him, and everlasting punishment if he disobeys Him and turns away from Him.

This understanding and certainty concerning the Unseen will thereupon endow the seeker with commitment to service, and with dedication to the worship of this Beneficent Master, whom he has sought and found, and with whom he has become familiar after he was ignorant of Him. He still does not know how to worship Him, however, nor what is required of him in serving Him with both his outer and his inner being. After the shock of this experience of Allāh (Glory be to Him and Exalted is He), the seeker must therefore exert himself strenuously, in order to learn what is required of him, in the way of duties imposed by the Sacred Law [*farā'iḍ shar'iyya*], both outwardly and inwardly.

The hurdle of repentance [*tawba*].

Once he has perfected the knowledge and understanding of the religious duties, the seeker will be prompted to engage in worship [*'ibāda*] and to preoccupy himself therewith. When he looks at himself, however, he will see that he is guilty of serious offences and sins, for this is the state of the majority of human beings, so he will say: "How shall I engage in worshipful service, when I am persistent in sinful disobedience, thoroughly stained thereby? It is therefore incumbent upon me, first of all, to repent to Him, so that He may forgive me my sins, deliver me from their captivity, and make me pure and free from their pollution. I shall then become fit for service and performance of duty."

At this point, therefore, the seeker is confronted by the hurdle of repentance [*tawba*], which he certainly needs to surmount, in order to arrive at what is intended thereby. He must set about fulfilling the rightful claims and preconditions of repentance, until he surmounts that hurdle.

The hurdle of the four impediments [*'awā'iq*].

Then, once he has experienced genuine repentance, and is no longer impeded by this hurdle, the seeker will yearn for worshipful service, eager to engage therein. When he examines his situation, however, he will see that he is completely surrounded by impediments [*'awā'iq*], each one of them obstructing him with some kind of hindrance from the worship he intends to perform. On closer inspection, he will notice that they are four in number: this world, his fellow creatures, the devil and the lower self [*nafs*]. He will therefore need to surmount them by four means: detachment from this world, isolation from his fellow creatures, combat with the devil, and conquest of the lower self.

As for the lower self, it is the most difficult of these impediments, since it is impossible for him to detach himself from it, nor can he conquer it once and for all, as he can subjugate the devil, because it is the means of transport and the instrument. There is also no hope of its readiness to accept and perform the worshipful service intended by the servant, since it is naturally disposed to the opposite of goodness, such as frivolity and indulgence therein. He therefore needs to bridle it with the rein of true devotion [*taqwā*], so that it will stay at his disposal and not break away, and be led by him and not rebel. He must employ it in good deeds and righteous works, and keep it away from dangers and causes of corruption.

He will thus embark on surmounting this hurdle, while appealing to Allāh (Glorious is His remembrance) for help in that task. Then, once he has succeeded in surmounting it, he will return to the intent of worshipful service.

The hurdle of the four hindrances [*ʿawāriḍ*].

Hindrances [*ʿawāriḍ*] will still obstruct him, however, distracting him from the performance of his intended worship, and preventing him from devoting himself properly to that purpose. Upon investigation, he will discover that these are four in number:

1. The sustenance [*rizq*] demanded by the lower self, which will say: "I cannot do without sustenance and provision. I have now become detached from this world, as well as being isolated from fellow creatures, so what will be the source of my provision and my sustenance?"

2. The risks inherent in everything he fears or hopes for, desires or detests. He does not know whether his course is right or wrong in that respect, because the consequences of all matters are obscure. His heart is concerned about them, for he might lapse into some depravity or perilous situation.

3. The hardships and misfortunes inflicted upon him from every side, especially now that he has committed himself to contradicting his fellow creatures, waging war on the devil, and opposing the lower self. Many a lump he must swallow! Many an ordeal will confront him! Many a care and sorrow will perplex him! Many a disaster will befall him!

4. The vicissitudes of fate from Allāh (Glory be to Him and Exalted is He), causing him to experience sweetness and bitterness on various occasions.

The lower self is quick to feel resentment and it promptly stirs up trouble, so the seeker is now confronted by these four hindrances [*ʿawāriḍ*]. He needs to surmount them by four means:

1. Absolute trust [*tawakkul*] in Allāh (Glory be to Him and Exalted is He) in the case of sustenance.
2. Deference [*tafwīḍ*] to His authority (Glorious and Almighty is He) in the case of risk.
3. Patience [*ṣabr*] in enduring the infliction of hardships.
4. Contentment [*riḍā*] in response to the advent of fate.

The hurdle of the incentives [*bawāʿith*].

The seeker has thus set about surmounting the hurdle of the four hindrances [*ʿawāriḍ*], with the permission of Allāh (Exalted is He) and the benefit of His assistance. As soon as he has succeeded in surmounting it, and returned to the intent of worshipful service, he will notice that the lower self is listless, weak and lazy. It displays no vim and energy, and no enthusiasm for goodness, as it rightly and properly should. Its inclination is always to nothing but heedlessness, relaxation, comfort and idleness, or indeed to wickedness, mischief, tribulation and ignorance. At this point, therefore, he needs a pilot who will steer it towards goodness and obedience, and who will stimulate it accordingly. He also needs an influence to restrain it from wickedness and sinful disobedience, and to discourage it therefrom.

The answer is hope and fear. Hope means expectation of the splendid reward of Allāh (Glory be to Him) and the excellent kinds of grace that He has promised. The recollection thereof is a pilot that will steer the lower self and spur it towards obedience, propelling it in that direction and arousing its enthusiasm. Fear means dread of the painful torment of Allāh (Almighty and Glorious is He) and the agony of all the types of punishment and disgrace that He has threatened. It is an influence that will restrain the lower self from sinful disobedience, diverting and discouraging it therefrom.

The seeker was thus confronted by the hurdle of the incentives [*bawāʿith*], so he needed to surmount it by the two means that have just been mentioned. He tackled it with the benefit of Allāh's enabling grace (Almighty and Glorious is He), so he succeeded in surmounting it. Then, as soon as he had done so, he returned his attention to the performance of worshipful service. He saw no obstacle and no distraction, and he found an incentive and a stimulus, so he applied himself eagerly to worship, performing it and embracing it with total enthusiasm and keenness, and he made it his regular practice.

The hurdle of the impairments [*qawādiḥ*].

Then, when he reviewed his situation, he noticed that this splendid worship, in which all of that was possible, could be affected by two terrible plagues, namely, hypocritical display [*riyāʾ*] and vain conceit [*ʿujb*]. He would at one time perform his act of obedience to impress other people, and thereby spoil it. On another occasion, he would refrain from that and blame his lower self, thereby indulging in self-conceit, so he would render the worship null and void, ruining and spoiling it.

The seeker was thus confronted by the hurdle of the impairments [*qawādiḥ*], and he needed to surmount it by refraining from taunting reference to his generosity, and suchlike, so that whatever good he had done would be preserved to his credit. He tackled this hurdle with Allāh's permission (Glory be to Him and Exalted is He), with diligence, caution, and awareness of the excellent protection of the All-Compelling One [*al-Jabbār*] (Exalted is He) and His support.

The hurdle of praise [*ḥamd*] and thankfulness [*shukr*].

Then, once he had completed all of this, it seemed that worshipful service was possible for him in its right and proper form, safe from every detriment. When he looked closely, however, he saw that he was immersed in the oceans of Allāh's blessings and His benefits (Exalted is He), because of the abundance of grace bestowed upon him by Allāh, in the way of enabling support, safekeeping, all kinds of assistance, protection and munificence. He was afraid that he might be guilty of neglecting thankfulness, and thereby lapse into ingratitude, so that he would sink from that lofty degree, the degree of the servants who are sincerely devoted to Allāh (Almighty and Glorious is He), and would lose those noble blessings, consisting of the various favours of Allāh (Exalted is He) and His excellent regard for him. He was thus confronted at this point by the hurdle of praise [*ḥamd*] and thankfulness [*shukr*].

He therefore tackled this hurdle and surmounted it with the means at his disposal, with abundance of praise and thankfulness for his many blessings. Then, once he had succeeded in surmounting this hurdle, and had alighted beyond it, he found himself at his destination. His aspired goal was now in front of him, so he had only a little distance to travel until he reached the plain of gracious favour, the desert of ardent longing and the open spaces of loving affection. He would then alight in the meadows of good pleasure and the gardens of intimate friendship, on the carpet of happiness, at the stage of close proximity, the session of confidential conversation and the bestowal of robes of honour and tokens of prestige.

Once the seeker has reached his destination, he will continue to enjoy these spiritual conditions, savouring their fragrance throughout the days of his survival and the rest of his life. With a bodily form in this world and a heart in the Hereafter, he will wait for the courier day by day, until he loses all interest in his fellow creatures, regards this world as unclean, yearns for death, and consummates the ardent longing for the heavenly host [*al-mala' al-a'lā*].

He is now in the presence of the Messengers of the Lord of All the Worlds. They will bring him refreshment and fragrant musk, good tidings and good pleasure from the presence of a Lord who is well-pleased, not angry. They will transport him to well-being, the perfection of joy and intimate friendship, from this fleeting and deceptive world to the Presence Divine and the abode of the Gardens of Paradise. He will then see that his poor weak self has a permanent blessing and a great and mighty dominion.

At this point, he will receive from his Master, the All-Compassionate, the Gracious, the Noble and Generous (Magnificent is His remembrance), such kindness and affection, such welcoming and hospitality, such benefaction and respect, that it cannot be encompassed by the description of the describers, nor by the characterization of the characterizers. His blessing will increase each day, for all eternity. Oh, what a splendid happiness! Oh, what a lofty state! Oh, what a fortunate servant, what an enviable man, and what a praiseworthy condition! Joy is for him, and bliss the journey's end!

We beseech Allāh, the Kind, the Compassionate (Glory be to Him and Exalted is He), to grant us—and you—this splendid bounty and momentous favour. That is not difficult for Allāh. We beseech Him not to include us among those who have no experience of this matter, but only a description, aural information, formal knowledge and unfulfilled desire. We beseech Him not to use the knowledge we have acquired as evidence against us on the Day of Resurrection [*Yawm al-Qiyāma*]. We beseech Him to enable us to act appropriately in all respects, and to perform our duty to His liking and approval. He is the Most Merciful of the merciful [*Arḥam ar-rāḥimīn*] and the Most Generous of the most generous [*Akram al-akramīn*].

May Allāh bless our chieftain, Muḥammad, his family and his Companions, and may He grant them peace, honour and nobility.

This is the sequential arrangement suggested to me by my Patron [*Mawlā*] in the path of worshipful service [*ʿibāda*]. You should now understand, therefore, through Allāh's enabling grace, that the hurdles [*ʿaqabāt*] add up to a total of seven:

1. The hurdle of knowledge [*ʿilm*].
2. The hurdle of repentance [*tawba*].
3. The hurdle of the impediments [*ʿawāʾiq*].
4. The hurdle of the hindrances [*ʿawāriḍ*].
5. The hurdle of the incentives [*bawāʿith*].
6. The hurdle of the impairments [*qawādiḥ*].
7. The hurdle of praise [*ḥamd*] and thankfulness [*shukr*].

These constitute the complete subject matter of "The Path of the Worshipful Servants to the Garden of the Lord of All the Worlds [*Minhāj al-ʿĀbidīn ilā Jannati Rabbi 'l-ʿĀlamīn*]." We shall now follow this list of hurdles with concise definitions, including all the important points. We shall devote a separate chapter to each hurdle, if Allāh so wills (Almighty and Glorious is He). Allāh (Glory be to Him) is the Guardian of enabling grace and guidance [*Waliyyu 't-tawfīq wa 't-tasdīd*], and there is no might nor any power except with Allāh, the All-High, the Almighty [*wa lā ḥawla wa lā quwwata illā bi'llāhi 'l-ʿAliyyi 'l-ʿAẓīm*].

The First Hurdle
The hurdle of knowledge [*ʿilm*]

Allāh is the Source of enabling grace! O seeker of salvation and worshipful service, as your first requirement, may Allāh enable you to gain knowledge [*ʿilm*], for it is the pivot [*quṭb*] on which everything turns.

You must understand that knowledge and worship [*ʿibāda*] are two essentials, which account for everything you see and hear from the literary work of the writers, the teaching of the teachers, the preaching of the preachers, and the research of the researchers. Indeed, it was because of them that the Books of Scripture [*Kutub*] were revealed and the Messengers [*Rusul*] were sent. Yes indeed, it was because of them that the heavens and the earth were created, as well as the creatures they contain.

You must also consider two verses in the Book of Allāh (Almighty and Glorious is He):

1. His saying (Magnificent is His remembrance):

> It is Allāh who has created seven heavens,
> *Allāhu 'lladhī khalaqa sabʿa samāwātin*
> and of the earth their like.
> *wa mina 'l-arḍi mithla-hunn:*
> The Command comes down between them gradually,
> *yatanazzalu 'l-amru baina-hunna*
> so that you may know that Allāh is Powerful over all things,
> *li-taʿlamū anna 'llāha ʿalā kulli shaiʾin Qadīr:*
> and that Allāh has encompassed everything in knowledge.
> *wa anna 'llāha qad aḥāṭa bi-kulli shaiʾin ʿilmā.* (65:12)

This Qurʾānic verse [*āya*] is sufficient proof of the nobility of knowledge, especially knowledge of the affirmation of Oneness [*Tawḥīd*].

2. His saying (More Glorious is He than any other sayer):

> I did not create the jinn and humankind
> *wa mā khalaqtu 'l-jinna wa 'l-insa*
> except to worship Me.
> *illā li-ya'budūn.* (51:56)

This Qur'ānic verse is sufficient proof of the nobility of worship, and the necessity of its performance.

These two matters [knowledge and worship] are thus of the utmost importance. They are the purpose of the creation of the two abodes [this world and the Hereafter]. It is therefore the servant's duty not to occupy himself with anything else, not to follow anything else, and not to look into anything else. You must know that anything apart from them is futile, devoid of benefit, and merely ineffectual nonsense. Once you have realized that, you must also understand that knowledge is the nobler of the two essentials, and the superior of the two. That is why the Prophet (Allāh bless him and give him peace) once said:

> The superiority of the scholar ['*ālim*] over the worshipper ['*ābid*] is like my superiority over the most inferior member of my Community [*Ummatī*].

He also said (Allāh bless him and give him peace):

> A glimpse of the scholar ['*ālim*] is dearer to me than the worship of a year, its fasting [*ṣiyām*] and its vigil [*qiyām*].

When he said (Allāh bless him and give him peace):

> Shall I show you the noblest of the people of the Garden [of Paradise]?

—they said: "Yes indeed, O Messenger of Allāh!" so he said:

> They are the scholars ['*ulamā'*] of my Community.

It is therefore clear to you that knowledge is nobler as an essential than worship. Nevertheless, worship is strictly necessary in conjunction with knowledge, for one's knowledge is otherwise no more than scattered particles of dust [*habā'an manthūrā*].[5] Knowledge is comparable to a tree, while worship is comparable to one of its fruits. Nobility belongs to the tree, since it is the fundamental element, but its usefulness derives from its fruit. The servant must therefore have a share and a portion of both. This is why al-Ḥasan al-Baṣrī (may Allāh

[5] An allusion to Q. 25:23.

bestow His mercy upon him) once said: "Seek this knowledge in a way that does no harm to worship, and seek this worship in a way that does no harm to knowledge."

While it has been established that the servant must have both of them together, knowledge undoubtedly takes precedence, because it is the basis and the guide. That is why the Prophet (Allāh bless him and give him peace) once said:

> Knowledge is the leader of the action, and the action is his follower.

There are two reasons why knowledge has become a basic principle, to which you are obliged to give priority over worship:

1. In order to be capable of worship, and to be safe and sound, it is necessary for you, first of all, to recognize the One deserving of worship [*Maʿbūd*], and then to worship Him. How can you worship One whom you do not recognize by His Names [*Asmāʾ*] and the attributes of His Essence [*Dhāt*], and what is rightly due to Him and what is inconceivable in His description? It may be that you believe in something false about Him and His attributes—Let us take refuge with Allāh from what is contrary to the Truth!—in which case your worship is nothing but scattered particles of dust [*habāʾan manthūrā*].[6]

Then you must learn what legal duties [*wājibāt sharʿiyya*] you are obliged to perform, in the manner prescribed for you, and what prohibitions you are obliged to refrain from violating. Otherwise, how can you perform acts of obedience, without knowing what they are and how they must be performed? How can you refrain from acts of disobedience, without knowing that they are acts of disobedience? You must learn the acts of worship required by the Sacred Law [*ʿibādāt sharʿiyya*], such as purification [*ṭahāra*], ritual prayer [*ṣalāt*], fasting [*ṣawm*] and so on, with their rules and preconditions, so that you perform them correctly. Otherwise, you may spend years in the practice of something that spoils your state of purity and your ritual prayers, and prevents them from conforming to the Sunna [the exemplary practice of the Prophet (Allāh bless him and give him peace)], without your being aware of it. You may encounter some problem, and find no one to consult about it, since you have not studied the matter.

[6] **Author's note:** We have warned elsewhere of the tremendous danger this poses. See the explanation of "coming to a bad end [*sūʾ al-khātima*]," in the Book of Fear [*Kitāb al-Khawf*], which is one of the Books of "The Revival of the Religious Sciences [*Iḥyāʾ ʿUlūm ad-Dīn*]."

This topic also includes the internal acts of worship [*ʿibādāt bāṭiniyya*], they being the endeavours of the heart, which you must also learn. Among them are absolute trust [*tawakkul*], delegation [*tafwīḍ*], contentment [*riḍā*], patience [*ṣabr*], repentance [*tawba*] and sincere devotion [*ikhlāṣ*], as well as others to be mentioned later, if Allāh (Exalted is He) so wills. You must also learn the corresponding prohibitions, like discontent [*sukhṭ*], overexpectation [*amal*], hyprocritical display [*riyāʾ*] and vain conceit [*kibr*], so that you will avoid committing such offences.

These duties are specifically enjoined by Allāh (Exalted is He, in His glorious Book and on the tongue of His Prophet (Allāh bless him and give him peace), as is the prohibition of their opposites. In the words of Allāh (Exalted is He):

> And put all your trust in Allāh,
> *wa ʿala ʼllāhi fa-tawakkalū*
> if you are true believers.
> *in kuntum muʾminīn.* (5:23)
>
> And give thanks to Allāh
> *wa ʼshkurū liʼllāhi*
> if you truly worship Him alone.
> *in kuntum iyyā-hu taʿbudūn.* (2:172)
>
> And endure with patience.
> *wa ʼṣbir*
> Your patient endurance is only
> *wa mā ṣabru-ka*
> by [the help of] Allāh.
> *illā biʼllāhi.* (16:127)
>
> And commit yourself to Him
> *wa tabattal ilai-hi*
> with intense commitment.
> *tabtīlā.* (73:8)

That is to say: "Devote yourself to Him with sincere devotion [*akhliṣ ilai-hi ikhlāṣā*]."

In these and other such Qurʾānic verses [*āyāt*], He has prescribed the internal acts of worship, just as He has prescribed the ritual prayer and fasting. So what is wrong with you, that you have omitted these duties, when their commandment comes from One Lord, in one Book? You have in fact been heedless of them, for you know nothing about them. You are classed as someone so enamoured of his worldly fortune, that he has turned what is right and proper [*maʿrūf*] into that which is wrong and improper [*munkar*], and vice versa. You are classed as someone who has neglected the forms of knowledge described by Allāh, in His Book, as light [*nūr*] and wisdom [*ḥikma*] and guidance [*hudā*]. You are classed as someone who has sought the means to acquire unlawful sustenance, and to net the ephemeral bounties of this world.

Are you not afraid, O seeker of right guidance, that you may be omitting something from these duties, or even the greater part of them? You may be engaging in voluntary prayer and supererogatory fasting, but to no avail. You may be persisting in one of these sinful acts of disobedience, for which you deserve the Fire of Hell. You may be abstaining from permissible food or drink or sleep, seeking nearness to Allāh (Almighty and Glorious is He), yet to no avail.

Worse than all of that, you may be caught in the snare of overexpectation, and overexpectation is an outright act of sinful disobedience. You think of it as good intention, due to your ignorance of the distinction between the two, and their close resemblance in certain aspects. You may likewise be entangled in worry and discontent, mistaking this for humble entreaty and supplication to Allāh. You may also be indulging in sheer ostentation, supposing it to be an expression of praise for Allāh (Glory be to Him and Exalted is He), or a way of inviting people to goodness.

This makes you guilty of counting acts of sinful disobedience to Allāh (Glory be to Him) as acts of worshipful obedience, and of reckoning the splendid reward instead of the dreadful punishments. You are thus in a mighty delusion and disgusting heedlessness, and this, by Allāh, is an appalling disaster for those who act without knowledge.

In addition to all the foregoing, external actions have links to the internal endeavours, which either improve them or corrupt them, such as sincere devotion [on the positive side], and ostentation, vain conceit, taunting [*dhikr al-manna*] and so on [on the negative side]. If someone does not recognize these internal endeavours, and the ways in which they affect the external acts of worship, and if he does not know how to be wary of them and take precautions against them, the conduct of his outer being is also unlikely to be safe and sound. He will therefore lose the acts of worship of both the outer and the inner being, and be left with nothing but misery and woe. This is the sheer loss.[7] This is why

[7] An allusion to Q. 22:11 and 39:15.

Allāh's Messenger (Allāh bless him and give him peace) once said, concerning the quality of knowledge:

> A sleep based on knowledge is better than a ritual prayer [*ṣalāt*] based on ignorance, for he who acts without knowledge spoils more than he improves.

On the subject of knowledge, Allāh's Messenger (Allāh bless him and give him peace) also said:

> The fortunate are inspired with it, and the wretched are deprived of it.

Since knowledge resides with Allāh (Glory be to Him), this means that he who is deprived suffers two misfortunes: He does not learn knowledge, then he is wretched and exhausted in worship that is futile, for there is nothing in it for him except hardship and toil. Let us take refuge with Allāh from useless knowledge and action!

This explains the meticulous care of the abstemious scholars who put their knowledge into practice (may Allāh be well pleased with them), as distinct from people in general. The scope of servitude [*ʿubūdiyya*] and the basis of worship and service to Allāh, the Lord of All the Worlds, are founded on knowledge. Such is the view of the perceptive, and of those endowed with support and enabling grace [from Allāh].

If it is clear to you now, from this succinct account, that the servant does not acquire obedience [*ṭāʿa*], and does not retain it securely, except through knowledge, it is therefore necessary to accord priority to knowledge [*ʿilm*] in the matter of worship [*ʿibāda*].

2. As for the second reason for giving priority to knowledge, it is that useful knowledge produces fear of Allāh (Exalted is He) and reverence for Him. As Allāh (Exalted is He) has said:

> Only those of His servants who have knowledge fear Allāh.
> *inna-mā yakhsha 'llāha min ʿibādi-hi 'l-ʿulamāʾ*. (35:28)

That is because, if someone does not recognize Him with the recognition He deserves, he will not revere Him with the reverence that He deserves, nor will he pay Him the honour and respect that He deserves. Through knowledge he will come to recognize Him, honour Him and revere Him.

Knowledge thus bears fruit in the form of all acts of worshipful obedience, and prevents all sinful disobedience, through Allāh's enabling grace.

Apart from these two [obedience and refraining from disobedience], the servant has no purpose in the worship of Allāh (Glory be to Him and Exalted is He). It is therefore incumbent upon you to acquire knowledge—May Allāh guide you aright, O traveller on the road of the Hereafter!—as the very first thing of all. Allāh is the Custodian of enabling grace, by His favour and His mercy!

Perhaps you will say: "The master of the Sacred Law (Allāh bless him and give him peace) is reported as having said:

> The quest for knowledge is a duty incumbent upon every Muslim.

—so what is that knowledge, the quest for which is an obligatory duty, and to what extent must the servant acquire it in the matter of worship?"

You must therefore know that the forms of knowledge, the pursuit of which is obligatory, are three in number: (1) knowledge of the affirmation of Oneness [*Tawḥīd*], (2) knowledge of the secret being [*sirr*], by which I mean what is connected with the heart and its endeavours, and (3) knowledge of the Sacred Law [*Sharīʿa*]. As for the extent to which each one of these is necessary:

1. In the case of knowledge of the affirmation of Oneness [*Tawḥīd*], its obligatory nature is determined by the extent of your familiarity with the basic principles of the religion, namely:

—That you have a God [*Ilāh*] who is All-Knowing [*ʿĀlim*], All-Powerful [*Qādir*], Purposive [*Murīd*], Ever-Living [*Ḥayy*], Speaking [*Mutakallim*], All-Hearing [*Samīʿ*], All-Seeing [*Baṣīr*], One [*Wāḥid*], Without partner [*lā sharīka la-h*], Described by the attributes of perfection [*Muttaṣif bi-ṣifāt al-kamāl*], Immune to deficiency, cessation, and the signs of novelty [*Munazzaʿ ʿani 'n-nuqṣān wa 'z-zawāl wa dalālāt al-ḥudūth*], Detached by sempiternity from every phenomenon [*Munfarid bi'l-qidam ʿan kulli muḥdath*].

—That Muḥammad (Allāh bless him and give him peace) is His servant and His Messenger, truthful in what he has brought from Allāh (Exalted and Sanctified is He), and in what has been conveyed on his tongue concerning the affairs of the Hereafter. [*wa anna Muḥammadan (ṣalla 'llāhu ʿalai-hi wa sallam) ʿabdu-hu wa Rasūlu-hu 'ṣ-ṣādiqu fī-mā jāʾa bi-hi ʿani'llāhi (taʿālā wa taqaddas) wa fī-mā warada ʿalā lisāni-hi min umūr al-ākhira*].

Then there are questions concerning the practices [*shaʿāʾir*] of the Sunna [exemplary conduct of the Prophet (Allāh bless him and give him peace)], with which you are also required to be familiar.

Beware of committing heretical innovation in the religion of Allāh (Glory be to Him and Exalted is He), by inventing doctrines communicated by no Book of Scripture nor any sound traditional report [*athar*]. If you are guilty of such heresy, you will be in the gravest danger in the presence of Allāh (Glory be to Him).

As for the proofs of the affirmation of Oneness [*Tawḥīd*], the root of them all is found in the Book of Allāh (Glory be to Him). They have also been mentioned by our Shaikhs (may Allāh be well pleased with them all), in the books they have compiled about the principles of religious subjects.

In short, whenever ignorance of something puts you in danger of perdition, the quest for knowledge thereof is an obligatory duty, which you are not permitted to abandon. This is our summary conclusion. Allāh is the Source of enabling grace!

2. As for knowledge of the secret being [*sirr*], its obligatory nature is determined by familiarity with its positive requirements and its prohibitions, so that you may acquire reverence for Allāh (Exalted is He) and sincere devotion to Him, as well as true intention and integrity in action. All of that will come later in this book of ours, if Allāh (Almighty and Glorious is He) so wills.

3. As for knowledge of the Sacred Law [*Sharīʿa*], its obligatory nature is determined by your familiarity with the practices it requires you to perform, such as purification [*ṭahārā*], the ritual prayer [*ṣalāt*] and fasting [*ṣawm*]. As for the pilgrimage [*ḥajj*], almsgiving [*zakāt*] and the sacred struggle [*jihad*], if their obligatory nature applies to you, it is incumbent upon you to acquire the knowledge needed to perform the relevant duty, but otherwise not.

This is undoubtedly the full extent to which it is necessary for the servant to acquire knowledge. Whenever particular knowledge is indispensable, its acquisition becomes an obligatory duty for you.

Suppose you ask:

"Is it obligatory for me to learn so much knowledge of the affirmation of Oneness [*Tawḥīd*], that I can use it to destroy all the communities of unbelief [*milal al-kufr*] and force them to accept the proof of Islām, as well as to destroy all heretical innovations [*bida*ʿ] and force their perpetrators to accept the proof of the Sunna?"

In answer to this question, you must know that this is a collective duty [*farḍ ʿala 'l-kifāya*].[8] Your personal responsibility applies to what enables you to confirm your belief in the basic principles of the religion, not to anything else. It is likewise not incumbent on you to be familiar with the branches and fine details of knowledge of the affirmation of Oneness [*Tawḥīd*], nor to investigate all its problematic questions. Of course, if you experience some doubt concerning the basic principles of the religion, so that you are afraid of impairing your conviction, it is incumbent on you to resolve that doubt, by means of any discussion that can lead to satisfaction. You must beware of contention and dispute, for they are a sheer sickness without remedy. You must guard against them with all your might, for if anyone indulges in them, he will not achieve salvation, unless Allāh (Exalted is He) shields him with His mercy and His grace.

Next, you should know what will happen if, in every land, there is a missionary [*dāʿī*] from the people of the Sunna, one who resolves all doubts and refutes the heretical innovators, one who is uniquely equipped with this knowledge, and who purifies the hearts of the people of the Truth by ridding them of heretical insinuations. In such a case, the duty [that he has fulfilled] will cease to apply to everyone other than him.

It is likewise unnecessary for you to be familiar with the subtle details of knowledge of the secret being [*sirr*], and the full interpretation of the marvels of the heart, with the exception of anything that is liable to spoil your worship, for then you need to be familiar with it in order to avoid it.

As for that which you are obliged to practise, such as sincere devotion [*ikhlāṣ*], praise [*ḥamd*], thankfulness [*shukr*] and absolute trust

[8] In Islāmic jurisprudence [*fiqh*], a distinction is drawn between *farḍ ʿain*, i.e., a religious duty that is incumbent on every individual Muslim, and *farḍ ʿala 'l-kifāya*, meaning a collective duty, incumbent on the Islāmic community as a whole, though not on every individual Muslim.

[*tawakkul*], you must be familiar with it in order to carry it out, though not in other cases.

It is likewise unnecessary for you to be familiar with all the subjects of jurisprudence [*fiqh*], such as buying and selling, renting and leasing, marriage and divorce, and criminal offences. All of that is a collective duty [*farḍ ʿala 'l-kifāya*].[9]

You may ask: "If this is the extent of knowledge of the affirmation of Oneness [*Tawḥīd*], can it be acquired by a person's own research, without a teacher?" You must therefore know that the teacher is an opener and a facilitator, and that studying with him is easier and more comfortable. Allāh (Exalted is He) bestows His gracious favour on whomever He will among His servants, so He is their Instructor [*Muʿallim*] (Glory be to Him and Exalted is He).

Then you must know that this hurdle, which is the hurdle of knowledge, is an almost insurmountable hurdle, yet through it one does reach the objective and the goal. Its usefulness is great, though traversing it is very hard and its danger is enormous. So many have deviated from it and gone astray. So many have stepped on it and slipped. So many have floundered on it in confusion. Many a non-Muslim cleric [*ḥabr*] has been cut off. Many a spiritual traveller [*sālik*] has crossed it in a short space of time, while another has hesitated in it for seventy years. The matter is entirely in the Hand of Allāh (Almighty and Glorious is He). As for its usefulness, we have already explained that the servant's need for it is urgent, and that the whole business of worship depends on it, especially on knowledge of the affirmation of Oneness [*Tawḥīd*] and knowledge of the secret being [*sirr*].

According to traditional report, Allāh (Exalted is He) spoke to David (peace be upon him) by way of inspiration [*waḥy*], saying:

> O David, learn useful knowledge![10]

David asked: "O my God [*Ilāhī*], and what is useful knowledge?" Allāh replied:

> That you recognize My Majesty, My Glory, My Grandeur, and the perfection of My Power over everything, for this is what will bring you near to Me.[11]

[9] See note 8 on p. 26 above.

[10] *yā Dāwudu taʿallimi 'l-ʿilma 'n-nāfiʿ.*

[11] *an taʿrifa Jalālī wa ʿAẓamatī wa Kibriyāʾī wa kamāla Qudratī ʿalā kulli shaiʾ: fa-inna hādha 'llādhī yuqarribu-ka ilayy.*

ʿAlī (may Allāh ennoble his countenance) is reported as having said: "I would not be happy if I had died as an infant, even if I had been admitted to the Garden of Paradise, instead of growing to maturity and so becoming intimately acquainted with my Lord."

The people who know Allāh best are those who are most fearful of Him, most frequent in worship, and most sincere in giving counsel for the sake of Allāh (Glory be to Him and Exalted is He).

Faced with the extreme difficulty of this hurdle, you must devote yourself sincerely to the quest for knowledge, and that quest must be the quest for first-hand comprehension [*dirāya*], not the quest for second-hand information [*riwāya*]. You must know that the danger is tremendous, for if someone seeks knowledge in order to attract people to him, to gain the company of the leaders, to win the applause of his fellows, and to hunt the vanities of this world, his trade is unprofitable and his transaction is a bad bargain.

Allāh's Messenger (Allāh bless him and give him peace) once said:

> If someone seeks knowledge in order to flaunt it before the scholars, or to argue with stupid fools, or to make people turn their faces towards him, Allāh will cause him to enter the Fire of Hell.

It was Abū Yazīd al-Bisṭāmī (may Allāh bestow His mercy upon him) who said: "I worked with dedicated striving for thirty years, and I found nothing harder on me than knowledge and its danger."

You must be on your guard, in case Satan paints you a pretty picture, and says to you: "Since knowledge entails this terrible danger, it is best left aside." You must not think like that, for Allāh's Messenger (Allāh bless him and give him peace) is reported as having said:

> On the night of the Heavenly Ascension [*Miʿrāj*], I was shown the Fire of Hell, and I saw that most of its occupants were the poor.

His listeners asked: "O Messenger of Allāh, were they short of property?" He said:

> No, but rather of knowledge.

If someone does not learn knowledge, he cannot master the rules that govern acts of worship, and he will fail to perform them correctly. Even if a man worshipped Allāh (Glory be to Him) with the worship of the angels of the heavens, but without knowledge, he would be among the losers. You must therefore rally all your forces in the quest for knowledge, through study, instruction and teaching, and you must avoid laziness and boredom. Otherwise, you are in danger of going astray. Let us take refuge with Allāh (Almighty and Glorious is He)!

Now for our summary conclusion:

If you examine the signs of Allāh's creation (Almighty and Glorious is He), and scrutinize them with care, you will know that you and we have a God [*Ilāh*] who is All-Knowing [*ʿĀlim*], All-Powerful [*Qādir*], Ever-Living [*Ḥayy*], Purposive [*Murīd*], All-Hearing [*Samīʿ*], All-Seeing [*Baṣīr*], Speaking [*Mutakallim*], Immune to the randomness of speech, knowledge and purpose [*Munazzaʿ ʿan ḥudūth al-kalām wa 'l-ʿilm wa 'l-irāda*], Sanctified against every deficiency and damage [*Muqaddas ʿan kulli naqṣ wa āfa*]. He is not qualified by the attributes of phenomena [*muḥdathīn*]. He is not subject to anything to which His creatures are subject. He does not resemble anything in His creation, and nothing resembles Him. Places and directions do not contain Him. Accidents and disasters do not befall Him.

I have examined the miracles [*muʿjizāt*] of the Prophet (Allāh bless him and give him peace), his signs [*āyāt*] and the emblems of his Prophethood [*Nubuwwa*]. I have acknowledged that he is Allāh's Messenger (Allāh bless him and give him peace) and His trusted custodian of His inspiration [*waḥy*]. I have also acknowledged what the righteous forebears [*salaf*] believed, namely:

—That Allāh (Exalted is He) will be seen in the Hereafter.

—That He exists without being confined to any limited direction,

—That the Qur'ān is the uncreated speech of Allāh (Exalted is He), and does not consist of separate letters and sounds, since if it were like that, it would be among the objects of creation.

—That in the worldly domain [*mulk*] and the Heavenly Kingdom [*Malakūt*], no event occurs and no glance is cast, except by the decree of Allāh (Exalted is He), His destiny, His purpose and His will, for He is the Source of good and evil, benefit and harm, and faith [*īmān*] and unbelief [*kufr*].

—That Allāh (Exalted is He) owes nothing to any of His creatures.

If He empowers someone, it is by His gracious favour, and if He punishes someone, it is in accordance with His justice.

—That which has come to us on the tongue of the Master of the Sacred Law (Allāh's blessings and peace be upon him) concerning the affairs of the Hereafter, such as the Gathering [*Ḥashr*] and the Resurrection [*Nashr*], the torment of the grave, the interrogation conducted by [the two angels] Munkar and Nakīr, and the Balance [*Mīzān*] and the Narrow Bridge [*Ṣirāṭ*].

These are principles established by the righteous forebears (may Allāh be well pleased with them all), as matters of belief and strict adherence. They were accepted by general consensus [*ijmāʿ*], before the diversity of heretical innovations [*bidaʿ*] and the emergence of sectarian tendencies [*ahwiya*]. We take refuge with Allāh from heretical innovation in the religion, and from the following of desire without proof.

I then examined the actions of the hearts, and the obligations and prohibitions imposed on the inner being. These will come later in this book, so that you may acquire the relevant knowledge.

You must also become familiar with everything you need to practise, like purification [*ṭahāra*], the ritual prayer [*ṣalāt*], fasting [*ṣawm*] and so on, for then you will have fulfilled the duty imposed on you by Allāh (Exalted is He), who has summoned you to obedience in the matter of knowledge. You will have come to be one of the scholars of the Community of Muḥammad (Allāh bless him and give him peace) who are firmly rooted in knowledge. If you put your knowledge into practice, and embark on the cultivation of your life in the Hereafter, you will be a knowledgeable servant, acting for the sake of Allāh (Exalted is He) with conscious understanding, not in ignorance, not as a mere follower of convention, and not in heedlessness. Yours will be the glorious honour. Your knowledge will have great worth and abundant reward. You will have surmounted this hurdle, left it behind you, and fulfilled its due, with the permission of Allāh (Exalted is He). Allāh (Glory be to Him) is responsible for assisting you and us with His enabling grace and His facilitation. He is the Most Merciful of the merciful [*Arḥam ar-rāḥimīn*], and there is no might nor any power except with Allāh, the All-High, the Almighty [*wa lā ḥawla wa lā quwwata illā bi'llāhi 'l-ʿAliyyi 'l-ʿAẓīm*].

The Second Hurdle
The hurdle of repentance [*tawba*]

Repentance [*tawba*] is your next obligation, O seeker of worshipful service [*ʿibāda*]—May Allāh enable you to succeed!—and that is for two reasons:

1. So that you may receive the blessing of obedience [*ṭāʿa*], for the evil of sins results in deprivation and leads to disappointment. The shackle of sins prevents progress towards obedience to Allāh (Almighty and Glorious is He) and rapid access to His service, because the weight of sins prevents agility in the performance of good deeds, and alacrity in acts of obedience. Persistence in sins contributes to the blackening of hearts, so you find them in darkness and hardness, devoid of clarity and purity, containing no joy and no sweetness.

If Allāh does not grant His mercy, sins will drag their perpetrator towards unbelief [*kufr*] and misery. It is hard to imagine how someone can be helped and guided to obedience, when he is embedded in evil and hard-heartedness. It is hard to imagine how someone can be summoned to service, when he is persistent in disobedience and addicted to dissension. It is hard to imagine how someone can be drawn close to intimate converse [*munājāh*], when he is stained with all kinds of filth and impurities. According to traditional report, the acknowledged teller of the truth, Allāh's Messenger (Allāh bless him and give him peace), once said:

> If the servant tells a lie, the two angels will recoil from the stench that comes out of his mouth.

How can such a tongue be fit for the remembrance of Allāh (Almighty and Glorious is He)? Without a doubt, someone who persists in sin is unlikely to find enabling grace, and his limbs will be too sluggish for the worship of Allāh (Exalted is He). If he does conform, it will be with trouble and toil, unaccompanied by sweetness and pure delight. All that is due to the evil of sins and the failure to repent. The truth was told by him who said: "If you cannot keep the night vigil and the daytime fast, you must know that you are shackled, for your transgression has shackled you."

2. Repentance is incumbent upon you so that your worship will be accepted of you, for the Lord of the religion will not accept it as a freewill offering. That is because repentance of sins, like the satisfaction of legal claimants, is an obligatory duty, whereas the worship you undertake is generally a work of supererogation [*nafl*]. How can your voluntary donation be accepted of you, when the debt you owe is a condition you have not fulfilled? How can you forsake the lawful [*ḥalāl*] and the permissible [*mubāḥ*], while you persist in doing what is forbidden [*maḥẓūr*] and unlawful [*ḥarām*]? How can you converse with Him, appeal to Him and extol Him, when He—the only refuge is with Allāh!—is angry with you? This is the obvious condition of sinners who persist in disobedience. Allāh is the One from whom help is sought!

You may ask: "What is the meaning of sincere repentance, and what must the servant do, in order to escape from all sins?"

This will be my reply: As for repentance, it is one of the endeavours of the heart. According to the gist of the teaching of the religious scholars (may Allāh be well pleased with them), repentance means cleansing the heart by ridding it of sin. Our own Shaikh [Abū Bakr aṭ-Ṭarṭūsī] (may Allāh bestow His mercy upon him) defined it as follows: "Repentance is renouncing, in honour of Allāh (Exalted is He) and in fear of incurring His displeasure, the option to commit a sin the like of which one has previously committed, the likeness being a matter of rank [in the legal scale], not actual form." On the basis of this definition, repentance has four conditions:

a. Renouncing the option of sin. In other words, the servant must resolve, firmly and decisively, that he will on no account revert to sin. If he renounces sin, but retains the feeling that he may return to it, or if he is hesitant rather than firmly resolved, he may suffer a relapse, for he is restraining himself from sin, not repenting it.

b. The servant must repent a sin the like of which he has previously committed. That is because, if he has not committed the like of it before, he is being wary [*muttaqī*], not penitent [*tā'ib*]. You must surely recognize the validity of the saying that the Prophet (Allāh bless him and give him peace) was wary of unbelief [*kufr*], and that it is not correct to say that he was penitent of unbelief, since he had never been guilty of any unbelief whatsoever. As for ʿUmar ibn al-Khaṭṭāb (may Allāh be well pleased with him), he was indeed penitent of unbelief, since he had previously been guilty thereof.

c. The sin a person has previously committed must resemble the one for which he is renouncing the option, in rank and degree, not in actual form.

Consider the case of a decrepit old man, on the verge of passing away, who has previously been guilty of sexual misconduct [*zinā*] and highway robbery [*qaṭʿ aṭ-ṭarīq*]. If he wishes to repent thereof, it is possible for him to do so, without a doubt, since the door to repentance has not been locked against him. It is not possible, however, for him to renounce the option of committing sexual misconduct and highway robbery. Since he is no longer capable of those offences, he is incapable of renouncing the option to commit them. It is therefore incorrect to describe him as renouncing and restraining himself from that of which he is incapable, and which is impossible for him. He is still capable, however, of committing offences comparable in rank and degree to sexual misconduct and highway robbery, such as lying, false accusation [*qadhf*],[12] backbiting [*ghība*] and slander [*namīma*]. That is because all of these are sinful acts of disbedience.

Even if the scope of the sin is different in each case, all these multifarious acts of disobedience are of one rank [in the legal scale], which is below the rank of heretical innovation [*bidʿā*], while the rank of heretical innovation is below the rank of unbelief [*kufr*]. Repentance is therefore correct for him, with regard to sexual misconduct, highway robbery, and all other previous sins, the likes of which he is now incapable of committing in actual form, [because he is still capable of committing sins of the same rank in the legal scale].

[12] In Islāmic law, the term *qadhf* usually refers specifically to an accusation of sexual misconduct [*zinā*], directed against a virtuous man or woman by a person who is unable to produce four reputable witnesses. The penalty incurred by making such an accusation is eighty lashes.

d. The penitent must renounce his option purely in honour of Allāh (Almighty and Glorious is He), and in dread of His displeasure and the agony of His chastisement, not on account of worldly advantage, fear of other people, praise or fame or prestige, personal weakness, poverty, or anything else.

These are the conditions and basic principles of repentance. If you meet them and fulfil them, your repentance will be real and genuine.

As for the incentives to repentance, they are three in number: (1) Remembering the extreme ugliness of sins. (2) Remembering the severity of Allāh's punishment (Almighty and Glorious is He), and the unbearable pain of His displeasure and His wrath. (3) Remembering your weakness and your lack of dexterity. If someone cannot bear the heat of the sun, a box on the ear from a policeman, or the bite of an ant, how will he endure the heat of the Fire of Hell, the impact of the iron rods wielded by the *zabāniya* [tormenting angels who stoke the Fire], the stinging bites of serpents resembling the necks of Bactrian camels, and of scorpions like mules, created of fire in the abode of wrath and perdition? We take refuge with Allāh! Then again, we take refuge with Allāh from His displeasure and His torment!

If you apply yourself diligently to these recollections, and make them your frequent practice by day and by night, they will surely prompt you to sincere repentance of sins. Allāh is the Source of enablement, through His gracious favour.

The question may be asked: "Is it not true that the Prophet (Allāh bless him and give him peace) once said:

> Remorse is a form of repentance [*an-nadam tawba*].

—and that he did not refer to any of the conditions you have mentioned and emphasized?"

The answer will be: You must know, first of all, that remorse [*nadam*] is not decreed for the servant. Remorse is a feeling that affects his heart, when he regrets certain matters and wishes they were not as they are, whereas repentance [*tawba*] is decreed for the servant, and he is commanded to perform it. Moreover, as we surely know, if someone feels remorse for sins, that does not cause him to lose his prestige among people, nor to expend his wealth in compensation, so that is certainly not a form of repentance. From this you will understand that the traditional report [*khabar*] contains a meaning you have not grasped from its surface. The inner meaning is that remorse, when it is felt in honour of Allāh (Glory be to Him) and in fear of His chastisement, is conducive to sincere repentance, for that is among the attributes of the penitents and of their spiritual state.

If the servant remembers the three incentives to repentance, he will feel remorse, and that feeling of remorse will induce him to renounce the option of committing sins. His remorse will remain in his heart in future, so it will encourage him to practise supplication and humble entreaty. Since that is among the causes of repentance and the attributes of the penitent, Allāh's Messenger (Allāh bless him and give him peace) called it by the name "repentance [*tawba*]." The point should now be within your grasp, if Allāh (Exalted is He) so wills.

Suppose you ask: "How is it possible for the human being to practise patience, so that he will never be guilty of any sin whatsoever, whether it be minor or major? What about the Prophets of Allāh (may Allāh's blessings and peace be upon them), who are the most noble of Allāh's creatures (Glory be to Him and Exalted is He)? The masters of knowledge have disagreed about them, so have they [the Prophets] attained to this degree, or not?"

In answer to this question, you must know that this matter is possible [for the human being], not inconceivable. It is actually quite easy, for Allāh confers distinction upon whomever He wills, by His mercy. One condition of repentance is that the servant must not commit a sin intentionally. If he sins absent-mindedly, or by mistake, he is pardoned for it by the gracious favour of Allāh (Exalted is He), so this is easy for someone who is helped and guided by Allāh (Exalted is He).

You may say: "Nothing keeps me from repentance, except that I know from myself that I shall return to sin, and that I shall not adhere to repentance, so there is no benefit in that."

You must recognize this as Satan's deception, and know where this "knowledge" comes from, for you may die as a penitent, before you revert to sin.

As for the fear of reverting to sin, you must be firmly resolved and truthful in that regard, and entrust the outcome to Allāh. If He grants complete success, the purpose will be fully achieved by His gracious favour. Even if He does not grant complete success, all your previous sins will have been forgiven, you will be delivered from them and purified, and you will not be guilty of any sin, except the one you have committed now. This is the mighty profit and the great and glorious benefit, so do not let the fear of reversion keep you from repentance. Where repentance is concerned, you are always entitled to one of those two good results. Allāh is the Custodian of enabling grace and guidance. This is the crux of the matter.

As for leaving sins behind, and achieving deliverance from them, you must know that sins in general are subdivided into three categories:

1. Omitting the obligatory duties imposed on you by Allāh (Glory be to Him and Exalted is He), such as the ritual prayer [*ṣalāt*], or fasting [*ṣawm*], or almsgiving [*zakāt*], or atonement [*kaffāra*], to mention a few examples. You must make up for such omissions, as far as you possibly can.

2. Sins between you and Allāh (Glory be to Him and Exalted is He), such as drinking alcoholic liquor [*khamr*], playing [musical instruments like] clarinets [*mazāmīr*], consuming usurious profit [*ribā*], and similar offences. You must feel remorse for that, and convince your heart to abstain forever from anything of the kind.

3. Sins between you and your fellow servants. These are the most problematic and most difficult, for they involve material property [*māl*], the person [*nafs*], reputation [*ʿirḍ*], the sanctity of family ties [*ḥurma*], and the sphere of religion [*dīn*].

In the case of material property [*māl*], you must restore it to him [its rightful owner] if you can. If you are unable to do so, because of destitution and poverty, you must ask him to absolve you. If you cannot do that, because of the absence or death of the person concerned, and it is possible to make a charitable donation [*taṣadduq*] on his behalf, you must act accordingly. If that is not possible, you must multiply your good deeds, and appeal to Allāh with supplication and humble entreaty, imploring Him to make your victim well pleased with you on the Day of Resurrection.

As for [offences against] the person [*nafs*], you must make it possible for the victim or his heirs to exact retaliation [*qiṣāṣ*], so that he [or they] may either take revenge or grant you exculpation. If you are unable to do so, you must appeal to Allāh (Glory be to Him) with humble entreaty, imploring Him to make your victim well pleased with you on the Day of Resurrection.

As for [offences against someone's] reputation [*ʿirḍ*], if you have backbitten him, or slandered him, or vilified him, you are obliged to declare yourself a liar before those in whose presence you did so. You must also seek absolution from the victim, if possible, but only if you are not afraid of provoking additional trouble and strife by your confession. If you are afraid of that, you must appeal to Allāh (Glory be to Him and Exalted is He), imploring Him to make your victim well pleased with you, and to bless him with abundant compensation. You must also beseech Him frequently to forgive your victim for any sins he may have committed.

As for the sanctity of family ties [*ḥurma*], which you have violated by cheating someone in connection with his wife, his son, or some other relative, there can be no question of seeking absolution for that offence, since confessing it will only give rise to trouble and strife. Instead, you must humbly implore Allāh (Glory be to Him), beseeching Him to make your victim well pleased with you, and to bless him with abundant compensation. Only in a very rare case, where you are truly safe from causing trouble and strife, should you seek absolution from your victim.

As for the sphere of religion [*dīn*], if you have accused someone of unbelief, or of heretical innovation, or of having gone astray, this is the most difficult problem of all. You need to call yourself a liar in the presence of anyone who heard you make those charges, and to seek absolution from your victim, if it is possible for you to do so. If that is not possible, you must appeal to Allāh (Exalted is He) in earnest, and feel remorse for your offence, so that He may cause your victim to be well pleased with you.

In short, you must do whatever you can to satisfy your legal claimants, and, when you cannot do that directly, you must appeal to Allāh (Glory be to Him and Exalted is He) with humble entreaty and charitable donation [*taṣadduq*], imploring Him to make your victim well pleased with you. Since that depends on the will of Allāh (Glory be to Him) on the Day of Resurrection, you can expect no immediate judgement. You must rely on His tremendous favour and His universal beneficence, in the hope that, when He recognizes the truthfulness in His servant's heart, he will satisfy his claimants from the treasury of His grace.

This is the crux of the matter, so you must understand it correctly. Then, if you act in the manner we have described, and rid your heart of the option to commit similar offences in future, you will have left all sins behind. If you succeed in purging the heart, but not in making up for omissions and in satisfying your legal claimants, you are responsible for the consequences, but other sins are forgiven.

This chapter calls for a lengthy commentary, which is beyond the scope of this synopsis. You should also consult the following Books from the work entitled "The Revival of the Religious Sciences [*Iḥyā' 'Ulūm ad-Dīn*]": (1) the Book of Repentance [*Kitāb at-Tawba*], (2) the Book of Nearness to Allāh (Exalted is He) [*Kitāb al-Qurba ila 'llāh (ta'ālā)*], and (3) the Book of the Ultimate Aim [*Kitāb al-Ghāyat al-Quṣwā*]. In them you will discover many benefits and a comprehensive commentary. As for what we have mentioned here, it constitutes the indispensable foundation. Allāh is the Source of enabling grace.

Subsection

Next, you must know for certain that this hurdle is a difficult hurdle, of which the importance is great and the potential harm is enormous.

Professor Abū Isḥāq al-Isfarā'īnī (may Allāh bestow His mercy upon him) was one of those who are firmly rooted in knowledge, and who put their knowledge into practice. According to a report that has reached us, he said:

"I appealed to Allāh (Glory be to Him) for thirty years, imploring Him to grant me sincere repentance. Then I began to wonder, so I said to myself: 'Glory be to Allāh! There is a need about which I have entreated Allāh for thirty years, and it has not been fulfilled until now. Then, in a dream, I saw someone speaking to me. He seemed to be saying: "Do you find that surprising? Do you realize what you are asking of Allāh? You are really asking Allāh (Glory be to Him) to love you! You must surely have heard His saying (Magnificent is His Majesty):

Truly, Allāh loves those who repent,
inna 'llāha yuḥibbu 't-tawwābīna
and He loves those who keep themselves clean.
wa yuḥibbu 'l-mutaṭahhirīn. (2:222)

""""Is this a trivial need?""""

You must pay attention to these leading figures [like Professor Abū Isḥāq], noting their diligent concern for the probity of their hearts, and the importance they attach to providing for the journey to their ultimate destination.

As for the dreadful harm that lurks in the postponement of repentance, the beginning of sin is hardness of heart, and the last of it—Let us take refuge with Allāh!—is calamity and disaster. Beware, therefore, of forgetting the affair of Iblīs and Bal'am ibn Bā'ūrā', for the beginning of their affair was a sin, and the end of it was unbelief [*kufr*], so they perished among those who perish for all eternity. It is incumbent upon you—May Allāh bestow His mercy upon you!—to practise wakeful alertness and dedicated striving, for then you may weed out from your heart the root of this persistence [in sin], and relieve your neck of these burdens.

Do not consider hardness of heart immune to sins, but reflect on your condition, for one of the righteous has said: "Darkness of the heart is caused by sins." The symptom of darkness of the heart is that you can find no refuge from sins, no room for obedience, and no resort for good advice. You must not underestimate the gravity of sins, so that you regard yourself as penitent, when you are actually persisting in major sins [*kabā'ir*]. We are informed that [Abū Abdi'llāh] Kahmas ibn al-Ḥasan once said: "I committed a sin, so I have been weeping over it for all of forty years." Someone asked: "What was it, O Abū Abdi'llāh?" He replied: "A brother for Allāh's sake paid me a visit, so I bought a fish for him, and he ate it. Then I went over to my neighbour's wall, and [without obtaining his consent] I took from it a piece of clay, which my visitor used to wipe his hand."

You must therefore examine yourself, call yourself to account, and hasten to repentance without delay, for the time of death is concealed, this world is an illusion, and the self and the devil are your enemies. You must humbly beseech and entreat Allāh (Glory be to Him), and remember the state of our father Adam (Allāh bless him and give him peace), whom Allāh (Exalted is He) created with His Hand, then breathed some of His Spirit into him, and conveyed him to His Garden on the necks of the angels. Adam committed only one sin, so he experienced what he experienced, until Allāh (Exalted is He) said to him, according to traditional report:

> O Adam, what kind of neighbour have I been for you?

Adam replied: "An excellent neighbour, O my Lord!" Allāh then said:

> O Adam, depart from My neighbourhood, and remove from your head the crown of My Noble Grace, for someone who disobeys Me cannot be My neighbour.

According to that same report, Adam then wept over his sin for two hundred years, until Allāh accepted his repentance and forgave him for his one and only sin.

This is how He treated His Prophet [*Nabī*] and His Special Friend [*Ṣafī*], on account of a single sin, so how will He treat others, on account of innumerable sins? This was the humble supplication and entreaty of the penitent [Adam], so how should it be for the persistently aberrant? How fine is the saying of the poet who said:

> Afraid for himself is someone who does repent,
> so how do you see the state of one who does not repent?

If you do repent, but then break your repentance and revert to sin, you must return to repentance in haste, and say to yourself: "Perhaps I shall die before I revert to sin this time." You must do likewise if this happens a third time and a fourth. Just as you have adopted sin and reversion to it as a profession, you must also adopt repentance and returning to it as a profession. You must not be less competent in repentance than you are in sin. You must not despair, nor let Satan bar you from repentance on that account, for that is the best profession. You have surely heard the saying of the Prophet (Allāh bless him and give him peace):

> The best of you is every sorely tempted person [*mutafattin*] who is devoutly penitent [*tawwāb*].

In other words: "[The best of you is] frequently afflicted with sin, yet frequent in repentance thereof, and in returning to Allāh (Magnificent is His Majesty) with remorse and the plea for forgiveness."

You must also remember His saying (Glory be to Him):

> If someone does evil or wrongs his own self,
> *wa man ya'mal sū'an aw yaẓlim nafsa-hu*
> then seeks forgiveness of Allāh,
> *thumma yastaghfiri 'llāha*
> he will find Allāh All-Forgiving, All-Compassionate.
> *yajidi 'llāha Ghafūran Raḥīmā.* (4:110)

This is the most important point, for Allāh is the Source of enabling grace.

Subsection

To put the whole matter in a nutshell:

—You must begin by absolving your heart of all sins. In other words, you must make it firmly resolved that you will absolutely never revert to sin, apart from any unintentional mistake. You must do this in such a manner that Allāh (Glory be to Him and Exalted is He) will acknowledge the truthfulness of your resolution, since it comes from a pure heart.

—You must do as much as you can to satisfy your legal claimants. You must make up for omissions to the best of your ability, and appeal to Allāh (Glory be to Him and Exalted is He) with humble supplication and entreaty, where the leftovers are concerned, so that they may receive sufficient attention.

—Then you must go and perform the complete ablution [*taghtasil*], wash your clothes, and perform four cycles [*raka'āt*] of ritual prayer in the proper manner. You must set your face on the ground in an empty place, where no one can see you except Allāh (Glory be to Him and Exalted is He).

—You must then lay dust on your head and rub it on your face, which is the most dignified member of your body, with streaming tears, a sad heart, and a loud lament. You must recall your sins one by one, as far as you are able, blaming and scolding your disobedient self for them, and saying: "Are you not ashamed, O lower self [*nafs*]? Is it not time for you to repent? Can you bear the torment of Allāh (Glory be to Him)? Do you need to incur the displeasure of Allāh (Glory be to Him)?" You must repeat this frequently, and weep profusely.

—Then you must raise your hands towards the All-Compassionate Lord (Glory be to Him), and say: "My God [*Ilāhī*], Your renegade servant has come back to Your door. Your disobedient servant has returned to righteousness. Your sinful servant has come to you with apology, so pardon me through Your noble generosity, accept me through Your gracious favour, and look upon me with Your mercy! O Allāh, forgive me for my previous sins, and preserve my innocence in what is left of the appointed time, for all goodness is in Your Hand, and with us You are Kind, Compassionate.

—Then you must offer the supplication of distress [*du'ā' ash-shidda*], which is expressed in the words:

O Manifestation of all things great!
yā Majlā 'aẓā'imi 'l-umūr:

O Goal of the ambition of the high-minded!
yā Muntahā himmati 'l-mahmūmīn:

O He who, when He wishes something,
yā Man idhā arāda amran
has only to say to it: "Be!" and there it is!
fa-inna-mā yaqūlu la-hu kun fa-yakūn:

Our sins have enveloped us,
aḥāṭat bi-nā dhunūbu-nā
but You are the Store for them.
Anta 'l-Madhkhūru la-hā

O Store for every distress,
yā Madhkhūran li-kulli shidda:
I have been keeping You in store for this moment,
kuntu addakhiru-ka li-hādhihi 's-sā'a:
so relent towards me,
fa-tub 'alayya
for You are the Ever-Relenting, the All-Compassionate!
inna-ka Anta 't-Tawwābu 'r-Raḥīm.

—Then you must shed many tears, abase and humble yourself, and say:

O He whom no business distracts from any business,
yā Man lā yashghalu-hu sha'nun 'an sha'n:
and no hearing from any hearing!
wa lā sam'un 'an sam':

O He who is not disconcerted by the multiplicity of problems!
yā Man lā tughalliṭu-hu kathratu 'l-masā'il:

O He who is not wearied by the importuning of the importunate!
yā Man lā yabramu-hu ilḥāḥu 'l-muliḥḥīn:

Let me taste the cool refreshment of Your pardon
adhiq-nī barda ʿafwi-ka
and the sweetness of Your forgiveness,
wa ḥalāwata maghfirati-k:
through Your mercy, O Most Merciful of the merciful.
bi-raḥmati-ka yā Arḥama 'r-rāḥimīn:
You are surely Capable of all things.
inna-ka ʿalā kulli shaiʾin Qādīr.

—Then you must invoke blessing on the Prophet (Allāh bless him and give him peace) and on his family.

—Then you must seek forgiveness for all the believing men [*muʾminīn*] and all the believing women [*muʾmināt*], and return to obedience to Allāh (Magnificent is His Majesty).

You have now repented with a sincere repentance [*qad tubta tawbatan naṣūḥā*]. You have left sins behind, and you are now as pure as on the day when your mother gave you birth. Allāh (Glory be to Him) has come to love you, and you are entitled to the recompense and the reward. You are endowed with blessing and mercy, such as cannot be encompassed by the description of the describers. You have attained to safety and salvation, and escaped from Allāh's wrath. You have been delivered from the agony of sinful acts of disobedience, and from their trial and tribulation in this world and the Hereafter. You have surmounted this hurdle, with the permission of Allāh (Glory be to Him and Exalted is He). Allāh is the Custodian of guidance through His grace and favour.

The Third Hurdle
The hurdle of the impediments [*ʿawāʾiq*]

As for your next duty, O seeker of worshipful service—may Allāh (Exalted is He) enable you to succeed!—it is disposing of the impediments [*ʿawāʿiq*], so that your worship will be right and proper. As we have mentioned earlier,[13] the impediments are four in number:

The First Impediment
This world and all that it contains

There is only one way to dispose of this impediment, and that is by detachment [*tajarrud*] and abstinence [*zuhd*] from this world. You are obliged to practise this detachment and abstinence for two reasons only:

1. First, so that your worship will be correct and frequent, for your interest in this world keeps you preoccupied.

As for your outer being, it is preoccupied with the acquisition of worldly goods, while your inner being is preoccupied with desire and the prattle of the lower self [*ḥadīth an-nafs*]. Both of these prevent worship. The self is single, and the heart is single, so, if either is preoccupied with one thing, it is cut off from the opposite. This world and the Hereafter can be compared to a couple of wives: if you please one of the pair, you will displease the other. They can also be compared to the east and the west, since you move away from one to the extent that you incline towards the other.

As for your preoccupation with the external world, we have heard that Abu 'd-Dardāʾ (may Allāh be well pleased with him) once said: "I tried hard to combine worship with trade, but they did not fit together, so I concentrated on worship and abstained from trade." ʿUmar [ibn al-Khaṭṭāb] (may Allāh be well pleased with him) is

[13] See p. 11 above.

reported as having said: "If these two were compatible for anyone other than me, they would be compatible for me, because of the strength and flexibility that Allāh (Glory be to Him) has granted me." In view of this saying, you must devalue the transitory world and choose safety. Peace [be on those who follow right guidance]!

As for this world's tendency to keep the heart, which is the inner being, preoccupied with desire, the Prophet (Allāh bless him and give him peace) is reported as having said:

> If someone loves his life in this world, he devalues his life in the Hereafter, and if someone loves his life in the Hereafter, he devalues his life in this world. You must therefore prefer what is lasting to that which is fleeting.

This should make it clear to you that, if your outer being is preoccupied with this world and your inner being with its desire, worship in its true form is impossible for you. On the other hand, if you abstain from this world, so that you are outwardly and inwardly free from attachment, worship will be possible for you, or even easy, since your limbs and organs will assist you in its performance. Salmān al-Fārisī (may Allāh be well pleased with him) is reported as having said: "If the servant abstains from this world, his heart will be enlightened with wisdom, and his limbs and organs will assist him in worship." This is the crux of the matter.

2. The second reason [for practising detachment and abstinence] is that it increases the value of your work, and magnifies its worth and its honour, for the Prophet (Allāh bless him and give him peace) has said:

> Two cycles of prayer [*rak'atān*] from a learned man, whose heart is abstinent, are better and dearer to Allāh (Magnificent is His Majesty) than the worship of all worshippers till the end of time, forever and eternally.

Since worship is thereby ennobled and multiplied, it is incumbent on someone who seeks worshipful service to abstain from this world, and to detach himself from it completely.

You may ask: "What is the meaning of abstinence [*zuhd*] from this world, and what is the real significance thereof?"

You should therefore know that, according to our scholars (may Allāh bestow His mercy upon them), abstinence is of two kinds: abstinence that is decreed for the servant, and abstinence that is not decreed.

As for that which is decreed, it involves three things: (1) abandoning the search for what is lacking from this world, (2) parting with everything collected from it, and (3) forsaking the desire and preference for it.

As for the abstinence that is not decreed for the servant, it is the feeling of coldness towards the thing [abstained from] in the heart of the abstainer.

With its three elements, the abstinence that is decreed for the servant precedes the abstinence that is not decreed for the servant. When the servant succeeds in abstaining—by not seeking what he lacks from this world, by parting with what he has gained from it, and by forsaking with his heart the desire and preference for it, for the sake of Allāh and His mighty reward, through his recollection of this world's misfortunes—that will instill the feeling of coldness towards this world in his heart. This, in my opinion, is the real abstinence.

Of the three elements, you must know that the most difficult is forsaking desire with the heart. Many a person has forsaken it with his outer being, though he loves it and longs for it with his inner being, so he is exposed to assaults and severe anguish from his lower self. The whole affair is rooted in this [desire]. You must listen to His saying (Glory be to Him, for He is More Glorious than any other sayer):

> As for that Ultimate Abode,
> *tilka 'd-dāru 'l-ākhiratu*
> We shall bestow it on those who do not desire
> *naj'alu-hā li'lladhīna lā yurīdūna*
> either exaltation on the earth, or corruption.
> *'uluwwan fi 'l-arḍi wa lā fasādā.* (28:83)

Note that He has made the bestowal dependant on the negation of desire, rather than abstinence from the search and the desired action.

You must also listen to His sayings (Glory be to Him and Exalted is He):

> If someone desires the harvest of the Hereafter,
> *man kān yurīdu ḥartha al-ākhirati*
> We shall give him an increase in his harvest,
> *nazid la-hu fī ḥarthi-hi*
> and whoever desires the harvest of this world,
> *wa man kāna yurīdu ḥartha 'd-dunyā*
> We shall give him some of it,
> *nu'ti-hi min-hā*
> but in the Hereafter he will have no share.
> *wa mā la-hu fi 'l-ākhirati min naṣīb.* (42:20)

> Whoever desires that which hastens away,
> *man kāna yurīdu 'l-ʿājilata*
> We shall hasten for him therein whatever We will.
> *ʿajjalnā la-hu fī-hā mā nashāʾu.* (17:18)
>
> And whoever desires the Hereafter,
> *wa man arāda 'l-ākhirata*
> and strives for it with the effort required,
> *wa saʿa la-hu saʿya-hā*
> while he is a true believer—
> *wa huwa muʾminun*
> for such, their effort is favourably received.
> *fa-ulāʾika kāna saʿyu-hum mashkūrā.* (17:19)

You will surely notice that the emphasis here is on desire, in every instance, so it must be the most important factor. Nevertheless, if the servant is diligent and correct in addressing the first two elements, by which I mean parting [with his worldly possessions] and abandoning [the search for what he lacks], there is still room for hope that Allāh (Glory be to Him) will enable him, through His gracious favour, to dispel this desire and preference from his heart, for He is the Noble Bestower (Almighty and Glorious is He).

As for the stimulus that will prompt you to abandon [the search for things you lack], and to part [with your possessions], and will make that easy for you, it is the recollection of the misfortunes and faults of this world. Many people have had something to say about that, for instance: "I have forsaken this world on account of the shortage of its wealth, the abundance of its trouble, the speed of its fading away, and the meanness of its partners."

This drew the following comment from my own Shaikh, Imām [Abū Bakr al-Warrāq] (may Allāh bestow His mercy upon him): "But from this comes the fragrant scent of longing, because, if a person complains about separation from someone, it means that he would love to be in contact with that individual. If he abandons something on account of the involvement of partners, it means that he would love to be its sole possessor."

The most eloquent saying on the subject is that of our Shaikh (may Allāh the Exalted bestow His mercy upon him): "This world is the enemy of Allāh (Almighty and Glorious is He). You are His lover, and he who loves someone detests his enemy." He also said: "Besides, this world is essentially a putrid cadaver. You must surely see that it is bound to end in filth, corruption, ruination, evanescence and waste, but it is a cadaver that is anointed with perfume and wrapped in adornment, so the heedless are deceived by its exterior, while the intelligent abstain from it."

The question may be asked: "So what is the legal status of abstinence from this world? Is it a compulsory duty [*farḍ*], or a supererogatory obligation [*nafl*]?"

You must therefore know that abstinence [*zuhd*] is incumbent upon us with regard to both what is lawful [*ḥalāl*] and what is unlawful [*ḥarām*]. In the case of what is unlawful, it is a compulsory duty, and in the case of what is lawful it is a supererogatory obligation.

For those who perform acts of obedience correctly, whatever is unlawful [*ḥarām*] belongs in the same category as carrion flesh [*maita*], which is considered unclean, and which can only be used in emergency, to the extent required for the prevention of serious harm.

As for abstinence from that which is lawful [*ḥalāl*], it is peculiar to the class of saints called *Abdāl*.[14] For them, what is lawful belongs in the same category as carrion flesh [*maita*], of which they can only use an indispensable quantity. Where they are concerned, whatever is unlawful [*ḥarām*] belongs in the same category as the Fire of Hell, so it never occurs to them, under any circumstance, to seek its acquisition.

This is the meaning of coldness in the heart, in the sense that the abstainer severs his ambition from this world, regards it as filthy and views it with extreme disgust, so that his heart retains no preference for it, and no desire.

You may ask: "How is it possible for this world, when its lustful delights and its marvellous pleasures are so desirable for the human being, to belong in the same category as the Fire of Hell, or in the absurd category of the putrid cadaver, when the human constitution is our constitution, and human nature is our nature?"

[14] *Abdāl* is the plural of *Badal*. In the Sixth Discourse of *Revelations of the Unseen*, Shaikh ʿAbd al-Qādir (may Allāh be well pleased with him) gives the following explanation: "Annihilation [*fanāʾ*] is the aim and object, the final destination of the journey of the saints. This was the direction sought by all previous saints and *Abdāl*: to become extinct to their own will, and let the will of the Almighty and Glorious Truth take its place, as a permanent transformation, lasting until death. That is why they came to be called *Abdāl* [lit: 'substitutes'] (may Allāh be well pleased with them all)."

You must know, therefore, that if someone is blessed with special enabling grace, and if he recognizes the evils of this world and its basic filth, it can indeed come to be like that in his sight. The only ones who find this surprising are the addicts of desire, those who are blind to the faults and evils of this world, deluded by its superficial charm and its adornment. Let me coin an allegory for you: This can be likened to the case of a person who concocts a sweet jelly [*khabīṣ*], using sugar and all the other necessary ingredients, and then throws a piece of deadly poison into the mixture. One man sees that happen, but another fails to notice it. The cook sets the jelly in front of the pair, beautifully decorated and adorned.

As for the man who saw the poison being added, he will abstain from that jelly, for it will not occur to him, under any circumstance whatsoever, to take it and eat it. In his sight, that would belong in the same category as the Fire of Hell. Considering what he knows about its dreadful consequences, he will hardly be deceived by its superficial charm and its beautiful adornment!

As for the other man, who failed to notice what had been added to the mixture, he will be deluded by its decorated surface, so he will be greedily impatient to taste it. When he sees to his surprise that his companion is abstaining from it, he will start wondering how he can be so stupid.

This is analogous to the unlawful contents [*ḥarām*] of this world, in relation to those who are knowledgeable and righteous, and to those who are ignorant and motivated by desire.

Suppose the cook does not throw poison into the jelly, but spits or blows his nose into it, then rubs it with oil and decorates it. The man who witnessed that action will recoil from that jelly with disgust. He will hardly go near it, except in emergency and pressing need. As for the man who failed to witness that, he is ignorant of what the jelly contains, deluded by its superficial charm, eager to eat it, addicted, admiring and enamoured.

This is analogous to the lawful contents [*ḥalāl*] of this world, in relation to the same two groups: the people of insight and understanding, and the people of desire and heedlessness.

The difference between the two men, despite their equivalence in nature and constitution, is due to nothing but the insight and knowledge belonging to one of the two, and the ignorance and coarseness belonging to the other. If the addict of desire had known and understood what the abstainer knew, he would have been abstinent like him. If the abstainer had been as ignorant and blind as the addict of desire, he would have been addicted to desire like him.

As I have thereby understood, this distinction is due to the perceptive faculties, not to the natural dispositions. This is a useful principle, and a clear and straightforward statement, acknowledged and confirmed by the intelligent.

Allāh (Exalted is He) is the Custodian of right guidance and enablement, through His gracious favour.

The question may be asked: "Some part of this world is indispensable for our sustenance, so how can we abstain from it?"

You must therefore know that abstinence [*zuhd*] applies to excess, meaning that which exceeds what is needed to sustain the human constitution. The purpose of acquiring sustenance and strength is to enable you to worship Allāh (Glory be to Him), not for the sake of eating, drinking, and enjoying worldly pleasures. If Allāh (Exalted is He) so wills, He may use a material thing and a physical instrument [*sabab*] to sustain the human constitution. If Allāh (Exalted is He) so wills, He may sustain it by other than physical means, such as the angels (peace be upon them). If He does wish to use a material thing, it is something readily available to you, or which you can seek and earn. If He so wills, it may be something else again, something He provides for you from sources you could never imagine, without any searching or earning on your part. As Allāh (Exalted is He) has said:

> And if someone is truly devoted to Allāh,
> *wa man yattaqi 'llāha*
> He will prepare a way out for him,
> *yaj'al la-hu makhrajā:*
> and He will provide for him
> *wa yarzuq-hu*
> from sources he could never imagine.
> *min ḥaithu lā yaḥtasib.* (65:2,3)

In that case, you have no need whatsoever for searching and for exercising the will. On the other hand, if you are incapable of that abstinence, and you search and exercise the will, your intention must be readiness and true devotion to the worship of Allāh (Glory be to Him and Exalted is He), not carnal lust and pleasure. If that is what you intend, it is good for you to search and to exercise the will, for the search is really for the Hereafter, not for this world, and it does not diminish your abstinence and your detachment.

You must recognize all this as pointing in the right direction. Allāh is the Source of enabling grace!

The Second Impediment [*ʿāʾiq*]
Your fellow creatures [*khalq*]

Your next obligation—may Allāh enable you and us to worship Him!—is to practise isolation from your fellow creatures [*khalq*]. There are two reasons for that:

1. Your fellow creatures distract you from the worship of Allāh (Almighty and Glorious is He). Consider this report from one of the scholars:

"I passed by a group of people who were engaged in an arrow-shooting contest. One man was sitting at a distance from them, so I wished to speak to him, but he said: 'The remembrance [*dhikr*] of Allāh is dearer to me than your speech.' When I asked him: 'Are you alone?' he replied: 'My Lord and my two angels are with me.' I then said: 'Which of these [contestants] are the winners?' He replied: 'Those whom Allāh has forgiven.' I said: 'Where is the path [to success]?' He pointed his hand towards the sky, then he got up and left me, saying [to Allāh]: 'Most of Your creatures are distracted from You.'"

That explains why your fellow creatures distract you from worship, and even prevent you from performing it. Worse still, they cause you to fall into wickedness and perdition. It was Ḥātim al-Aṣamm (may Allāh bestow His mercy upon him) who said:

"I sought five things from these creatures, but I did not find them: I sought obedience and abstinence, but they did not practise them, so I said: 'Help me to practise them, even if you do not,' but they did not [help me]. I said: 'Approve of me if I practise them,' but they refused.

I said: 'Then do not prevent me from practising them,' but they did prevent me. I said: 'Do not invite me to that which displeases Allāh the Almighty, and do not treat me with hostility if I do not follow you.' They rejected my request, so I abandoned them and concentrated on my own private interest [in obedience and abstinence]."

You must also know, O brother in the religion, that your Prophet Muḥammad (Allāh bless him and give him peace) described the time of seclusion [*ʿuzla*], explained its character, and commanded its observance in solitary isolation. There is no doubt that he (Allāh bless him and give him peace) knew more about what is right and proper, and was more sincere in counselling us, than we ourselves. If you find that your present time corresponds to his description and his explanation, you must comply with his command (Allāh bless him and give him peace) and accept his wise counsel. Have no doubt that he (Allāh bless him and give him peace) was well aware of what would be best for you in your own time. Do not invent excuses, and do not deceive yourself, otherwise you are doomed and inexcusable.

Part of the above-mentioned description is contained in the well-known report from ʿAbdu'llāh ibn ʿAmr ibn al-ʿĀṣ (may Allāh be well pleased with him and his father), who said:

"We were in the company of the Prophet (Allāh bless him and give him peace), when mention was made of corruption [*fitna*]. He said: 'If you see that people break their contracts, and their trusts carry little weight, they are like this...,' and he intertwined his fingers. I said: 'What should I do in that case? May Allāh make me your ransom!' He said:

> Stick to your home and keep your tongue to yourself. Accept what you know to be right, and leave what you know to be wrong. You must adopt the pattern of the élite [*khāṣṣa*], and discard the pattern of the common herd [*ʿāmma*]."

According to another report, the Prophet (Allāh bless him and give him peace) once said:

> Those are the days of turmoil [*harj*].

When someone asked: "And what are the days of turmoil?" he replied:

> [They are the days] when a man cannot trust his close companion [*jalīs*].

According to yet another report, Ibn Masʿūd (may Allāh be well pleased with him) told al-Ḥārith ibn ʿAmīra that the Prophet (Allāh bless him and give him peace) once said to him:

> If you are granted a long life, you will live through a time when preachers are many, though scholars are few, and when questioners are many, though few can answer their questions. It will be a time when caprice is the director of knoweldge.

When Ibn Masʿūd asked: "And when will that be?" he replied (Allāh bless him and give him peace):

> When the ritual prayer [*ṣalāt*] has been put to death, bribery has been accepted as the norm, and the religion has been sold for a tiny slice of this world. Seek salvation! Seek salvation! Woe unto you! Then again, seek salvation!

You can see everything mentioned in these reports with your own eye, in your own time and its people, so take good care of yourself!

The righteous forebears [*salaf*] (may Allāh be well pleased with them) were unanimous in being on guard against their own time and its people. They preferred seclusion [*ʿuzla*], enjoined its practice and urged it on one another. There is no doubt that they were most perceptive and most sincere in their advice, and that the times have not become better after them, but even worse and more bitter. Yūsuf ibn Asbāṭ is reported as having said: "I once heard ath-Thawrī say: 'By Allāh—there is no god but He!—seclusion has become lawful at this time.' I said: 'Well, if it became lawful in his time, in this time of ours it has come to be necessary and obligatory!'"

Sufyān ath-Thawrī is also said to have written to ʿAbbād al-Khawwāṣ (may Allāh bestow His mercy upon them both): "You are at a time from which, we have been told, the Companions of Muḥammad (Allāh bless him and give him peace) sought refuge with Allāh, lest they should reach it. They had knowledge that we do not possess, so how is it for us, when we have reached it with little knowledge, little patience, and few assistants to help us do well, along with misery from this world and corruption from its people?"

According to ʿUmar ibn al-Khaṭṭāb (may Allāh be well pleased with him): "In seclusion [*ʿuzla*] there is welcome relief from bad associates." In similar vein, a poet has said:

> This is the time of which we needed to beware,
> according to Kaʿb and according to Ibn Masʿūd.

It is an age in which Truth is rejected entirely,
while wrong and injustice are not rejected at all.

Blind and deaf are those confused by such times,
when Iblīs has the chance to succeed and ascend.

If this lasts long, and nothing happens to change it,
no death will be lamented and no birth celebrated.

I have discovered that Sufyān ibn ʿUyaina said: "I asked ath-Thawrī to give me some good advice, so he told me: 'Devote very little time to acquiring familiarity with people.' I said: 'May Allāh bestow His mercy upon you! Surely we have been told, in the traditional report [*khabar*]: 'Devote a great deal of time to acquiring familiarity with people, for every believer has a right to intercede [on another's behalf].' He then went on to say: 'I suppose you have never experienced something you detest, except from someone you know well!' I said: 'Yes, that is true!'

"Then he died (may Allāh bestow His mercy upon him), and I saw him in a dream some years later, so I said: 'O Abū ʿAbdi'llāh, give me some good advice!' He told me: 'Devote little time to familiarity with people, as little as you can, for deliverance from them is very hard to achieve.'"

The meaning of this report has also been expressed in poetry:

Ever since greyness first appeared in the parting of my hair,
I have not ceased to examine and investigate these creatures.

The more I have come to know human beings,
the more I have found fault with them.
May Allāh grant a good reward to everyone I have not come to know!

There is no sin for which I deserve to be treated with aversion,
except that I have loved someone who did not act justly.

It has also been said that these words were inscribed on the door of ath-Thawrī's house: 'May Allāh grant a good reward to those who do not know us well, and may He not grant that to our friends, for we have never suffered harm except from them!'

The sense of this inscription has also been expressed in poetic verse:

May Allāh grant a good reward, on our behalf,
to those with whom we share no affection,
and with whom we are not mutually acquainted,

for no grief has afflicted us, and no harm has befallen us,
from any people except those we love and know well.

It was al-Fuḍail (may Allāh bestow His mercy upon him) who said: "This is a time when you must guard your tongue, conceal your status, cure your heart, accept what you know to be right, and leave what you know to be wrong."

Sufyān ath-Thawrī said: "This is the time of silence, staying at home, and being content with basic nourishment until you die."

According to Dāwūd aṭ-Ṭā'ī (may Allāh bestow His mercy upon him): "You must fast from this world, devote your nature to the Hereafter, and flee from people as you would flee from the lion."

According to Abū 'Ubaida: "I have never met a wise man who did not tell me, at the end of his speech: 'If you love to be unknown, you are sure to receive Allāh's favour!'"

Traditional reports on this subject are too numerous for this book to contain them all. We have compiled a separate book devoted to it, which we have entitled: "The Book of the Morals and Ethics of the Righteous, and of Salvation from the Wicked [*Kitāb akhlāq al-abrār wa 'n-najāt mina 'l-ashrār*]." You should consult it, for you will discover wonders and marvels. A hint is enough for the intelligent person! Allāh is the Custodian of enabling grace, and right guidance is due to His favour.

2. As for the second factor that requires you to practise isolation from people, it is that people will corrupt the worship you succeed in performing, unless Allāh (Glory be to Him) grants immunity. They will do so by means of the incentives they offer, encouraging hypocrisy and ostentation. Yaḥyā ibn Mu'ādh ar-Rāzī (may Allāh bestow His mercy upon him) spoke the truth when he said: "The desire to impress other people is the doormat of hypocrisy."

These righteous abstainers [many of whose sayings we have quoted above] were afraid for themselves in this context, so they refrained from meeting socially and exchanging visits. We are told that Harim ibn Ḥayyān once said to Uwais al-Qaranī (may Allāh bestow His mercy upon them both): "O Uwais, connect with us through visiting and meeting together!" Uwais replied: "I have connected with you through something far more valuable than either of those two, that being supplication [*du'ā'*] in private, because visiting and meeting together can easily give rise to ostentation and hypocrisy."

When Sulaimān al-Khawwāṣ was in the vicinity of Ibrāhīm ibn Ad'ham, he was asked: "Will you not go to him?" He said: "To overthrow a rebellious devil [*shaiṭān mārid*] would be dearer to me than meeting with him!" They disapproved of his saying that, so he explained: "I am afraid that, if I met him, I would put on a show to impress him, whereas, if I met a devil, I would hold myself aloof from him."

My own Shaikh, Imām [Abū Bakr al-Warrāq], once met with one of the experts in direct knowledge [*'ārifīn*], and they engaged in a lengthy discussion, then, at the end of their conversation, they appealed to Allāh for His blessing. My Shaikh said to the expert: "I do not think I have ever attended a meeting more hope-inspiring than this one!" The expert said to him: "But I have never attended a meeting more fear-inspiring than this one! Were you not intent on showing your speech and your knowledge in the most favourable light, in order to impress me? I was doing likewise, so we are guilty of hypocritical display [*riyā'*]." My Shaikh wept profusely, then he fell into a faint. In the wake of that experience, he would often cite these poetic verses:

Alas for a prosperous man, for whom nothing
is more dreadful than the justice of the Judge!

I confess his disobedience to Allāh,
for none but He treats me with mercy.

O my Lord, grant pardon to a sinner,
who has transgressed but is remorseful.

When the night grows dark, he says:
"Oh for a sin condoned by the All-Knowing!"

Such is the state of those who practise abstinence and spiritual training, when they meet together, so what is the state of those addicted to desire and vanity, let alone the state of those addicted to evil and ignorance?

You must know that the time has dawned on enormous corruption, and people have become the source of great harm, for they distract you from the worship of Allāh (Exalted is He), to the point where you hardly practise it at all. Then they corrupt what little you do practise, so that hardly any part of it remains intact for you. You must therefore resort to seclusion and isolation from people, and to seeking refuge with Allāh from the evil of this time and its folk. Allāh (Exalted is He) is the Protector [*Ḥāfiẓ*], through His gracious favour and His mercy.

You may ask: "So what is the definition of seclusion and isolation from people? Will you explain to us the condition of the various classes of people in this regard, and the extent to which they must be avoided?"

You must therefore know—may Allāh bestow His mercy on you and on us!—that people in this context are of two types:

—First, there is a man who has no need of his fellow creatures, for the sake of knowledge and the explanation of a rule of law. The best course for this man is isolation from other people. He should not mingle with them, except in a congregational prayer [*jumʿa*], a customary gathering [*jamāʿa*], a Festival [*ʿĪd*], a Pilgrimage [*Ḥajj*], a session of traditional learning, or an unavoidable situation connected with the needs of livelihood. Otherwise, he should disguise his personal identity, and keep his place of residence from becoming known.

If this man wishes to cut himself off from people entirely, and not to mix with them in any situation whatsoever, whether it be religious or worldly, including customary gatherings, congregational prayers and so on—because he considers that in his best interest and conducive to his detachment—he can only accomplish that by one of two means: (1) He may settle in a place where these duties are not incumbent upon him, such as the mountain peaks and the depths of the desert valleys. This may well be one of the factors that attract the servants [of the Lord] to those places, far away from people. (2) He may be truly convinced that the harm inflicted on him, because of these duties, is much more serious than [the harm resulting from] their abandonment. In that case, he has a valid excuse for abandoning them.

When I was in Mecca (may Allāh keep it safe), I saw one of the learned elders who practise isolation. He did not attend gatherings at the Sacred Mosque [*al-Masjid al-Ḥarām*], in spite of his closeness to it and the safety of his situation. I brought that up with him one day, on one of my frequent visits to him, and he explained his excuse in the terms I have indicated above. In other words, the spiritual reward he obtained, from going out to the Mosque and meeting with people, did not compensate for the sins and bad consequences that affected him.

All things considered, no blame attaches to one who is excused, and Allāh (Exalted is He) knows best what the excuse is worth.

> Allāh is Aware of what the breasts contain.
> *wa 'llāhu ʿAlīmun bi-dhāti 'ṣ-ṣudūr.* (3:154)

Nevertheless, the correct approach is to start by participating in the congregational prayer, customary gatherings and various good activities, and by staying aloof from people in every other situation. If someone prefers the second approach, which means cutting himself off from people entirely, the way to accomplish it is by moving to places where these obligations are not incumbent upon him. As for the third approach, which is to live among the people in a particular town, but not to attend any congregational prayer or customary gathering—with the excuse that such attendance imposes a burden of sin, or some other bad consequence—the person concerned needs to make a very intense and detailed scrutiny, so that he may be relieved of that option. This third approach is fraught with the risk of error, so the first two are safer and more secure. Allāh is the Custodian of right guidance, through His gracious favour.

—As for the second type, he is a man to be regarded as an exemplar of knowledge, inasmuch as people need him in the sphere of their religion. They may need him to explain the Truth, or to refute the heretical innovator, or to summon them to goodness in action or in speech, or for some other purpose of the kind. For a man like this, there can be no question of seclusion from his fellow human beings. Far from it! He must install himself in their midst, as a wise counsellor for Allāh's creatures (Exalted is He), a defender of Allāh's religion (Exalted is He), and an interpreter of Allāh's laws.

According to traditional report, Allāh's Messenger (Allāh bless him and give him peace) once said:

> If heresies [*bidaʿ*] appear, but the scholar holds his tongue, may the curse of Allāh be upon him!

This is relevant if the exemplary scholar is among the people, but even if he goes out from their midst, seclusion is still not permissible for him.

It is related that Professor Abū Bakr ibn Fawrak (may Allāh bestow

His mercy upon him) decided to isolate himself from people, in order to worship Allāh. While he was on one of the mountains, he suddenly heard a voice crying: "O Abū Bakr, you have come to be one of Allāh's proofs against His creatures, yet you have forsaken Allāh's servants!" He promptly went back to the town, and this experience was the cause of his companionship with his fellow creatures.

As I was told by Ma᾽mūn ibn Aḥmad (may Allāh bestow His mercy upon him), Professor Abū Isḥāq (may Allāh bestow His mercy upon him) said to the worshippers secluded on Mount Lebanon: "O consumers of dry herbs [*ḥashīsh*]! You have left the Community of Muḥammad (Allāh bless him and give him peace) in the hands of the heretics, and busied yourselves here with the consumption of dry herbs." They said to him: "We lack the strength required for keeping people company. Allāh has given you such strength, so that is incumbent on you!" After hearing this, Professor Abū Isḥāq compiled his book "The Compendium of the Visible and the Concealed [*al-Jāmiʿ li'l-jalī wa 'l-khafī*]." They were thus equipped (may Allāh bestow His mercy upon them) not only with abundance of knowledge, but also with plentiful practice, and with a clear-sighted view of the journey on the path of the Hereafter.

You must also know that this man, the kind people need in the context of religion, has two urgent needs of his own in the company of his fellow creatures: First of all, he needs long-enduring patience, enormous tolerance, a kind and gracious attitude, and constant readiness to seek help from Allāh (Exalted is He). Secondly, he needs to be inwardly detached from people, even though he is together with them in physical form. If they talk to him, he will talk to them. If they visit him, he will treat them with all due respect, and he will thank them. If they say nothing to him, and turn away from him, he will take advantage of that opportunity. If they are engaged in something right and good, he will assist them. If they indulge in foolish talk and bad conduct, he will contradict them and shun them, or he may chide them and rebuke them, if he hopes to improve their hearts.

He will also fulfil all their entitlements, including social visits and special visits to the sick, as well as the satisfaction of needs presented to him, to the best of his ability. He will not demand any form of remuneration from them, nor will he expect that of them. He will not expose them to alienation because of that [failure to remunerate him]. He will spend on them generously, if he can, and he will be shy of accepting gifts from them. He will be tolerant of any annoyance they cause him, showing them a cheerful face and letting them see him in fine form. He will hide his own needs from them, enduring them by himself and dealing with them in his heart and his inner being.

He also needs to pay special attention to his own person, by giving it an opportunity to engage in devout worship. As ʿUmar ibn al-Khaṭṭāb (may Allāh be well pleased with him) once said: "If I sleep through the night, I am bound to neglect my own person, and if I sleep through the day, I am bound to neglect the flock, so how is it for me to sleep between these two?" In this context, I am also reminded of the following verses of poetry:

If you are eager for the guidance of the spiritual leaders,
you must be determined that events will find you endowed

with a dignified bearing towards everything unpleasant,
and with a patient heart, for that is a safeguard in the breast.

Your tongue must be kept in reserve, your gaze reined in,
your inner being concealed, except in the presence of the Lord,

your remembrance covered over, your door locked shut,
your mouth wearing a smile, your stomach hungry,

your heart sorely wounded, your market stagnant,
your merit buried, and your disrepute widespread.

Each day must find you swallowing a painful torment
from the time and the brethren, while your heart is obedient.

Your day must be devoted to people, without taunting,
and your night to love [of the Lord], in the absence of prying eyes.

This night is an opportunity, so use it to prepare a pretext
for a dismal Day when pretexts will be few and far between.

Yes indeed, this man will be together with people in person, but his heart will be so far removed from them! That, upon my life, is a difficult matter and a hard way to live. Our Shaikh (may Allāh bestow His mercy upon him) had this to say about it, in the advice he bequeathed [to his son]: "O my son, live with the people of your time, but do not follow their example." Then he said: "How hard it is to live with the living, while following the example of the dead!"

According to Ibn Masʿūd (may Allāh be well pleased with him): "You must both mingle with people and stay apart from them, and do not injure your religion." This is a pleasantly witty remark!

If temptations come surging in a series of waves, so that the state of affairs deteriorates, and people turn their backs on the matter of religion, they treat a believer with ruthless disrespect, and they pay no attention to a scholar. They ignore any source of benefit, and the matter of their religion does not concern them at all. You see that corruption not only pervades the common herd, but also creeps in among the élite. This gives the scholar a valid excuse to practise seclusion and isolation and the burial of knowledge.

I am afraid that what we have mentioned is an accurate description of this tough and difficult time. Allāh is the One to whom we must turn for help, and in Him we must place our trust!

This [that we have described above] is the legal status of seclusion and isolation from people, so you must understand it correctly, for, if it is misunderstood, the error will be serious and very harmful. Allāh is the Source of enabling grace!

You may say: "Surely the Prophet (Allāh bless him and give him peace) has told us:

> You must attend the customary gathering [*jamāʿa*], for the Hand of Allāh (Exalted is He) is upon the customary gathering. Satan is the wolf of the human being, for he snatches the sheep that is lonely, separate, remote and solitary.

Satan is together with the solitary individual, but he is far removed from the pair."

You must therefore know that, along with those you have cited, this Prophetic saying has also come down to us:

> Stick to your own home, attend to your personal affairs, and leave the business of the common herd.

The command to practise seclusion and isolation is applicable in the time of evil, so there is no contradiction in what he has said (Allāh bless him and give him peace), and the two reports must be combined, through the power of Allāh and His enabling grace. As for his saying (Allāh bless him and give him peace):

> You must attend the customary gathering [*jamāʿa*].

—it can be understood in three ways:

Firstly, it may mean: "[You must gather together] for the sake of the religion and the law." Since this Community does not concur in error, violation of the consensus [*ijmāʿ*] and the rule of law [*ḥukm*] is contrary to the principle upheld by the majority of the Community, and separation from them is invalid and erroneous. However, in the case of someone who secludes himself from them for the sake of some benefit to his religion, his conduct has nothing to do with any of that [erroneous separation].

Secondly, it may mean: "You must attend the customary gathering, so that you do not cut yourself off from them in their congregational prayer, their religious assemblies and the like, for these contain the strength of the religion, the perfection of Islām, and the displeasure of the unbelievers [*kuffār*] and the apostates [*mulḥidīn*]." That [attendance] also includes blessings and merciful favour from Allāh (Almighty and Glorious is He). That is why we say: "For the solitary individual, it is right and proper to join with other people in general assemblies for good purposes, and to avoid their company and social intercourse in all other matters, because of the various kinds of harm involved."

Thirdly, that commandment applies under normal conditions, but not, in the time of corruption, to the man who is weak in the matter of religion. As for the man who is keenly perceptive, and strong in the matter of Allāh's religion (Exalted is He), he will recognize the time of corruption, which the Prophet (Allāh bless him and give him peace) has warned the Community against, and in which he has commanded them to practise seclusion [*ʿuzla*]. He will see that seclusion is preferable, because of the corruption and perils inherent in social intercourse. He must not cut himself off from the assemblies of Islām and those devoted to the common good. If he wishes to isolate himself from people for a period of time, he should settle on a mountain peak, or in a desert hollow, for the sake of what he considers to be in the best interest of his religion.

Wherever this man may be, I cannot see him failing to be enabled by Allāh (Almighty and Glorious is He) to attend the customary gatherings, congregational prayers and other assemblies of Islām. He will therefore attend them, to avoid losing his share of the blessing they confer, for the assemblies of Islām are of the same importance, in the sight of Allāh (Exalted is He), even if people change and become corrupt.

From what we have heard, this applies to the state of the saints called *Abdāl*,[15] for they attend the assemblies of Islām wherever they may be. They travel wherever they wish on this earth, and the earth for them is but a single step from end to end. According to the reports at our disposal, the earth is rolled up for them, they call out to one another with salutations, and they are blessed with all kinds of gifts and charismatic talents. They deserve congratulations for what they have achieved! May Allāh grant good patience to those who do not focus on their personal salvation, and may He help those seekers, such as the likes of us, who have not yet arrived at the goal!

Where my own state is concerned, I am reminded of these verses of poetry:

The seekers have triumphed, the contact has been made,
and the lovers have attained to the loved ones.

We are left here wavering in perplexity, meanwhile,
between the boundaries of contact and avoidance.

We hope for nearness with distance combined, and this
is the very essence of absurdity for mental faculties.

So quench our thirst with a drink that removes distress,
and that will guide us to the path of rightness,

O Physician of the sick, O Healing Ointment for wounds,
and O my Saviour from all chronic illnesses!

I know not by what means to cure my sickness,
nor how I may succeed on the Day of Reckoning.

Let us now grasp the reins of the fingertips, and return to the subject of seclusion, for we have strayed from the main topic of the section!

Someone may say: "Surely the Prophet (Allāh bless him and give him peace) has told us:

> The monasticism [*rahbāniyya*] of my Community is the habit of sitting in the mosques.

—and this implies stern disapproval of isolation."

[15] See note 14 on p. 48 above.

You must therefore understand that this applies under normal conditions, but not in the time of corruption, as we have previously explained. Besides, when someone sits in the mosque, without mingling with people or intruding upon them, he is still with them in physical form, though he is inwardly isolated from them. This is the true meaning of seclusion. As for the isolation we have been describing, it is not isolation in physical form and place, so try to understand that, and may Allāh bestow His mercy upon you! In the words of Ibrāhīm ibn Ad'ham (may Allāh bestow His mercy upon): "Be comprehensively singular, with your Lord be intimate, and from people be estranged."

Someone may ask: "What do you say about the colleges of the scholars of the Hereafter, and the convents of the Ṣūfīs, those travellers on the path of the Hereafter, and what about residence in such places?"

In this business, you must therefore understand, that procedure [establishing and residing in such institutions] is ideally suited to most of the experts in knowledge and independent judgement [*ijtihād*]. That is because it combines the two aspects and the two benefits, one of which is seclusion from people and isolation from them in the sphere of companionship, social intercourse and involvement in their affairs. The second is participation with them in their congregational prayers and their customary gatherings, and augmenting the ceremonies [*sha'ā'ir*] of Islām. Safety is thereby secured for those who practise isolation, as well as great benefit for the Muslims in general, since they [the scholars of the Hereafter] provide the ordinary people with exemplary guidance, blessing and wise counsel. This means that residence in those places is a very equitable procedure, a very fine condition, and a very safe path.

This explains why most of the experts in direct knowledge [*'ārifīn*] reside among the people, because of their usefulness to the servants of Allāh (Exalted is He) in the sphere of religion, the slightness of the harm they suffer, and the fine example they provide, by letting their fellow creatures witness their good manners and their excellent modes of conduct. The language of the spiritual state [*lisān al-ḥāl*] is more eloquent than the language of speech [*lisān al-maqāl*], so that is a very fine arrangement in the matter of religion, for the sake of knowledge and worship, and a very wise idea.

You may ask: "So where does the seeker stand, in relation to the scholars who exercise their independent judgement, and to those who practise spiritual training? Does he keep them company, or does he seclude himself from them?"

You must therefore know that if they are firmly committed to their basic principles, and to the path they have inherited from their righteous predecessors, they are truly splendid as brothers for the sake of Allāh (Almighty and Glorious is He), as friendly companions, and as helpers in the worship of Allāh (Exalted is He). Seclusion and isolation are out of the question in your relationship with them. Their likeness is best described by what you hear about the ascetics of Lebanon and others, namely, that they form groups to help one another in righteousness and true devotion, and to advise one another to recognize the Truth and endure with patience.

On the other hand, if they have altered their way of life, forsaken their principles, and deserted the path they inherited from their righteous predecessors, in relation to them, the position of this independent scholar and spiritual trainee is like his relationship with ordinary people. He must stick to his corner and guard his tongue, participating with them in their good works, but avoiding them in the rest of their affairs and their misfortunes. He will thus be in seclusion from the people of seclusion, isolated from those who practise isolation!

You may ask: "What if this independent scholar and spiritual trainee prefers to depart from their midst, and move to another place, for the sake of some benefit he sees for himself, and to avoid a disaster that threatens to befall him in their compnay?"

You must therefore know that these colleges and convents are similar to an impregnable fortress, protected by the independent scholars from highway robbers and thieves. If anyone ventures outside, he will find himself in a zone of the desert, patrolled by the horsemen of the devils, troop upon troop, who will rob him or take him captive. What state will he be in, if he goes out into the desert, and the enemies control him from every side, able to treat however they wish? In the case of this weak man, he has no choice but to stick to the fortress. As for the man who is strong and perceptive, whom the enemies cannot overcome, and in whose sight the fortress and the desert are equal, he has nothing to fear if he goes out. Nevertheless, to be in the fortress is safer in any case, since he cannot be secure from slips and accidents in the presence of the comrades of evil.

Since this is the actual state of affairs, it is better for the spiritual trainee to be with the men of Allāh, to endure the discomfort of fellowship with patience, and to seek what is best in every situation. As for the strong man, who has reached the full degree of rectitude, there is nothing to prevent him from isolating himself from them.

You must understand this whole discussion, and reflect upon it, for then you may profit and be safe, if Allāh (Exalted is He) so wills.

You may ask: "So what do you say about visiting those who are brethren for the sake of Allāh (Almighty and Glorious is He), and about the connection between friends, in meeting and conversing with one another?"

In answer to this question, you must know that visiting those who are brethren for the sake of Allāh (Almighty and Glorious is He) is one of the precious elements of the worship of Allāh (Exalted is He). It contains the noble grace of nearness to Allāh (Almighty and Glorious is He), as well as various other benefits and the welfare of the heart, but only on two conditions:

—Firstly, you must not overdo that [visiting] and carry it to excess. The Prophet (may Allāh bless him and his family, and may He give them peace) once said to Abū Huraira (may Allāh be well pleased with him):

> Visit at decent intervals, for then you will share more love.

—Secondly, you must preserve the correctness of that [visiting], by avoiding hypocritical display and ostentation, idle talk and backbiting, and everything of that kind, for it will have dire consequences for you and your brother. It is related that al-Fuḍail and Sufyān (may Allāh bestow His mercy upon them) engaged each other in conversation, then they both wept. Sufyān said: "O Abū ʿAlī, I hope that we have never attended a meeting more hope-inspiring for us than this one!" Then al-Fuḍail said: "I have never attended a meeting more fear-inspiring for me than this one!" When Sufyān asked him: "How can that be, O Abū ʿAlī?" he replied: "Were you not intent on presenting your speech in the most favourable light, in order to impress me? I was also intent on doing my best to impress you with my speech, so you put on a show for me, and I put on a show for you." Sufyān broke into tears.

When you meet and converse with the brethren, you must do so with moderation, caution and careful consideration, for then it will not impair your seclusion and isolation from people. Far from bringing harmful and unfortunate consequences upon you and your brother, it will produce much good and great benefit. Allāh is the Source of enabling grace!

You may ask: "So what will give me the incentive to practise seclusion and isolation from people, and make that easy for me?"

You must therefore know that three things will make that easy for you:

—The first is to immerse all your moments in worship, for worship is a profitable occupation, whereas socializing with people is one of the symptoms of bankruptcy. If you see yourself indulging in meeting and talking with people, in the absence of need and emergency, you should recognize that as a waste of time, prompted by idle curiosity and self-conceit. How appropriate is the saying of the poet:

Idle curiosity has led me to greet you,
for the idly curious seldom does any work.

Once you have truly embraced worship, you will discover the sweetness of intimate conversation [with the Lord], for you will become familiar with the Book of Allāh (Glory be to Him), distracted from your fellow creatures, and estranged from their company and their chatter. According to traditional report, when Moses (peace be upon him) returned from intimate conversation [with the Lord], he would feel estranged from people. He would plug his fingers into his ears, so that he could not hear their talk. At that time, he viewed their talk with aversion and alienation, comparing it to the braying of donkeys.

You must heed the poetic saying of our Shaikh (may Allāh bestow His mercy upon him):

Be content with Allāh as a friend,
and leave human beings aside.

Be true to your love, whether present
amongst them or absent.

However you wish to view people,
you will find them to be scorpions.

—The second [way to make seclusion easy for you] is detaching your ambition from them, once and for all, since their business is quite worthless for you. If it is pointless to hope for something useful from a person, and there is no reason to fear his harmfulness, his existence and his non-existence are indistinguishable.

—The third is that you should carefully observe their disastrous misfortunes, remember that and impress it repeatedly on your heart.

If you strictly adhere to these three principles, they will drive you away from the company of your fellow creatures. They will drive you to the door of Allāh (Exalted is He) and exclusive dedication to His worshipful service. They will make Him dear to you, and cause you to cling to His door. Allāh is the Source of enabling grace and protection!

The Third Impediment [*ʿāʾiq*]
The Devil Satan [*ash-shaiṭān*]

Your next obligation, O my brother, is to combat Satan and conquer him. There are two good reasons for that:

1. Satan is an obvious and misleading enemy, who has no interest in your welfare and preservation. Indeed, nothing short of your destruction will satisfy him in the least, so there can be no question of feeling safe from such a foe, nor of being off guard against him. Consider these two verses from the Book of Allāh (Exalted is He):

> Did I not make a covenant with you, O you sons of Adam,
> *a-lam aʿhad ilai-kum yā Banī Ādama*
> that you should not worship Satan?
> *al-lā taʿbudu 'sh-shaiṭān:*
> Surely he is an obvious enemy to you.
> *inna-hu la-kum ʿaduwwun mubīn.* (36:60)

> Surely Satan is an enemy to you,
> *inna 'sh-shaiṭāna la-kum ʿaduwwun*
> so treat him as an enemy.
> *fa-'ttakhidhū-hu ʿaduwwā.* (35:6)

This is warning at its utmost extreme!

2. Satan is naturally disposed to enmity towards you, and always committed to waging war against you. Through the watches of the night and all the daylight hours, he pelts you with his darts, but you are heedless of him, so something must be done about the situation!

There is another fine point worthy of your close attention: namely, that you are engaged in the worship of Allāh (Exalted is He), and in summoning your fellow creatures to Allāh's door (Glory be to Him) through your action and your speech. Since this is the direct opposite of Satan's work, his ambition, his purpose and his profession, it is as if you have fastened your belt and prepared to infuriate the Devil, trick him and oppose him. He also girds himself in readiness to attack you, fight you and outwit you, bent on causing mischief. The refuge is with Allāh, so do your duty!

Satan will not be satisfied until he destroys you utterly, since he does not yet feel safe from you. As for those who neither enrage him nor oppose him, but actually befriend him and agree with him, like the unbelievers and the addicts of desire, he still mistreats them and tries to destroy them in some cases. What does this say about his attitude to those who deliberately enrage him, and who dedicate themselves to opposing him? It means that he nurses a general hostility towards the rest of humankind, and towards you, O devotee of worship and knowledge, a special enmity. Your situation is of great concern to him, and he has assistants to help him against you, the worst of them being your lower self [*nafs*] and your passionate desire [*hawā*]. He also has various means and entrances and doors of which you are quite unaware.

Yaḥyā ibn Muʿādh ar-Rāzī spoke the truth when he said: "Satan is idle, while you are busily employed. Satan sees you, but you do not see him. You forget him, but he does not forget you. Satan also has helpers against you, enlisted from your own lower self. This makes it essential for you to wage war on him and conquer him, otherwise you cannot be safe from corruption and destruction."

You may ask: "With what can I wage war on Satan, and with what can I conquer him and drive him away?"

You must therefore know that the masters of this craft have two ways of dealing with this problem: (1) As one of them has said: "The only effective means of repelling Satan is to seek refuge with Allāh (Glory be to Him), for Satan is a dog that Allāh (Glory be to Him) has set on you. If you preoccupy yourself with fighting him and trying to subdue him, you will wear yourself out, your time will be wasted, and he will defeat you by inflicting injuries and wounds upon you. It is therefore better to resort to the Lord of the dog, so that he may keep the beast away from you." (2) As others have said: "The method is dedicated striving, and getting the better of him by means of repulsion, rejection and opposition."

In my personal opinion, the balanced and comprehensive approach is to combine these two methods. That is to say, you should first seek refuge with Allāh (Exalted is He) from Satan's evil, as He has commanded us,[16] for He is the Protector against his evil. Then, if we see that he is prevailing against us, we shall recognize it as a trial from Allāh (Exalted is He), designed to test our dedicated striving and the strength of our commitment to His cause (Glory be to Him and Exalted is He), and to examine our patience. In similar fashion, He has set the unbelievers on us, despite His ability to prevent their mischief and their wickedness, so that we may have the opportunity to wage the sacred struggle [*jihād*], to practise patience, to pass the test, and to bear witness. As Allāh (Exalted is He) has said:

> So that Allāh may know those who truly believe,
> *wa li-ya'lama 'llāhu 'lladhīna āmanū*
> and may choose witnesses from among you.
> *wa yattakhidha min-kum shuhadā'*. (3:140)
>
> Or did you suppose that you would enter the Garden,
> *am ḥabistum an tadkhulu 'l-jannata*
> while Allāh does not yet know those of you who really strive,
> *wa lammā ya'lami 'llāhu 'lladhīna jāhadū min-kum*
> and does not know those who are patiently enduring?
> *wa ya'lama 'ṣ-ṣābirīn*. (3:142)

According to our religious scholars (may Allāh bestow His mercy upon them), three things are involved in fighting and conquering Satan: (1) You must get to know and understand his cunning wiles and tricks in thorough detail, for then he will not dare to abuse you. Like the thief, if he knows that the owner of the house is aware of him, he will flee

[16] In the Qur'ān, where Allāh (Exalted is He) has said:

> Seek refuge with Allāh from Satan the accursed.
> *fa-'sta'idh bi'llāhi mina 'sh-shaiṭāni 'r-rajīm*. (16:98)

away. (2) You must scorn his tempting invitation. Do not attach your heart to that, and do not go along with him, for he is just like the barking dog: if you take an interest in the beast, it will be crazy about you and keep pestering, but it will fall silent if you shun it. (3) You must be constant in the remembrance of Allāh (Glory be to Him), with your tongue and your heart, for the Prophet (Allāh bless him and give him peace) once said:

> In Satan's side, the remembrance of Allāh (Exalted is He) is like gangrene in the side of the son of Adam [the human being].

You may ask: "So how do you get to know his cunning wiles, and how can one learn what that really means?"

You must therefore know that Satan uses whispered temptations [*wasāwis*], shooting them like arrows. That will only become clear to you through familiarity with notions [*khawāṭir*] and their various types. He also uses tricky devices [*ḥiyal*], planting them like snares. That will only become clear to you through familiarity with cunning wiles [*makāyid*], their properties and their functions.

Our scholars (may Allāh bestow His mercy upon them) have devoted whole chapters to the subject of notions [*khawāṭir*], and we have compiled a book entitled "The Deceit of Iblīs [*Talbīs Iblīs*]." This present book of ours does not contain a vast amount of information [about notions], but we shall provide you, if Allāh (Exalted is He) so wills, with a basic understanding of each type, and this should be enough, provided you adhere to it closely.

As for the origin of notions, you should know that Allāh (Exalted is He) has entrusted the heart of the human being to an angel, whose task is to invite him to goodness. That angel is called *al-Mulhim* [the Inspirer] and his invitation is called *ilhām* [inspiration]. In confrontation with him, Allāh has also appointed a devil, who invites the servant [of the Lord] to evil. That devil is called *Waswās* [Whisperer], and his invitation is called *waswasa* [whispering].

The Inspirer invites the servant to nothing but goodness, while the Whisperer invites him to nothing but evil, in the opinion of most of our scholars. According to one report, however, our own Shaikh (may Allāh bestow His mercy upon him) maintained that Satan sometimes invites to goodness, though he does so with evil intent. He may invite someone to do what is *mafḍūl* [of inferior merit], in order to keep him from doing what is *fāḍil* [of superior merit], or he may invite him to do something good, in order to drag him into a serious sin, such as arrogant pride [*ʿujb*], so that his good deed does not compensate for that evil.

These two [the Inspirer and the Whisperer] are thus a pair of summoners, stationed on the servant's heart, where they issue their invitations to him, and he hears his heart experiencing that. According to the traditional reports, the Prophet (blessing and peace be upon him) once said:

> Whenever a child is born to the human being, Allāh (Glory be to Him) assigns an angel to that child, and Satan assigns a devil to him [or her]. The devil is perched on the left ear of a human being's heart, while the angel is perched on the right ear of his heart, and that is how they issue their invitations to him.

The Prophet (may Allāh bless him and his family and grant them peace) also said:

> The devil has a lodging [*lamma*] in the human being, and the angel has a lodging too.

In other words, each of them has a place to stay. The noun *lamma* is derived from the same root as the verb[s] used in the expression: *lamma* (or *alamma) bi'l-makān*, meaning: "He settled in the place."

Allāh (Exalted is He) has also installed, in the constitution of the human being, a natural instinct inclined towards carnal desires and the enjoyment of pleasures, whether they be good or bad. That is the passion of the lower self [*nafs*], which is conducive to disasters. The human being is therefore influenced by these three summoners [the angel, the devil and the lower self].

After this introduction, you must understand that notions [*khawāṭir*] are influences that occur in the heart of the servant [of the Lord], prompting and inviting him to actions and abstentions. They are called *khawāṭir* because they are disturbing, like the *khaṭarāt* [dangers] of the wind and similar perils. In reality, their occurrence in the servant's heart is entirely due to Allāh (Glory be to Him and Exalted is He), but we need to distinguish four types: (1) Allāh (Exalted is He) causes some of them to occur in the heart directly, so a notion of this type is called a *khāṭir* [sing. of *khawāṭir*], and not by any other name. (2) He causes a second type to occur in accordance with the nature of the human being, so it is called the passion of the lower self [*hawa 'n-nafs*], and it is ascribed thereto. (3) He causes a third type to occur in response to the invitation issued by the angelic Inspirer [*al-Mulhim*], so it is ascribed to him and called *ilhām* [inspiration]. (4) He causes a fourth type to occur in response to the invitation issued by the devil [*shaiṭān*], so it is ascribed to him and called *waswasa* [whispering]. Notions are often ascribed to him directly, as *khawāṭir mina 'sh-shaiṭān* [notions from the devil], though in reality, they only occur when he issues his invitation, for he is like the instrument [*sabab*] in the process.

After this fourfold classification of notions [*khawāṭir*], you must also know this about the notion [*khāṭir*] that comes directly from Allāh (Exalted is He): It may be a good idea, worthy of respect and thoroughly convincing, or it may be a bad idea, calling for scrutiny and rigorous testing.

As for the notion that comes by way of the angelic Inspirer [*al-Mulhim*], it can only be a good idea, since he is a wise counsellor and guide, sent with no other mission than that.

As for the notion that comes by way of the devil [*shaiṭān*], it can only be a bad idea, designed to mislead and cause error, though it may sometimes seem to be a good suggestion, in which case it is actually a cunning device and a form of temptation.

As for the notion that comes by way of the passion of the lower self [*hawa 'n-nafs*], it is always a bad idea, a suggestion containing nothing good, intended to obstruct right progress and cause deviation. According to one of the righteous predecessors [*salaf*], the passion of the lower self may also offer a good suggestion, but with a bad intention, like the devil.

Next, you need to be familiar with three subdivisions that are absolutely essential for you: (1) The difference between the good notion and the bad notion in general. (2) The difference between a bad notion that is inspired directly and one that is satanic or passionate. It is important to know what differentiates them, because each one of them requires a different kind of rebuttal. (3) The difference between a good notion that is directly inspired and one that is angelic, or satanic, or passionate. These distinctions will enable you to accept what comes from Allāh (Exalted is He), or from the angelic Inspirer, and to reject what comes from the devil (and from passion, according to those who include it in this context).

1. Concerning the first subdivision, our scholars (may Allāh bestow His mercy upon them) have said: "If you wish to know the good notion from the bad notion, and to distinguish between them, you must weigh it in one of the three balances, so that its condition will become clear to you:

—"First, you must refer the matter that has occurred to you to the Sacred Law. If it is compatible therewith, it is a good idea. If it is at variance, depending on a special concession [*rukhṣa*] or a doubtful point [*shubha*], it is a bad idea.

—"If the first balance fails to give you a clear answer, you must refer the matter to guidance. If acting on the notion would be consistent with the guidance of the righteous, it is a good idea. If, by sharp contrast, it would mean following the wicked, it is a bad idea.

—"If the second balance also fails to give you a clear answer, you must refer the matter to the lower self and passion, then study the reaction. If this shows that it is something to which the lower self is averse, with a natural aversion, not one of fear and dread, you should recognize it as a good idea. If it is something to which the lower self is favourably disposed, with a natural and instinctive disposition, not one of hope and desire to please Allāh (Exalted is He), it is a bad idea. Since the lower self is always instigating evil [*ammāra bi's-sū'*],[17] it is absolutely not disposed to goodness."

By means of these three balances, if you look and study closely, the difference between the good notion and the bad notion will become quite obvious to you. Allāh (Exalted is He) is the Custodian of right guidance, through His gracious favour. He is truly Generous and Noble.

2. Concerning the second subdivision, our scholars have said: "If you wish to differentiate between the bad notion that comes by way of the devil, and the bad notion that comes by way of the passion of the lower self, or directly from Allāh (Exalted is He), you must study it carefully from three perspectives:

—Firstly, if you find it unambiguous and unequivocal, it is either

[17] An allusion to Q. 12:53.

from Allāh (Exalted is He), or from the passion of the lower self, but if you find it vacillating and confused, you should know that it is from the devil.

According to one of the righteous (may Allāh the Exalted bestow His mercy upon him): "The likeness of the passion of the lower self is that of the tiger; when it fights, it does not withdraw without a complete triumph and a clear victory. It can also be likened to the fanatical rebel [*khārijī*] who fights with religious zeal, and is unlikely to withdraw until he is slain. The likeness of the devil is that of the wolf; if you chase it away from one side, it will come back from another side."

—Secondly, if you find it in the wake of a sin you have committed, it is from Allāh (Exalted is He), intended as an insult and a chastisement for the wickedness of that sin. Allāh (Exalted is He) has said:

> No indeed; but what they have been earning
> *kallā bal rāna ʿalā qulūbi-him*
> has rusted upon their hearts.
> *mā kānū yaksibūn.* (83:14)

According to my own Shaikh, Imām [Abu 'l-Warrāq] (may Allāh bestow His mercy upon him): "This is how sins result in hardness of the heart: The process begins with a notion [*khāṭir*], then it leads to hardness and rust."

If this notion is not preceded by a sin you have committed, you should know that it comes by way of the devil. This is true in most cases, because he starts with the invitation to evil, and seeks to mislead in every case.

—Thirdly, if you do not find it weak, lacking in remembrance of Allāh (Exalted is He), and quick to fade away, it is from the passion [of the lower self]. If you do find it weak and lacking in remembrance of Allāh (Glory be to Him), it is from the devil. As explained the commentary on His saying (Exalted is He):

> from the evil of the slinking whisperer....
> *min sharri 'l-waswāsi 'l-khannās.* (114:4)

—the devil is crouching on the heart of the human being. When the latter remembers Allāh (Exalted is He), the devil slinks away, and when he is forgetful, the devil whispers.

3. As for the third subdivision, if you wish to differentiate between a good notion that comes from Allāh (Exalted is He) and one that comes from the angel, you must study it carefully from three perspectives:

—Firstly, if your study shows the notion to be strong and unequivocal, it is from Allāh (Exalted is He), but if it is somewhat ambiguous, it is from the angel. Since the angel is in the position of a counsellor, he explores every aspect and facet with you, and offers you every kind of sound advice, to encourage your compliance and your interest in goodness.

—Secondly, if the notion has come in the wake of serious effort and obedience on your part, it is from Allāh (Exalted is He), for Allāh (Exalted is He) has said:

> And as for those who strive in Our cause,
> *wa 'lladhīna jāhadū fī-nā*
> surely We shall guide them in Our ways.
> *la-nahdiyanna-hum subula-nā.* (29:69)
>
> And those who are guided aright,
> *wa 'lladhīna 'htadaw*
> He increases them in guidance.
> *zāda-hum hudan.* (47:17)

If the notion is not preceded [by such effort on your part], it is most probably from the angel.

—Thirdly, if the notion relates to the basic principles [of belief], and to the actions of the inner being, it is from Allāh (Glory be to Him). If it relates to the branches [of belief] and to external actions, it is from the angel in most cases, since the angel has no access to knowledge of the servant's inner being, according to most of the scholars. As for the good notion that comes by way of the devil, as a temptation to greater evil, our Shaikh (may Allāh bestow His mercy upon him) has said: "See if you find that your lower self is interested in the action that has occurred to your heart, with enthusiasm, not with timidity, with alacrity, not with hesitation, with a sense of security, not with fear, and with a blindness to the outcome, not with a clear perception thereof. If that is what you discover, you should know that the notion is either from Allāh (Glory be to Him) or from the angel."

To this I would add: It seems that enthusiasm is a flightiness in the human being, a tendency to act without clear understanding and consideration of the consequences. As for the slow approach, it is recommended in all but a few well-known instances. According to the traditional report, the Prophet (may Allāh bless him and his family and grant them peace) once said:

> Haste is from the devil, except in five instances: (1) giving the virgin in marriage, as soon as she has reached puberty; (2) settling a debt, as soon as it has fallen due; (3) preparing the corpse for burial, as soon as the person concerned has died; (4) entertaining the guest, as soon as he has arrived, and (5) repenting the sin, as soon as it has been committed.

As for fear, it is likely to be experienced in connection with putting the notion into practice, and doing that in a right and proper manner, acceptable to Allāh (Exalted is He). As for consideration of the outcome, it is a matter of reflecting and ascertaining that the notion is truly right and good. It may also involve the prospect of reward in the Hereafter, and the hope of earning that reward.

May you grasp all that successfully, for these three subdivisions contain what you need to know and understand on the subject of notions [*khawāṭir*]. You must study them carefully, and examine them as closely as you can, for they are among the subtle items of knowledge and the noble secrets contained in this chapter. Allāh is the Source of enablement, through His gracious favour.

More on the subject of tricks and deceptions from the devil:

In his effort to keep the human being from worshipful service [*ʿibāda*], the devil employs these seven cunning devices:

1. He simply forbids him to practise it. Then, if Allāh (Exalted is He) protects him, the human being will refuse to comply with Satan's prohibition, saying: "I am very much in need of that [worship], since I must obtain provision from this world, which is impermanent, in preparation for the journey to the Hereafter, which has no final conclusion."

2. Satan will then command him to procrastinate. If Allāh (Exalted is He) protects him again, the human being will refuse to comply with Satan's command, saying: "My appointed term is out of my control, so, if I postpone today's work till tomorrow, when shall I do tomorrow's work? Each day has its own job of work!"

3. Satan will then command him to make haste [in finishing his daily work], saying: "Make haste, make haste, so that you will have time to spare for such-and-such and such-and-such!" This time, if Allāh (Exalted is He) protects him, the human being will again reject Satan's command, saying: "A little work brought to completion is better than a lot of work marred by imperfection!"

4. Satan will then command him to complete the work, but only to gain people's admiration. Once again, if Allāh (Exalted is He) protects him, the human being will refuse to comply, saying: "What shall I do with people's admiration? Surely the approval of Allāh (Exalted is He) is all that I need!"

5. Satan will then try to make him lapse into vain conceit, by saying: "How splendid you are! How wide awake you are! How excellent you are!" If Allāh (Exalted is He) protects him, the human being will reject this flattery, saying: "The credit for that belongs to Allāh (Exalted is He), not to me, for He is the One who singled me out by His helpful guidance, and has given my work a tremendous value by His gracious favour. Were it not for His gracious favour, what would be the value of this work, considering the blessing conferred on me by Allāh (Exalted is He) and my disobedience towards Him?"

6. Satan's sixth attempt will be the most cunning of all, and none but the consciously alert will be able to resist it. He will say: "You must work hard in your inner being, for Allāh (Exalted is He) will make that show in your outward appearance." Satan meddles with the work of every worker, trying to insert an element of pretentiousness, but, if Allāh (Exalted is He) protects him, the human being will reject that interference, saying: "Until now, O accursed one, you have been approaching me with the obvious intention of corrupting my work. Now you are urging me to do it correctly, though your purpose is still to corrupt it! I am the servant of Allāh (Exalted is He), for He is my Master. If He wishes, He will reveal, and if He wishes, He will conceal. If He wishes, He will make me important, and if He wishes, He will make me insignificant. That is up to Him. It is all the same to me, whether He lets people see that [inner work of mine], or whether He does not reveal it, for nothing is at their disposal."

7. Satan will then try a seventh approach, saying: "You have no need for this work, because, if you have been created as a fortunate being, refraining from work will cause you no harm, and if you have been

created as a wretched being, doing it will give you no benefit." If Allāh (Exalted is He) protects him, the human being will reject this approach, saying: "I am merely a servant, and the servant is obliged to comply with the commandment governing his servitude. The Lord knows best about His Lordship. He decrees whatever He wills, and does whatever He wishes. The work is useful to me, however I may be. If I am fortunate, I need it to increase the reward. If I am wretched, I need it so that I shall not blame myself. Allāh (Exalted is He) will not punish me or hurt me for obedience. In any case, I would much prefer to be admitted to the Fire of Hell as an obedient servant, rather than enter it as a disobedient sinner, but what should I expect, when His promise is true and His word is genuine? Since He has promised reward for acts of obedience, if the servant meets Allāh (Exalted is He) in faith and obedience, he will definitely not enter the Fire. That servant will enter the Garden of Paradise, not because his work has entitled him to the Garden, but because of Allāh's true promise (Exalted is He and Sanctified is He)."

In this context, Allāh (Exalted is He) has said of the fortunate ones:

> And they say: "Praise be to Allāh,
> *wa qālu 'l-ḥamdu li'llāhi 'lladhī*
> who has fulfilled His promise to us."
> *ṣadaqa-nā wa'da-hu.* (39:74)

You must therefore be consciously alert—may Allāh bestow His mercy upon you!—for the matter is as you see and hear. You must compare it with other states and actions, appeal to Allāh (Exalted is He) for help and seek refuge with Him, for the matter is in His hand, and He is the Source of enabling grace. There is no might nor any power except with Allāh, the All-High, the Almighty.

The Fourth Impediment [*'ā'iq*]
The lower self [*nafs*]

O seeker of the acts of worship, may Allāh grant you and us protection from this self that is always instigating evil [*an-nafs al-ammāra bi's-sū'*] for it is the most harmful of enemies; its tribulation is the hardest form of tribulation, its treatment is the most difficult of all things, its sickness is the most perplexing form of sickness, and its remedy is the most problematic means of healing. There are two reasons for all that:

1. It is an enemy from within. When the thief is from within the house, it is very hard to outwit him, and the damage is very great. The poet spoke the truth when he said:

My lower self tempts me to do what harms me,
multiplying my diseases and my aches and pains.

How can I outwit an enemy, when
my enemy is lodged between my ribs?

2. It is a beloved enemy, and the human being is blind to the fault of his loved one. He hardly notices his fault, as the poet said:

You see no fault in one endowed with love and brotherhood,
not even a trace of one, since you are happily content.

The eye of happy contentment is blind to every fault,
but the eye of displeasure brings shortcomings to light.

This explains why the human being takes a positive view of everything bad in his own lower self, and hardly notices any fault belonging to it, regardless of its hostility and all the harm it causes. It is always on the verge of plunging him into disgrace and destruction, yet he is quite unaware of this, unless Allāh (Exalted is He) protects him by His gracious favour, and helps him against it by His mercy.

You must take special note of one sharp-witted and persuasive observation, namely this: If you look closely, you will discover that this lower self is the root of every temptation, disgrace, ignominy, ruin, sin and disaster that has ever occurred in Allāh's creation (Exalted is He), or will ever occur, from the beginning of creation till the Day of Resurrection. Those evils are either due to the lower self alone, or brought about with its help, its participation and its assistance.

The very first sin of disobedience against Allāh (Exalted is He) was committed by Iblīs, and the cause of it—after the preceding decree [of

Allāh]—was the passion of the lower self, with its arrogant pride and its envy. It seized Iblīs, after eighty thousand years of worshipful service, we are told, and cast him into the ocean of error, where he has been drowned for all eternity. He had no world, no fellow creatures and no devil to influence him, but only the lower self with its arrogant pride and its envy, so it did with him what it did.

Then came the sin of Adam and Eve (peace be upon them both). They were motivated by the passion of the lower self, and by their greed for perpetuity and life, until they were deluded by the words of Iblīs. That delusion thus came about with the help of the lower self and its participation, until, because of that, the couple fell from the proximity of Allāh (Exalted is He) and the habitation of Paradise [*Firdaws*]. They fell into this world, which is contemptible, troublesome, transitory and destructive. They encountered what they encountered, and their children encountered what they encountered, [and the process will continue] from that day until the eternity of the everlasting.

Then we have the story of Cain [*Qābīl*] and Abel [*Ābīl*], the cause of whose [fratricidal] affair was envy and avarice. Then there is the story of Hārūt and Mārūt, the cause of whose problem was carnal desire. This pattern is destined to continue until the Day of Resurrection.

If you find your fellow creatures guilty of any corruption, immorality, erroneous conduct or sinful disobedience, the root thereof can only be the lower self and its passsion. Otherwise, your fellow creatures are in a state of safety and goodness.

Since he is dealing with an enemy capable of all this harm, it is right and proper for the intelligent person to be concerned about his situation. Allāh (Exalted is He) is the Custodian of right guidance and enablement, through His gracious favour.

You may ask: "Well then, what stratagem should we employ in dealing with this enemy? Explain that to us clearly!"

You must therefore know that, as we have mentioned earlier, the lower self poses a thorny and difficult problem, for it cannot be conquered once and for all, like other enemies, since it is the means of transport [*dābba*; lit., riding animal] and the instrument. It is said that an Arab nomad [*Aʿrābī*] once urged a person to do something good, so he said: "Allāh (Exalted is He) has subdued every enemy of yours, except your own lower self." It is not possible for you to dispose of it once and for all, due to the extent of its harm, so you need to choose one of two approaches: (1) You should develop it and strengthen it, to the extent of its capacity for doing good. (2) You should weaken it and restrict it to a limit it must not trangress. In either case, you need to combine a very tough treatment with a subtle understanding. Then, as we have already mentioned, you must rein it with the bridle of true devotion [*taqwā*] and pious caution [*wara*ʿ], in order to obtain both benefits combined.

You may ask: "This is an unruly riding animal and a difficult, surly beast, which cannot be led to the bridle, so what device would enable us to control it?"

You must therefore know that what you say is quite correct, and that the device is to humble it, until it is ready to accept the bridle. According to our scholars (may Allāh bestow His mercy upon them), three factors contribute to the humbling of the lower self, and to the breaking of its passion, namely:

1. Deprivation of its appetites, for the stubborn riding animal becomes tractable when it is short of its fodder.
2. Making it carry the burdens of acts of worship, for, when the donkey's load is increased, while it is short of its fodder, it becomes humble and easy to lead.
3. Appealing to Allāh (Almighty and Glorious is He) for help, and imploring Him to assist you, for otherwise there is no salvation. You have surely heard the saying of Joseph (peace be upon him):

> "Surely the self is always inciting to evil,
> *inna 'n-nafsa la-ammāratun bi's-sūʾi*
> except inasmuch as my Lord has mercy."
> *illā mā raḥima Rabbī.* (12:53)

If you apply yourself diligently to these three matters, the unruly lower self will submit to your leadership, with Allāh's consent (Almighty and Glorious is He). You must then be quick to control it and bridle it, and so become safe from its mischief.

You may say: "Now, explain to us what is meant by true devotion [*taqwā*], so that we may understand it."

You must therefore know, first of all, that true devotion [*taqwā*] is a splendid treasure. If you succeed in acquiring it, you will find that its contents include many a noble jewel and precious object, abundant good and generous sustenance, great victory and vast booty, and tremendous authority. It is as if all the good things of this world and the Hereafter have been combined and subsumed under this single category, meaning true devotion [*taqwā*].

You must also reflect on what is said about it in the Qur'ān, for Allāh (Exalted is He) has attached so much good to it, promised so much recompense and reward for it, and added so much happiness to it. Out of all the Qur'ānic references, let me select these twelve quotations for you:

1. The first is an expression of praise and commendation, for Allāh (Exalted is He) has said:

> But if you practise patience and true devotion,
> *wa in taṣbirū wa tattaqū*
> that belongs to the steadfast heart of things.
> *fa-inna dhālika min ʿazmi 'l-umūr.* (3:186)

2. The second is about safekeeping and protection from the enemies, for Allāh (Exalted is He) has said:

> But if you practise patience and true devotion,
> *wa in taṣbirū wa tattaqū*
> their guile will never harm you.
> *lā yaḍurru-kum kaidu-hum shai'ā.* (3:120)

3. The third is about support and assistance, for Allāh (Exalted is He) has said:

> Surely Allāh is with those who are truly devout,
> *inna 'llāha maʿa 'lladhīna 'ttaqaw*
> and those who are active in goodness.
> *wa 'lladhīna hum muḥsinūn.* (16:128)
>
> And Allāh is the Custodian of those who are truly devout.
> *wa 'llāhu Waliyyu 'l-muttaqīn.* (45:19)

4. The fourth is about deliverance from hardships, as well as the provision of lawful sustenance, for Allāh (Exalted is He) has said:

> And if someone is truly devoted to Allāh,
> *wa man yattaqi 'llāha*
> He will prepare a way out for him,
> *yajʿal la-hu makhrajā:*

and He will provide for him
wa yarzuq-hu
from sources he could never imagine.
min ḥaithu lā yaḥtasib. (65:2,3)

5. The fifth is about the improvement of work, for Allāh (Exalted is He) has said:

O you who believe, be truly devoted to Allāh,
yā ayyuha 'lladhīna āmanu 'ttaqu 'llāha
and speak words that get straight to the point.
wa qūlū qawlan sadīdā.
He will improve your works for you.
yuṣliḥ la-kum a'māla-kum. (33:70,71)

6. The sixth is about the forgiveness of sins, for Allāh (Exalted is He) has said:

And He will forgive you your sins.
wa yaghfir la-kum dhunūba-kum. (33:71)

7. The seventh is about Allāh's love, for Allāh (Exalted is He) has said:

Allāh loves those who are truly devout.
inna 'llāha yuḥibbu 'l-muttaqīn. (9:4)

8. The eighth is about acceptance, for Allāh (Exalted is He) has said:

Allāh accepts only from those who are truly devout.
inna-mā yataqabbalu 'llāhu mina 'l-muttaqīn. (5:27)

9. The ninth is about the bestowal of nobility and honour, for Allāh (Exalted is He) has said:

Surely the noblest among you, in Allāh's sight,
inna akrama-kum 'inda 'llāhi
is the one of you who is most truly devout.
atqā-kum. (49:13)

10. The tenth is about good news at the time of death, for Allāh (Exalted is He) has said:

Those who truly believe, and practise true devotion,
alladhīna āmanū wa kānū yattaqūn:
for them there are glad tidings
la-humu 'l-bushrā
in the life of this world and in the Hereafter.
fi 'l-ḥayāti 'd-dunyā wa fi 'l-ākhira. (10:63,64)

11. The eleventh is about deliverance from the Fire of Hell, for Allāh (Exalted is He) has said:

> Then We shall rescue those who practised true devotion,
> *thumma nunajji 'lladhīna 'ttaqaw*
> and We shall leave the evildoers crouching there.
> *wa nadharu 'ẓ-ẓālimīna fī-hā jithiyyā.* (19:72)
>
> And far removed from it will be the righteous.
> *wa sa-yujannabu-ha 'l-atqā.* (92:17)

12. The twelfth is about everlasting life in the Garden of Paradise, for Allāh (Exalted is He) has said:

> [The Garden] has been prepared for those who are truly devout.
> *uʿiddat li'l-muttaqīn.* (3:133)

In these Qur'ānic quotations, all that is good and fortunate in both abodes [this world and the Hereafter] is explained in terms of true devotion [*taqwā*], so do not forget your share of it, O man! Then, in relation to the matter of worship, you must consider three basic principles:

1. Divine enablement and support are available to the truly devout, as Allāh (Exalted is He) has said:

> And know that Allāh is with the truly devout.
> *wa 'ʿlamū anna 'llāha maʿa 'l-muttaqīn.* (2:194)

2. Improvement of work and completion of deficiency are also available to the truly devout, as Allāh (Exalted is He) has said:

> He will improve your works for you.
> *yuṣliḥ la-kum aʿmāla-kum.* (33:71)

3. Acceptance of work is also available to the truly devout, as Allāh (Exalted is He) has said:

> Allāh accepts only from those who are truly devout.
> *inna-ma yataqabbalu 'llāhu mina 'l-muttaqīn.* (5:27)

The sphere of worship is centred on these three points: (1) Divine enablement, so that you may set to work; (2) improvement of shortcoming, so that the work may be completed, and (3) acceptance [of the work] once it has been completed. These are the three matters about which His servants must humbly entreat and beseech Allāh (Exalted is

He), saying: "Our Lord, enable us to act in obedience to you, complete our shortcoming, and accept from us!"

Allāh (Exalted is He) has promised all that in return for true devotion, and He has generously bestowed it on the servant who is truly devout, whether he asks for it or does not ask. It is therefore incumbent upon you to practise this true devotion, if you seek to worship Allāh (Exalted is He), and indeed, if you seek the happiness of this world and the Hereafter. The poet spoke the truth when he said:

> He who is truly devoted to Allāh, that is the one
> to whom profitable merchandise is made available.

One of the poets wrote this verse:

> Nothing follows a man to his grave,
> except true devotion and righteous work.

Another said:

> He who knows Allāh well, but whose knowledge of Allāh
> does not enrich him, that is a miserable wretch.
>
> How should the servant treat the glory of wealth,
> when glory, all glory, belongs to the truly devout?
>
> No harm will come to one who practises obedience,
> from what he receives and experiences in obedience to Allāh.

One of them inscribed this on a tomb:

> There is no provision for the journey, except true devotion,
> so take some of it, or leave it [and bear the consequences].

Next, you must contemplate one basic principle: Suppose that you laboured all your life in worship, and struggled and endured, until you obtained what you desired. Would not the value of it all depend upon acceptance? You know that Allāh (Exalted is He) has said:

> Allāh accepts only from those who are truly devout.
> *inna-mā yataqabbalu 'llāhu mina 'l-muttaqīn.* (5:27)

This means that the crux of the whole matter is true devotion. That explains the saying attributed to ʿĀʾisha (may Allāh be well pleased with her): "Allāh's Messenger (may Allāh bless him and his family, and may He grant them peace) was so happy with anything belonging to this world, and no one is happy with it except a person endowed with true devotion."

Qatāda is reported as having said: "It is written in the Torah [*Tawrāh*]: 'O son of Adam, practise true devotion to Allāh, and sleep wherever you wish.'"

I have heard that ʿĀmir ibn ʿAbd Qais wept at the time of his death. He used to perform a thousand cycles of prayer every day and night, then come to his bed and say: "O shelter of every evil! By Allāh, I am not pleased with you for Allāh's sake, not for the twinkling of an eye!" He spent a whole day weeping, so he was asked: "What makes you weep?' He replied: "His saying (Exalted is He):

> Allāh accepts only from those who are truly devout."
> *inna-mā yataqabbalu 'llāhu mina 'l-muttaqīn.* (5:27)

Next, you must contemplate another fine point, for it is the basis of all basic principles. Consider the following: It is related that one of the righteous said to one of his Shaikhs: "Give me a piece of good counsel!" His Shaikh replied: "I shall give you the same counsel that Allāh, the Lord of all the worlds, has given to those of former and of later times, in His saying (Exalted is He):

> And We counselled those who received the Book before you,
> *wa la-qad waṣṣaina 'lladhīna ūtu 'l-Kitāba min qabli-kum*
> and you, to practise true devotion to Allāh."
> *wa iyyā-kum ani 'ttaqu 'llāh.* (4:131)

Surely Allāh knows, better than anyone, what is beneficial to the servant! Surely He gives him more sincere advice, and treats him with more compassion and kindness than anyone! If there were any virtue in the universe more beneficial to the servant, more comprehensive of goodness, worthy of greater reward, more splendid in terms of servanthood, greater in value, more meritorious in the present, and more conducive to success in the future, than this virtue that is true devotion, Allāh (Exalted is He) would have ordained it for His servants. He would have made that incumbent on his special friends [*khawāṣṣ*], because of the perfection of His wisdom and the extent of His mercy.

Since He has enjoined this one virtue [true devotion], including the first and the last of His servants in that commandment, and confining Himself thereto, you know it to be the ultimate goal and the only target. You also know that He (Almighty and Glorious is He) has included every exhortation, guidance, direction, admonition, instruction, teaching and training, in this single injunction, as befits His wisdom and His mercy. You also know that this virtue, meaning true devotion, is the comprehensive container of all that is good in this world and the Hereafter, the means of resolving all serious concerns, and the means of attaining to the highest degrees in servanthood. The poet expressed it beautifully, when he said:

> Surely true devotion is nothing but glory and honour,
> and your love of this world is merely abasement and loss.
>
> There is no shortcoming in the servant who is devout,
> so long as his devotion is true, even if he works as a weaver or cupper.

This is a principle that cannot be surpassed, and it contains sufficiency for someone who sees the light, is rightly guided, acts accordingly, and is satisfied with that. Allāh is the Custodian of right guidance and enablement, through His gracious favour.

You may say: "Enormous is the worth of this virtue, glorious is its rank, and urgent is the need to experience it, so it must now be explained in detail."

You should therefore know that the matter is just like that, so it is entitled to have its worth exalted, its pursuit is obligatory, and the need to experience it is urgent. As you are well aware, however, the procurement of any serious and important matter necessitates much searching, a great deal of weary labour, a lofty aspiration, and a very intense effort. Since this virtue is a great and splendid virtue, the effort required in seeking it, the fulfilment of its due, and the care devoted to its procurement, also amount to a great work and a tremendous undertaking. Noble deeds are just as difficult as those one finds repugnant, and pleasures are commensurate with inconveniences. Allāh (Exalted is He) tells us:

> And as for those who strive in Our cause,
> *wa 'lladhīna jāhadū fī-nā*
> surely We shall guide them in Our ways.
> *la-nahdiyanna-hum subula-nā:*
> Allāh is surely with those who are active in goodness.
> *wa inna 'llāha la-maʿa 'l-muḥsinīn.* (29:69)

He is the Kind One [*ar-Raʾūf*], in whose Hand is the easing of every difficulty, so listen, take note, and try hard to grasp the explanation of this virtue, until you know and understand it well. Then set about putting it into practice, and appeal to Allāh (Almighty and Glorious is He) for assistance, so that you may act in accordance with what you know, for that is what it is all about. Allāh is the Custodian of enablement and guidance, through His gracious favour.

You must know first of all—may Allāh bless your religion and increase your certitude!—that true devotion [*taqwā*], according to our Shaikhs (may Allāh bestow His mercy upon them), means keeping the heart innocent of any sin the like of which you have never committed, so that, through the strength of your determination to abstain therefrom, you acquire a protective shield [*wiqāya*] between you and sinful acts of disobedience. Such is the opinion of our own Shaikh [Abū Bakr al-Warrāq] (may Allāh bestow His mercy upon him).[18]

In the Qur᾽ān, three nuances of meaning are conveyed by the noun *taqwā* [and its corresponding verbs and other linguistic forms]:

1. Fear [*khashya*] and awe [*haiba*]. Allāh (Exalted is He) has said [using imperative verbs in the Arabic]:

> And treat Me with dutiful devotion [with fear and awe].
> *wa iyyā-ya fa-'ttaqū-n.* (2:41)

> And be on your guard [in fear and awe] against a day
> *wa 'ttaqū yawman*
> in which you will be brought back to Allāh.
> *turja῾ūna fī-hi ila 'llāh.* (2:281)

2. Obedience [*ṭā῾a*] and worshipful service [*῾ibāda*]. Allāh (Exalted is He) has said:

> O you who truly believe,
> observe your duty to [obey and worship] Allāh,
> *yā ayyuha 'lladhīna āmanu 'ttaqu 'llāha*
> with the devotion that is truly due to Him.
> *ḥaqqa tuqāti-hi.* (3:102)

[18] ***Author's linguistic note***: In the Arabic language, the origin of the term *taqwā* is *waqwā* (with *wāw* as the initial letter), a verbal noun synonymous with *wiqāya* [protection]. The corresponding verbs are *waqā* [past tense] and *yaqī* [present or future tense]. The initial *wāw* is converted to a *tā᾽* in several other cases, such as *wuklān* <*tuklān* [trust].

Thus, when the servant acquires a *wiqāya* [protection] between himself and sinful acts of disobedience, through the strength of his determination to abstain therefrom, and the dedication of his heart to that firm resolve, he is aptly described by the participial adjective *muttaqī* [lit., careful to be on guard]. The verbal noun *taqwā* is applied to that abstinence, determination and dedication.

According to Ibn ʿAbbās (may Allāh be well pleased with him and his father), this means: "Obey Allāh with the obedience that is truly due to Him." According to Mujāhid: "It means that He must be obeyed and not disobeyed, that He must be remembered and not forgotten, and that He must thanked and not treated with ingratitude."

3. Keeping the heart pure and free from sins. This is the real meaning of *taqwā*, rather than the first two. Consider the words of Allāh (Exalted is He):

> He who obeys Allāh and His Messenger,
> *wa man yuṭiʿi 'llāha wa Rasūla-hu*
> and fears Allāh, and is truly devoted to Him:
> *wa yakhsha 'llāha wa yattaq-hi*
> such are indeed the victorious.
> *fa-ulāʾika humu 'l-fāʾizūn.* (24:52)

Allāh (Exalted is He) has mentioned obedience and fear, then [using the verb *yattaq*] He has mentioned *taqwā*. You should therefore know that the real meaning of *taqwā* is something other than obedience and fear. It actually means keeping the heart pure, as we have previously explained.

Our Shaikhs (may Allāh bestow His mercy upon them) have also maintained that the degrees of *taqwā* are three in number: (1) *taqwā* in the sense of devout abstinence from *shirk* [polytheism; attributing partners to Allāh]; (2) *taqwā* in the sense of devout abstinence from *bidʿa* [heretical innovation], and (3) *taqwā* in the sense of devout abstinence from the multifarious acts of sinful disobedience. Allāh (Glory be to Him) has referred to all three in a single Qurʾānic verse [*āya*], in His saying (More Glorious is He than any other sayer):

> There shall be no sin on those who believe
> *laisa ʿala 'lladhīna āmanū*
> and do good works, for what they may have eaten,
> *wa ʿamilu 'ṣ-ṣāliḥāti junāḥun fī-mā ṭaʿimū*
> so long as they practise true devotion,
> *idhā ma 'ttaqaw*
> and believe and do good works,
> *wa āmanū wa ʿamilu 'ṣ-ṣāliḥāti*
> then practise true devotion and believe,
> *thumma 'ttaqaw wa āmanū*
> then practise true devotion and do good.
> *thumma 'ttaqaw wa aḥsanū.*

> Allāh loves those who are active in goodness.
> *wa 'llāhu yuḥibbu 'l-muḥsinīn.* (5:93)

From this it is clear that the first *taqwā* is *taqwā* in the sense of devout abstinence from *shirk* [attributing partners to Allāh], for the belief [*īmān*] that stands in contrast to polytheism is the affirmation of Oneness [*Tawḥīd*].[19] It is equally clear that the second *taqwā* is *taqwā* in the sense of devout abstinence from *bid'a* [heretical innovation], for the belief [*īmān*] that is mentioned in connection with *taqwā* is acceptance of the doctrines of the Sunna and the Community.[20] It is also clear that the third *taqwā* is *taqwā* in the sense of devout abstinence from the multifarious acts of sinful disobedience. There is no reference to belief at this point, for Allāh (Exalted is He) has linked *taqwā* with doing good [*iḥsān*], and that signifies obedience and the correct performance thereof.

The Qur'ānic verse has thus combined reference to the three degrees: (1) the degree of belief; (2) the degree of the Sunna, and (3) the degree of correct performance of worshipful obedience.

This is what the scholars (may Allāh bestow His mercy upon them) have said, in explanation of the meaning of *taqwā*. As for my own opinion, I have discovered that *taqwā* may also apply to abstinence from excessive consumption of lawful sustenance [*ḥalāl*]. This is consistent with the well-known report, according to which the Prophet (Allāh bless him and give him peace) once said:

> The truly devout [*muttaqūn*, lit., those who practise *taqwā*] are so called only because of their abstinence from that which contains nothing harmful, as a precaution against that which does contain something harmful.

I would like to combine the opinions of our scholars (may Allāh bestow His mercy upon them) with the reported saying of the Prophet (Allāh bless him and give him peace), for that should provide a comprehensive definition and a profoundly far-reaching explanation of the meaning [of *taqwā*]. I shall therefore state my opinion as follows:

[19] According to this interpretation, the beginning of the Qur'ānic verse [5:93] could be translated:

> There shall be no sin on those who believe
> [that there is no god but Allāh]....

[20] On the basis of this interpretation, part of the Qur'ānic verse [5:93] could be translated:

> so long as they practise true devotion, and believe
> [in the doctrines of Sunna and the Community] and do good works....

The meaning of *taqwā* is the avoidance of everything from which you fear harm to your religion. Consider the case of the invalid who takes wise precautions: It is said that he *yattaqī* [practises *taqwā*], since he avoids everything that would cause him physical harm, such as a particular foodstuff, drink or fruit. As for that from which harm is feared in the matter of religion, it falls into two categories: (1) that which is unquestionably unlawful [*ḥārām*] and sinfully disobedient, and (2) excessive indulgence in that which is lawful [*ḥalāl*], since preoccupation with such excess, and total immersion therein, will drag the person concerned into unlawful conduct and sheer disobedience.

That is because of the gluttony and exorbitance of the lower self, and the rebelliousness and disobedience of passion. If someone wishes to be safe from harm in the matter of his religion, he must therefore avoid the danger and refrain from excessive indulgence in that which is lawful. If he does not take this precaution, he will be drawn into conduct that is unquestionably unlawful. Let us recall the saying of the Prophet (Allāh bless him and give him peace):

> ...because of their abstinence from that which contains nothing harmful, as a precaution against that which does contain something harmful.

In other words: "...because of their abstinence from excessive indulgence in that which is lawful, as a precaution against falling into that which is unlawful."

In the fully comprehensive sense, therefore, *taqwā* is the avoidance of everything injurious to the welfare of religion, and that is sinful disobedience and excessive indulgence.

If we wish to define *taqwā* in terms of the science of the Sacred Law [*Shar*ʿ], we shall put it like this:

The comprehensive definition of *taqwā* is keeping the heart innocent of any evil the like of which you have never committed, so that, through the strength of your determination to abstain therefrom, you acquire a protective shield [*wiqāya*] between you and every evil.

Evils are of two kinds: (1) A fundamental evil, meaning that which Allāh has forbidden with an absolute prohibition [*taḥrīm*], such as acts of outright disobedience. (2) A non-fundamental evil, meaning what He has forbidden as a matter of strict discipline [*taʾdīb*], that being excessive indulgence in what is lawful [*ḥalāl*], such as permissible opportunities [*mubāḥāt*] that are exploited with carnal desire.

In the first case, *taqwā* is an obligatory duty [*farḍ*], so the penalty for its omission is the torment of the Fire of Hell. In the second case, *taqwā* is a matter of good behaviour and propriety [*adab*], so the penalty for its omission is confinement, calling to account, reproach and blame.

If someone practises the first kind, he is at the lower degree of *taqwā*, that being the stage of those who correctly observe obedience [*ṭāʿa*]. If someone practises the second kind, he is at the higher degree of *taqwā*, that being the stage of those who correctly abstain from that which is permissible [*mubāḥ*]. If the servant combines the two, meaning the avoidance of every act of disobedience and excessive indulgence, he has experienced the full significance of *taqwā*, practised it correctly, and combined every benefit therein. This is the perfect piety [*waraʿ*], which is fundamental to the matter of religion. That is also the station of propriety [*adab*] at the door of Allāh (Exalted is He).

Such is the meaning of *taqwā* and its general explanation, so you must understand it successfully, if Allāh (Exalted is He) so wills.

You may say: "So now let us have a specific explanation of this meaning [of *taqwā*] as it relates to the lower self [*nafs*], and how it should be employed in that connection. To progress from this point, we need to know how to bridle this lower self with *taqwā* in this sense, which, as you have explained, is the real meaning of the term."

Yes [that is in fact what you need]. The specific explanation [of *taqwā*], in the context of this lower self, is that you must control the latter with the strength of firm resolve, so that you deter it from every act of sinful disobedience, and preserve it from every form of excessive indulgence. If you do that, you will have practised true devotion to Allāh (Exalted is He) in your eye, your ear, your tongue, your heart, your stomach, your genitals and all your other organs, and you will have reined them all with the bridle of *taqwā*.

This subject requires a lengthy commentary, and we have given some indication of it in the book entitled: "Revival of the Religious Sciences [*Iḥyāʾ ʿUlūm ad-Dīn*]."

As for what is essential to you here and now, we may state it as follows: If someone wishes to practise true devotion to Allāh, he must supervise the five basic members of the body: namely, the eye, the ear, the tongue, the heart and the stomach. He must guard them zealously against everything from which harm is feared in the matter of religion, such as sinful disobedience, unlawful sustenance, and excessive and extravagant indulgence in that which is lawful. If he succeeds in safeguarding these five members, he is likely to protect the rest of his physical organs, and he will thus have devoted the whole of his body to Allāh (Exalted is He) with comprehensive *taqwā*.

The need [that you have expressed] calls for an explanation of each of these five members of the body, and a detailed account of what is unlawful in respect of each one of them, to the extent appropriate to this present book. We shall deal with this in five subsections:

First subsection
The eye [*ʿain*]

It is incumbent upon you—may Allāh grant you, and us, His enabling grace!—to safeguard the eye, for it is the cause of every disorder and disaster. I shall mention three basic principles that ought to be sufficient in this context:

1. First of all, consider the saying of Allāh (Glory be to Him):

> Tell the believing men to lower their eyes
> *qul li 'l-muʾminīna yaghuḍḍū min abṣāri-him*
> and guard their private parts.
> *wa yaḥfaẓū furūja-hum:*
> That is purer for them
> *dhālika azkā la-hum.*
> Allāh is Aware of what they do.
> *inna 'llāha Khabīrun bi-mā yaṣnaʿūn.* (24:30)

You should know that I have studied this Qurʾānic verse [*āya*] with close attention, and in it, for all its brevity, I have discovered three significant nuances: (1) a strict injunction [*taʾdīb*], (2) a notification [*tanbīh*], and (3) an intimidation [*tahdīd*].

—As for the strict injunction, it is His saying (Exalted is He):

> Tell the believing men to lower their eyes.
> *qul li 'l-muʾminīna yaghuḍḍū min abṣāri-him*

The servant is obliged to comply with the master's command, and to observe his rules of conduct. Otherwise, he will be guilty of impropriety, so he will be excluded, for he will not be permitted to attend the meeting [held by his master] and be present in the audience. You must therefore understand this important point, and consider its implications.

—As for the notification [*tanbīh*], it is His saying (Exalted is He):

> That is purer for them
> *dhālika azkā la-hum.*

This may be understood in two senses, though Allāh knows best: (1) "That is cleaner [*aṭhar*] for their hearts." Purity [*zakāh*] is synonymous with cleanliness [*ṭahāra*], and purification [*tazkiya*] is synonymous with cleansing [*taṭhīr*]. (2) "That is more productive [*anmā*] of their goodness." The basic meaning of *zakāh* is *numuww* [growth].

Allāh (Exalted is He) has thus served notice that lowering the eyesight is conducive to the cleansing of the heart and the multiplication of obedience and goodness. That is because, if you do not lower your gaze, and if you slacken its reins, you will look at things that do not concern you, so your eye is bound to fall on something unlawful. Then, if you look at it deliberately, that will be a great sin. Perhaps your heart will become attached to that, so you will perish, unless Allāh (Exalted is He) bestows His mercy.

It is related that the servant looks with a look in which his heart is spoiled, just as the skin is spoiled in the process of tanning, so his heart becomes useless forever. Even if what you look at is something permissible [*mubāḥ*], perhaps your heart will become preoccupied with it, with the result that whisperings [*wasāwis*] and notions [*khawāṭir*] come your way. Perhaps you will not obtain it [the permissible object], so you will be left with your heart preoccupied, cut off from all that is good. If you had not seen that [permissible object], you would be relieved of all that trouble. Relevant in this context is the saying attributed to Jesus (may Allāh's blessings be upon him):

> Beware of the gaze, for it sows lustful desire in the heart, and it causes its owner nothing but trouble.

It was Dhu'n-Nūn [al-Miṣrī] who said: "Lowering the eyes is an excellent screen against lustful desires." The poet expressed it beautifully when he said:

When you sent your gaze out searching
on your heart's behalf one day, the sights exhausted you.

You could not grasp the whole of what you saw,
and you lacked the patience to deal with part of it.

Whenever you are lowering the gaze and safeguarding the eye, you are not looking at things that do not concern you, and in which you have no real interest. You are pure in the breast, free in the heart, relieved of many whispered temptations, safe from self-inflicted disasters, and steadily increasing in good things. You must therefore take careful note of this important point. Allāh (Almighty and Glorious is He) is the Source of enablement, through His gracious favour and His noble generosity.

—As for the intimidation [*tahdīd*], it is His saying (Exalted is He):

> Allāh is Aware of what they do.
> *inna 'llāha Khabīrun bi-mā yaṣna'ūn.* (24:30)

—and also in His saying (Exalted is He):

> He knows the treachery of the eyes,
> *ya'lamu khā'inata 'l-a'yuni*
> and what the breasts conceal.
> *wa mā tukhfi 'ṣ-ṣudūr.* (40:19)

This is sufficient as a warning to anyone who fears the dignity of his Lord, so this is one basic principle from the Book of Allāh (Almighty and Glorious is He).

2. The second principle is contained in the saying attributed to Allāh's Messenger (Allāh bless him and give him peace):

> Ogling the charms of a woman is a poisoned arrow, one of the arrows of Iblīs. If someone refrains from it, Allāh (Exalted is He) will let him taste a meal of worship that will delight him.

He will also discover that the sweetness of worship and the pleasure of intimate converse [with Allāh] are on an equal footing, as far as worshippers are concerned. This is something to be tested by experience, for it is recognized and verified by one who puts it into practice. That is because, if he refrains from looking at things that do not concern him, he will discover a joy in worship, a sweetness in obedience, and a pure clarity in the heart, such as he has never found before.

3. The third principle is that you must look at each member of your body, to see what purpose it is meant to serve and where it needs attention. You can then take the necessary measures to protect it and keep it safe. The purpose of the foot is to walk in the meadows and

mansions of the Garden of Paradise. The purpose of the hand is to hold the cup containing the drink, and to pluck the fruit [of the Garden]. The other members of the body are for similar purposes, apart from the eye, which is solely for the purpose of beholding the Lord of All the Worlds (Glory be to Him). There is no honour more glorious and greater than that, in either of the two abodes [this world and the Hereafter], so, if an honour like this can be expected and hoped for, because of something in particular, that thing deserves to be protected and preserved, respected and revered.

There you have the three basic principles. If you study them with proper care, you will have all the provisions you need in this subsection [concerning the eye].

Second subsection
The ear [*udhun*]

You must protect your hearing against obscene language and superfluous talk. That is for two reasons:

1. According to traditional report, the listener is the speaker's partner [*al-mustamiʿ sharīk al-mutakallim*]. To this effect, the poet says:

> Of all the ways, seek the middle ways,
> and steer well clear of the doubtful side.
>
> Keep your ears from hearing ugly talk,
> as the tongue must be kept from its utterance.
>
> For you are, when you listen to ugly talk,
> a partner of its speaker, so take heed.

2. That [careless listening] stirs up notions [*khawāṭir*] and whisperings [*wasāwis*] in the heart, then preoccupation with the body sets in, so there is nothing left over for worship.

You must also know that speech, when it enters the heart and hearing of the human being, is comparable to the food that enters his belly, for some of it is harmful and some of it is beneficial, some of it is nourishment and some of it is poison. Indeed, the effect of speech is greater and more lasting than that of food, because of the time it takes to digest. Food passes from the stomach during a sleep, for instance.

A trace of it may remain for a while, but it soon disappears. It also has a remedy, which removes its effect from the body of the human being.

As for the speech that enters his heart, it may stay with him for the rest of his life, and he may never forget it. If it is bad, it will constantly make him suffer trouble and distress, and cause notions and whisperings to arise in his heart. He will need to reject these influences, keep his heart from dwelling on them, and seek refuge with Allāh from their evil. Because of that [bad speech], he is in danger of being subjected to trial and tribulation, and finally brought to the point where he suffers a terrible calamity.

If you have kept your hearing detached from things that do not concern you, only then will you be relieved of these troubles, so the intelligent person must pay serious attention to what is at stake. Allāh is the Source of enabling grace!

Third subsection
The tongue [*lisān*]

Your next obligation is to safeguard the tongue, control it and restrict it, for it is the member of the body most prone to recalcitrance and rebelliousness, and the most frequent cause of corruption and hostility.

We have been told that Sufyān ibn ʿAbdi'llāh once said: "I said: 'O Messenger of Allāh, what do you fear the most, where I am concerned?' He took hold of his own tongue (blessing and peace be upon him), then he said: 'This!'"

According to Yūnus ibn ʿUbaidu'llāh: "I found myself enduring the trouble of fasting in the intense heat in Baṣra, but I could not bear to abstain from speech that did not concern me."

You must therefore be very careful to safeguard the tongue, sparing no effort in the process, and you must remember these five basic principles:

1. The tradition reported by Abū Saʿīd al-Khudarī (may Allāh be well pleased with him):

> As soon as the human being enters the morning time, all the members of his body turn quickly to the tongue, and they say to it: "We implore you to behave correctly, for if you behave correctly, we shall behave correctly, and if you misbehave, we shall also misbehave."

The meaning implied in this—Allāh knows best, of course—is that the speech of the tongue affects all the members of the human body, either helping them or causing them disappointment. This interpretation is confirmed by the saying attributed to Mālik ibn Dīnār: "If you notice a hardness in your heart, a feebleness in your body, and a deprivation in your sustenance, you should know that you have spoken about something that does not concern you."

2. The second principle is making good use of your time, for most of what the human being talks about is devoid of the remembrance of Allāh (Exalted is He), so it is mostly idle gossip and a waste of time. We are told that Ḥassān ibn Abī Sinān once passed by a room that had recently been constructed, so he asked: "How long is it since this was built?" Then he scolded himself, saying: "O my deceptive self, you are asking about something that does not concern you, and the penalty for that is a year-long fast."

Congratulations to those who pay due attention to their own lower selves, and woe to the heedless ones, who throw off all restraint and loosen the reins! Allāh is the One from whom help must be sought!

The poet spoke the truth and expressed it beautifully, when he said:

> Seize two cycles [of prayer] in the dark of the night,
> if you are unemployed and comfortably at ease.
>
> And if you are not involved in useless chatter,
> perform in its stead a glorification [*tasbīḥ*] [of Allāh].
>
> The need for silence is better than speaking,
> even if you are very eloquent in speech.

3. The third principle is the preservation of righteous deeds, for if someone fails to safeguard his tongue, and does too much talking, he will undoubtedly lapse into backbiting people. As the Prophet (Allāh bless him and give him peace) has said:

> If someone talks too much, he will often lapse [into sin].[21]

As for backbiting [*ghība*], it is the thunderbolt that ruins acts of worshipful obedience, in accordance with the saying: "The likeness of someone who backbites people is the likeness of someone who wields a catapult, using it to fling his merits to the east and the west, to right

[21] *man kathura lafẓu-hu kathura saqṭu-h.*

and left." We have heard that someone told al-Ḥasan [al-Baṣrī]: "O Abū Saʿīd, so-and-so has backbitten you," so al-Ḥasan sent the backbiter a bowl filled with ripe dates, and he said: "It has come to my notice that you have made me a gift of your merits, so I wish to recompense you!"

The subject of backbiting was mentioned in the presence of [ʿAbd ar-Raḥmān] ibn al-Mubārak [ibn al-Wāḍiḥ al-Ḥanẓalī], so he said: "If I were to backbite anyone, I would backbite my mother, because she is most deserving of my merits."

We are told that Ḥātim al-Aṣamm missed keeping vigil one night, so his wife found fault with him. He said: "Some people prayed last night, then, when the morning came, they slandered me, so their prayer will be in my balance on the Day of Resurrection."

4. The fourth principle is safety from the terrors of this world, in accordance with the saying of Sufyān [ath-Thawrī]: "Do not utter with your tongue what will cause your teeth to break!" Someone else said: "Do not exercise your tongue, for it will spoil your state of being." In the words of a poet:

> Safeguard your tongue and do not speak, for you will be afflicted.
> Affliction is guaranteed as the consequence of speech.

According to Ibn al-Mubārak (may Allāh be well pleased with him):

> You must safeguard your tongue, for the tongue
> is quick to kill the man it targets.
>
> The tongue is also the guide of the heart,
> guiding men to its understanding.

According to Ibn al-Muṭīʿ (may Allāh bestow His mercy upon him):

> A man's tongue is a lion in a den;
> if he sets it loose, it will attack him.
>
> So restrain it from obscenity with the bridle of silence,
> for then you will have protection from afflictions.

According to the popular refrain: "Many a word says to its owner: 'Leave me! We shall ask Allāh for assistance, through His mercy!'"

5. The fifth principle is to remember the terrors of the Hereafter and its dreadful consequences. I shall mention one important point in this connection: namely, that you must beware of saying something that is

forbidden and unlawful, or something that would otherwise be permissible, but which transgresses into matters that do not concern you. If it is forbidden and unlawful, it entails the torment of Allāh (Exalted is He), to an extent that is unbearable for you. As we know from traditional report, Allāh's Messenger (Allāh bless him and give him peace) once said:

> On the night when I was transported beyond this world, I saw that some people in the Fire of Hell were eating corpses, so I said: "O Gabriel, who are these?" He said: "These are the ones who eat the flesh of their fellow human beings."

The Prophet (Allāh bless him and give him peace) told Muʿādh:

> Keep your tongue from [maligning] the bearers of the Qurʾān and the seekers of knowledge, and do not tear people to shreds with your tongue, for [if you do so], the dogs of the Fire of Hell will tear you to shreds.

According to Abū Qilāba: "Backbiting separates the heart from right guidance, so we beg Allāh (Exalted is He) for protection from that, through His gracious favour."

This applies to forbidden speech. As for that which is permissible [but indulged in to excess], there are four cases to consider:

1. The interest taken by the Noble Recording Angels [*al-Kirām al-Kātibīn*] in that which contains nothing good and nothing beneficial. The human being is obliged to relate to them with humble modesty, so that he does not offend them. Allāh (Exalted is He) has said:

> Not a word does he utter,
> *mā yalfiẓu min qawlin*
> without there being an observer at the ready by his side.
> *illā ladai-hi raqībun ʿatīd.* (50:18)

2. The sending to Allāh (Glory be to Him and Exalted is He) of a record of idle talk and babble. The servant must beware of that, and he must be afraid of offending Allāh (Almighty and Glorious is He).

We are told that one of the righteous predecessors said, when he noticed that a man was using obscene language: "Woe unto you! You are dictating a record to your Lord, so consider what you are dictating!"

3. The reading of the servant's record before the All-Compelling Sovereign [*al-Malik al-Jabbār*] on the Day of Resurrection, in the presence of the witnesses, between the hardships and the terrors, while

he is thirsty, naked, hungry, cut off from the Garden of Paradise and excluded from blessing.

4. The blame and reproach for what you have said, the conclusive nature of the evidence [against you], and the sense of shame before the Lord of Might and Glory [*Rabb al-ʿIzza*]. As someone put it: "Beware of excess, for its reckoning will be prolonged!"

These principles are sufficient as an admonition for someone who can bear to be admonished. We have treated the subject extensively in the book entitled: "Secrets of Religious Practices [*Asrār Muʿāmalāt ad-Dīn*]," so examine its contents and you will find the medicine you need.

Fourth subsection
The heart [*qalb*]

Your next obligation is to safeguard and improve the heart, and to do that with the greatest care, sparing no effort in the process. Of all these members of the body, the heart is the one most fraught with danger, most effective in its influence, most delicate in subtlety, most awkward to improve, and most difficult by nature. I shall mention five principles in this connection, sufficient for the present purpose:

1. The first principle is represented by His sayings (Exalted is He):

> He knows the treachery of the eyes,
> *yaʿlamu khāʾinata ʾl-aʿyuni*
> and what the breasts conceal.
> *wa mā tukhfi ʾṣ-ṣudūr*. (40:19)
>
> Allāh knows what is in your hearts.
> *wa ʾllāhu yaʿlamu mā fī qulūbi-kum*. (33:51)
>
> He is indeed Aware of the hidden content of the breasts.
> *inna-hu ʿAlīmun bi-dhāti ʾṣ-ṣudūr*. (11:5)

He has mentioned this, and repeated the mention of it, so often in the Qurʾān. The watchfulness of the All-Knowing, the All-Aware, is sufficient as a warning and a threat for the special few among His servants, because dealing with the Knower of the Unseen is a very grave danger. You must therefore consider what He knows about your heart!

2. The second principle is represented by the saying of Allāh's Messenger (Allāh bless him and give him peace):

> Allāh (Exalted is He) does not look at your outer forms and your skins. He looks only at your hearts.

The heart is therefore the focal point of the gaze of the Lord of All the Worlds, so it is strange that someone could attach importance to his face, when that is the focal point of the gaze of his fellow creatures! He washes and cleans his face, ridding it of dirt and stains, and makes it as beautiful as he possibly can, so that no creature will detect any fault in it, but he pays no attention to his heart, though it is the focal point of the gaze of the Lord of All the Worlds. He ought to purify his heart, adorn it and perfume it, so that the Lord (Magnificent is His Majesty) will not see it marred by any filth, dirt, stain or fault. Instead, he allows it to accumulate a mass of rubbish, filth and squalor, so disgusting that if his fellow creatures caught a glimpse of any part of it, they would avoid him, shun him and chase him away. Allāh is the One from whom help must be sought!

3. The third principle is that the heart is a sovereign who must be obeyed, and a leader who must be followed. All the members of the body are followers, so, if the one that is followed is sound, the followers will also be sound. If the sovereign is on the right path, his subjects will also be on the right path. That will be made clear to you by the saying attributed to the Prophet (Allāh bless him and give him peace):

> The body contains a chunk of flesh. If that chunk is sound, the whole body is sound, but if it is unhealthy, the whole body is unhealthy. That chunk is the heart, of course!

Since the soundness of the whole depends on that one part, it must surely be treated with the utmost care.

4. The fourth principle is that the heart is the treasury of every precious jewel belonging to the servant, and of every item of real importance to him. The first of these is the intellect [*ʿaql*], and the most splendid of them is direct knowledge [*maʿrifa*] of Allāh (Exalted is He), which is the cause of bliss in the two abodes [this world and the Hereafter]. Then come the faculties of perception [*baṣāʾir*], which are the means of advancement and distinction in the sight of Allāh (Almighty and Glorious is He). Then comes sincere intention [*niyya khāliṣa*] in acts of obedience, on which depends the reward of eternity. Then come the various forms of knowledge and wisdom, which endow

the servant with honour and all noble qualities, including the praiseworthy attributes that enable men to achieve superiority, as we have explained with detailed commentary in the book entitled: "Secrets of Religious Practices [*Asrār Muʿāmalāt ad-Dīn*]."

A treasury like this deserves to be to kept safe, preserved from pollution and damage, guarded and protected against thieves and robbers, and honoured and dignified with every mark of respect. That will prevent any filth from staining those precious jewels, and keep any foe from seizing them. Let us take refuge with Allāh!

5. The fifth principle is this: I have carefully studied the condition of the heart, and discovered that it has five characteristics belonging to none of the other members of the human body:

—The first is that the enemy is intent on it, focused on it and firmly attached to it, for the devil is perched on the heart of the human being. The heart is the place of inspiration [*ilhām*] and whispering [*waswasa*], the two invitations that are always issued to it by the angel and the devil, respectively.

—The second is that the heart has more to keep it preoccupied. Intelligence and passion are both contained within it, so it is the battle ground of the two armies: passion and its troops, and intelligence and its troops. It is always in the midst of their mutual combat, fighting and conflict, so its fortress must be defended, protected and never neglected.

—Thirdly, the heart has more distractions to contend with, for notions [*khawāṭir*] never cease to descend upon it like arrows, or like rain that falls unceasingly by night and day, while you are powerless to bring this to a stop.

The heart is not in the same position as the eye, for it is between the eyelids, which can be closed to let you rest. You may also be in an empty place, or a dark night, so the sight of the eyes will be protected.

Nor is the heart like the tongue, which is behind the two barriers: the teeth and the cheeks. You are also capable of restraining it and keeping it silent, whereas the heart is a target for notions [*khawāṭir*], which you have no way of preventing and guarding against, and which do not grant you respite for one moment. The lower self is also quick to follow them, and preventing that is a very difficult matter and a tremendous test.

—Fourthly, the treatment required to remedy the heart is difficult to apply, since the heart is invisible to you. Almost without your being aware, some affliction invades it and some problem affects it, so you need to investigate that thoroughly, with prolonged effort, scrupulous examination and intense training.

—Fifthly, the heart [*qalb*] is more rapidly affected by disasters, for it is closer to capsizing [*inqilāb*]. As the saying goes: "The heart is quicker to capsize than the kettle on the boil." That is why the poet said:

> The heart is only called the *qalb* because of its *taqallub* [unsteadiness],
> while the mind affects the human being in various ways.

If the heart slips—the refuge is with Allāh!—its slip is more serious [than that of any other member of the body], and its lapse is more abominable, since the least of it is hardness and an inclination towards something other than Allāh (Glory be to Him and Exalted is He), and the worst of it is a final seal of unbelief [*kufr*]. The refuge is with Allāh (Exalted is He). You have surely heard His saying (Exalted is He):

> He refused and gave a display of arrogant pride,
> *abā wa 'stakbara*
> and so he came to be one of the unbelievers.
> *wa kāna mina 'l-kāfirīn*. (2:34)

This means that arrogant pride was in his heart, so it brought him to the outward display of denial and unbelief.

You have surely heard His saying (Exalted is He):

> But he clung to the earth
> *wa lākinna-hu akhlada ila 'l-arḍi*
> and followed his own passion.
> *wa 'ttabaʿa hawā-h*. (7:176)

The inclination to follow passion was in that man's heart, so it induced him to commit that shameful sin with his outer self.

You have surely heard His saying (Exalted is He):

> We confound their hearts and their eyes.
> *wa nuqallibu af'idata-hum wa abṣāra-hum*
> As they did not believe therein at first,
> *ka-mā lam yu'minū bi-hi awwala marratin*
> We let them wander blindly on in their contumacy.
> *wa nadharu-hum fī ṭughyāni-him yaʿmahūn*. (6:110)

For this reason, O man, the special servants of Allāh (Exalted is He) are afraid for their hearts, weep over them, and devote their caring attention to them. Allāh (Glory be to Him) described these special servants when He said:

> They fear a day when hearts and eyeballs will be overturned.
> *yakhāfūna yawman tataqallabu fī-hi 'l-qulūbu wa 'l-abṣār.* (24:37)

May Allāh include you, and us, among those who heed the admonitions, who are cautious in places of danger, and who succeed in improving their hearts with scrupulous attention. He is the Most Merciful of the merciful.

You may say: "This matter of the heart is very important indeed, so inform us of the factors that improve it, and of the evils that obstruct it and corrupt it. Perhaps we shall then succeed in making the necessary effort to act accordingly."

You must therefore know that the detailed explanation of these points is very lengthy indeed, beyond the scope of this book. None but the scholars of the Hereafter have undertaken that research, and compiled written works devoted to this subject. In connection with what is needed in that respect, they have mentioned about ninety praiseworthy virtues, as well as their blameworthy opposites. They have also described in detail the actions and procedures that are obligatory or forbidden.

By my life, if someone is seriously concerned about the state of his religion, if he is alarmed by the slumber of the heedless, and if he examines himself with care, it will not be too much for him to acquire all that knowledge and put it into practice, so long as Allāh (Exalted is He) enables him to succeed. We have mentioned a fraction of it in the account of the marvels of the heart, in the book entitled: "Revival of the Religious Sciences [*Iḥyā' ʿUlūm ad-Dīn*]." We have also provided a detailed account of the whole subject, its nature and its treatment, in the book entitled: "Secrets of Religious Practices [*Asrār Muʿāmalāt ad-Dīn*]." Though insignificant in itself, the latter book is extremely useful, if only to those heroic scholars who are firmly rooted in knowledge.

As for the content of this present book, it should prove useful to both the novice and the graduate, to the strong and the weak alike. We have examined the principles that cannot go unmentioned, concerning the remedial treatment of the heart, since the need for them is pressing, and they are absolutely indispensable in the sphere of worship. We have found that these four matters require particular attention: (1) the stumbling blocks of the worshippers and (2) the mishaps of those who strive hard; in other words: (3) the disturbances of hearts and (4) the vices of the lower selves, which impede, disgrace, corrupt and spoil.

Each of these four has a countermeasure, the first three being the uprightness of the worshippers, the correct performance of worship, and the righteousness of hearts. The vices [of the lower selves] are subdivided into four: (1) excessive expectation, (2) haste, (3) envy, and (4) arrogant pride. There are four corresponding virtues: (1) minimal expectation, (2) proceding at a moderate pace in all matters, (3) wishing the best for one's fellow creatures, and (4) humble submissiveness and modesty.

Such are the basic principles concerning the righteousness of hearts and their corruption. As for the central point at issue, you must spare no effort in guarding against these vices and acquiring these virtues. You will then have sufficient provisions and achieve the goal, if Allāh (Exalted is He) so wills. I shall now inform you about these vices, in statements that are brief but satisfactory:

1. As for excessive expectation [*ṭūl al-amal*], it is the impediment to every good deed and act of obedience, and the incentive to everything wicked and corrupt. It is the incurable disease that afflicts human creatures with all kinds of trials and tribulations. You must therefore know that, if your expectation is excessive, you will suffer these four consequences:

—First, the neglect of obedience and laziness in its performance. You say: "I shall act in due course, for the days are in front of me, and I shall not miss that opportunity." Dāwūd aṭ-Ṭā'ī (may Allāh bestow His mercy upon him) spoke the truth when he said: "If someone fears the threat, that which is remote will draw close to him. If someone's expectation is excessive, his work will be bad." According to Yaḥyā ibn Mu'ādh ar-Rāzī (may Allāh bestow His mercy upon him): "Overexpectation is an obstacle to everything good, greed is a barrier to every truth, patience is a route to every victory, and the lower self is a summoner to every evil."

—The second consequence is refraining from repentance and putting it off till later. You say: "I shall repent in due course, for the days lie ahead in abundance. I am young and my age is insignificant. Repentance is at my disposal, and I am capable of it whenever I am ready." Perhaps death will catch you by surprise, while you persist [in sin], so the appointed term will seize you before your work has been corrected.

—The third consequence is greed for the accumulation of wealth, and preccupation with this world to the exclusion of the Hereafter. You say: "I am afraid of poverty in my old age, and that I may be too weak to acquire property. I must have something extra, something to keep in store for sickness, senility or poverty." This is the kind of outlook that stimulates desire and greed for this world, and implacable anxiety about the means of survival. You say: "What am I going to eat? What am I going to drink? What am I going to wear? The winter is here, the summer is coming, and I have nothing. Perhaps my life will be long, so I shall be in need. With old age the need will be severe. I cannot do without nourishment and sufficient provision from other people." This is the kind of attitude that stimulates desire for this world, the accumulation of its wealth, and the refusal to share whatever part of it you possess. At the very least, this will keep your heart preoccupied, waste your life or your moment of opportunity, and multiply your grief and sorrow, all to no avail and no advantage.

Consider the saying of Abū Dharr (may Allāh be well pleased with him): "I was killed by the worry of a day I had not reached." Someone asked: "How was that, O Abū Dharr?" He said: "My expectation went beyond my appointed term."

—The fourth consequence is hardness of the heart and forgetfulness of the Hereafter. This is because, if you expect long life, you will fail to remember death and the grave. As ʿAlī ibn Abī Ṭālib (may Allāh ennoble his countenance) once said: "There are two things that I fear for you the most: excessive expectation and the following of passion." There is no doubt that excessive expectation causes forgetfulness of the Hereafter, and the following of passion blocks acceptance of the Truth. Your thoughts and your business are mostly concerned with the news of this world, the means of livelihood, the company of people, and so on. That makes the heart turn hard. Gentleness and pure serenity of the heart can only come about through remembrance of death and the grave, the reward and the punishment, and the conditions of the Hereafter. In the absence of any of that, from whence can your heart obtain gentleness and pure serenity? Allāh (Exalted is He) has said:

> But the term was prolonged for them,
> *fa-ṭāla ʿalai-himu 'l-amadu*
> and so their hearts were hardened.
> *fa-qasat qulūbu-hum.* (57:16)

If you overextend your expectation, your obedience will be too little, your repentance will be delayed, your disobedience will increase, your greed will intensify, your heart will harden, and your heedless disregard of the outcome will be magnified—the refuge is with Allāh!—so, unless Allāh (Exalted is He) bestows His mercy, the blessing of the Hereafter will be lost to you. What state of affairs could be worse than this? What calamity could be more disastrous than this? All of this is due to excessive expectation. You must therefore curtail your expectation, consider your death to be close at hand, and remember the condition of your close relatives and brethren, whom death took by surprise, at a moment they did not anticipate, for your condition may be similar to theirs. Beware, O my deceptive self, and remember the saying of ʿAwf ibn ʿAbdi'llāh (may Allāh bestow His mercy upon him): "How many a one has looked forward to a day he did not complete, and how many a one has waited for a tomorrow he did not reach. If you saw the appointed term and its arrival, you would loathe expectation and its deceptiveness."

You have surely heard the saying of Mary's son Jesus (peace be upon him): "This world consists of three days: (1) a yesterday that has passed, and there is nothing of it in your hand; (2) a tomorrow that you may or may not reach, and you do not know either way, and (3) a today, in which you are present, so make good use of it!"

Then there is the saying of Abū Dharr al-Ghifārī (may Allāh be well pleased with him): "This world consists of three hours: (1) an hour that has already passed; (2) an hour in which you are present, and (3) an hour that you may or may not reach, and you do not know either way." This means that you only have one hour, in actual fact, since death is at the ready from hour to hour.

Then there is the saying of our own Shaikh (may Allāh bestow His mercy upon him): "This world consists of three breaths: (1) a breath that has passed, in which you did whatever you did; (2) a breath in which you are present, and (3) a breath that you may or may not reach, and you do not know either way."

How many an inhaler has been snatched by death before exhaling that last breath! In actual fact, you have only one breath, not a day and not an hour, so be quick to devote this one breath to worship and repentance, before the opportunity is lost, for perhaps you will die in the next breath. Do not worry about sustenance, for perhaps you will not live long enough to need it, so your time will be wasted and the worry superfluous. The human being should not worry about sustenance for a single day, a single hour, or a single breath. Remember what the Prophet (Allāh bless him and give him peace) said to Usāma:

> You must wonder about Usāma, the buyer of a month's patience.[22] Usāma is guilty of excessive expectation. By Allāh, I have never set a foot on the ground, and assumed that I would raise it again. I have never taken a morsel, and assumed that I would swallow it before death overtook me. By the One who holds my soul in His hand, what you are promised will surely come to pass, and you cannot escape.[23]

If you remember these sayings, O man, and diligently contemplate the message they convey, by considering it over and over again, your expectation will be curtailed, if Allāh (Exalted is He) so wills. You will then see yourself attending promptly to acts of obedience, and hastening your repentance, so your sinful disobedience will fall away from you, and you will abstain from this world and its pursuit. Your reckoning and your penalty will be lightened, and your heart will concentrate on remembering the Hereafter and its terrors. That will happen from breath to breath, as you move towards it and survey it [the Hereafter] one breath at a time. Hardness of heart will leave you, to be replaced by gentleness and pure serenity, and you will then experience the fear

[22] ***Commentator's note***: According to Abū Sa'īd al-Khudarī, Usāma ibn Zaid bought an infant slave-girl [*walīda*] from Zaid ibn Thābit, for the price of one hundred dīnārs, on the understanding that the deal would be settled in a month's time.

[23] The Prophet (Allāh bless him and give him peace) was quoting the Qur'ānic verse [*āya*]:

> What you are promised will surely come to pass,
> *inna mā tū'adūna lā-ātin*
> and you cannot escape.
> *wa mā antum bi-mu'jizīn.* (6:134)

of Allāh (Exalted is He) and the dread of offending Him. The matter of your worship will be rectified for you, the hope of your being prepared for your ultimate outcome will be strengthened, and you will achieve the desired goal in your ultimate outcome. All of that will come in the wake of the gracious favour of Allāh (Exalted is He), by means of this virtue, which is curtailment of expectation [*qiṣar al-amal*].

It is related that Zurāra ibn Awfā (may Allāh bestow His mercy upon him) was asked in the sleep after his death: "Which deeds have made the greatest contribution to what you now enjoy?" He said: "Contentment and curtailment of expectation."

You must therefore examine yourself, O brother, and devote every effort to this great principle, for it is the most important and the most effective in improving the heart and the lower self. Allāh (Exalted is He) is the Custodian of enabling grace, through His favour and His mercy.

2. As for envy [*ḥasad*], it is the spoiler of acts of obedience and the incentive to sinful errors. It is the chronic disease with which most of the Qur᾽ān-reciters and scholars are afflicted, not to mention the common folk and the ignorant, to the point where it destroys them and dooms them to the Fire of Hell. You have surely heard the saying of Allāh's Messenger (Allāh bless him and give him peace):

> Six [sets of people] will enter the Fire of Hell because of six [offences]: (1) the Arabs because of sinful disobedience; (2) the rulers because of tyranny; (3) the local chiefs because of arrogant pride; (4) the merchants because of cheating; (5) the country bumpkins because of ignorance, and (6) the scholars because of envy.

If an affliction is so disastrous that it dooms the scholars to the Fire of Hell, it is truly something to be guarded against!

You must also know that envy stirs up five things:

—First of all, the corruption of acts of obedience. Allāh's Messenger (Allāh bless him and give him peace) once said:

> Envy consumes fine qualities, just as the fire consumes wood.

—Secondly, the commission of acts of sinful disobedience and wicked deeds. According to Wahb ibn Munabbih (may Allāh bestow His mercy upon him): "The envier has three distinctive features: (1) he flatters [the person he envies] when he is present; (2) he backbites him when he is absent, and (3) he takes pleasure in the misfortune when it occurs.

It is enough for you that Allāh (Exalted is He) has commanded us to seek refuge from the evil of the envier, for He has said (Glory be to Him):

> ...and from the evil of an envier when he envies.
> *wa min sharri ḥāsidin idhā ḥasad.* (113:5)

He has likewise commanded us to seek refuge from the evil of the devil and the sorcerer. Consider how much evil and corruption envy must contain, since He has equated it with the devil and the sorcerer, so that help against it can only be sought from Him, and there is no refuge except with Allāh, the Lord of All the Worlds!

—Thirdly, tiresome labour and concern, not merely to no avail, but accompanied by a burden of sin and disobedience. According to Ibn as-Sammāk (may Allāh bestow His mercy upon him): "I have never seen a wrongdoer more similar to the victim of wrongdoing than the envier. He has a wretched personality, a baffled mind, and an implacable distress."

—Fourthly, the heart is so blind that it can hardly understand any of the laws of Allāh (Glory be to Him and Exalted is He). According to Sufyān ath-Thawrī (may Allāh bestow His mercy upon him): "You must observe protracted silence, for you will then possess pious caution [*wara*ʿ]. You must not be greedy for this world, so that you may be a trustworthy guardian. You must not be a fault-finder, so that you may be safe from people's tongues. You must not be envious, so that you may be quick to understand."

—Fifthly, deprivation and disappointment. The envier can hardly achieve any goal, nor be helped to defeat any foe. According to Ḥātim al-Aṣamm (may Allāh bestow His mercy upon him): "The spiteful person is not religious, the fault-finder is not a worshipful servant, the slanderer is not worthy of trust, and the envier is not victorious."

How can the envier achieve his goal, when his goal is the removal of Allāh's blessings (Exalted is He) from His Muslim servants? How can he be helped against his enemies, when they are the believing servants of Allāh? Abū Yaʿqūb (may Allāh bestow His mercy upon him) expressed it beautifully, when he said: "O Allāh, cause us to wait patiently for the completion of blessings on Your servants, and improve their conditions!"

Envy is a disease that corrupts your obedience, increases your wickedness and your sinful disobedience. It prevents you from achieving the sense of comfort and the understanding of the heart, victory over the enemies and the accomplishment of success. What sickness could be worse? You must treat yourself with an effective remedy! Allāh is the Custodian of enablement, through His gracious favour and His noble generosity.

3. As for haste and impetuosity [*nazaq*] in the pursuit of piety [*birr*], it is the vice that causes the proper targets to be missed, and that results in sinful acts of disobedience. It gives rise to four regrettable consequences:

—First of all, the worshipful servant aims to achieve a particular degree of goodness and rectitude, and he strives hard to that end, but he may be too hasty and the timing may be inappropriate. If that is the case, he may either slacken and despair, abandoning the effort and forfeiting that degree, or else he may overdo the effort and exhaust himself, and this will also deprive him of that degree. He is caught between excess [*ifrāṭ*] and negligence [*tafrīṭ*], each of them being the result of haste. According to the traditional report, the Prophet (Allāh bless him and give him peace) once said:

> This religion of ours is firm terrain, so travel in it at a gentle pace, for the stranded traveller covers no ground and keeps no camel to ride.

As the popular saying goes: "If you do not hurry, you will arrive." In the words of a poet:

> He who acts unhurriedly gains part of what he needs,
> while he who acts in haste is beset with errors and mistakes.

—Secondly, the worshipful servant has some need, so he appeals to Allāh (Exalted is He) to satisfy it, with frequent and urgent supplication. Perhaps he is trying to hasten the response, before its proper time, so he will not receive it. If that is the case, he grows weary and bored, and refrains from supplication, so he forfeits his need and is deprived of what he seeks.

—Thirdly, someone wrongs the worshipful servant, making him furiously enraged, so he hurriedly invokes a curse on the wrongdoer, causing a Muslim to perish. Perhaps he has transgressed the limit, thereby falling into sinful disobedience and perdition. Allāh (Exalted is He) has said:

> Man prays for evil as he prays for good,
> *wa yadʿu 'l-insānu bi'sh-sharri duʿāʾa-hu bi'l-khair:*
> for the human being is ever hasty.
> *wa kāna 'l-insānu ʿajūlā.* (17:11)

—Fourthly, the basis and foundation of worshipful service is pious caution [*waraʿ*]. The basis of pious caution is thorough examination of everything. Complete research means investigating absolutely everything, including food and drink, clothing, speech and action. If a man is hasty in dealing with matters, rather than unhurried and scrupulously thorough, he will not exercise the necessary hesitation and attentiveness. He will be hasty in speech, so he will lapse into error. He will be hasty in eating every kind of food, so he will lapse into that which is unlawful and dubious. He will be equally hasty in every matter, so pious caution will elude him, and what good is there in worshipful service without pious caution? He is in the state of separation from the degrees of goodness, guilty of the deprivation of needs, the perdition of the Muslims and his own perdition. There is also the risk of losing the caution that is essential to material welfare.

The human being is therefore obliged to deal with the vice of haste, by removing it and then improving the lower self. Allāh is the Custodian of enablement, through His grace and favour.

4. As for arrogant pride [*kibr*], it is the vice that is immediately destructive. You have surely heard the saying of Allāh (Exalted is He):

> He refused and gave a display of arrogant pride,
> *abā wa 'stakbara*
> and so he came to be one of the unbelievers.
> *wa kāna mina 'l-kāfirīn.* (2:34)

This vice is not of the same order as other vices, which degrade an action and cause harm by indirect means, for it causes harm at the very root, degrading religion and belief. If it grows strong and becomes predominant, it cannot be rectified. The refuge is with Allāh!

At the very least, the servant who is guilty of arrogant pride will suffer these four disastrous consequences:

—First, preclusion from the truth and blindness of the heart, preventing recognition of the signs of Allāh (Exalted is He), which contain the laws of Allāh (Exalted is He). Allāh (Exalted is He) has said:

> I shall turn away from My signs those who
> *sa-aṣrifu ʿan āyāti 'lladhīna*
> magnify themselves wrongfully in the earth.
> *yatakabbarūna fi 'l-arḍi bi-ghairi 'l-ḥaqq*. (7:146)

> This does Allāh print on every arrogant, disdainful heart.
> *ka-dhālika yaṭbaʿu 'llāhu ʿalā kulli qalbi mutakabbirin jabbār*. (40:35)

—Second, hatred and loathing from Allāh (Exalted is He). Allāh (Exalted is He) has said:

> He does not love the arrogantly proud.
> *inna-hu lā yuḥibbu 'l-mustakbirīn*. (16:23)

Moses (peace be upon him) is reported as having said: "O my Lord, which of Your creatures is most hateful to You?" His Lord replied: "The one whose heart is arrogantly proud, whose tongue is coarse, who shifts his eye, whose hand is niggardly, and whose morality is bad."

—Third, disgrace and chastisement in this world and the Hereafter. It was Ḥātim (may Allāh bestow His mercy upon him) who said: "Beware of letting death overtake you in three conditions: arrogant pride, avarice and conceit. If someone is arrogantly proud, Allāh (Exalted is He) will not remove him from this world, until He exposes him to contempt from the meanest of his relatives and servants. If someone is avaricious, Allāh (Exalted is He) will not remove him from this world, until He puts him in need of a crust of bread or a drop of water, and he cannot find anything to swallow. If someone is conceited, Allāh (Exalted is He) will not remove him from this world, until He smears him with his urine and his excrement." It has also been said: "If someone is proud without justification, Allāh (Exalted is He) will justifiably make him suffer humiliation."

—Fourth, the Fire of Hell and torment in the Hereafter. According to traditional report, Allāh (Exalted is He) has said:

> Grandeur is My robe and splendour is My waist-wrapper, so if anyone competes with Me in either one of them, I shall cause him to enter the Fire of Hell.[24]

[24] This is a Sacred Tradition [*Ḥadīth Qudsī*], not a Qurʾānic verse [*āya*].

In other words: "Splendour and grandeur are among the attributes peculiar to Me, so they are not appropriate for anyone but Me, just as the robe and waist-wrapper of the individual human being are peculiar to him, and they are not shared by anyone else."

The foundation of the whole business [of religion] is recognition of the Truth, and grasping the meanings of the signs and laws of Allāh (Exalted is He). A vice that deprives you thereof will expose you to hatred from Allāh (Glory be to Him and Exalted is He), disgrace in this world, and the Fire of Hell in the Hereafter. An intelligent person must not neglect his own self, so that he fails to correct it by removing the vice. He must be alert and on his guard, and seek refuge with Allāh (Almighty and Glorious is He), for He is the Custodian of safekeeping and enablement, through His gracious favour.

This is some of what we have come to know about the disastrous consequences of these four vices. One of them is enough for the intelligent person, let alone all four of them, since the matter of his heart is important to him, and he must defend the cause of his religion. Allāh is the Source of enabling grace!

You may say: "If this is the state of affairs, with regard to the disastrous consequences of these vices, and the need to be on our guard against them, it is essential to understand their real nature and their exact definition. Explain that to us, therefore, so that we may recognize the means of protection against them."

You must therefore know that much has been said about each one of these vices, and we have treated this discussion in great detail in the books entitled: "Revival of the Religious Sciences [*Iḥyā᾽ ʿUlūm ad-Dīn*]" and "Secrets of Religious Practices [*Asrār Muʿāmalāt ad-Dīn*]." We shall now mention that which cannot go unmentioned, for it is simply indispensable—Allāh is the Source of enabling grace!—so this is what we have to say:

—As for overexpectation [*amal*], most of our scholars (may Allāh bestow His mercy upon them) have said: "Overexpectation is the desire for life to be of indeterminate duration. Curtailment of expectation means that you restrict it by making it contingent on the will of Allāh and His knowledge [by saying: 'If Allāh wills (*in shā᾽a 'llāh*)'], or making it conditional on the correctness of the wish. If you mention your life, by saying with firm conviction: 'I shall still be alive after another breath, or another hour, or another day,' you are being excessively expectant. That is a sinful act of disobedience on your part, since it is a judgement on the Unseen. If you make it contingent on the will and knowledge of Allāh, by saying: 'I shall still be alive, if Allāh wills,' or, 'if Allāh knows that I shall still be alive,' you have departed from the category of overexpectation, and you are innocent of that offence."

Likewise, if you wish your life to last for another moment, as a matter of certainty, you are being excessively expectant. On the other hand, if you make your wish contingent on its correctness, you have departed from the category of overexpectation, and curtailment of expectation is rightly ascribed to you, since you have refrained from making a definite prediction. You must therefore refrain from making any such prediction, by mentioning survival and the desire for it—mentioning with the heart, that is to say. This means that you must keep the heart firmly committed to that abstinence. You must understand all that correctly, if Allāh (Almighty and Glorious is He) so wills.

Furthermore, overexpectation is of two kinds: the overexpectation of the common folk, and that of the élite.

As for the overexpectation of the common folk, it means that you wish for life and survival in order to accumulate worldly goods and enjoy them. This is sheer sinful disobedience. Its opposite is curtailment of expectation. Allāh (Exalted is He) has said:

> Let them eat and enjoy life, and let expectation beguile them,
> *dhar-hum ya'kulū wa yatamatta'ū wa yulhi-himu 'l-amalu*
> for they will soon come to know!
> *fa-sawfa ya'lamūn.* (15:3)

As for the overexpectation of élite, it means that you wish for survival in order to complete some good work, about which there is an element of doubt; that is to say, the servant is not certain about its appropriateness for him. To undertake a particular good work, or bring it to completion, may sometimes be inappropriate for the servant, since it may cause him to lapse into vain conceit, in which case the harm will outweigh the benefit.

When the servant embarks on a ritual prayer [*ṣalāt*], or a fast [*ṣawm*], or some other act of obedience, it is therefore incorrect for him to predict that he will bring it to completion, since that is a mystery [*ghaib*]. Nor must he intend that [completion] absolutely, because that may not be appropriate for him. He should rather make that contingent on Allāh's will, or on the appropriateness [of what he intends], for he will then be innocent of the fault of overexpectation. Allāh (Exalted is He) said to His Prophet (Allāh bless him and give him peace):

> And do not say of anything: "I shall do that tomorrow,"
> *wa lā taqūlanna li-shaiʾin innī fāʿilun dhālika ghadā:*
> without adding: "if Allāh so wills."
> *illā an yashāʾa 'llāh.* (18:23,24)

The opposite of this overexpectation, according to the scholars, is praiseworthy intention [*niyya maḥmūda*]. They say that in a broad sense, because, if someone acts with praiseworthy intention, he cannot be guilty of overexpectation.

We have already explained the nature of overexpectation [in the passages above]. As for praiseworthy intention, it is necessary to understand it well, since it is the basic principle [to be observed in guarding against overexpectation]. The scholars (may Allāh bestow His mercy upon them) have defined it precisely and comprehensively in the following terms: "Correct and praiseworthy intention is the decisive proposal to perform a deed immediately, before all other deeds, as well as the wish to bring it to completion, combined with *tafwīḍ* [entrustment to Allāh] and *istithnāʾ* [making it contingent on Allāh's will, by saying: 'If Allāh wills (*in shāʾa 'llāh*)']."

Someone may ask: "Why is it permissible to make a decisive proposal concerning the beginning [of the deed], whereas *tafwīḍ* and *istithnāʾ* are strictly required where completion is concerned?"

The answer to this will be: Because of the absence of risk at the outset, since you are ready to begin immediately, and there is nothing to make you delay, and because of the presence of risk where completion is concerned, since that will occur at an indeterminate moment. There are two risks, in fact: (1) the risk of failure to arrive, since you do not know whether or not you will reach that point [of completion], and (2) the risk of incorrectness, since you do not know whether or not that is appropriate for you. That is why *istithnāʾ* is necessary, because of the risk of failure to arrive, as well as *tafwīḍ*, because of the risk of incorrectness. If the proposal is made on these conditions, the intention will be praiseworthy, exempt from overexpectation and its dire consequences. You must therefore consider all this with very great care.

You must also know that the fortress of curtailment of expectation is the remembrance of death, and the stronghold of its fortress is the remembrance of the suddenness of death, and the fact that it may snatch the servant by surprise and unawares, while he is in a state of delusion and lassitude. You must therefore pay careful attention to all this advice, and apply it successfully, for it is sorely needed. You must desist from wasting time on tittle-tattle and quarrelling with people. Allāh is the Source of enablement, through His gracious favour!

—As for vicious envy [*ḥasad*], it is the wish to see your Muslim brother deprived of Allāh's blessings (Exalted is He), meaning everything containing benefit for him. If you do not wish to see him deprived of those blessings, but wish to have the like of them for yourself, that is harmless envy [*ghibṭa*]. This probably explains the saying of the Prophet (Allāh bless him and give him peace):

> There is no envy [*ḥasad*] except in two [senses]....

In other words, he used the term *ḥasad* loosely, to include the meaning of *ghibṭa*, because of the close connection between the two.

If you wish to see your Muslim brother deprived of things that contain no benefit for him, that is solicitude [*ghaira*]. Such is the distinction between these concepts.

As for the opposite of envy [*ḥasad*], it is well-wishing [*naṣīḥa*]. In other words, it is the wish to see your Muslim brother retain the blessings of Allāh (Exalted is He), meaning everything containing benefit for him.

You may ask: "How do we know whether something is to his benefit or to his detriment, so that we may wish him well, or envy him?"

You must therefore understand that we can make a reasonable assumption about that, and our reasonable assumption is tantamount to knowledge in such cases. If the matter is still doubtful to you, on no account must you wish to see any Muslim lose or retain a blessing, unless your wish is qualified by *tafwīḍ* [entrustment to Allāh] and contingent on correctness. You will then be innocent of envy, and you will obtain the benefit of well-wishing.

As for the fortress of well-wishing [*naṣīḥa*], which provides protection from envy, it is remembrance of the duty to befriend the Muslims, which Allāh (Exalted is He) has strictly imposed. The stronghold of this fortress is remembrance of the worth of the true believer, whom Allāh (Exalted is He) has magnified and exalted, and of the splendid favours Allāh has in store for him in the Hereafter, as well as the splendid benefits he offers you in this world, such as mutual help and assistance, and company in congregational gatherings [*jamāʿāt*], especially the Friday prayers [*jumuʿāt*]. You should also remember that you can hope for his intercession in the Hereafter.

These considerations, and others of the kind, should encourage you to wish the best for every Muslim, and deter you from envying him for any blessing bestowed on him by Allāh (Exalted is He). Allāh (Glory be to Him) is the Custodian of enablement, through His gracious favour!

—As for haste [*ʿajala*], it is the tendency, rooted in the heart, that urges precipitous action in response to the very first notion that occurs, instead of hesitation and careful exploration. Its opposite is deliberateness [*anāh*], another tendency rooted in the heart, which promotes a cautious approach to all matters, thorough investigation of their significance, and a steady pace in following and acting upon them. As for hesitation [*tawaqquf*], its opposite is recklessness [*taʿassuf*].

According to our own Shaikh (may Allāh bestow His mercy upon him): "Deliberateness means hesitation before involvement in the matter, until its rightness becomes clear to the person concerned. It also means hesitation after involvement, so that he may give every part of the matter its proper due." As for the prerequisites of hesitation, they are: (1) remembering the risky aspects of affairs, which hinder the progress of the human being, and the various disasters to be feared as a result; (2) remembering to make sure that safety [from those disasters] is well and truly established, and (3) remembering the remorse and censure inherent in recklessness and haste.

These considerations, and others like them, are incentives to deliberateness and hesitation in the conduct of affairs, and deterrents from haste and recklessness. Allāh (Exalted is He) is the Custodian of safekeeping, by His mercy!

—As for arrogant pride [*kibr*], you should know that it is an inclination to exalt and magnify the self, and *takabbur* means following that inclination. Its opposite is an inclination to humble and belittle the self, and *tawāḍu*ʿ means following that inclination. Each of these two terms [*takabbur* and *tawāḍu*ʿ] has a general and a particular signification. The general signification of *tawāḍu*ʿ is being satisfied with the most inferior quality in clothing, housing and means of transport. In sharp contrast, *takabbur* signifies a snobbish attitude to that kind of satisfaction. As for *tawāḍu*ʿ in the particular sense, it means training the self to accept the truth from anyone, whether he be a lowly person or a nobleman. Again in sharp contrast, *takabbur* is a major sin of disobedience and a very serious error.

The fortress of *tawāḍu*ʿ, in the general sense, is remembering your starting point and your final destination, as well as your present state in relation to vices and impurities. As one of the scholars said: "Your first condition is that of a putrid sperm, and your last is that of filthy corpse. You are now between the two, carrying the excrement." The fortress of *tawāḍu*ʿ, in the particular sense, is remembering the punishment in store for the deviant from the Truth, the persistent in falsehood.

We have now provided a concise treatment of the subject, sufficient for those endowed with discernment. Allāh is the Source of enabling grace and the Custodian of helpful guidance!

Fifth subsection
The stomach [*baṭn*] and its preservation

Your next obligation, O seeker of worshipful service, is the preservation and improvement of the stomach. Of all the members of the body, it is the hardest for the dedicated seeker to improve, the most difficult and troublesome, the greatest cause of harm and bad effects. That is because it is the well and the mine, and from it the other members derive strength and weakness, chastity and sexuality, and so on and so forth. You must therefore keep it from consuming sustenance that is unlawful [*ḥarām*] and dubious [*shubha*], first of all, and then from excessive consumption of lawful sustenance [*ḥalāl*], in second place, if you truly aspire to the worshipful service of Allāh (Exalted is He).

As for that which is unlawful and dubious, you are obliged to avoid it for three reasons:

1. As a precaution against the Fire of Hell, for Allāh (Exalted is He) has said:

> Those who devour the wealth of orphans wrongfully,
> *inna 'lladhīna ya'kulūna amwāla 'l-yatāmā ẓulman*
> they do but swallow fire into their bellies,
> *inna-mā ya'kulūna fī buṭūni-him nārā:*
> and they will be exposed to burning flame.
> *wa sa-yaṣlawna sa'īrā.* (4:10)

The Prophet (Allāh bless him and give him peace) once said:

> If any piece of meat comes from a forbidden source, the Fire of Hell is more entitled to it [than the Garden of Paradise].

2. The consumer of unlawful and dubious sustenance is an outcast, incapable of worship, since no one is fit for the service of Allāh (Exalted is He) except every clean and purified individual. We are surely aware that Allāh (Exalted is He) has barred any *junub* [person in a state of major impurity] from entering His house [the mosque], and any *muḥdith* [person in a state of minor impurity] from touching His Book. He has said (More Glorious is He than any other sayer):

> ...nor when you are in a state of major impurity,
> *wa lā junuban*
> except when journeying on the road, till you have bathed.
> *illā 'ābirī sabīlin ḥattā taghtasilū.* (4:43)

> [In a Book kept hidden]
> [*fī Kitābin maknūn:*]
> which none shall touch except the purified.
> *lā yamassu-hu illa 'l-muṭahharūn.* (56:78,79)

This is despite the fact that major impurity [*janāba*] and minor impurity [*ḥadath*] are both classed as permissible [*mubāḥ*], so how will it be for someone who is immersed in the filth of the unlawful, and the pollution of that which is forbidden and dubious? How will it be for him, when he is summoned to the service of Allāh, the All-Glorious, and to His noble remembrance (Glory be to Him)? Surely that can never be!

According to Yaḥyā ibn Mu'ādh ar-Rāzī (may Allāh bestow His mercy upon him): "Obedience is stored in the treasuries of Allāh

(Exalted is He). Its key is supplication [*duʿāʾ*] and the teeth [of that key] consist of lawful sustenance [*ḥalāl*]. If the key does not have teeth, the door will not be opened, and if the door of the treasury is not opened, how will someone reach the obedience it contains?"

3. The consumer of unlawful and dubious sustenance is deprived of the ability to do what is good. Even if he happens to do a good deed, it will be rejected and not accepted of him. He will therefore get nothing from it, except trouble and toil and waste of time. The Prophet (Allāh bless him and give him peace) once said:

> Many a keeper of vigil [*qāʾim*] gets nothing but insomnia from his vigil [*qiyām*], and many a keeper of the fast [*ṣāʾim*] gets nothing but hunger and thirst from his fasting [*ṣiyām*].

According to Ibn ʿAbbās (may Allāh be well pleased with him and his father): "Allāh does not accept the ritual prayer of [*ṣalāt*] of a man who has an unlawful substance in his belly."

As for the excessive consumption of lawful sustenance [*fuḍūl al-ḥalāl*], it is the plague of worshipful servants and the scourge of those who work hard. From my thorough study, I have found that it entails the following ten disastrous consequences, which are the basic elements in this matter:

1. Overeating results in hardness of the heart and the loss of its radiant light. According to traditional report, the Prophet (Allāh bless him and give him peace) once said:

> Do not cause the heart to die from too much food and drink, for the heart dies like the seed when it gets too much water.

Some of the righteous have likened the stomach to a cooking pot underneath the heart. When the pot comes to the boil, the steam rises up towards the heart, which is clouded and besmirched by too much steam.

2. Overeating causes disorder in the members of the body, exciting them and stimulating them to indulge in excess and corruption. When a man is inordinately satiated, his eye takes a passionate interest in things that do not concern him, and which are either unlawful or excessive. His ear is keen on listening to such things, and his tongue on talking about them. His genitals are itching with lust for them, and his

feet are eager to walk in their direction. When he is hungry, by contrast, all the members of the body are calm and tranquil, with no appetite for any of this and no energy to pursue it. According to Professor Abū Jaʿfar (may Allāh bestow His mercy upon him): "Such is the nature of the stomach, as a member of the body, that if it is hungry, the other members are satiated."

The gist of the matter is that a man's words and deeds are in keeping with his food and drink. If what is lawful enters, out goes the unlawful. If virtue comes in, out goes excess. Food is like the seeds of actions, and actions are the plants that grow from those seeds.

3. Overeating results in paucity of understanding and knowledge, for the stomach discards intelligence. [Abū Sulaimān] ad-Dārānī (may Allāh bestow His mercy upon him) spoke the truth when he said: "If you wish for something you need, from this world or the Hereafter, do not eat until you have satisfied that need, for eating alters the mind." This is an obvious fact, well-known by anyone who has put it to the test of experience.

4. Overeating results in paucity of worshipful service, for, when the human being eats too much, his body grows heavy, his eyes take charge of him, and the rest of his physical organs are enfeebled. Nothing comes from him, even if he tries to work, except sleeping like a laid-out corpse. Someone said: "If you are fat-bellied, prepare yourself for chronic illness."

In the story of Yaḥyā [John the Baptist] (peace be upon him), we are told that Iblīs appeared to him, carrying a load of meat-hooks. Yaḥyā said to him: "What are these?" Iblīs replied: "These are the carnal desires that I use to hunt human beings." Yaḥyā then asked him: "Do you find them of any use in dealing with me?" Iblīs said: "No, except that you were satiated one night, so we made you too sluggish to perform the ritual prayer." Yaḥyā (peace be upon him) said: "I shall certainly never satiate myself again after that!" Iblīs said: "Without a doubt, I shall never admonish anyone again after that!"

This story is about someone who was satiated only one night in his life, so how will it be for someone who does not go hungry for one night in his life, yet aspires to worshipful service?! According to Sufyān ath-Thawrī (may Allāh bestow His mercy upon him): "Worshipful service is a craft, its workshop is seclusion, and its instrument is hunger."

5. Overeating causes the sweetness of worship to be lost. According to Abū Bakr aṣ-Ṣiddīq [the Champion of Truth] (may Allāh be well pleased with him): "I have never eaten my fill since I accepted Islām, so I could enjoy the sweetness of worshipping my Lord. Nor have I ever drunk my fill since I accepted Islām, because of ardent longing to meet my Lord."

These are the attributes of the discoverers [to whom the Divine secrets are revealed], for Abū Bakr (may Allāh be well pleased with him) was a discoverer [*mukāshaf*], and the Prophet (Allāh bless him and give him peace) referred to him when he said:

> Abū Bakr does not excel you in the merit of fasting or ritual prayer, but only in something established within himself.

It was ad-Dārānī who said: "How sweet is worshipful service, when my stomach clings to my back!"

6. Overeating carries the risk of the lapsing into the dubious and the unlawful, because lawful sustenance comes to you only as essential nourishment [*qūt*]. According to traditional report, the Prophet (Allāh bless him and give him peace) once said:

> Lawful sustenance comes to you only as essential nourishment, whereas that which is unlawful comes to you hapazardly and at random.

7. Overeating keeps the heart and the body preoccupied: (1) with the procurement of the food it demands; then (2) with its preparation; then (3) with its consumption; then (4) with clearing it from the bladder and the bowels; then (5) with the need to recover from it, due to the appearance of some harmful effect on the body, or rather, of plagues and diseases in this world. The Prophet (Allāh bless him and give him peace) once said:

> The root of every disease is indigestion, and the root of every cure is starvation.

We are told that Mālik ibn Dīnār [al-Baṣrī] used to say: "O these [people of Baṣra], I paid frequent visits to the toilet, until I felt ashamed before my Lord, on account of overeating. If only Allāh would place my sustenance in a pebble, for me to suck until I die!"

It must be obvious, from all of this, that overeating results in the pursuit of this world, greed for what other people possess, and the wasteful use of time.

8. Overeating has unfortunate consequences in the Hereafter, and it intensifies the agonies of death. As related in the traditional reports [*akhbār*]: "The intensity of the agonies of death is commensurate with the pleasures of this world." In other words, if someone overindulges in the latter, he will suffer more of the former.

9. Forfeiture of the reward in the Hereafter. Allāh (Exalted is He) has said:

> You squandered your good things
> *adhhabtum ṭayyibāti-kum*
> in the life of this world and sought comfort therein.
> *fī ḥayāti-kumu 'd-dunyā wa 'stamtaʿtum bi-hā*
> Now this Day you are rewarded with the doom of ignominy,
> *fa 'l-yawma tujzawna ʿadhāba 'l-hūni*
> because you were disdainful in the land without a right,
> *bi-mā kuntum tastakbirūna fi 'l-arḍi bi-ghairi 'l-ḥaqqi*
> and because you used to transgress.
> *wa bi-mā kuntum tafsuqūn*. (46:20)

In other words, to the extent that you indulge in the pleasures of this world, you will forfeit the pleasures of the Hereafter. It was in this context that Allāh (Exalted is He) said to His Prophet (Allāh bless him and give him peace), when He put this world at his disposal:

> I shall not cause you to forfeit any part of your [reward in the] Hereafter.[25]

Allāh made him unique in that regard, and He indicated that forfeiture applies to all others, unless Allāh bestows that same gracious favour upon you.

It is related that Khālid ibn al-Walīd received ʿUmar ibn al-Khaṭṭāb as his guest (may Allāh be well pleased with them both), and he prepared a meal for him, so ʿUmar said: "This is for us, but what is there for those poor Emigrants [*Muhājirīn*], who have died without eating their fill of barley bread?" Khālid replied: "For them there is the Garden of Paradise, O Commander of the Believers!" ʿUmar then said: "If they have achieved the Garden of Paradise, and this is our share of this world, they have distinguished themselves from us with a clear distinction!"

[25] This is a Sacred Tradition [*Ḥadīth Qudsī*], not a Qurʾānic verse [*āya*].

It is also related that ʿUmar (may Allāh be well pleased with him) was thirsty one day, so he called for some water. A man gave him a leather bag containing water, in which dates had been pressed. When ʿUmar brought it close to his mouth, he found the water cold and sweet, so he refrained from drinking it, saying: "Ugh!" The man exclaimed: "By Allāh, I have not neglected to sweeten it, O Commander of the Believers!" ʿUmar (may Allāh be well pleased with him) said: "That is what kept me from drinking it. Woe unto you! But for the Hereafter, we would participate with you in your worldly life!"

10. Overeating results in confinement and punitive reckoning, and in blame and condemnation for the lack of propriety involved in excessive acquisition and the pursuit of lustful desires. The Prophet (Allāh bless him and give him peace) once said:

> As for this world, its lawful sustenance is a trial, its unlawful sustenance is a torment, and its charm leads to perdition.

There you have all the ten dire consequences. Any one of them should be enough for someone who looks after himself. It is therefore incumbent upon you, O diligent worshipper, to exercise the utmost caution with regard to nourishment, so that you do not lapse into anything unlawful or dubious, for that would make you suffer torment. You must also restrict your consumption of lawful sustenance, to the amount required in preparation for the worship of Allāh (Exalted is He), so that you do not lapse into misconduct and remain in confinement. Allāh is the Custodian of enabling grace!

You may say: "Explain to us, first of all, the nature of the unlawful and the dubious, and give us their precise definition."

Let me therefore tell you, by Allāh's eternal life, that we have treated the subject exhaustively in the book entitled: "Secrets of Religious Practices [*Asrār Muʿāmalāt ad-Dīn*]." We have also discussed it in a separate chapter in the book entitled: "Revival of the Religious Sciences [*Iḥyāʾ ʿUlūm ad-Dīn*]." Nevertheless, we shall now provide some abbreviated quotations, so that you may achieve the understanding of the feeble novice, since the present book is intended to benefit the novice in worshipful service, and to assist the seeker.

Subsection

Concerning the remedial treatment of this world, your fellow creatures, the devil and the lower self.

It is your duty, O man, to make every effort to surmount this enormous and lengthy hurdle, for it is the most difficult and troublesome of all the hurdles, and the one most fraught with tribulation and temptation. Whenever creatures come to perdition, the cause of their separation from the path of Truth is either a worldly influence, a fellow creature, a devil, or a lower self. We have explained the importance of that [effort to surmount this hurdle] in the books we have compiled under the titles: "Revival of the Religious Sciences [*Iḥyāʾ ʿUlūm ad-Dīn*]," "Secrets of Religious Practices [*Asrār Muʿāmalāt ad-Dīn*]," and "The Approach to Allāh [*al-Qurba ila 'llāh*]."

As for the purpose of the present book, I asked Allāh to show me the secret of the remedial treatment of the lower self, to improve me, and to use me as the means of improving others. In this noble book, I have confined myself to points that are brief in words but rich in meaning, sufficient for those who study them with care and providing a clear view of the path, if Allāh (Exalted is He) so wills. This subsection is devoted to points concerning the remedial treatment of this world, fellow creatures, the devil and the lower self.

—As for this world, it is incumbent on you to be wary of it and abstain from it, because you are sure to fit one of three descriptions:

1. You are one of those endowed with faculties of perception and discernment, in which case it is enough for you that this world is the enemy of Allāh (Glory be to Him), while He is your Friend and your Custodian, and that this world is contrary to your intelligence, while your intelligence is your valuable asset.

2. You are one of those endowed with aspirations and dedication to the worship of Allāh (Exalted is He), in which case it is enough for you that this world's bad luck can prevent you from fulfilling your worthy intention. Just thinking about it distracts you from worship and goodness, so what can be expected of this world itself?

3. You are one of the heedless, with no perceptive faculty by which to discern the true facts, and with no aspiration to urge you to noble

deeds. In this case, it is enough for you that this world will not last forever: either you will part from it, or it will part from you. In the words of al-Ḥasan [al-Baṣrī]: "If this world lasts for you, you will not last for it, so what benefit is there for you in seeking it, and in spending your precious life in its pursuit?" The poet expressed himself well, when he said:

Donate this world [to charity], for then you will obtain a pardon.
This world is surely headed for complete extinction.

What can you expect from a life that will not last?
The nights will soon alter your expectation.

This world of yours is just like a fleeting shadow:
It shades you for a while, then announces its departure.

The intelligent person must therefore not be deceived by this world. The poet spoke the truth when he said:

[This world is] a muddled dream, or like a fleeing shadow.
The clever man should not be deceived by that kind of thing.

—As for the devil, it is enough for you to consider what Allāh (Exalted is He) said to His Prophet Muḥammad (Allāh bless him and give him peace):

And say: "My Lord, I seek refuge with You
wa qul Rabbi aʿūdhu bi-ka
from the suggestions of the devils,
min hamazāti 'sh-shayāṭīn.
and I seek refuge with You, my Lord,
wa aʿūdhu bi-ka
lest they be present with me."
Rabbi an yaḥḍurū-n. (23:97,98)

This [Prophet Muḥammad (Allāh bless him and give him peace)] is the best of all creatures, the most knowledgeable, the most intelligent and the most meritorious in the sight of Allāh (Exalted is He), so how about you, with your ignorance, your shortcoming and your heedlessness?

—As for your fellow creatures, this is all you need to know: If you mixed with them and shared their passions, you would be guilty of sin and spoil your stake in the Hereafter. If you oppose them, on the other hand, you will suffer their insults and their rude remarks, and you will make your worldly life a misery. You cannot be sure that they will not trap you in their hostility and animosity, so that you fall into their wickedness. If they treat you with praise and respect, I fear that you are in danger of corruption and vain conceit. If they blame and belittle you, I fear that you will sometimes be sad, and sometimes angry, though not for the sake of Allāh. In either case, the consequence is devastating.

Remember how your relationship with them will be, after you have been in the grave for three days: how they will forsake you, avoid you and forget you, and hardly ever mention you, as if you had never seen them and they had never seen you. There [in the grave], you will have no one left but Allāh (Glory be to Him).

It is surely a great mistake to waste your days with these fellow creatures, in spite of the lack of fidelity and the lack of constancy in your relationship with them. You are forsaking the service of Allāh (Exalted is He), though everything will return to Him, and to Him alone, so that nothing but He will survive for all eternity. All needs are for Him. All reliance is on Him. All safekeeping, in every situation, and in every difficulty and danger, depends on Him alone, the One who has no partner. You must therefore consider all this most carefully, O miserable wretch, for then you may be guided aright, if Allāh (Exalted is He) so wills. Allāh is the Custodian of right guidance, by His gracious favour.

—As for the lower self, it is enough for you to consider what you observe about its states, its wickedness, its wilfulness, and its preference for evil. In the state of carnal desire, it is a domestic animal. In the state of anger, it is a savage beast. In the state of misfortune, you see it as a little child. In the state of good fortune, you see it as a Pharaoh. In the state of hunger, you see it as a lunatic. In the state of satiety, you see it arrogantly conceited. If you satisfy its appetite, it becomes cocky and cheerful, but if you let it starve, it screams and moans, for it is as the poet said:

> Like the bad donkey, if you satisfy its appetite,
> it kicks at people, and if it is hungry, it brays.

One of the righteous spoke the truth when he said: "Such is the wickedness and ignorance of this lower self, that when it contemplates an act of sinful disobedience, or responds to the urge of a carnal desire, it will neither comply with your instruction nor forsake its desire, even if you try to dissuade it, or intercede on its behalf with Allāh (Glory be to Him), then with His Messenger (peace be upon him) and all His Prophets and Books, and with all the righteous predecessors among His servants. You may also remind it of death, the grave, the Resurrection, the Garden of Paradise and the Fire of Hell, but still to no avail. Then, if you threaten to deprive it of a loaf of bread, it will calm down and abandon its desire, so you will recognize its vileness and its ignorance."

You must therefore beware of neglecting it, O man, for it is as its Creator (Magnificent is His Majesty), He who knows it well, has said:

> Surely the self is always instigating evil.
> *inna 'n-nafsa la-ammāratun bi's-sū'.* (12:53)

This is sufficient as an admonition for anyone who is intelligent.

We are told that one of the righteous, called Aḥmad ibn Arqam al-Balkhī (may Allāh bestow His mercy upon him), once said: "My lower self told me to set out on a military campaign [*ghazw*], so I said: "Glory be to Allāh! Allāh says:

> Surely the self is always instigating evil.
> *inna 'n-nafsa la-ammāratun bi's-sū'.* (12:53)

"—yet this [lower self of mine] is commanding me to do what is good. This would never happen, but it is lonely, so it is looking for more contact with people. It wants to relax in their company, and to have them get to know it, so that they will treat it with respect, reverence and honour. I said to it: 'I shall not settle you in civilized society, nor shall I put you in a position to make acquaintances.' I disapproved of its response, and I said: 'Allāh (Exalted is He) is the Most Truthful of all speakers.' Then I told it: 'I shall fight the enemy stark naked, so you will be the first casualty.' As before, I disapproved of its response."

Aḥmad ibn Arqam went on to enumerate the good things he wished to accomplish, and his lower self responded to all that [in a manner of which he disapproved]. His account continues:

"I said: 'O my Lord, forbid me to take notice of it, for I am suspicious of it, and I give credence to You.' I then seemed to hear it say: 'O Aḥmad, you kill me every day, by repeatedly preventing me from satisfying carnal desires, and by your opposition, yet no one knows about it. If you fight [the unbelievers], and I am slain immediately, I shall escape from you. People will hear about me, and they will say: "Aḥmad has been martyred," and for me there will be honour and good repute.'" In conclusion, Aḥmad said: "So I stayed at home, and did not join the military campaign that year."

Notice the treachery and deceptiveness of the lower self. It seeks to impress people after death, with a deed that has not yet occurred! The poet spoke the truth, and expressed it beautifully, when he said:

> Beware of your lower self! Do not feel safe from its perils,
> for the lower self is more mischievous than seventy devils.

Be well aware—may Allāh bestow His mercy upon you!—of this treacherous instigator of evil, and commit your heart to opposing it in every situation, for then you will take the right path and be safe, if Allāh (Exalted is He) so wills. You must also bridle it with the reins of true devotion [*taqwā*], for there is no other means of outwitting it.

In this context, you must recognize a basic principle: namely, that worshipful service has two facets: (1) the facet of earning [*iktisāb*] and (2) the facet of avoidance [*ijtināb*]. Earning is the performance of acts of worshipful obedience, while avoidance is refraining from acts of sinful disobedience and all bad things. Taken together, these constitute true devotion [*taqwā*].

In every case, the facet of avoidance is safer, more virtuous, more meritorious and more honourable for the servant than the facet of earning. That is why the novices among the people of worship, those at the first stage of dedicated striving, are chiefly concerned with the facet of earning. Their whole endeavour is to fast during the daytime, to keep vigil during the night, and so on. As for the graduates among the people of worship, those endowed with faculties of discernment, they are chiefly concerned with the facet of avoidance. Their only endeavour is to preserve their hearts from inclining towards anything other than Allāh (Exalted is He), their stomachs from overeating, their tongues from idle talk, and their eyes from looking at things that do not concern them.

It was in this connection that the second of the seven worshippers said to Jonah (peace be upon him): "O Jonah, there are some people to whom the ritual prayers [*ṣalawāt*] have been made dear, so they prefer nothing to them, for the ritual prayers are the pillar of worship, in constancy to Allāh, in truthfulness, and in humble submissiveness and entreaty. There are some to whom fasting [*ṣawm*] has been made dear, so they prefer nothing to that. There are some to whom charitable giving [*ṣadaqa*] has been made dear, so they prefer nothing to that. O Jonah, you are our interpreter in these matters, so dedicate the length of your ritual prayer to patient endurance of hardships, and submission to the commandment of Allāh (Glory be to Him and Exalted is He). Dedicate your fasting to saying nothing about anything bad, and dedicate your charitable giving to the prevention of harm, for you can give nothing worthier than that, and you can fast for nothing purer than that."

Since you know that the side of avoidance is more deserving of cultivation and dedicated effort, if you are able to combine the two facets, earning and avoidance, your condition is perfected, your purpose is achieved, and you are safe and prosperous. If you can only accomplish one of the two, let it be that side of avoidance, for then you will be safe, if not prosperous. Otherwise, you will fail on both counts, so you will obtain no benefit from keeping vigil at night and all the weariness involved. You may also spoil your vigil with a single desire, just as you may be enriched by a long day of fasting, only to ruin what you have gained with a single word.

According to traditional report, someone asked Ibn ʿAbbās (may Allāh be well pleased with him and his father): "What do you say about two men, one of them responsible for much that is good and much that is bad, and the other responsible for little of either?" He replied: "I do not set anything on a par with blamelessness."

The state of the invalid is similar to what we have said [about the two facets of worship], inasmuch as there are two halves to the remedial treatment of the invalid, one half being medicine and one half being protective care. If the two are combined, you will soon see the invalid restored to good health. If they cannot be combined, protective care is preferable, since medicine is useless in the absence of protective care, whereas protective care is always beneficial, even if medicine is unavailable. The Prophet (Allāh bless him and give him peace) once said:

> The root of every medicine is protective care.

By this he presumably meant—Allāh knows best, of course!—that it is an effective substitute for any medicine.

That explains why the remedial treatment employed by the people of India is said to consist mainly of protective care, together with preventing the invalid from eating, drinking and talking for a number of days, since that is the only means by which he will be restored to good health.

It should thus be clear to you that true devotion [*taqwā*] is the basis of the matter and its very essence. Its practitioners are the highest class of worshipful servants. It is therefore incumbent on you to spare no effort in that endeavour, and to give it all the attention you can muster. Allāh (Glory be to Him) is the Custodian of enabling grace, through His mercy!

Subsection

Concerning the need to monitor the eye, the tongue, the stomach and the heart

Your next duty is to monitor these four members of the body: the eye, the tongue, the stomach and the heart, for they are the basic elements.

1. The eye. It is enough for you to know that the sphere of religion and this world is centred on the heart, and that the eye is responsible for most of the dangerous, distracting and corrupting influences that affect the heart. That is why ʿAlī (may Allāh be well pleased with him) said: "If someone does not control his eye, the heart as no value for him."

2. The tongue. It is enough for you to know that your profit and your booty, and the fruit of your labour and your exertion, are all for the sake of worship and obedience, and that the tongue is responsible for most of the dangerous, damaging and corrupting influences that spoil worship, such as affectation, pretentiousness and backbiting. With a single utterance, the tongue can ruin everything at which you have laboured for one year, or even five or ten. That is why someone said: "Nothing is more deserving of long imprisonment than the tongue."

It is related that one of the seven worshippers said to Jonah (peace be upon him): "O Jonah, when the worshippers exert themselves in worship, they have no better source of strength in their worship than prolonged abstinence from speech." He then went on to say: "You certainly have nothing more effective than the preservation of your tongue, and you have no better means of caring for the soundness of your breast."

You must also remember all those breaths in which you spoke too much that was harmful to you. It would be better for you if you said: "I seek Allāh's forgiveness [*astaghfiru 'llāh*]," for your plea may coincide with a precious moment, so that Allāh forgives you and you profit from your capital investment. Or if you said: "There is no god but Allāh [*lā ilāha illa 'llāh*]," for you may obtain such reward and treasure as your imagination cannot conceive. Or you may say: "I beg Allāh for well-being," for that may be well received, so that Allāh (Exalted is He) responds to your supplication, and you are delivered from the affliction of this world and the Hereafter.

It is surely a great loss and an awful stupidity, that you should cause yourself to lose all these noble benefits, by wasting your breath and your time on superfluous talk. At the very least, that will condemn you to blame, punitive reckoning and confinement on the Day of Resurrection. The poet expressed it beautifully when he said:

> Whenever you intend to utter idle talk,
> replace it with a glorification [of the Lord].

3. The stomach. It is enough for you to know that your purpose is worshipful service, and that food is the seed and the water from which work sprouts and grows. If the seed is rotten, the crop will not be good; indeed, it threatens to ruin your land, so you will never prosper.

In this connection, we are told that Maʿrūf al-Karkhī said: "When you fast, consider what you are eating to break your fast, the person in whose company you are breaking fast, and whose food you are eating. Many a one eats a morsel, and his heart is so transmuted that it never returns to its former state. Many a morsel has invalidated a night vigil, and many a stray glance has prevented the recitation of a Sūra [of the Qur'ān]. By eating a morsel, the servant may invalidate the religious observance of one whole year."

You must therefore pay careful attention to your diet, O man, and treat it with extreme caution, if your heart contains any concern and aspiration for the worship of your Lord. This cautious attention must be applied to the diet itself, to ensure that it is lawful. Then you must observe propriety in its consumption, otherwise you will be a porter of food and a waster of days, for we know for certain—indeed, we have seen with our own eyes—that nothing comes from worship when the stomach is full.

If you find this advice repugnant, and use all kinds of sly devices to avoid it, you will experience no delight and no sweetness in worship. That is why someone said: "Do not hope to combine the sweetness of worship with overeating. What light is there in a soul without worship, and in worship without delight and without sweetness?"

In this same context, Ibrāhīm ibn Ad'ham (may Allāh bestow His mercy upon him) has said: "I made friends with most of the men of Allāh (Exalted is He) on Mount Lebanon, so they used to give me this advice: 'When you return to the sons of this world, provide them with four admonitions. Say to them: "(1) If someone indulges in overeating, he will not discover the delight of worship. (2) If someone sleeps too much, he will find no blessing in his life. (3) If someone seeks to please other people, he cannot look forward to the Lord's good pleasure. (4) If someone talks too much, and engages in backbiting, he will not leave this world in the religion of Islām."'"

According to Sahl [at-Tustarī] (may Allāh bestow His mercy upon him): "Goodness in its entirety resides in these four virtues, and through them the [saints called] Abdāl have come to be Abdāl:[26] (1) keeping the bellies empty; (2) silence; (3) isolation from people, and (4) staying awake at night."

According to one of those who know by direct experience: "Hunger is our capital investment. In other words, whatever we obtain in the way of relief, security, worship, sweetness, knowledge and useful work, it is due to hunger and the patient endurance thereof, for the sake of Allāh (Glory be to Him)."

4. As for the heart, it is enough for you to know that it is the root of everything. If you corrupt it, everything is corrupted, and if you improve it, everything is improved. The heart is the tree, while the other members of the body are branches. From the tree the branches drink, and either grow well or decay. The heart is the king, while the other members of the body are followers and supporters. If the king is

[26] See n. 14 on p. 48 above.

righteous, the subjects are righteous, and if he is corrupt, the subjects are corrupt. The righteousness of the eye, the tongue, the stomach and so on, is therefore evidence of the righteousness and well-being of the heart. On the other hand, if you see any flaw and corruption in them, you must recognize that as due to some flaw and corruption in the heart. Since corruption in the heart is much more serious, you must devote your attention to improving it, for then the whole body will be healthy, so you will be able to relax.

The problem posed by the heart is subtle and difficult, since it is built on notions [*khawāṭir*], and they are not under your control. To prevent the following of notions, you need every effort you can muster, for that involves the utmost trouble and toil. For this reason, improvement of the heart becomes a very hard task for those who strive with dedication, and the chief preoccupation of those endowed with faculties of discernment. According to Abū Yazīd [al-Bisṭāmī] (may Allāh bestow His mercy upon him): "I applied remedial treatment to my heart for ten years, to my tongue for ten, and to my lower self for ten, and it seemed that my heart was the most difficult of the three."

Next, you must concentrate on the four vices we have mentioned earlier:[27] (1) excessive expectation, (2) haste, (3) envy, and (4) arrogant pride.

We have singled these four out from among the other vices, and paid special attention to protection against them, for the simple reason that they afflict all human beings in general, and the Qur'ān-reciters in particular, so they are more ugly and abominable [than other vices].

1. Notice how the Qur'ān-reciter indulges in excessive expectation, though he counts it as a good intention, so it causes him to lapse into laziness and slackness in work. 2. Notice how he is in great haste to achieve the ranks of goodness, so he is excluded from them, or to receive a response to a righteous supplication, so he is deprived of that response, or to invoke a curse on someone, so he suffers remorse for that, as mentioned in the story of Noah (peace be upon him).

3. Notice how he envies his peers for the gracious favour that Allāh has bestowed upon them, sometimes to the point where envy makes him guilty of abominations and atrocities, such as no profligate or debauchee would commit.

[27] See pp. 107-21 above.

In this connection, Sufyān ath-Thawrī (may Allāh bestow His mercy upon him) once said: "I fear no threat to my blood, apart from the Qur᾿ān-reciters and the scholars." His listeners disapproved of this remark, so he said: "I did not say it. I was simply quoting Ibrāhīm an-Nakha῾ī (may Allāh the Exalted bestow His mercy upon him)."

According to ῾Aṭā᾿ [al-Qurashī]: "Sufyān ath-Thawrī (may Allāh bestow His mercy upon him) told me: 'Beware of the Qur᾿ān-reciters, and beware of me in their presence, for if I contradict the dearest of them to me, by saying that a pomegranate is sweet, when he says it is sour, I cannot be sure that he will not carry my blood to a tyrannical ruler.'"

According to Mālik ibn Dīnār: "I accept the testimony of the Qur᾿ān-reciters against people in general, but I do not accept the testimony of one of them against another, because I have found them to be enviers."

We are told that al-Fuḍail once said to his son: "Buy me a house far away from the Qur᾿ān-reciters. I want nothing to do with a set of people who will expose me if I make a slip, and who will envy me if I receive a blessing."

4. Notice how the Qur᾿ān-reciter treats people with arrogant pride, belittling them with a contemptuous expression and a scowling face. He acts as if he is doing people a favour, by performing two extra cycles of ritual prayer, or as if he has received good news from Allāh (Exalted is He) about the Garden of Paradise or deliverance from the Fire of Hell, or as if he is certain of happiness for himself and misery for the rest of humankind. Then, regardless of all that, he dresses in the clothing of the humble, in garments of wool and the like, and pretends to be virtually dead. This is not consistent with haughtiness and arrogant pride; it is the very opposite, in fact, but the blind do not see.

We are told that Farqad as-Sabakhī once entered the presence of al-Ḥasan [al-Baṣrī], while Farqad was wearing a simple sheet [*kisā᾿*] and al-Ḥasan was dressed in a fine suit of clothes [*ḥulla*]. Farqad started fingering that suit, so al-Ḥasan said: "Why are you taking such an interest in my attire? My attire is the attire of the people of the Garden of Paradise, whereas your attire is the attire of the people of the Fire of Hell. I have heard that most of the people of the Fire are the owners of sheets." Then al-Ḥasan went on to say: "They put abstinence in their clothes, and arrogant pride in their breasts. By Him who is sworn by, one of your kind is prouder of his sheet than the owner of the silk shawl [*miṭraf*] is proud of his silk shawl!"

Dhu 'n-Nūn [al-Miṣrī] (may Allāh bestow His mercy upon him) alluded to this concept when he said:

He wished to be a Ṣūfī,
so he foolishly took pride in wool [*ṣūf*],
while some folk wear it as a clownish prank,

to give you the impression of humility
and treat you with arrogant pride,
though arrogant pride bears no resemblance to humility.

He wished to be a Ṣūfī,
so that he would be called trustworthy,
though trustworthiness is not what his Ṣūfism signifies,

and he is not seeking God [*al-Ilāh*] through it, but
through it he is seeking the path to breach of faith.

You must therefore be on your guard, O man, against these four disastrous vices we have mentioned, especially arrogant pride. The first three are pitfalls, by slipping into which you will fall into sinful disobedience. Arrogant pride is also a pitfall, by slipping into which you will fall into the oceans of unbelief and transgression. Do not forget the story of Iblīs and his temptation, and how:

He refused and gave a display of arrogant pride,
abā wa 'stakbara
and so he came to be one of the unbelievers.
wa kāna mina 'l-kāfirīn. (2:34)

The only recourse is to Allāh (Almighty and Glorious is He), so that He may protect us all with His gracious care. He is indeed the Munificent, the Noble and Generous.

Subsection

The gist of the matter, O man, is that if you apply your intelligence, you will recognize that this world has no permanence, and that its benefit is not equal to its harm. Its bad consequences include weariness of the body and preoccupation of the heart, in this world, and painful torment and lengthy punitive reckoning in the Hereafter, which you lack the strength to endure. If you know that really well, you will abstain from its superfluity, and take from it only what you need for the worshipful service of your Lord. You will leave enjoyment and pleasure to the Garden of Paradise, the permanent abode of bliss, in the vicinity of the Lord of All the Worlds, the All-Powerful, the Independent, the Noble and Generous.

You know that your fellow creatures have no fidelity, and that their trouble is greater than their helpfulness. You have withdrawn from mingling with them, except for essential purposes. You take advantage of their goodness, while avoiding their harmfulness. You share your company with Him in whose company you suffer no loss, the One you serve without regret. Your intimate friendship is with His Book, and your close attachment is to Him, so He is with you in every situation. From Him you receive every handsome gift and gracious favour, and you find Him in the presence of every misfortune, in this world and the Hereafter. As the Prophet (Allāh bless him and give him peace) once said:

> Be ever heedful of Allāh, for then you will find Him wherever you turn.

You know that the devil is wicked, completely devoted to being your enemy, so seek refuge with your Lord, the All-Powerful, the All-Compelling, from this accursed hound. Do not be heedless of his cunning tricks and his snares. You must repel him with the remembrance of Allāh (Glory be to Him), and do not consider that too difficult, for it is easy, if you show the determination of real men. As Allāh (Exalted is He) has said:

> Surely he has no authority over those who believe
> *innahu laisa la-hu sulṭānun ʿala ʾlladhīna āmanū*
> and put all their trust in their Lord
> *wa ʿalā Rabbi-him yatawakkalūn*. (16:99)

Abū Ḥāzim spoke the truth when he said: "What is this world, and what is Iblīs? As for this world, what has passed from it is but a dream, and what remains is nothing but desires. As for the devil, by Allāh, he has been obeyed, but to no avail, and he has been disobeyed, yet done no harm."

You know the ignorance of this lower self, and its insatiable appetite for things that will harm it and destroy it. You have therefore viewed it with compassion, with the view of the intellectuals and the scholars, who consider the ultimate outcomes, not with the view of the ignoramuses and the immature, who consider only the present, who do not understand the risk of harm, and who flee from the bitterness of the medicine. You must bridle it with the reins of true devotion [*taqwā*], by restraining it from everything it does not really need, such as excessive talking, gazing and eating. You must keep it from involvement in any corruptive vice, whether it be excessive expectation, haste, envy of a Muslim, pride that is out of place, or eating from sheer lust and gluttony. You must give it only what it simply cannot do without, and from which there is no fear of harm, since there is no need for superfluity. Allāh (Exalted is He) has provided for His servants in abundance, by His mercy, and He has made them independent of everything harmful to them in the matter of their religion, so what need is there for that excessive indulgence?

As one of the righteous put it: "True devotion [*taqwā*] is a very easy thing: If something arouses my suspicion, I abstain from it, for the lower self will then become submissive, and accustomed to what you make it get used to." It is just as the poet said:

> The lower self is desirous, if you encourage its desire,
> but if it is reduced to very little, it will be satisfied.

Someone else said: "As for the lower self, it will bear whatever burden you impose upon it."

Another poet said:

> I patiently abstained from pleasures, until they went away,
> then I forced my lower self to do without them, so they stayed.
>
> The lower self is whatever the hero makes of it,
> so if it is fed, it longs for more, and if not, it is satisfied.

If you understand what we have described, you are counted among those who abstain from this world and yearn for the Hereafter. You must also know that, if someone is called by the name az-Zāhid [the Abstainer], he has been called by a thousand praiseworthy names, and you are one of those exclusively devoted to Allāh (Glory be to Him), those who enjoy His intimate friendship, and who serve the Lord of All the Worlds. You are just as the poet said:

Some people are addicted to this world of theirs,
and some are devoted solely to their Master,

so He has attached them to the door of His approval,
and made them independent of all other creatures.

By night they set their feet in line [for prayer],
and the eye of the Guardian watches over them.

So congratulations to them,
and congratulations to them again,
since He has greeted them with the salutation!

You are one of those abstainers who wage the sacred struggle for the cause of Allāh, the élite of Allāh's servants (Exalted is He), of whom He has said Allāh (Glory be to Him):

As for My servants,
inna ʿibādī
you shall have no authority over any of them.
laisa la-ka ʿalai-him sulṭānun (15:42)

You are also one of the truly devout, those who enjoy the bliss of the two abodes [this world and the Hereafter]. This means that you have become more virtuous than many of the angels drawn near [to the Lord], since they have no carnal desire to summon them to evil, and no wicked lower self.

You have now left this long and difficult hurdle behind you, and gone ahead of all the impediments to reach your goal. This should not surprise you, for it is an easy matter, when accompanied by seeking Allāh's help and taking refuge with Him. We ask Allāh (Exalted is He), for He is the Best to be asked, to support you and us with the blessing of His enabling grace, His assistance and His facilitation. He is Capable of solving every problem, and His help can be invoked in every difficult situation, for the power to create and ordain is in His hand, and He is Omnipotent over all things. There is no might nor any power, except with Allāh, the All-High, the Almighty.

The Fourth Hurdle
The hurdle of the four hindrances [*ʿawāriḍ*]

O seeker of worshipful service, may Allāh enable you to succeed! Your next obligation is to stop the hindrances that distract you from the worshipful service of Allāh (Exalted is He), and to block their access to you, so that they do not divert you from your goal. As we have mentioned earlier,[28] they are four in number:

The First Hindrance [*ʿāriḍ*]
Sustenance [*rizq*]

The first hindrance is sustenance [*rizq*] and the demand of the lower self for its provision. Absolute trust [*tawakkul*] in Allāh (Glory be to Him) is the only protection from this hindrance. You must therefore put all your trust in Allāh (Glory be to Him), in the matter of sustenance and in every case of need. That is for two reasons:

—Freedom to engage in worship, and to receive the benefit of truly good provision. If someone is not absolutely trusting [*mutawakkil*], he is bound to be distracted from the worship of Allāh, because of the need for livelihood and welfare, either outwardly or inwardly. He is distracted either by the physical effort to acquire and to earn, like the common folk who are addicted to this world, or by desire and temptation [*waswasa*] experienced in the heart, like those who endeavour to worship but are still attached to this world.

Worshipful service needs freedom of the heart and the body, if it is to obtain its rightful due. Such freedom is peculiar to those who are absolutely trusting. I will even say, of everyone who is weak at heart, that his heart will scarcely be at ease without something known for sure, so it will hardly be satisfied with anything else, however great its

[28] See p. 12, 13 above.

importance in this world and the Hereafter. My Shaikh, Abū Muḥammad (may Allāh the Exalted bestow His mercy upon him), would often say in my hearing: "The business of this world goes well for two men: one who is absolutely trusting [*mutawakkil*], and one who is daring [*mutahawwir*]."

In my opinion, this statement is comprehensive in its meaning, since a person who is daring tackles affairs on the strength of habit and courage of heart, paying no attention to any obstacle that might prevent him, or any notion [*khāṭir*] that might weaken him, so things go well for him. As for someone who is absolutely trusting, he tackles affairs on the strength of conviction, discernment, perfect certitude concerning the promise of Allāh (Glory be to Him), and complete reliance on His guaranty. He pays no attention to anyone who tries to scare him, or to any devil who tries to tempt him, so he achieves his goals and succeeds in his endeavour.

As for the feeble creature, he is always caught between absolute trust, on the one hand, and hesitation, slackness and confusion, on the other. He is like a donkey in its manger and a hen in its cage, noticing what its owner usually provides, and seldom bothering to look for anything else. His lower self takes no interest in lofty matters, and his aspiration is cut off, so he is unlikely to embark on any noble project. Even if he does so, he is unlikely to succeed in its accomplishment.

As you have surely noticed, the ambitious sons of this world have not achieved any major degree or important rank, except through their hearts' detachment from their lower selves, their properties and their families.

As for the kings, they engage in wars and in doing battle with their enemies, to the point of destruction or triumph, in order to obtain the rank of sovereignty and the authority of government. When Muʿāwiya ibn Sufyān saw the armies on the day of [the battle of] Ṣiffīn, he said: "If someone wishes for something of great worth, he must run the great risk involved."

As for the travelling merchants, they ride dangers and perils by land and by sea, and they cast their persons and their properties into risky places in the east and in the west. They concentrate on one of two matters: either the deliverance of their spirits [*arwāḥ*], or the acquisition of profits [*arbāḥ*], in order to obtain every mighty profit, every massive property, and every precious object.

As for the market tradesman, whose heart is feeble and whose resolve is flimsy, he is unlikely to sever his heart from its attachment to his lower self and his property. He spends all his life between his home and his shop, so he never achieves a noble rank, like the kings, nor an enormous profit, like the merchants who dare to take risks. If, in his market, he makes the profit of a dirham [silver coin] on his goods, that is a great deal for him, because of his heart's attachment to something known for sure.

Up to this point, we have been discussing this world and its sons. As for the sons of the Hereafter, their capital investment is this virtue of absolute trust [in Allāh] and severance of the heart from all attachments. Once they have consolidated this virtue and achieved it really and truly, they become free to worship Allāh (Exalted is He). They become capable of isolation from fellow creatures, of travelling in the land, of penetrating the deserts, and of dwelling on the mountains and in the canyons. They have become the strong servants, the heroes of the religion, the freemen of humanity and the kings of the earth. They really do travel wherever they wish, and settle wherever they wish. They embark on tremendous undertakings, with knowledge and in worshipful service, as they see fit. They encounter no impediment, and no barrier stands in their way. All places for them are one, and all times are one in their view. This is indicated by the saying of the Prophet (Allāh bless him and give him peace):

> If someone takes pleasure in being the strongest of human beings, let him put all his trust in Allāh. If someone takes pleasure in being the noblest of human beings, let him practise true devotion to Allāh. If someone takes pleasure in being the richest of human beings, let him be more reliant on what is at Allāh's disposal than on what is at his own disposal.

According to Sulaimān al-Khawwāṣ: "If a man puts all his trust in Allāh (Glory be to Him), with truthful intention, he has no need of the worldly commanders and those beneath them. How could he need them, when his Master is the Independent, the Praiseworthy?"

According to Ibrāhīm al-Khawwāṣ: "I met a young man in the wilderness, and he seemed like an ingot of silver, so I said to him:

'Where are you going, O young man?' He said: 'To Mecca.' I said: 'Without provision for the journey, and without a camel? He said: 'O weak in certitude, He who can preserve the heavens and the earth is Capable of bringing me to Mecca, without provision for the journey and without a camel!' When I entered Mecca, there he was, performing the *ṭawāf* [circumabulation of the Kaʿba] and saying:

O self of mine, keep travelling forever,
and do not fall in love with anyone,

except the Majestic Lord, the Everlasting.
O self of mine, die of heartsickness.

"When he saw me, he said: 'O Shaikh, you are still in that state of weakness!'"

Abū Muṭīʿ said to Ḥātim al-Aṣamm: "I have heard that you traverse the deserts with absolute trust [in Allāh], without any provision for the journey." Ḥātim replied: "My provision for the journey consists of four things." Abū Muṭīʿ asked: "What are they?" He said: "I regard this world and the Hereafter as a dominion belonging to Allāh (Exalted is He). I regard all creatures as the servants of Allāh and His dependants. I see the means of sustenance, and all other means, at the disposal of Allāh (Almighty and Glorious is He). I see that Allāh's decree is effective in all of Allāh's earth."

The poet expressed it well, when he said:

I see the abstainers enjoying fragrance and comfort.
Their hearts are far removed from this world.

When you look at them, you are looking at people
who are kings of the earth, their mark being tolerance.

—As for the second factor that necessitates absolute trust in Allāh (Glory be to Him and Exalted is He) in this matter [of sustenance], it is the tremendous danger and risk involved in the omission of that trust. Allāh (Glory be to Him) has surely linked the provision of sustenance to the act of creation, for He has said (Exalted is He):

Allāh is the One who created you, then provided for you.
Allāhu 'lladhī khalaqa-kum thumma razaqa-kum. (30:40)

This indicates that sustenance comes from Allāh (Glory be to Him), not from any other source, such as creatures. He did not confine

Himself to the indication, however, for He added the promise (Almighty and Glorious is He):

> Allāh is indeed the All-Provider.
> *inna 'llāha Huwa 'r-Razzāqu.* (51:58)

Nor did He confine Himself to the promise, for He added the guaranty:

> There is no beast upon the earth
> *wa mā min dābbatin fi 'l-arḍi*
> for which Allāh does not provide.
> *illā ʿala 'llāhi rizqu-hā.* (11:6)

Nor did confine Himself to the guaranty, for He went on to swear:

> And by the Lord of the heavens and the earth,
> *fa-wa Rabbi 's-samāʾi wa 'l-arḍi*
> it is the truth, even as that you speak.
> *inna-hu la-ḥaqqun mithla mā anna-kum tanṭiqūn.* (51:23)

Then, in addition to all that, He commanded absolute trust, and emphasized it with the admonition:

> And put all your trust in the Living One who never dies.
> *wa tawakkal ʿala 'l-Ḥayyi 'lladhī lā yamūtu.* (25:58)

He also said (Glory be to Him):

> And put all your trust in Allāh,
> *wa ʿala 'llāhi fa-tawakkalū*
> if you are true believers.
> *in kuntum muʾminīn.* (5:23)

If someone fails to consider His saying, and is not content with His promise, and is not satisfied with His guaranty, and is not convinced by His oath, and then ignores His commandment, His promise and His threat, imagine what his state will be! What tribulation will result from this? This, by Allāh, is a serious affliction, and we are guilty of great heedlessness if we ignore it. The truthful and trustworthy Messenger (Allāh bless him and give him peace) once said to Ibn ʿUmar:

> How will it be for you, if you are left among a set of people who hoard their annual supply of sustenance, because of the weakness of their certitude?

We are told that al-Ḥasan [al-Baṣrī] (may Allāh bestow His mercy upon him) once said: "May Allāh curse any groups of people to whom their Lord swears an oath, yet they do not believe Him. When this

Qur'ānic verse was revealed:

> And by the Lord of the heavens and the earth....
> *fa-wa Rabbi 's-samā'i wa 'l-arḍi....* (51:23)

—the angels said: 'Perish the sons of Adam [human beings]! They angered the Lord until He swore that He would provide their sustenance.'"

According to Uwais al-Qaranī (may Allāh be well pleased with him): "Even if you worship Allāh with the worshipful service of the people of the heavens and the earth, He will not accept it from you, until you acknowledge that He speaks the truth." Someone asked: "And how shall we acknowledge that He speaks the truth?" Uwais replied: "You must be convinced of what Allāh has destined for you, in the matter of your sustenance, and set your body free to worship Him." Harim ibn Ḥayyān said to him: "Where do you command me to reside?" Uwais pointed his hand towards Damascus, then Harim asked: "What is the cost of living there?" Uwais said: "Ugh! Alas for these hearts! Suspicion has infected them, so they derive no benefit from good advice."

We have heard that a body-snatcher [*nabbāsh*] repented at the hand of Abū Yazīd al-Bisṭāmī (may Allāh the Exalted be well pleased with him), so Abū Yazīd asked him about his condition, and he said: "I snatched bodies from a thousand graves, and I did not see their faces turned towards the *Qibla* [direction of prayer], except the faces of two men." Abū Yazīd exclaimed: "Wretched are all those others, for doubt concerning sustenance turned their faces away from the *Qibla*!"

One of our companions (may Allāh bestow His mercy upon him) told me that he saw a man who was one of the people of righteousness, so he asked him about his spiritual state, saying: "Are you secure in your faith?" The man replied: "Faith is only secure for those who are absolutely trusting [in Allāh]."

We beg Allāh (Exalted is He) to improve us by His gracious favour, and not to chastise us for our mistakes. He is indeed the Most Merciful of the merciful.

You may say: "Tell us what is the real meaning of absolute trust, what is its legal status, and to what extent is it incumbent on the servant in the matter of sustenance?"

This will be explained to you in four subsections, concerning: (1) the linguistic derivation of the term *tawakkul* [absolute trust]; (2) its use in context; (3) its definition, and (4) its stronghold or fortress.

—As for its linguistic derivation, *tawakkul* is a verbal noun formed on the pattern *tafaʿʿul*, derived from the same root, *w–k–l*, as *wakāla* [trusteeship; agency]. If a person is *mutawakkil* [trusting] in someone, he is appointing him as the *wakīl* [trustee; agent] in charge of his business, as the guarantor of its good management and as its caretaker, without imposing inconvenience and anxiety.

—As for its use in context, you should know that *tawakkul* is an appropriate term in three contexts: (1) In the context of destiny [*qisma*], where it signifies confidence in Allāh, because you will not lose what has been destined for you, since His judgement does not change, and this is established by hearing [the Qurʾān]. (2) In the context of help, where it signifies belief and confidence in the help you will receive from Allāh (Almighty and Glorious is He), if you help Him and strive in His cause. Allāh (Exalted is He) has said:

> And when you are firmly resolved,
> *fa-idhā ʿazamta*
> put all your trust in Allāh.
> *fa-tawakkal ʿala 'llāh.* (3:159)

> O you who truly believe,
> *yā ayyuha 'lladhīna āmanū*
> if you help Allāh, He will help you.
> *in tanṣuru 'llāha yanṣur-kum* (47:7)

> It is incumbent on Us to help the true believers.
> *wa kāna ḥaqqan ʿalai-nā naṣru 'l-muʾminīn.* (30:47)

This is established by the promise He has given. (3) In the context of sustenance and need, for Allāh (Exalted is He) is responsible for whatever will make your physical constitution fit for His service, and whatever will enable you to worship Him. We know that from His saying (Exalted is He):

> And if someone puts all his trust in Allāh,
> *wa man yatawakkal ʿala 'llāhi*
> He will suffice him.
> *fa-Huwa ḥasbuh.* (65:3)

The truthful and trustworthy Messenger (Allāh bless him and give him peace) once said:

> If you put your trust in Allāh, with the trust He fully deserves, He will sustain you as He sustains the birds, which leave their nests hungry in the morning, and return in the evening with their bellies full.

This is a binding duty for the servant, as indicated by the intellect and the Sacred Law together. This is the most obvious and compelling conclusion with regard to absolute trust [*tawakkul*] in the context of sustenance, and it is the purpose of this subsection.

Sustenance is guaranteed, according to those who are well versed in the knowledge of Allāh (Exalted is He), but this will only be made clear to you by explaining the several categories of sustenance. You must therefore know that sustenance is subdivided into four categories: (1) that which is guaranteed; (2) that which is destined; (3) that which is already possessed, and (4) that which is promised [by Allāh].

—As for the sustenance that is guaranteed [*maḍmūn*], it is the nourishment by which the physical constitution is sustained without other means. The guaranty from Allāh (Exalted is He) applies to this kind of sustenance, and absolute trust is necessary in relation to it, as indicated by the intellect and the Sacred Law. Since Allāh (Exalted is He) has charged us with service and obedience to Him, with our bodies, He has guaranteed whatever will prevent deficiency in the physical constitution, so that we may perform what He has imposed upon us.

One of the Shaikhs of the Karrāmiyya sect expressed himself fluently, on the basis of his heretical doctrine, when he said: "The guaranty of the servants' means of sustenance is necessary, in accordance with the wisdom of Allāh (Exalted is He), for three reasons: (1) He is the Master and we are the servants, and it is incumbent on a master to provide for his servants, just as the servants must work for their master. (2) He has created them needy of sustenance, and He has not given them any means to obtain it, since they do not know what constitutes their sustenance, where it is, and when it is available. It is therefore incumbent on Him to supply that need of theirs, and to enable them to obtain their sustenance. (3) He has made them responsible for service, and the search for sustenance is a distraction from that. It is therefore incumbent on Him to supply them with sufficient provision, so that they can devote themselves to service."

This is the saying of someone who has not grasped the secrets of Lordship [*Rubūbiyya*]. If someone maintains that the provision of sustenance is incumbent on Allāh, he is in error, as we have explained in the discussion of [orthodox Islāmic] theology [*fann al-kalām*].

Let us now return to our explanation of the four types of sustenance:

—As for the sustenance that is destined [*maqsūm*], it is that which Allāh (Glory be to Him) has foreordained and inscribed on the Well-kept Tablet [*Lawḥ Maḥfūẓ*]. It consists of what each individual will eat, drink and wear, in a predetermined quantity and at a particular time. It will neither increase nor diminish, and neither be brought forward nor delayed, from what has been inscribed as its destiny. As the Prophet (Allāh bless him and give him peace) once said:

> Sustenance is unalterably foreordained. The righteousness of a righteous person cannot increase it, not can the profligacy of a profligate diminish it.

—As for the sustenance that is already possessed [*mamlūk*], it is the worldly property owned by every individual, inasmuch as Allāh (Exalted is He) has decreed and foreordained that he should possess it, for it is part of the sustenance of Allāh (Exalted is He). He has said (Exalted is He):

> Spend from that with which We have provided you.
> *anfiqū mimmā razaqnā-kum*. (2:254)

In other words: "[Spend] from that which We have put in your possession."

—As for the sustenance that is promised [*maw'ūd*], it is that which Allāh has promised to His truly devoted servants, on the condition of true devotion, as lawful sustenance obtained without trouble and toil. Allāh (Exalted is He) has said:

> And if someone is truly devoted to Allāh,
> *wa man yattaqi 'llāha*
> He will prepare a way out for him,
> *yaj'al la-hu makhrajā:*
> and He will provide for him
> *wa yarzuq-hu*
> from sources he could never imagine.
> *min ḥaithu lā yaḥtasib*. (65:2,3)

We have now described the four types of sustenance. Absolute trust is obligatory only in relation to the type that is guaranteed [*maḍmūn*], so understand that well!

—As for the definition of absolute trust [*tawakkul*], according to one of our Shaikhs: "It is the heart's reliance [*ittikāl*] on Allāh, with exclusive dependence on Him and despair of everything other than Him."

One of them said: "[It is] total commitment of the heart to Allāh, in relation to welfare, by abandoning its attachment to anything other than Him."

According to Shaikh al-Imām Abū ʿUmar (may Allāh bestow His mercy upon him): "Absolute trust [*tawakkul*] is the abandonment of attachment [*taʿalluq*], and attachment means attributing the maintenance of your physical constitution to something other than Allāh (Exalted is He)."

According to my own Shaikh, Imām [Abū Bakr al-Warrāq] (may Allāh bestow His mercy upon him): "Absolute trust and attachment are two attributions. Absolute trust means attributing the maintenance of your physical constitution to Allāh (Exalted is He), while attachment means attributing its maintenance to someone other than Allāh."

In my opinion, these sayings all refer to one basic principle: namely, that you must make your heart firmly convinced that the maintenance of your physical constitution, the satisfaction of your need, and your sufficient provision, all come directly from Allāh (Almighty and Glorious is He), not by way of someone other than Allāh, not by way of any ephemeral things of this world, and not by any secondary means whatsoever. Then, if Allāh (Glory be to Him) so wills, He may put some created material or worldly means at His servant's disposal, or, if He so wills, He may suffice him directly with His power, without secondary means and indirect methods. If you remember that with your heart, and are firmly convinced that it is true, and if the heart is completely devoted to Allāh (Glory be to Him) and to Him alone, to the exclusion of created objects and secondary means, you will then have attained to the reality of absolute trust. Such is its definition.

—As for the stronghold of absolute trust, which supports its attainment, it is the remembrance of Allāh's guaranty. The stronghold of its stronghold is the remembrance of Allāh's majesty and His perfection, in His knowledge, His sustenance, His power, and His total freedom from breaking promises, absent-mindedness, inadequacy and deficiency. If the servant is diligent in remembering all these points, he will attain to absolute trust in Allāh (Glory be to Him) where the matter of sustenance is concerned.

You may ask: "Is there in any situation whatsoever, in which the servant is obliged to search for sustenance?"

You must therefore know that guaranteed sustenance is that which provides nourishment and support [for the physical constitution]. We cannot search for it, since it is part of what Allāh (Glory be to Him) does for His servant. Like life and death, the servant can neither procure it nor drive it away. As for that which is allotted by indirect means, the servant is not obliged to search for it, since he has no need for that search. His only need is for that which is guaranteed, and that comes directly from Allāh (Exalted is He) and within the guaranty of Allāh (Exalted is He).

As for His saying (Exalted is He):

> And seek the gracious favour of Allāh.
> *wa 'btaghū min faḍli 'llāhi.* (62:10)

—it refers to [the search for] knowledge and spiritual reward, though some say: "No, it is a special concession, since it is a commandment in the wake of the prohibition,[29] so it is meant in the sense of permission, not in the sense of necessity and obligation."

Someone may say: "But this guaranteed sustenance is provided by indirect means. It is necessary for us to seek those means?"

The answer will be: That is not required of you, since the servant has no need of it. Allāh (Glory be to Him) does His work by indirect means and without indirect means, so why should you need to seek the indirect means? Besides, Allāh (Exalted is He) has given you an absolute guaranty, without the condition of seeking and earning. Allāh (Exalted is He) has said:

> There is no beast upon the earth
> *wa mā min dābbatin fi 'l-arḍi*
> for which Allāh does not provide its sustenance.
> *illā ʿala 'llāhi rizqu-hā.* (11:6)

[29] That is to say, it follows the prohibition included in the preceding Qurʾānic verse [*āya*]:

> And leave trading aside.
> *wa dharu 'l-baiʿ.* (62:9)

That being the case, how can it befit Him to command the servant to search for something, when he does not know where to look for it? Of all the available means, he has no idea which will give him access to his sustenance, not to something else. He cannot tell which will be his means of nourishment and growth, not something else. Not one of us can identify the particular means required for that purpose, so it would not make sense to impose that search upon him. Consider this correctly, for it is very clear.

Besides, it should be enough for you to know that the Prophets (may Allāh's blessings be upon them) and the saints who put all their trust in Allāh [*al-awliyā' al-mutawakkilīn*] did not seek any sustenance, in most cases and in general, and they devoted themselves exclusively to worshipful service. The consensus is that they would never fail to comply with Allāh's commandment (Exalted is He), and they would never disobey Him (Exalted is He) in that respect. It must therefore be clear to you that searching for sustenance and its means of obtainment is not a necessary undertaking for the servant.

You may ask: "Is sustenance increased by searching, and is it reduced by the failure to search?"

My answer will be: Certainly not, for it is inscribed on the Well-kept Tablet, foreordained and fixed in time. There is no changing of Allāh's decree, and no altering of His destiny and His inscription. This is correct according to our scholars (may Allāh be well pleased with them), contrary to the opinion held by some of the companions of Ḥātim [al-Aṣamm] and Shaqīq [al-Balkhī], who said: "Sustenance is not increased or diminished by the action of the servant, but property [*māl*] does increase and diminish." This is incorrect, because the evidence in both cases is one and the same, that being the inscription [on the Well-kept Tablet] and destiny [*qisma*], and it is indicated by His saying (Exalted is He):

> So that you do not grieve for what has escaped you,
> *li-kai-lā ta'saw 'alā mā fāta-kum*
> nor exult because of what you have been given.
> *wa lā tafraḥū bi-mā ātā-kum.* (57:23)

If it was indeed increased by searching and reduced by the failure to search, it would be a cause of grief or exultation, since the servant would be slack and lazy until it escaped him, or vigorous and energetic until he acquired it. The Prophet (Allāh bless him and give him peace) said to a beggar [who asked him for a dry date]:

> Here you are! If you do not come and get it, it will surely come to you!

It may be said: "The reward and the punishment are also inscribed on the Well-kept Tablet, and we are obliged to seek the reward and refrain from the cause of punishment, so are reward and punishment increased by seeking or reduced by refraining?"

You must therefore know that seeking the reward is necessary only because Allāh has commanded it with a definite commandment, and threatened punishment for its omission. He has not guaranteed the reward without any action on our part, and increasing the reward and the punishment depends on the action of the servant. The difference between the two is a subtle point, for according to one of our scholars: "The inscription on the Well-kept Tablet is in two parts:

—The first part is inscribed absolutely and unconditionally, with no dependence on the action of the servant. This is the list of the provisions of sustenance [*arzāq*] and the appointed terms of life [*ājāl*]. Notice how Allāh (Exalted is He) has mentioned both of them absolutely and without condition. He has said (Exalted is He):

> There is no beast upon the earth
> *wa mā min dābbatin fi 'l-arḍi*
> for which Allāh does not provide its sustenance.
> *illā ʿala 'llāhi rizqu-hā.* (11:6)

> When their term comes, they shall neither tarry
> *fa-idhā jāʾa ajalu-hum lā yastaʾkhirūna*
> for a moment nor forge ahead.
> *sāʿatan wa lā yastaqdimūn.* (7:34)

The master of the Sacred Law (peace be upon him) once said:

> Four things have been finally determined: (1) the creation [*khalq*]; (2) nature [*khuluq*]; (3) sustenance [*rizq*], and (4) the appointed term [*ajal*].

—The second part is inscribed with a condition, making it dependent on the action of the servant. This is the list of the reward and the punishment [to be meted out at the Resurrection]. Notice how Allāh (Exalted is He) has mentioned them both in His Book [the Qurʾān], where He makes them dependent on the action of the servant. He has said (Exalted is He):

> If only the People of the Book would believe
> *wa law anna ahla 'l-Kitābi āmanū*
> and practise true devotion,
> *wa 'ttaqaw*
> We would remit their sins from them
> *la-kaffarnā ʿan-hum sayyiʾāti-him*
> and We would bring them into Gardens of Delight.
> *wa la-adkhalnā-hum jannāti 'n-naʿīm.* (5:65)

This is very clear, so understand it well!

Someone may say: "In our experience, the seekers find provisions and properties, while the abstainers are deprived and impoverished!"

He will be told: From what you say, it seems that you do not find a seeker deprived and poor, or an abstainer at leisure, prosperous and rich. Yes indeed, this is the most common state of affairs! You should know that this is the foreordainment of the Almighty, the All-Knowing, and the management of the Sovereign, the All-Wise.

Abū Bakr Muḥammad ibn Sābiq, the preacher from Ṣaqalliyya in Syria (may Allāh bestow His mercy upon him), recited these poetic verses:

> From many a strong man, strong in his versatility
> and mentally acute, sustenance veers away,
>
> while many a weakling, weak in his versatility,
> seems to be scooping plenty from the ocean gulf.
>
> This is a sign that God has secret knowledge
> of His creatures, a secret that is not disclosed.

You may ask: "Should you enter the desert without provision for the journey?"

The answer is that, if you have strength of heart in relation to Allāh (Exalted is He), and complete reliance on Allāh's promise, you should enter [without provision]; if not, stay with the common folk and their attachments. I heard Imām Abu'l-Maʿālī (may Allāh bestow His mercy upon him) say: "If someone stays close to Allāh (Exalted is He), while following the custom of the common folk, Allāh will stay close to him in supplying sufficient provision." This is a very fine saying, containing abundant benefits for those who consider it with care.

You may ask: "Does not Allāh say (Exalted is He):

> So make provision for yourselves,
> *wa tazawwadū*
> for the best provision is true devotion.
> *fa-inna khaira 'z-zādi 't-taqwā.* (2:197)?"

You must therefore know that this contains two statements: (1) That it [the provision you must make for yourselves] is the provision of the Hereafter. That is why He said: "The best provision is true devotion," and He did not say: "the vanities of this world and its material means." (2) That some people did not take provision for themselves on the journey to the Pilgrimage, relying on other people instead. They would beg and complain, pestering and annoying other people, so they were commanded to make provision for themselves, with an admonition to the effect that taking provision from your own property is better than taking other people's property and relying on them.

You may also ask: "Does this mean that, if someone is absolutely trusting [in Allāh], he should still carry provision with him on journeys?"

You must therefore know that he may carry provision, but he should not attach his heart to it, with the conviction that it is undoubtedly his sustenance, and that it contains his physical support. He should attach his heart solely to Allāh (Exalted is He), put all his trust in Him, and say: "Sustenance is allotted by destiny, unalterably predetermined. If Allāh (Exalted is He) so wills, He will support my physical constitution with this or with something else." He may also carry provision with some other intention, to assist a fellow Muslim, for instance.

The essence of the matter is not about taking provision or travelling without it, but rather about the heart. You must not attach your heart to anything but the promise of Allāh (Exalted is He), the excellence of His sufficiency, and His guaranty. Many a traveller carries provision, though his heart is with Allāh, not with the provision. Many a traveller leaves provision behind, though his heart is with the provision, not with Allāh (Exalted is He). What really matters, therefore, is the heart. You must understand these principles, for then you will have enough to meet your needs, if Allāh (Exalted is He) so wills.

Someone may say: "The Prophet (Allāh bless him and give him peace) used to carry provision for the journey, as did the Companions and the righteous predecessors."

He will be told: That is unquestionably permissible [*mubāḥ*], not unlawful [*ḥarām*]. The only thing that is unlawful is attaching the heart to the provision, and forsaking absolute trust in Allāh (Glory be to Him), so understand that well! Besides, what do you think of Allāh's Messenger (Allāh bless him and give him peace), considering that Allāh (Exalted is He) told him:

> And put all your trust in the Living One who never dies.
> *wa tawakkal ʿala 'l-Ḥayyi 'lladhī lā yamūtu.* (25:58)

Did he disobey Him in that? Did he attach his heart to food and drink, or to a dirham [silver coin] or a dīnār [gold coin]? Of course not, and Allāh forbid that it should be so! No indeed, his heart was with Allāh (Exalted is He), and his absolute trust was in Allāh (Exalted is He), as He had commanded him, for he is the one who paid no attention whatsoever to this world, and never extended his hand to the keys of all the earth's treasuries. When he and the righteous predecessors took provision with them, they did so because of good intentions, not because their hearts were inclined towards the provision instead of towards Allāh (Exalted is He). The important point is the intention, as we have informed you, so understand that well. Wake up from your slumber, arise from your heedlessness, and try to understand, for then Allāh will guide you aright.

You may ask: "Which is more meritorious, taking provision for the journey, or leaving it behind?"

You must therefore know that this varies as the situation varies. If he is leading a caravan, the traveller may wish to demonstrate that taking provision is permissible, or he may intend to use it to assist a fellow Muslim, or to succour someone in distress. In cases such as these, taking provision is more meritorious. If he is travelling alone, and he is strong of heart in relation to Allāh (Glory be to Him), provision for the journey may distract him from the worshipful service of Allāh (Glory be to Him and Exalted is He), so leaving it behind is more meritorious.

Try to understand all this, and practise it correctly. Allāh is the Source of enabling grace!

The Second Hindrance [*ʿāriḍ*]
Perils and dangers [*akhṭār*]

The only protection from perils and dangers resides in delegation [*tafwīḍ*]. You must therefore delegate the whole business to Allāh (Glory be to Him), and that is for two reasons:

1. The immediate calming of the heart. When situations are dangerous and dubious, so that you cannot distinguish what is right about them from what is wrong, you experience disturbance in your heart and confusion in your natural instincts. You cannot tell whether you are becoming involved in something virtuous, or in something corrupt. Then, when you delegate the whole business to Allāh (Exalted is He), you know that you will not become involved in anything that is not virtuous and good. You will thus feel safe from danger, mischief and transgression, as your heart becomes tranquil at once. This tranquillity, security and comfort in the heart is a tremendous advantage. Our Shaikh (may Allāh bestow His mercy upon him) would often say, during his meeting: "Leave the management to the One who created you, for then you may relax!" He also recited these poetic verses on the subject:

> When someone cannot tell whether his benefit
> resides in what is pleasing or what is unpleasant,
>
> it befits him to delegate what he cannot handle
> to the One who will look after all his needs,
>
> the Caring Diety [*Ilāh*], the One who is Kinder
> in compassion than his father and his mother.

2. The acquisition of what is right and good in the future. That is because conditions at the hurdles are ambiguous. Many an evil appears in the form of something good, many a disadvantage assumes the guise of an advantage, and many a poison takes the shape of a honeycomb. You are ignorant of the hurdles and their mysteries. If you take matters at face value, and engage in them of your own volition, as you see fit, how quickly you will fall into perdition, while you are unaware!

It is related that one of the worshippers asked Allāh to let him see Iblīs, so he was told: "Ask for well-being!" He refused to accept anything other than that [the sight of Iblīs], so Allāh (Exalted is He) showed Iblīs to him. As soon as he saw Iblīs, the worshipper aimed a blow at him, so Iblīs said to him: "Were it not that you will live for a hundred years, I would surely destroy you and punish you!" The worshipper was deluded by these words, and he said to himself: "My life will be very long, so I shall do whatever I wish, then repent later on." He lapsed into depravity, abandoned worshipful service, and perished.

This should admonish you to refrain from making definite predictions, and from insisting on the fulfilment of your desire. It should also warn you against excessive expectation, for that is the great disaster. The poet spoke the truth when he said:

> Beware of lustful desires and cravings,
> for many a craving has resulted in death.

If you delegate your business to Allāh (Glory be to Him), and ask Him to choose for you what is in your best interest, you will encounter only that which is good and correct. Quoting the words of the righteous servant, Allāh (Exalted is He) said:

> "And I delegate my business to Allāh.
> *wa ufawwiḍu amrī ila 'llāh:*
> Allāh is Ever-Perceptive of the servants."
> *inna 'llāha Baṣīrun bi'l-ʿibād.* (40:44)

Then He went on to say:

> So Allāh warded off from him the evils which they plotted,
> *fa-waqā-hu 'llāhu sayyiʾāti mā makarū*
> while a dreadful doom encompassed Pharaoh's folk.
> *wa ḥāqa bi-āli Firʿawna sūʾu 'l-ʿadhāb.* (40:45)

Notice how He made the servant's delegation [to Him] result in protection from evils, assistance against the enemies, and achievement of the goal. You must consider this successfully, if Allāh (Exalted is He) so wills.

You may say: "Explain to us the meaning of delegation [*tafwīḍ*] and its legal status."

You must therefore know that the term is best explained under two headings: (1) The context in which delegation [*tafwīḍ*] is appropriate, and its legal status. (2) Its meaning, its definition and its opposite.

—As for its proper context, you must know that objectives are three in number:

1. An objective about which you know for certain that it is wicked and evil, absolutely without doubt, like the Fire of Hell and the torment, and such actions as unbelief [*kufr*], heretical innovation [*bid*ʿ*a*] and sinful disobedience [*ma*ʿ*ṣiya*]. There can be no question of intending to achieve that objective.

2. An objective about which you know for certain that it is right and proper, like the Garden of Paradise, true belief, and the Sunna [exemplary practice of the Messenger (Allāh bless him and give him peace)], for instance. You are entitled to intend the attainment of such objectives, without reservation. Delegation is out of place in this context, since there is no danger involved, and no doubt that the objective is good and proper.

3. An objective about which you do not know for certain that it is right for you, or wrong: for instance, the performance of supererogatory devotions [*nawāfil*] and making use of things that are permissible [*mubāḥāt*]. This is the proper context of delegation. You are not allowed to intend such objectives without reservation, but only by making the intention contingent on the will of Allāh [by saying: "If Allāh wills (*in shā*ʾ*a 'llāh*)"] and conditional on goodness and correctness. If you restrict your intention by making it contingent on the will of Allāh, that constitutes an act of delegation [*tafwīḍ*]. If you make your intention without saying: "If Allāh wills (*in shā*ʾ*a 'llāh*)," that constitutes a blameworthy and forbidden desire.

Delegation is therefore appropriate in the context of every objective in which there is an element of danger, since you cannot be certain that it contains what is correct for you.

—As for the meaning of delegation [*tafwīḍ*], according to one of our Shaikhs (may Allāh bestow His mercy upon them): "It is abstaining from the choice that involves some risk, and leaving it to the One who is qualified to choose and manage, the One who knows the best interest of His creatures. There is no god but He!" According to Shaikh Abū Muḥammad as-Sijzī (may Allāh bestow His mercy upon him): "It is leaving your risky choice to the One who is qualified to choose [*al-Mukhtār*], so that He may choose what is best for you, on your behalf."

According to Shaikh Abū ʿUmar (may Allāh bestow His mercy upon him): "It is the abandonment of ambitious desire, and ambitious desire is the unconditional intention to achieve something risky."

Such are the definitions offered by the Shaikhs. Our own view is expressed as follows:

Delegation is the wish to have Allāh (Exalted is He) take care of your interests, in those cases where you do not feel safe from the danger involved. The opposite of delegation is ambitious desire [*ṭamaʿ*], but there are two aspects to the general concept of ambitious desire:

1. It signifies hope, in the sense that you wish for something that involves no danger, or for something risky, in which case you make your intention contingent on the will of Allāh. That is praiseworthy, not blameworthy. As Allāh (Exalted is He) has said:

> And who, I ardently hope, will forgive me
> *wa 'lladhī aṭmaʿu an yaghfira lī*
> my sin on the Day of Doom.
> *khaṭīʾatī yawma 'd-dīn.* (26:82)
>
> "We ardently hope that our Lord will forgive us our sins,
> *innā naṭmaʿu an yaghfira la-nā Rabbu-nā khaṭāyā-nā*
> because we are the first of the believers."
> *an kunnā awwala 'l-muʾminīn.* (26:51)

This aspect is not the one that concerns us here.

2. It signifies blameworthy ambition, as in the saying of the Prophet (Allāh bless him and give him peace):

> Beware of ambitious desire, for it is a present poverty.

Someone said: "Ambitious desire is the destruction and corruption of the religion, and pious caution is its firm foundation." According to our Shaikh (may Allāh bestow His mercy upon him): "Blameworthy ambition is twofold: (1) the heart's attachment to a suspicious benefit, and (2) the unconditional intention to achieve something risky."

As for the stronghold of delegation, it is remembering the danger inherent in situations, and the possibility of ruination and corruption they contain. The stronghold of its stronghold is remembering your inability to guard against the various kinds of peril, and to prevent yourself from falling into them, through your ignorance, your heedlessness and your weakness. Diligence in these two efforts of remembrance will induce you to delegate all matters to Allāh (Glory be to Him), to beware of predicting their achievement without reservation, and to refrain from intending them without making the intention contingent on goodness and correctness. Allāh is the Source of enabling grace!

You may be asked: "What is this danger, because of which you consider delegation necessary in our affairs?"

You must therefore know that danger is a general term, covering two specific dangers:

1. The danger of doubt as to whether something will or will not be, and whether you will or will not achieve it. This requires *istithnāʾ* [making your intention contingent on the will of Allāh], and it falls within the chapter of intention [*niyya*] and overexpectation [*amal*].

2. The danger of erroneous conduct, inasmuch as you are not certain that it contains what is right and proper for you. This is the situation in which delegation is necessary.

The leading scholars have provided differing explanations of danger. According to one of them: "The danger in taking an action is that there may be salvation in not taking it, for it may possibly involve a sin. There is no danger in true belief, right conduct and adherence to the Sunna, since salvation is absolutely impossible without true belief, and right conduct does not involve any sin. Where true belief and right conduct are concerned, it is therefore correct to intend their observance unconditionally."

According to the Professor [Abū Isḥāq al-Isfarānī] (may Allāh bestow His mercy upon him): "The danger in taking an action is that the danger may possibly present a hindrance, so that dealing with the hindrance becomes the main concern, rather than proceeding with the action. That may happen in connection with permissible actions [*mubāḥāt*], customary practices [*sunan*] and obligatory observances [*farāʾiḍ*]. Consider the case of someone who has barely enough time for the ritual prayer, so he intends to perform it, but he is suddenly threatened by a fire or a flood, from which it is possible for him to escape. In that situation, preoccupation with his escape is more appropriate than embarking on his ritual prayer. Unconditional intention is not correct, therefore, with regard to permissible and supererogatory practices and many obligatory observances."

Someone may ask: "How can it be fitting for Allāh to impose something on His servant, and threaten him with punishment for its omission, if there is no benefit for him in its performance?"

You should therefore know that our Shaikh (may Allāh bestow His mercy upon him) has said: "Allāh (Exalted is He) does not command the servant to do something, unless it is to his benefit and he is free from hindrances. He does not bind His servant to the performance of an obligatory duty so strictly that he has no exemption from it, unless there is also benefit for him in that. Allāh (Exalted is He) may sometimes grant him an excuse, on the grounds that attending to one of two commandments is better than preoccupation with the other, as we have mentioned above. In that case, the servant is not only excused, but rewarded, not for omitting one obligatory duty, but for performing the other, which is more important."

I heard the Imām [Abu'l-Ma'ālī] (may Allāh bestow His mercy upon him) say this about this question: "In everything that Allāh has imposed on His servants, such as the ritual prayer, the fast and the pilgrimage, there is undoubtedly some benefit for the servant, and it is correct to intend their performance unconditionally." He added: "Our opinion on this is generally agreed." This means that permissible and supererogatory observances are subject to this rule [of delegation], so understand that well, for it is one of the abstruse topics of the chapter. Allāh is the Source of enabling grace!

Someone may ask: "Is the delegator [*mufawwiḍ*] safe from perdition and maltreatment, when the abode [of this world] is the abode of trial and tribulation?"

You must therefore know that, in most cases, the delegator is only treated well. His treatment is rarely anything but good. If he does happen to be treated badly, he may be disappointed and so fall from the rank of delegation, though there is no benefit for the servant in disappointment and falling from the rank of delegation. This is the opinion of Shaikh Abū 'Umar (may Allāh bestow His mercy upon him).

It has also been said: "The delegator is treated only with what is to his benefit, in relation to what he has delegated to Allāh (Glory be to Him). As for disappointment and falling short of the rank of delegation, they are out of the question in this context, since there is no doubt as to their wrongness. Delegation applies only to something about which there is uncertainty concerning its wrongness and its rightness." This is the better of the two opinions, according to our own Shaikh (may Allāh bestow His mercy upon him), since the incentive to delegation would otherwise not be strong.

It may be asked: "Is it obligatory for the delegator to receive the most excellent treatment?"

You must therefore know that obligation is absurd in reference to Allāh (Exalted is He), for He is under no obligation to His servants. He may treat the servant with what is most beneficial, rather than what is most excellent, as an act of wisdom on His part. Consider how He decreed that the Prophet (Allāh bless him and give him peace) and his Companions should sleep throughout the night until the rising of the sun, on one of their journeys, so that they missed the ritual prayer of the night and the ritual prayer of the dawn, even though prayer is more excellent than sleep. He would sometimes ordain that he should be preoccupied with wives and children, even though exclusive devotion to the worship of Allāh (Almighty and Glorious is He) is more excellent, for:

> He is Ever-Aware of His servants, All-Seeing.
> *inna-hu bi-ʿibādi-hi Khabīrun Baṣīr*. (42:27)

This is just like the case of the skilled and wise physician, who chooses barley water for the invalid, even though sugar water is more excellent and sweeter, since he knows that barley water is more beneficial in treating his illness. The goal for the servant is salvation from perdition, not that which is [apparently] most excellent and most noble, though combined with corruption and destruction.

It may be asked: "Is the delegator free to choose?"

You must therefore know that the correct opinion, according to our scholars, is that he is free to choose, and is not subject to reproach concerning his delegation. That is because, if there is some benefit for him in surplus and what is more excellent, he will wish for Allāh (Exalted is He) to provide him with what is most excellent, just as the invalid will say to the physician: "Let my medicine be sugar water, instead of barley water, if there is some benefit for me in both, so that I may obtain the surplus and the benefit together." The case of the servant is similar, if he asks Allāh (Exalted is He) to include his benefit in what is most excellent, and to provide him therewith, so that He will grant him the surplus and the benefit together. This request must be made subject, however, to the condition that, if Allāh chooses the benefit for him in some form other than the most excellent, he will be perfectly content with that.

It may be asked: "Why is the servant free to choose what is most excellent, though he is not free to choose what is most beneficial?"

You must therefore understand that this is the difference between the two: The servant can distinguish the most excellent from the inferior, but he cannot distinguish the beneficial from the harmful, in order to seek it with unconditional intention. Besides, the meaning of his choosing the most excellent is that he wishes for Allāh (Exalted is He) to provide him with his benefit included in what is most excellent, and for Him to choose and ordain that on his behalf. It does not mean that the servant has any control over anything in that regard, so understand that well!

There you have the gist of the subtle knowledge of this subject [of delegation] and its mysteries. Had the need for it not been so pressing, we would not have ventured on its exposition, because it is like the clashing waves of the oceans of the sciences of revelatory disclosure [*mukāshafa*]. In this book, I have confined myself to providing the essential information, with the intention of explaining it for the benefit of both the master scholars and the novices, if Allāh (Exalted is He) so wills. Allāh is the Source of enabling grace!

The Third Hindrance [*ʿāriḍ*]
Destiny's decree [*qaḍāʾ*]
and the various forms in which it is experienced

The only protection from destiny's decree is contentment [*riḍā*] therewith. You must therefore be content with Allāh's decree (Almighty and Glorious is He), for two reasons:

1. Freedom to worship. That is because, if you are not content with destiny's decree, you will always be worried, for your heart will keep

wondering: "Why was it like that, and why is it like this?" If your heart is preoccupied with these concerns, how can it be free to worship? You have only one heart and you have filled it with anxieties, with questions about the past and future state of this world, so what space is left in it for the remembrance of Allāh, for His worship, and for thinking about the Hereafter?

Shaqīq [al-Balkhī] (may Allāh bestow His mercy upon him) spoke the truth when he said: "By regretting things past and trying to manage those yet to come, you have lost the blessing of your present moment."

2. The danger of incurring the wrath of Allāh (Exalted is He) through discontent. As we learn from traditional reports, one of the Prophets complained to Allāh (Exalted is He) about something unpleasant that had happened to him, so Allāh (Exalted is He) addressed him by way of inspiration, saying: "Do you lodge a complaint against Me, when I am not deserving of blame and complaint? This is how your situation appeared in the knowledge of the Unseen, so why are you displeased with My decree for you? Do you wish Me to alter this world for your sake, or to change the Well-kept Tablet [*al-Lawḥ al-Maḥfūẓ*] because of you, and so decree what you wish, instead of what I wish, and that it should be as you find pleasing, not as I find pleasing? By My Might and Glory, I swear that if you repeat this within your breast another time, I shall divest you of the garb of Prophethood and transport you to the Fire of Hell, and I shall not care!"

Let the intelligent person listen to this awesome admonition and the terrifying threat. If Allāh can be like this with His Prophets and His chosen friends, how will He be with others? Listen again to His saying (Almighty and Glorious is He): "If you repeat this in your breast another time.... " This relates to the prattle of the lower self and the vacillation of the heart, so how will it be for someone who screams and cries for help, who complains to his Lord, the Noble and Generous Benefactor, moaning and yelling over the heads of the congregation, and who attracts supporters and companions? This applies to someone who has been displeased on one occasion, so how will it be for someone who spends his whole life in displeasure with Allāh (Exalted is He)? This applies to someone who complains to Him, so how will it be for someone who complains to others?

We take refuge with Allāh from the evils of our lower selves, and from the wickedness of our deeds. We beg Him to pardon us and forgive us for our misconduct, and to improve us with the excellence of His caring attention. He is indeed the Most Merciful of the merciful.

Someone may ask: "What is the meaning of contentment with destiny's decree? How can it be realized, and what is its legal status?"

You should therefore know that the scholars have said: "Contentment is the abandonment of displeasure. Displeasure is expressed by asserting that something other than what Allāh (Exalted is He) has decreed would be better and more beneficial for you, though you do not know for certain whether it is good or bad." This [abandonment of displeasure] is a precondition of contentment, so understand that well.

You may say: "Surely all evils and sins are due to the decree and foreordainment of Allāh (Exalted is He), so how can the servant be content with evil, and how can that be incumbent upon him?"

You should therefore know that contentment with the decree is all that is incumbent. The decreeing of evil is not itself an evil. The evil is what has been decreed, so contentment is not with the evil [but only with the fact that Allāh has decreed it].

According to our Shaikhs (may Allāh the Exalted be well pleased with them): "Four things have been divinely decreed: (1) a benefit [*niʿma*], (2) an adversity [*shidda*], (3) something good [*khair*] and (4) something evil [*sharr*].

"In the case of a benefit, there must be contentment with the One who decrees [*al-Qāḍī*], the decree [*al-qaḍāʾ*] and what is decreed [*al-maqḍī*]. There must also be gratitude for it, inasmuch as it is a blessing, and the servant must acknowledge its blessedness by demonstrating the effect of the benefit.

"In the case of an adversity, there must also be contentment with the One who decrees, the decree and what is decreed. There must also be patience, since an adversity is hard to endure.

"In the case of something good, there must also be contentment with the One who decrees, the decree and what is decreed. The servant must also acknowledge the favour, since it is a boon that he has been fortunate to obtain.

"In the case of something evil, there must also be contentment with the One who decrees, the decree and what is decreed, inasmuch as it has been decreed, not inasmuch as it is evil. The fact that it has been decreed is attributable, in reality, to the decree and the One who decrees."

This last case is similar to the situation where you are content with the doctrine [*madhhab*] of the proponent of a different school, in the sense that you are content to have knowledge of it, not to adopt it as your own doctrine. The fact that it is known [*maʿlūm*] is attributable to knowledge [*ʿilm*], so you are actually content and pleased with the knowledge of that doctrine, not with the doctrine itself.

Someone may ask: "If someone is content, is he entitled to ask for more?"

The answer will be: Yes, if he does so with the stipulation that it must be good and proper, not unconditionally. That will not dislodge him from contentment. It is actually a sign of contentment, so it is better [than not asking for more], because, if something delights a person and he is content with it, he will naturally ask for more of the same. The Prophet (Allāh bless him and give him peace) used to say, when milk was available:

> O Allāh, grant us Your blessing in it, and provide us with more of it!

He would also say, when referring to [food or drink] other than milk:

> [O Allāh, grant us Your blessing in it], and provide us with more of something better than it!

In neither case did he indicate that he was not content with what Allāh (Exalted is He) had foreordained for him in that particular instance.

You may ask: "Has it not been reported that the Prophet (Allāh bless him and give him peace) made his request contingent on Allāh's will, and conditional on its being good and proper?"

You must therefore know that these matters are peculiar to the heart, and there is no need to express them with the tongue. Failure to express them verbally is therefore unimportant, provided they are stipulated by the heart, so understand that unequivocally.

The Fourth Hindrance [*ʿāriḍ*]
Adversities [*shadāʾid*] and misfortunes [*maṣāʾib*]

There is only one protection from adversities and misfortunes, and that is patience [*ṣabr*]. You must therefore practise patience in all situations. That is for two reasons:

1. The achievement of worshipful service and the accomplishment of its purpose. The whole business of worshipful service is founded on patience and the endurance of adversities, so, if someone is not patient, he will not achieve any part of it in reality. That is because, if someone intends to worship Allāh (Exalted is He), and genuinely devotes himself to that worship, he will be confronted by adversities, trials and misfortunes from several directions:

—First of all, there is no worshipful service in which hardship is not an essential element. That accounts for all this encouragement to perform it, and the promise of reward. The performance of worship is impracticable without the curbing of passion and the subjugation of the lower self, since the lower self is an obstacle to all that is good. Resistance to passion and the subjugation of the lower self are among the most difficult challenges confronting the human being.

—Secondly, if the servant does good work, in spite of the hardship involved, he is obliged to act with caution, so that his work will not be spoiled, and prudence is more exacting than the work itself.

—Thirdly, the abode [of this world] is the abode of trial and tribulation, so its inhabitant will inevitably be afflicted with its adversities and misfortunes. There are several types of misfortune:

Misfortune afflicting the family, close relatives, spiritual brethren and companions with death, loss and separation.

Physical misfortune, in the form of diseases and ailments.

Misfortune affecting a person's reputation, so that people attack him, envy him, belittle him, and indulge in backbiting and telling lies about him.

Misfortune affecting property, by causing it to be lost and cease to exist.

Each of these misfortunes inflicts a particular kind of ordeal and torment, so it is necessary to endure them all with patience. Anxiety and grief will otherwise deprive the servant of the freedom to worship.

—Fourthly, the seeker of the Hereafter is always more severely afflicted and subject to more trial and tribulation. The closer someone is to Allāh, the more he suffers misfortunes in this world, and the more severely he is tested. You have surely heard the saying of the Prophet (Allāh bless him and give him peace):

> Of all human beings, those most severely tested are the Prophets, then the scholars, then those who are most exemplary....

If someone intends to do good work, and devotes himself completely to the path of the Hereafter, these trials and tribulations are therefore bound to confront him. If he does not endure them with patience, and fails to avoid preoccupation with them, he will be cut off from the path and distracted from worshipful service, so he will not achieve any part thereof. Allah (Glory be to Him and Exalted is He) has told us to be on our guard against trials, tribulations and misfortunes, and the suffering they inflict upon us. He confirmed and emphasized that admonition, for He said (Exalted is He):

> Surely you will be tried in your property
> *la-tublawunna fī amwāli-kum*
> and in your persons, and you will hear much wrong
> *wa anfusi-kum: wa la-tasmaʿunna*
> from those who were given the Book before you,
> *mina 'lladhīna ūtu 'l-Kitāba min qabli-kum*
> and from the idolaters.
> *wa mina 'lladhīna ashrakū adhan kathīrā.* (3:186)

Then He went on to say:

> But if you endure with patience
> *wa in taṣbirū*
> and practise true devotion,
> *wa tattaqū*
> that represents the resolute handling of things.
> *fa-inna dhālika min ʿazmi 'l-umūr.* (3:186)

It is as if He were saying: "Convince yourselves firmly that you must inevitably suffer various kinds of trial and tribulation, then, if you endure with patience, you will be real men, and your resolutions will be the resolutions of real men." If someone is determined to worship Allāh (Glory be to Him), he must therefore resolve, first of all, to practise patience for a very long time, and to commit himself firmly to enduring the terrible adversities that will follow one another in succession until death. He will otherwise lose the means to achieve his goal, and approach it from the wrong direction.

We are told that al-Fuḍail (may Allāh bestow His mercy upon him) once said: "If someone is determined to traverse the road to the Hereafter, let him install within himself these four colours of death: the white, the red, the black and the green. The white death is hunger, the black is tolerance of blame from other people, the red is opposition to the devil, and the green is [indifference to] the succession of misfortunes, one after the other."

2. As for the second of the two reasons for patience, it is the benefit conferred by patience in this world and the Hereafter, including salvation and success. Allāh (Exalted is He) has said:

> And if someone is truly devoted to Allāh,
> *wa man yattaqi 'llāha*
> He will prepare a way out for him,
> *yaj'al la-hu makhrajā:*
> and He will provide for him
> *wa yarzuq-hu*
> from sources he could never imagine.
> *min ḥaithu lā yaḥtasib.* (65:2,3)

In other words: "If someone is truly devoted to Allāh (Exalted is He), with patience, He will grant him a way out of adversities, including victory over the enemies." Allāh (Exalted is He) has said:

> So endure with patience, for the outcome
> *fa-'ṣbir inna 'l-'āqibata*
> is in favour of the truly devout.
> *li'l-muttaqīn.* (11:49)

Allāh (Exalted is He) has also said:

> And the fair word of the Lord was fulfilled
> *wa tammat kalimatu Rabbi-ka 'l-ḥusnā*
> for the Children of Israel,
> *'alā Banī Isrā'īla*
> because of their patient endurance.
> *bi-mā ṣabarū.* (7:137)

Joseph is said to have written, in response to Jacob (peace be upon them both): "Your forefathers endured with patience, so they triumphed.

You must therefore endure with patience, as they endured with patience, and triumph as they triumphed."

In this same context, a poet has said:

Do not despair, even if suffering is prolonged.
If you seek help with patience, you will find relief.

The patient sufferer well deserves to satisfy his need,
and he who keeps knocking at the doors deserves refuge.

One of the benefits of patience is that it confers precedence and leadership. Allāh (Exalted is He) has said:

And We appointed them to be leaders
wa ja'alnā-hum a'immatan
guiding by Our command,
yahdūna bi-amri-nā. (21:73)

Those benefits include commendation from Allāh (Glory be to Him and Exalted is He), for He has said (Glory be to Him and Exalted is He):

We found him patiently enduring.
innā wajadnā-hu ṣābirā:
An excellent servant indeed [was the Prophet Job],
ni'ma 'l-'abd:
for he was ever returning [in repentance to his Lord]!
inna-hu awwāb. (38:44)

They include glad tidings, blessing and mercy, for Allāh (Exalted is He) has said:

And give glad tidings to those who are patiently enduring.
wa bashshiri 'ṣ-ṣābirīn:
to those who say, when a misfortune strikes them:
alladhīna idhā aṣābat-hum muṣībatun
"To Allāh we belong, and to Him we are returning."
qālū innā li'llāhi wa innā ilai-hi rāji'ūn:

Such are they on whom are blessings
ulā'ika 'alai-him ṣalawātun
from their Lord, and mercy.
min Rabbi-him wa raḥma:
Such are the rightly guided.
wa ulā'ika humu 'l-muhtadūn. (2:155-7)

They include love from Allāh (Exalted is He), for He has said (Exalted is He):

> Allāh loves those who are patiently enduring.
> *wa 'llāhu yuḥibbu 'ṣ-ṣābirīn.* (3:146)

They include the highest levels in the Garden of Paradise, for Allāh (Exalted is He) has said:

> Those shall be awarded the highest heaven,
> *ulā'ika yuzjawna 'l-ghurfata*
> for having endured with patience.
> *bi-mā ṣabarū.* (25:75)

They include the tremendous honour, for Allāh (Exalted is He) has said:

> Peace be upon you, because you endured with patience.
> *salāmun ʿalai-kum bi-mā ṣabartum* (13:24)

They also include a reward without limit and without end, far beyond the imaginings of creatures, their reckoning and their comprehension, for Allāh (Exalted is He) has said:

> Surely the patiently enduring will be paid
> *innamā yuwaffa 'ṣ-ṣābirūna*
> their wages in full without reckoning.
> *ajra-hum bi-ghairi ḥisāb.* (39:10)

Glory be to a Deity [*Ilāh*] who is a Noble Master! How Generous is He, for He bestows all these gracious favours on His servant, in this world and the Hereafter, in reward for the patience of an hour! It must now be clear to you that the benefit of this world and the Hereafter resides in patience. The Prophet (Allāh bless him and give him peace) once said:

> All that is good for the true believers resides in the patience of one hour.

The poet spoke well when he said:

> Patience is the key to what is hoped for,
> and everything good is because of it,
>
> so endure with patience, even if the nights are long,
> for the stubborn horse may then prove manageable,
>
> and through patience you may find attainable
> what once made you say: "Alas, it will never be!"

Another poet said:

I endured with patience, and patience became part of my nature.
Let it suffice you that Allāh has commended patience!

I shall endure with patience, until Allāh judges between us,
whether it be a matter of ease, or a matter of difficulty.

You must therefore take advantage of this noble and praiseworthy virtue, and spare no effort in its constant practice, for then you may be numbered among the successful. Allāh (Exalted is He) is the Custodian of enabling grace!

You may ask: "What is the real meaning of patience, and what is its legal status?"

You should therefore know that, in classical Arabic, the term *ṣabr* [patience] is synonymous with *ḥabs* [confinement; restraint]. Allah (Exalted is He) has said:

> And restrain yourself
> *wa 'ṣbir nafsa-ka*
> along with those who cry unto their Lord
> *ma'a 'lladhīna yad'ūna Rabba-hum*
> in the morning and the evening,
> *bi'l-ghadāti wa 'l-'ashiyyi*
> seeking His countenance;
> *yurīdūna Wajha-hu*
> and do not let your eyes overlook them,
> *wa lā ta'du 'ainā-ka 'an-hum*
> desiring the pomp of the life of this world.
> *turīdu zīnata 'l-ḥayāti 'd-dunyā.*
> And do not obey someone
> *wa lā tuṭi' man*
> whose heart We have made heedless
> *aghfalnā qalba-hu*
> of Our remembrance, who follows his own lust
> *'an dhikri-nā wa 'ttaba'a hawā-hu*
> and whose case has been abandoned.
> *wa kāna amru-hu furuṭā.* (18:28)

Patience [*ṣabr*] is attributed to Allāh (Exalted is He), but only in the sense of restraint [*ḥabs*], since He restrains the torment from the sinful offenders, instead of inflicting it upon them immediately [in this world]. In relation to the endeavours of the heart, the term *ṣabr* is used because it signifies restraining the lower self from anguish [*jaza'*], and *jaza'*, according to some of the scholars, means expressing your perturbation in the face of adversity. Others maintain, however, that *jaza'* means seeking to escape from adversity without making the intention contingent on the will of Allāh, whereas *ṣabr* means refraining from it [from *jazaʿ* in the latter sense].

The stronghold of patience [*ṣabr*] is remembering the extent and the timing of adversity, that it will neither increase nor diminish, and that it will neither be brought forward nor postponed. There is no benefit in anguish [*jazaʿ*], but only harm and danger.

The stronghold of this stronghold is remembering the excellence of Allāh's recompense for patience, and the generous favour that is held in store for it in His presence (Exalted is He). Allāh is the Source of enabling grace!

Subsection

It is incumbent upon you to surmount this difficult and obstructive hurdle, by repelling these four hindrances [*ʿawāriḍ*] and removing their cause. If you fail to do so, they will not let you remember the worshipful service that is your goal. They will not allow you to think about it, let alone enable you to accomplish it. Each one of them presents a distracting preoccupation, in both the short term and the long term.

The most serious and problematic of them all is the business of sustenance [*rizq*] and its management. That is the greatest trial for the majority of people. It wearies their natural aptitudes, preoccupies their hearts, multiplies their cares, narrows their lives, and magnifies their liabilities and their burdens. It diverts them away from Allāh (Exalted is He) and His service, towards the service of this world and the service of creatures, so they live in this world in heedlessness and darkness, weariness and exhaustion, abasement and humiliation. They approach the Hereafter bankrupt, facing the reckoning and the torment, unless Allāh (Exalted is He) bestows His mercy through His gracious favour.

Notice how many a Qurʾānic verse [*āya*] Allāh (Exalted is He) has revealed on that subject [of sustenance], and how often He has mentioned His promise, His guaranty and His oath concerning it. The Prophets and the scholars have not ceased to admonish people and make them aware of the path. They have compiled books, coined allegories for them, and put them in fear of offending Allāh (Exalted is He), yet, in spite of all that, they are not rightly guided, do not practise true devotion, and do not experience tranquillity. No indeed, they are plunged in a flood of anxious concern, constantly afraid of missing a lunch or a supper.

The root of all that is too little reflection on the signs of Allāh (Glory be to Him), too little meditation on the works of Allāh, failure to consider the speech of Allāh's Messenger (Allāh bless him and give him peace), and failure to ponder the sayings of the righteous, combined with receptivity to the whisperings of the devil, listening to the speech of the ignorant, and being misled by the habits of the negligent. The devil thereby gains control of them, and bad habits take root in their hearts, so that reduces them to weakness of the heart and frailty of certitude.

As for the best of people, those who are endowed with faculties of discernment, and who are masters of earnest endeavour and dedicated striving, they clearly discern the path of Heaven, so they do not toy with the material means of the earth. They cling to the lifeline of Allāh,[30] so they take no interest in the attachments of their fellow creatures. They are fully convinced by the signs of Allāh (Exalted is He) and they recognize His path, so they take no notice of the temptations of the devil, their fellow creatures and the lower self. If a devil, a selfish instinct or a person tempts them to do something, they engage the tempter in dispute, repudiation and contradiction, until people turn away from them, the devil leaves them alone, the lower self submits to them, and the right path is straight ahead of them.

We are told that Ibrāhīm ibn Ad'ham (may Allāh bestow His mercy upon him) was intending to enter the desert, when Satan came to him and tried to scare him, by saying: "This is a perilous desert, and you have no provision with you and no means [of survival]!" Ibrāhīm thereupon resolved (may Allāh bestow His mercy upon him) that he would traverse the desert without that [provision for the journey], and that he would not traverse it without performing a thousand cycles of prayer beneath each and every milestone. He acted in accordance with his resolution, and stayed in the desert for twelve years. In one of those

[30] An allusion to Q. 3:103.

years, [the Caliph] ar-Rashīd went on the Pilgrimage [*Ḥajj*], and he saw Ibrāhīm praying beneath a milestone. He was told: "This is Ibrāhīm ibn Ad'ham, performing the ritual prayer," so he approached him and said: "How are you, O Abū Isḥāq?" Ibrāhīm gave the poetic response:

We patch this world of ours by shredding our religion,
so our religion does not last, and neither does what we patch.

Congratulations to a servant who prefers Allāh, his Lord,
and donates his worldly interest to whatever lies in store!

We are told that one of the righteous (may Allāh bestow His mercy upon him) was in a certain desert, when Satan told him in a seductive whisper: "You are without provision, and this is a perilous desert, devoid of any cultivation and unpopulated." He thereupon resolved that he would travel in spite of his lack of provision, that he would follow the path without receiving anything from people, and that he would eat nothing until butter and honey were placed in his mouth. Then he turned aside from the main road, and went on his way.

He said (may Allāh bestow His mercy upon him): "I travelled as Allāh willed, and I came upon a caravan that had gone astray. When I saw the people in that caravan, I threw myself down on the ground, so that they would not notice me, but Allāh (Almighty and Glorious is He) caused them to travel until they reached me. I closed my eyes as they approached me, and they said: "This is someone lost, who has fainted from hunger and thirst. Fetch some butter and some honey, and put them in his mouth. Perhaps he will recover consciousness!" They promptly fetched some butter and some honey, so I clenched my mouth and my teeth. Then they brought a knife, intending to use it to pry my mouth open, so I laughed and opened my mouth. When they saw me act like that, they said: 'Are you a lunatic?' I said: 'No, and praise be to Allāh (Exalted is He)!' I then told them something about what had happened to me with the devil, and they found that truly amazing."

According to one of our Shaikhs (may Allāh bestow His mercy upon them): "In the course of one of my journeys, I paused to spend days of learning in a mosque far removed from the populace. I was travelling without provision, in accordance with the custom of our saints, so the devil whispered to me: 'This is a mosque far distant from the populace.

If you travel to a mosque in a populated area, its people will notice you and attend to your needs.' I said: 'I shall not break my journey anywhere but here. I am under oath to Allāh that I shall not eat anything except sweetmeat, and that I shall not eat that until it is put into my mouth, morsel by morsel.' I then performed the late evening prayer, and locked the door.

"When an early segment of the night had passed, I suddenly heard a person knocking on the door, and he was holding a lamp. Since the knocking went on and on, I opened the door, to find myself facing an old woman accompanied by a young man. She came inside and set before me a dish of sweet jelly, saying: 'This young man is my son. I prepared this sweet jelly for him, but an argument occurred between us, so he swore that he would not eat until a strange man ate with him.' (Or she may have said: 'This is the stranger who is in the mosque, so eat, and may Allāh bestow His mercy upon you!') She then started putting a morsel into my mouth, and a morsel into her son's mouth, until we were satisfied. The pair of them then departed, and I locked the door, while feeling amazed at what had happened."

Stories like this describe the dedicated strivings of the righteous, and their defiant opposition to the devil. That should contain three benefits for you:

1. You should understand that sustenance will not escape, in any case whatsoever, from someone for whom it has been predestined.

2. You should understand that the matter of sustenance and absolute trust [*tawakkul*] is very important indeed, and that the devil resorts to very sly tricks and temptations in this arena. Even the likes of those ascetic Imāms [in the stories above] were not immune to that, and the devil did not despair of them. Even after those long spiritual exercises and the many dedicated efforts they had previously expended, they still needed to ward him off with these refutations. By my life, even if someone struggled against the lower self and the devil for seventy years, he could not feel sure that they would not tempt him, just as they tempt the novice in worshipful service. They would even tempt him as they tempt a heedless individual, who has never devoted an hour to spiritual exercise. Then, if they got the better of him, they would surely disgrace him and destroy him, with the destruction suffered by the heedlessly

deluded. In that there is a warning for those endowed with faculties of discernment.

3. You should understand that the matter is not brought to completion, except through absolute commitment and the utmost endeavour, for they [those ascetic Imāms] were just like you in flesh and blood and body and spirit. As a matter of fact, they were more fragile than you in body, weaker in limbs and organs, and more delicate in bones, but they had the strength of knowledge, the light of certitude, and aspiration in the matter of religion. This made them capable of such dedicated efforts, and of attaining to such high stations. You must therefore attend to your lower self. May Allāh bestow His mercy upon you, and us, and may he cure it [the lower self] of this chronic disease, so that you may prosper, if Allāh (Exalted is He) so wills!

Subsection

Now, after all that has been said above, I shall single out certain important items for your attention, since they will benefit the heart if you reflect on them. They will furnish you with the substance of this chapter, and leave you with a clear understanding of the truth, if you consider them carefully and put them into practice. Allāh (Glory be to Him) is the Source of enabling grace.

1. You must know that Allāh (Exalted is He) has guaranteed sustenance for His servants in His Book. He has guaranteed your sustenance and pledged Himself to provide you with it. What would you say, if one of the kings of this world promised to welcome you as his guest at night, and to entertain you at dinner, assuming that you believed him to be truthful, so that he would not lie or break his promise? What would you say, for that matter, if you received such a promise from a commoner, or a Jew, or a Christian, or a Magian, who was apparently honest and sincere in what he said? Would you not rely on him and his promise, feel comfortable with what he said, and have no worry about your supper that night, because of your trust in him?

Well then, what do you think of the fact that Allāh (Exalted is He) has not only guaranteed your sustenance for you, and pledged Himself to provide it, but has solemnly sworn an oath to that effect in several places [in the Qur'ān]? How is it that you do not feel comfortable with His promise, that you do not rely on His word and His guaranty, that you pay no attention to His solemn oath, and that your heart is actually disturbed and ill at ease? What a disgrace, if only you could see its evil consequences! What a misfortune, if only you knew what it really means!

ʿAlī ibn Abī Ṭālib (may Allāh be well pleased with him) is said to have uttered these poetic verses:

> Do you seek Allāh's sustenance from someone other than Him,
> and do you wake up feeling no fear of the consequences?
>
> Are you content with a money changer, even if he is a polytheist,
> though you are not content with your Lord as a guarantor?
>
> It seems that you have not read what is in His Book,
> so you have become extremely weak in certitude.

This attitude to the matter [of sustenance] is conducive to doubt and suspicion, and the person concerned is in danger—the refuge is with Allāh!—of being deprived of true knowledge and religion. This is the context in which He said (Glory be to Him):

> And put all your trust in Allāh,
> *wa ʿala 'llāhi fa-tawakkalū*
> if you are indeed believers.
> *in kuntum mu'minīn.* (5:23)
>
> And in Allāh let the believers put all their trust.
> *wa ʿala 'llāhi fa-l'-yatawakkili 'l-mu'minūn.* (3:122)

This single item is therefore sufficient for the believer who is seriously interested in the state of his religion. There is no might nor any power except with Allāh, the All-High, the Almighty.

2. You must know that sustenance is foreordained. That is clearly stated in the Book of Allāh (Exalted is He) and the traditions of Allāh's Messenger (Allāh bless him and give him peace). You must also know that His foreordainment [*qisma*] does not alter and does not change. If you refuse to acknowledge foreordainment, or accept the idea of its cancellation, you are knocking on the door of unbelief. (We take refuge with Allāh!) If you know it to be a true fact that does not change, what can be gained from anxious concern and searching, except humiliation

and degradation in this world, and agony and loss in the Hereafter? That is why the Prophet (Allāh bless him and give him peace) once said:

> "[This is] the sustenance of so-and-so, the son of so-and-so" is inscribed on the back of the whale and the bull, so the greedy person gets nothing extra except trouble.

Our own Shaikh (may Allāh bestow His mercy upon him) had this to say on the subject: "Whenever something has been predestined for your pair of jaws, no one but you will ever chew it, so eat your sustenance—woe unto you!—with dignity, and do not eat it with shame." This item is also sufficient for real men.

3. I heard from my Shaikh, the Imām [al-Ḥaramain] (may Allāh bestow His mercy upon him), that the Professor [Abū Isḥāq] (may Allāh bestow His mercy upon him) used to say: "Concerning the matter of sustenance, I have found satisfaction in pondering and telling myself: 'Surely this sustenance is for life and livelihood, for the corpse does nothing with sustenance. The life of the servant is in the treasury of Allāh (Exalted is He) and at His disposal, and the same is true of sustenance: if He wills, He gives it to me, and if He wills, He withholds it from me. It is concealed from me, entrusted to Allāh (Exalted is He), who manages it as He wills, and I am comfortable with that." This is a subtle item, sufficient for the masters of verification.

4. Allāh (Exalted is He) has guaranteed the servants' sustenance, but He has only guaranteed the sustenance that provides essential nourishment and growth, including physical stamina and preparation [for worshipful service].

Concerning the material means of sustenance [*asbāb*]

As for the material means of sustenance, in the form of food and drink, if the servant devotes himself to the worshipful service of Allāh (Exalted is He), and puts all his trust in Allāh, the material means may sometimes be withheld from him. He must not be concerned about that, however, and he must not be troubled by it, because the fact of the matter, as he well knows, is that the guaranty applies to support of the physical constitution. Absolute trust in Allāh (Glory be to Him) is relevant only in this sense, not in any other, and this [support of the physical constitution] is what can be expected from Allāh (Exalted is He). Allāh (Exalted is He) will undoubtedly assist the servant to fulfil the duty of worship and service, so long as his term of life and his obligation to worship continue, for this is the purpose [for which He created His servant].

Allāh is Capable of whatever He wills. If He so wills, He supports the physical constitution of His servant with food and drink, or with clay and soil, or with *tasbīḥ* [the glorification of Allāh] and *tahlīl* [the affirmation that there is no god but Allāh], as in the case of the angels. If He so wills, He uses some other means, different from all of these. The servant needs only the stamina and strength for worshipful service, not eating and drinking, the intensity of carnal desire and the enjoyment of pleasure. There is no reason, therefore, to be concerned about the means of sustenance.

This explains how the worshippers and ascetics found the strength to pursue their journeys, travelling by night and day. Some of them did not eat for ten days at a stretch, and some of them did not eat for a month or two months, yet they had the strength to carry on. Some of them used to swallow sand, so Allāh (Exalted is He) would convert it into nourishment for them. For instance, in the case of Sufyān ath-Thawrī (may Allāh bestow His mercy upon him), it is related that his funds ran out in Mecca, so he survived for fifteen days by swallowing sand. According to Abū Muʿāwiya al-Aswad: "I saw Ibrāhīm ibn Ad'ham eating clay for twenty days." According to al-Aʿmash: "Ibrāhīm at-Taimī (may Allāh the Exalted bestow His mercy upon him) said to me: 'I have not eaten for a month.' I exclaimed: 'For a month?!' He said: 'It would have been two months, except that a person implored me by Allāh to accept a bunch of grapes, so I ate them, and now I am complaining about my stomach!'" You should not find any of that surprising, for Allāh (Exalted is He) has the power to do whatever He wills.

Consider the case of this invalid, who does not eat for a month, yet he stays alive, even though the invalid is inevitably weaker and more fragile in nature than someone who is strong and healthy. As for someone who dies of hunger, that is because his appointed term has arrived, as in the case of someone who dies of overeating and indigestion. I am told that Abū Saʿīd al-Kharrāz (may Allāh bestow His mercy upon him) once said: "My relationship with Allāh (Glory be to Him) was such that He would feed me once every three days, so I entered the desert and went for three days without eating any food. Then, on the fourth day, I felt weak, so I stayed sitting in my place. Suddenly, I heard an invisible caller crying: 'O Abu's-Saʿīd, which is dearer to you, a means of sustenance, or strong energies?' I said: 'Strong energies!' Then I stood up at once. Three days seemed like a very short time to me now, so I spent twelve days without eating, and I suffered no pain on that account."

As for the situation where the servant experiences the withholding of the means of sustenance, and he knows how to put all his trust in Allāh, he must be firmly convinced that Allāh (Exalted is He) will support him with strength, so he must not be dismayed. It is his duty, in fact, to express his gratitude to Allāh (Exalted is He) by giving Him very many thanks for that experience. Allāh (Exalted is He) has treated him with gracious favour and kindness, since He has relieved him of trouble and granted him assistance. Through that gift of grace, the servant has achieved the essential purpose and the goal, and Allāh has relieved him of the burden [of sustenance] and the indirect means [of obtaining it], ruptured the ties of custom for his sake, shown him the way of power, likened his state to the state of the angels, and raised him above the condition of animals and the common folk. You must therefore contemplate this great principle, so that you may gain vast profit, if Allāh (Exalted is He) so wills.

Perhaps you will say: "You have gone to excess in this subsection, violating the conciseness stipulated for the present book."

My response will be: By Allāh's Everlasting Life, what I have included here is very little, compared with what is needed in this context, since it is most important in relation to worshipful service. Indeed, it is central to the whole subject of this world and servanthood. If someone has a serious interest in this subject, let him realize that and give it all the attention it deserves, for, unless he does so, he is missing the target.

If you need proof of the discernment of the scholars of the Hereafter and those who truly know Allāh, it is that they founded their business on absolute trust in Allāh, devotion to the worshipful service of Allāh, and the severance of all attachments. They compiled so many books and offered so much wise advice! Allāh sent them helpers from among the leaders, and companions, to provide them with pure goodness, so long as they did not join one of the sects of the ascetic Imāms known as the Karrāmiyya, for they built their doctrine on foundations that were not correct.

We did not cease to be worthy of honour, so long as we adhered to the path [*minhāj*] of our own Imāms, graduating from our places of worship and our colleges, every time, either as a leader in knowledge, like Professor Abū Isḥāq [al-Isfarānī], Abū Ḥāmid [al-Isfarānī ash-Shāfiʿī], Abu'ṭ-Ṭayyib [aṭ-Ṭabarī], Ibn Fawrak [al-Isbahānī], our own Shaikh [Imām Abū Bakr al-Warrāq], and other chieftains like them, or as a champion of truth [*ṣiddīq*] in worshipful service, like Abū Isḥāq ash-Shīrāzī, Abū Saʿīd aṣ-Ṣūfī, Naṣr al-Maqdisī, and other such leaders distinguished in knowledge and abstinence.

[We did not cease to be worthy] until some of our hearts became weak, and we were sullied by some of those attachments that are more harmful than beneficial. It was then that matters deteriorated, aspirations retreated, blessings flew away, and joys and sweet delights departed, to the point where hardly anyone is likely to be sincere in his worship, or to obtain any knowledge and experience of reality. Whatever light beams from us now, it shines only from those who have kept to the path of our righteous predecessors and our earlier Shaikhs, like al-Ḥārith al-Muḥāsibī, Muḥammad ibn Idrīs ash-Shāfiʿī, [Abū Ibrāhīm] al-Mazanī, Ḥarmala [at-Tajībī], and other leaders of the religion (may Allāh bestow His mercy upon them all), for, as the poet said:

They did not spend their days except in virtuous restraint,
and for the love of their Master they found no substitute.

They were the best, champions of Truth, models of sainthood,
who made the Master of masters the target of their quest.

From every one who patiently endured, the knot of patience was untied,
but the days did not loosen any knot from their contract [with Allāh].

We were kings in the early period of our history, but then we became subjects. We were knights on horseback, but then we became pedestrians. If only we would never be separated from the path!

Allāh is the One to whom we appeal for help against misfortunes, and He is the One whom we implore, begging Him not to deprive us of this spark of life. He is indeed Munificent, Generous, Gracious and Compassionate.

Concerning delegation [*tafwīḍ*]

As for delegation [*tafwīḍ*], there are two essential points for you to consider:

1. You should know that the exercise of choice is appropriate only for someone who is knowledgeable about affairs in all their aspects, both outwardly and inwardly, both in their present condition and in their eventual outcome. Otherwise, he risks choosing something bad and destructive, instead of something inherently good and beneficial. As you are surely aware, if you said to a bedouin, or a villager, or a keeper of sheep and goats: "Examine these dirhams [silver coins] for me, and sort out the good ones from the bad," he would not do that correctly. If you made the same request of a townsman who was not a money changer, the task would probably be just as difficult for him. Your only safe course, therefore, is to present those coins to the money changer, who is skilled in handling gold and silver, and who knows their peculiarities and their secret characteristics. As for the knowledge that embraces all affairs, from all directions, it is available only to Allāh, the Lord of All the Worlds, so no one is entitled to the exercise of choice and management, except Allāh, Alone without any partner. That is why He says (More Glorious is He than any other sayer):

> Your Lord creates and chooses whatever He wills.
> *wa Rabbu-ka yakhluqu mā yashā'u wa yakhtār:*
> They never have any choice.
> *mā kāna la-humu 'l-khiyara.* (28:68)

Then He has said (Exalted is He):

> Your Lord knows what their breasts conceal,
> *Rabbu-ka ya'lamu mā tukinnu ṣudūru-hum*
> and what they publish.
> *wa mā yu'linūn.* (28:69)

It is related that one of the righteous was told by Allāh (Exalted is He): "Ask and you shall receive!" He was blessed with right guidance, so he said: "One who knows all aspects tells someone who is ignorant of all aspects: 'Ask and you shall receive!' What do I know about what is good for me? So I ask Him, saying: 'You choose for me!'"

2. Suppose a man told you: "I shall take charge of all your affairs and manage all your necessary interests, so delegate the whole business to me, and focus your attention on the matter that truly concerns you." Assume that you considered him the most knowledgeable of all the people of your time, the wisest, the strongest, the most compassionate, the most righteous, the most honest and the most trustworthy. Would you not seize that opportunity and regard it as a tremendous blessing? Would you not feel the greatest sense of appreciation for him, and offer him the most abundant thanks and the finest praise? Then, if he chose for you something in which you did not recognize the benefit, instead of finding that disturbing, you would rely on his management and feel comfortable. You would understand that whatever he chose for you could only be good, and whatever he saw fit for you could only be in your best interest, after you had entrusted the business to him, and he had guaranteed all that.

Well then, what keeps you from delegating the business to Allāh, the Lord of All the Worlds (Glory be to Him)? He is the One who manages the entire universe, from heaven to the earth, for He is the Most Knowledgeable of the knowledgeable, the Most Capable of the capable, the Most Merciful of the merciful, and the Richest of the rich. Given the brilliance of His knowledge and the excellence of His management, His choice on your behalf will surely transcend your knowledge and understanding, so you must focus your attention on the matter that concerns you in preparation for your life in the Hereafter. If His choice on your behalf has a mysterious aspect, which you do not comprehend, you must be content with that and feel comfortable with it, however it may be, for it is surely good and beneficial.

You will draw the right conclusions from all this, if Allāh wills. Allāh is the Source of enabling grace.

Concerning contentment with destiny [*ar-riḍā bi'l-qaḍā'*]

As for contentment with destiny, you must consider two essential points, to which nothing further need be added:

1. The benefit of contentment in the present and the future. As for its benefit in the present, it is freedom of the heart and relief from useless anxiety. That is why one of the ascetics (may Allāh bestow His mercy upon him) once said: "Since destiny is a true fact, anxiety is redundant." According to the traditional report, the Prophet (Allāh bless him and give him peace) said to Ibn Masʿūd (may Allāh be well pleased with him):

> Let your anxiety be very slight, for whatever has been predestined will come about, and whatever has not been predestined will not come to you.

This Prophetic saying is comprehensive, conveying much valuable meaning in very few words.

As for the benefit of contentment in the future, it is the reward of Allāh (Exalted is He) and His good pleasure. Allāh (Exalted is He) has said:

> Allāh is well pleased with them,
> *raḍiya 'llāhu ʿan-hum*
> and they are well pleased with Him.
> *wa raḍū ʿan-h.* (5:119)

By contrast, discontent is fraught with anxiety, sorrow and distress in the present, and with the burden of sin and punishment in the future. It has no benefit, since destiny's decree is effective, so it will not be cancelled by your anxiety and your discontent. As the poet said:

> Whatever is decreed, O self, endure it with patience,
> and may you be safe from that which is not foreordained.
>
> You must realize that what is predestined will come about
> for certain, regardless of whether or not you practise patience.

The intelligent person will not choose useless anxiety, combined with the burden of sin and punishment, instead of the heart's comfort and the reward of the Garden of Paradise!

2. Discontent is fraught with the dire threat of danger and injury, unbelief [*kufr*] and hypocrisy [*nifāq*], unless Allāh (Exalted is He) overtakes you [with His mercy]. Reflect on His saying (Exalted is He):

> But, by your Lord, they will not believe
> *fa-lā wa Rabbi-ka lā yu'minūna*
> until they make you judge of what is in dispute
> *ḥattā yuḥakkimū-ka fī-mā shajara*

> between them and find within themselves
> *baina-hum thumma lā yajidū fī anfusi-him*
> no dislike of what you decide,
> *ḥarajan mimmā qaḍaita*
> and submit with full submission.
> *wa yusallimū taslīmā.* (4:65)

He has thus denied their claim to belief, by solemnly swearing that belief is absent from those who are discontented, and who find within themselves a dislike of the decision of Allāh's Messenger (Allāh bless him and give him peace). What then is the condition of someone who is displeased with Allāh's decree (Exalted is He)? According to traditional report, Allāh (Exalted is He) says:

> If someone is not content with My decree, if he is not patient with My tribulation, and if he is not grateful for My blessing, let him choose a deity [*ilāh*] apart from Me.[31]

Someone said: "It is as if He is saying: 'This person will not be content with Me as a Lord, as long as he is displeased, so let him choose another lord, with whom he is content.'"

For the intelligent person, this [saying attributed to Allāh] is the ultimate threat and warning. One of the righteous predecessors spoke the truth, when he was asked: "What is servanthood [*ʿubūdiyya*] and what is Lordship [*Rubūbiyya*]?" and he replied: "It is for the Lord to decree, and for the servant to be content." This means that if the Lord decrees, but the servant is not content, it is pointless to speak of servanthood and Lordship. You must consider this principle, and scrutinize yourself, for then you may be safe, with Allāh's help and His enabling grace.

Concerning patience [*ṣabr*]

As for patience, it is a bitter medicine and a blessed though distasteful potion. It procures every benefit and protects you from every harm. Since the medicine fits this description, the intelligent person forces the lower self to drink it and gulp it down. He chokes on its bitterness and its sharpness, but he says: "The bitterness of an hour is the comfort of a year."

As for the benefits procured by patience, you should know that patience is fourfold: (1) patience in worshipful obedience, (2) patience

[31] This is a Sacred Tradition [*Ḥadīth Qudsī*], not a Qurʾānic verse [*āya*].

in abstaining from sinful disobedience, (3) patience in avoiding the excesses of this world, and (4) patience in enduring trials and misfortunes.

If someone endures the bitterness of patience, and practises patience in these four areas, he will attain to acts of obedience, to their stations of righteousness, and to their generous reward in the Hereafter. He will not lapse into acts of sinful disobedience, their afflictions in this world and their dire consequences in the Hereafter. He will not be tried by the search for this world, by preoccupation with it in the present, and by the consequence in the future. His recompense will not be lost because of the tribulation he had to suffer. By virtue of patience, he will thus attain to worshipful obedience, its noble stations and its reward. He will attain to righteousness, abstinence, and generous recompense and reward from Allāh (Glory be to Him). The full extent thereof is a matter known only to Allāh (Glory be to Him and Exalted is He). As for protection from causes of harm, he will be relieved of the trouble and hardship of impatience in this world, first of all, then of its burden and punishment in the Hereafter.

If he is too weak to practise patience, and follows the path of anguish, he will forfeit every benefit, and every cause of harm will adhere to him. There are several possibilities: (1) He will lose the benefit of worshipful obedience, since he does not endure its hardship with patience, does not put it into practice, and lacks the patience to maintain it. (2) He lacks the patience to refrain from sinful disobedience, so he lapses into it, or to avoid extravagance, so he becomes preoccupied with it. (3) He fails to endure a misfortune with patience, so he is deprived of the reward for patience. (4) Perhaps he will multiply his anguish, to the point where he forfeits the recompense [for patience], so he will suffer two misfortunes, one being the loss of the thing [that made him feel anguish in the first place], and the other being the loss of the reward and recompense.

Someone said: "Lack of patience in enduring a misfortune is worse than the misfortune itself. What benefit is there in something that robs you of what you stand to gain, and does not restore to you what you have lost? If one of the two escapes you, try to make sure that the other does not escape you as well!"

We are told that ʿAlī (may Allāh be well pleased with him) consoled a man by saying: "If you are patient, the decrees of destiny will befall you, and you will be rewarded, but if you are impatient, the decrees of destiny will befall you, and you will bear the burden of sin."

The gist of the matter is that you must detach the heart from its usual ties, and prevent the lower self from following its regular habits. This calls for absolute trust in Allāh (Glorious is His Name), forsaking the management of affairs and delegating them to Allāh (Glory be to Him), without knowing the secret concealed within them. You must restrain the lower self from discontent and from impatience, despite its tendency to rush in that direction. You must curb it with the reins of contentment, and by swallowing the drink of patience, despite its aversion to that treatment. This task is bitter, painful and hard to bear, but it is an effective procedure and a rightly guided method. It has a praiseworthy outcome, with fortunate and blessed results.

What would you say about a kind and wealthy father, if he prevented his dear son from eating a date or an apple, when the boy was sore-eyed, then handed him over to his harshly strict teacher, who confined him in his presence all day long, upset his feelings, and took him to the cupper to undergo a blood-letting operation, causing him pain and distress? Would you suppose that he withheld that fruit because of stinginess? How could that be, when he gives to strangers and treats them generously? Did he withhold it because of contempt for this son of his? How could that be, when he keeps everything he possesses in store for him? Did he intend to trouble and hurt him, out of hatred for the lad? How could that be, when the boy is the solace of his eye and the fruit of his heart, and it would worry him if a wind blew on his son? By no means! He acted as he did because he knew it to be in his son's best interest, and that this slight inconvenience would lead to an excellent result and enormous benefit [by curing his eye disease].

What would you say about a skilful, wise and loving physician, if he withheld a drink of water from a seriously ill patient, when the invalid was so thirsty that his liver was roasting, and made him drink a distasteful fruit juice, repugnant to his nature? Would you suppose that he was motivated by animosity and spite? By no means! His action was wise and beneficent, because he knew for certain that giving the invalid what he craved would damage him immediately and ruin him completely, whereas withholding that from him would result in his recovery and his survival.

You must therefore reflect with care, O man, if Allāh withholds from you a loaf of bread or a silver coin, since you know for certain that He possesses what you desire, that He can cause it to reach you, and that He is the Lord of generosity and gracious favour. He knows your condition, for nothing is hidden from Him, so there is no question of deficiency, inadequacy, concealment or stinginess [where He is concerned]. Exalted is He beyond all that, and Sanctified is He, for He is the Richest of the rich, the Most Powerful of the powerful, the Most Knowledgeable of the knowledgeable, and the Most Generous of the generous. You must therefore know for a fact that he would not withhold something from you, except in your best interest. How could it be otherwise, when He says:

> He is the One who created for you
> *Huwa 'lladhī khalaqa la-kum*
> all that is in the earth.
> *mā fi 'l-arḍi jamīʿā.* (2:29)?

How could it be otherwise, when He is the One who has generously endowed you with knowledge of Him, with knowledge beside which this world in its entirety amounts to nothing? According to the well-known traditional report, Allāh (Exalted is He) says:

> I keep My friends away from the bounty of this world, just as I keep the herdsman who cares for his camels away from the puddles of dung.[32]

When He tries you severely, you must therefore know for certain that He has no need of your trial and tribulation, that He knows your condition and sees your weakness, and that He treats you with kindness and compassion. You have surely heard the saying of the Prophet (Allāh bless him and give him peace):

> Allāh (Exalted is He) is More Compassionate with His servant than the tender mother with her child.

If you know this, you will understand that He would not inflict this unpleasant trial upon you, except in your best interest. You may be ignorant of its benefit, but He knows that full well. This explains why you see Him multiplying the trial and tribulation of His saints and His

[32] This is a Sacred Tradition [*Ḥadīth Qudsī*], not a Qurʾānic verse [*āya*].

chosen friends, those who are the most distinguished of His servants. In the words of the Prophet (Allāh bless him and give him peace):

> When Allāh loves a set of people, He tries them.
>
> The people most severely tried are the Prophets, then the martyrs, then the worthiest and the worthiest....

If you see Allāh withholding this world from you, and inflicting more and more hardships and suffering upon you, you must therefore know that you are noble in His sight, that you hold a lofty rank in His presence, and that He is making you tread the path of His saintly friends, for He sees you and He does not need that [withholding of this world...]. You have surely heard His saying (Exalted is He):

> So wait patiently for your Lord's decree,
> *wa 'ṣbir li-ḥukmi Rabbi-ka*
> for you are surely in Our sight.
> *fa-inna-ka bi-aʿyuni-nā.* (52:48)

You must acknowledge the gracious favour He bestows upon you, by looking after your best interest, multiplying your recompense and your reward, and appointing you to the ranks of the righteous and those who are distinguished in His sight. You will discover so many praiseworthy results and noble gifts! Allāh is the Custodian of helpful guidance, through His favour and His grace.

Subsection

In summary, if you know for certain that Allāh (Exalted is He) is the Guarantor of your sustenance, which you need for your survival and your performance of His worshipful service, that He is Capable of what He wills however He wills, and that He is Aware of your need in every situation and at every moment, you will put all your trust in His true guaranty and His genuine promise. Your heart will feel at ease with that, and you will forget about worldly attachments and material means, and your heart's addiction to them.

Worldly attachments do not enrich you or suffice you, without Allāh (Almighty and Glorious is He), for He (Exalted is He) is the One who makes it easy for you to eat and drink. It is He who makes your food and drink wholesome and enjoyable. It is He who supplies you with their energy and benefit, and protects you from their heaviness and harmfulness. He (Exalted is He) may also enrich you and suffice you without them, if He wills. The whole business depends on Him, Alone without any partner, so put all your trust in Him, not in any other.

You must likewise leave the management of your affairs to the One who manages the heavens and the earth. You must rid yourself of concern about anything beyond your knowledge, and of thinking about tomorrow's business. You must stop wondering whether something will happen tomorrow, or whether it will not happen, and how it will be [if it does happen]. You must stop saying "perhaps..." and "if...," since there is nothing in that except worrying the heart and wasting time. Maybe things will unfold in ways you never imagined, so that all your previous thinking and planning will prove to be a waste of precious time, nothing but a useless game. Worse still, you may suffer a loss that you sorely regret, for your heart may become preoccupied with it, and you may waste your whole life in the process. One of the pious ascetics (may Allāh be well pleased with him) gave this poetic admonition:

The ordainments of God [*al-Ilāh*]
and His judgement are predetermined,
so relieve your heart of "perhaps..." and "if...."

Another said:

Whatever is going to happen will happen in its own time,
yet the brother of ignorance is worried and sorrowful,
for perhaps what he fears will never come to be,
and perhaps what he hopes for will never happen.

In short, you must say to yourself:

"Nothing will ever befall us
lan yuṣība-nā
except what Allāh has decreed for us.
illā mā kataba 'llāhu la-nā
He is our Protecting Friend."
Huwa Mawlā-nā. (9:51)

He is Sufficient for us, and excellent is the Custodian, since He is Powerful with no end to His Power, Wise with no end to His Wisdom, Compassionate with no end to His Compassion. Since He possesses these attributes, He deserves to receive all your trust, and to have the whole business delegated to Him. Delegation [*tafwīḍ*] is therefore incumbent upon you. You must likewise convince your heart that whatever Allāh has decreed, and whatever He decrees for you, is most appropriate and most beneficial, even if the nature thereof is a mystery beyond our knowledge.

You must also tell yourself: "Whatever is predestined will undoubtedly come to be, so there is no benefit in discontent. You have no choice in what Allāh does, so it is pointless to be displeased. Do you not say: 'I am well pleased with Allāh as a Lord'? So how can you not be content with His decree, when the decree is part of the business of Lordship and its privilege?! Contentment [*riḍā*] is therefore incumbent upon you."

In similar fashion, when a misfortune befalls you and you experience something unpleasant, you must persuade your lower self to view it from the right perspective, and calm your heart so that it does not become perturbed. You must not succumb to complaining and impatient agitation, especially at the first shock. That is the crucial moment, when the lower self tends to react at great speed with habitual impatience, so you must tell it: "This misfortune has already occurred, so there is no expedient to ward it off. Allāh (Exalted is He) has prevented a much greater misfortune, for there are many kinds of trial and tribulation in His storehouses. This one will soon be over, so it will not last forever. It is a cloud that will surely disperse, so resign yourself to patience for a little while, for you will derive prolonged happiness from that."

You will receive a generous reward, once you have understood that there is no way of preventing what is destined to befall, that there is no benefit in impatient agitation, and that there no misfortune, in actual fact, in the presence of equanimity and patience. You must therefore occupy your tongue with *istirjāʿ* [saying: "We belong to Allāh, and to Him we are all returning (*innā li'llāhi wa innā ilaihi rājiʿūn*)"],[33] and your heart with remembering the reward you will receive from Allāh (Exalted is He). You must also remember how patiently the most terrible misfortunes were endured by those possessed of constancy [*ulu 'l-ʿazm*],[34] meaning the Prophets and the saintly friends of Allāh (Exalted is He).

[33] Q. 2:156.

[34] Q. 46:35.

If this world is withheld from you for a time, you must tell your lower self: "He knows the situation best, and He is Most Compassionate with you and Most Generous. He is the One who feeds the dog in spite of its vileness, and feeds the unbeliever in spite of his hostility. I am His servant, acknowledging His Lordship and affirming His Oneness, so am I not worth a loaf of bread in His sight?! This is inconceivable, so recognize the fact that He has not withheld this world from you except for some enormous benefit. As He has said (Exalted is He):

> Allāh will surely grant ease after hardship.
> *sa-yajʿalu 'llāhu baʿda ʿusrin yusrā.* (65:7)

Be patient for a little while, for then you will see the marvellous refinement of His work. You have surely heard the saying of the poet:

> Wait for the work of your Lord, for it will bring
> what you desire in the form of relief near at hand,
>
> and do not despair, if nothing special has yet occurred,
> for there are so many wondrous marvels in the Unseen.

Another poet said, in similar vein:

> O man beset with care,
> if hardship affects you severely,
> you must think of: "Did We not expand...."[35]
>
> Then hardship will come between two easements,
> if you repeat [the Sūra],
> so be happy!

If you take these admonitions to heart, as well as others like them, and make a regular practice of repeating them, that will soon ease your hardships for you, provided you have a lofty aspiration and a serious dedication.

You have now learned how to protect yourself from these four hindrances, and obtained complete relief from the trouble they cause. In the sight of Allāh (Exalted is He) you have come to be one of those who put all their trust in Him, who delegate their affairs to Him, who are content with His decree, and who patiently endure His trial and tribulation. You have gained comfort of heart and body in this world, splendid reward and treasure in the Herafter, and magnificent worth

[35] This is a reference to the Sūra of Relaxation [*Inshirāḥ*] Q. 94:1-8

and affection in the sight of the Lord of All the Worlds. You have thus acquired the best of both abodes. The path of worshipful service lies straight ahead of you, since there is no impediment and no distraction. You have now surmounted this difficult hurdle!

We beseech Allāh (Exalted is He) to support you, and us, with the blessing of His enabling grace, for the whole business is at His disposal, and He is the Most Merciful of the merciful. There is no might nor any power except with Allāh, the All-High, the Almighty.

The Fifth Hurdle
The hurdle of the incentives [*bawā'ith*]

It is now incumbent upon you, O my brother, to travel ahead, since the path lies straight before you, the way has been made easy, the impediments have been removed, and the hindrances have disappeared.

In order to travel the straight path, you have no option but to feel both fear and hope, and to persist in experiencing their true significance to the fullest extent.

Concerning fear [*khawf*]

In the case of fear, there are two reasons for clinging to it:

1. Deterrence from sinful acts of disobedience. This lower self that is always instigating evil [*an-nafs al-ammāra*] is strongly disposed towards wickedness, constantly looking for trouble. It will not desist from that, unless it receives a tremendously fear-inspiring shock and an extremely intimidating threat. It is not free [from slavery], so it is not concerned about loyalty and restrained from offensive conduct by a sense of shame. As the poet said:

> The slave is thrashed with the stick,
> while blame is enough for the freeman.

To manage the lower self, you must thrash it with the whip of intimidation, in word and deed and thought. We are told that the lower self of one of the righteous tempted him to commit an act of sinful disobedience, so he went and stripped off his clothes, rolled in the sun-baked dust, and said to his lower self: "Taste [the hot dust], for the Fire of Hell is far hotter than this!" Yes indeed, the lower self is a corpse by night and an idle mischief-maker by day.

2. The servant must not take pride in acts of worshipful obedience, for he will perish if he does so. He must curb the lower self with blame and criticism, finding fault with its vices and sins, which contain all sorts of dangers. It is reported that the Prophet (Allāh bless him and give him peace) once said:

> If Jesus and I were taken to task for what these two [lower selves of ours] have earned, we would suffer a torment suffered by no other creature.

—and he pointed with two of his fingers [to represent each of their lower selves].

We are told that al-Ḥasan [al-Baṣrī] used to say: "Not one of us is safe from having committed a sin, so the door of forgiveness may be locked in his face, for he acts in a way that is improper."

Ibn al-Mubārak used to say, while rebuking his lower self: "You talk like the pious ascetics, but you act like the hypocrites, and you long for the Garden of Paradise. Alas and alack! Another set of people are entitled to the Garden of Paradise, for they perform deeds quite different from those you perform."

These admonitions, and others like them, are examples of how the servant must rebuke the lower self, and scold it repeatedly, so that it will not take pride in an act of worshipful obedience, or commit an act of sinful disobedience. Allāh is the Source of enabling grace!

Concerning hope [*rajā*ʾ]

As for hope, you must maintain the feeling of it for two reasons:

1. It provides an incentive to acts of worshipful obedience. That is because goodness is a heavy burden. The devil tries to deter you from it, and passion invites you to its opposite. The state of the heedless, who constitute the majority of people, is obviously a natural disposition to gratify the lower self. The reward for acts of obedience is out of their sight, and the distance to its achievement seems very remote to them. This being the case, the lower self feels no incentive to goodness, and has no desire to accord it the respect it deserves.

If anything can make the lower self interested in goodness, it must be something that matches and equals these obstacles, or rather outweighs them. That something is strong hope for the mercy of Allāh, and intense longing for the blessing of His reward and His noble recompense. According to our own Shaikh (may Allāh bestow His mercy upon him): "Sadness prevents the consumption of food. Fear prevents sins. Hope reinforces acts of worshipful obedience. The remembrance of death leads to abstinence from excess."

2. Hope makes it easier for you to bear difficulties and hardships. If someone truly understands what he is seeking, he finds it easy to make the necessary effort. If someone is pleased by something, and feels a genuine longing for it, he readily endures the difficulty involved, and thinks nothing of the trouble he encounters in its pursuit. If a person loves someone with genuine affection, he also loves to endure the ordeal his loved one imposes, to the point where he discovers all kinds of delight in that ordeal.

Consider how the beekeeper thinks nothing of the stings inflicted by the bees, because the sweetness of the honey is fresh in his memory. Consider the hired workman, who cares nothing about climbing that tall ladder with a heavy load, throughout the long, hot summer day, because he remembers that he is due to collect a couple of silver coins in the evening. Consider the peasant farmer, who does not let his thinking dwell on the harshness of the heat and the cold, and the year-long drudgery and toil out in the fields, because he remembers the time of produce on the threshing floor.

Consider likewise, O my brother, those worshipful servants who are committed to dedicated striving, for they remember the Garden of Paradise, that delightful place of rest with its many kinds of comfort, including its dark-eyed maidens [*ḥūr*], its palaces, its food and drink, its ornaments and fine clothes, and everything else that Allāh (Exalted is He) has prepared for its inhabitants. They find it easy to bear any toil involved in worshipful service, or the loss of any pleasure and enjoyment in this world, or anything they suffer in the form of injury, humiliation, affliction or adversity, for the sake of the Garden of Paradise.

It is related that the companions of Sufyān ath-Thawrī (may Allāh the Exalted be well pleased with him) once told him what they thought about his fear, his dedicated striving, and the shabbiness of his outer condition. They said: "O teacher, even if you reduced this strenuous exertion, you would still reach your intended goal, if Allāh (Exalted is

He) so willed." Sufyān said: "How can I fail to strive with dedicated effort, when I have heard that the people of the Garden of Paradise will be in their places, and a light will appear to them, illuminating the eight Gardens. They will suppose that light comes from the Lord (Glory be to Him), so they will fall down in prostration. Then they will hear the call: 'Raise your heads! It is not what you suppose. It is merely the light of a young woman, smiling in the face of her husband.'" Sufyān then recited these poetic verses:

He whose abode is Paradise will not be harmed
by any wretchedness or poverty that he must bear.

See how he walks sadly, in fear and in dread,
walking to the mosques in tatters and rags.

O lower self, how patiently can you endure a flame?
The time is near when you must advance after retreating.

The business of servanthood hinges on two things: the performance of worshipful obedience, and the avoidance of sinful disobedience. None of that can be achieved, however, in the company of this lower self that is always instigating evil [*an-nafs al-ammāra bi's-sū'*], except through inducement and intimidation, inspiring hope and instilling fear. The stubborn mule needs a leader to lead it, and a driver to drive it. If it falls into a danger spot, it may need to be beaten with a whip from one side, and offered barley from another side, until it gets up and moves away from whatever it fell into. The delinquent youth will not attend school classes, without inducement from his parents and intimidation from the teacher.

This lower self is likewise a stubborn mule that has stumbled into the pitfall of this world, so fear is its whip and its driver, while hope is its barley and its leader. It is the delinquent youth, who must be moved to attend the classes of worship and righteousness, so its intimidation is the reminder of the Fire of Hell and the punishment [of the Hereafter], and its inducement is the reminder of the Garden of Paradise and its reward.

For the servant who seeks worshipful service and spiritual training, it is likewise necessary to make the lower self conscious of two feelings, they being fear and hope. Otherwise, the unruly lower self will not assist him in that endeavour. For this reason, [the Qur᾽ān, which Allāh has called] the Wise Remembrance [*adh-Dhikr al-Ḥakīm*][36] has coupled the promise [*wa῾d*] and the threat [*wa῾īd*], meaning the inducement and the intimidation, and has laid great stress on both of them. It has described the noble reward in terms that make its forfeiture unbearable, and described the painful punishment in terms that make its agony intolerable. You must therefore maintain these two feelings [fear and hope], for then you will achieve your goal of worshipful service, and the endurance of hardship will become easy for you. Allāh (Exalted is He) is the Custodian of helpful guidance, through His grace and His mercy.

You may ask: "What is the real meaning of hope and fear, and what is their classification?"

You must therefore know that, according to our scholars (may Allāh bestow His mercy upon them), fear and hope fall into the same category as *khawāṭir* [spontaneous feelings; random notions],[37] and the servant is only obliged to cultivate their stimulants. Our scholars have said: "Fear [*khawf*] is a shudder that occurs in the heart, in reaction to an unpleasant thought. Dread [*khashya*] is almost synonymous, but it implies a kind of reverential awe. The opposite of fear is boldness [*jarā᾽a*], but it may also be contrasted with the sense of security [*amn*]. The adjectives *khā᾽if* [fearful, afraid] and *āmin* [secure] correspond to the nouns *khawf* [fear] and *amn* [security]. The *āmin* is someone who is bold in relation to Allāh (Glory be to Him). Boldness [*jarā᾽a*] is therefore the true opposite of fear."

The stimulants of fear are four in number:

1. Remembering the many sins that have previously been committed, and the multitude of victims who have accused the wrongdoer, while you are in suspense, for the means of redemption is not yet clear to you.

2. Remembering the severity of Allāh's punishment (Glory be to Him), which you lack the strength to bear.

3. Remembering that your lower self is too weak to endure the punishment.

4. Remembering that Allāh (Exalted is He) has the power to deal with you whenever He wills and however He wills.

[36] Q. 3:58.

[37] See pp. 71-77 above.

As for hope [*rajā*ʾ], it is the heart's delight in the knowledge of Allāh's gracious favour (Glory be to Him), and its happiness with the abundance of Allāh's mercy (Exalted is He). This kind of hope is included in the category of spontaneous feelings [*khawāṭir*], so it has not been ordained for the servant. Another kind of hope has been ordained for the servant, and that is remembering the gracious favour of Allāh, His abundant generosity and His mercy. The term *rajā*ʾ is also applied to the intention that is made contingent on Allāh's will.[38]

Our present subject is the first kind of hope, which is the feeling of delight and happiness. Its opposite is despair, which is the sense of losing Allāh's mercy and His gracious favour, and the heart's detachment from that feeling. Such despair is a sinful act of sheer disobedience. This kind of hope must be a strict duty [*farḍ*], if the servant has no other means of guarding against despair. If he does have other means, it is a supererogatory duty [*nafl*], additional to the general belief in Allāh's gracious favour, His abundant generosity and His mercy.

The stimulants of hope are also four in number:

1. Remembering the gracious favours that Allāh has previously bestowed upon you, without any action [on your part] or any intercessor [on your behalf].
2. Remembering what Allāh has promised, as your share of His plentiful reward and His enormous favour, commensurate with His abundant grace and His noble generosity, and that your entitlement thereto does not depend on your action, since, if it did depend on your action, it would be a lesser thing and a smaller matter.
3. Remembering the abundance of Allāh's blessing, conferred on you in your religion and your worldly life, at the present time, in the form of all kinds of support and kindnesses, without any claim to entitlement or any request [on your part].
4. Remembering the vast extent of Allah's mercy (Exalted is He), that His mercy has outstripped His wrath, and that He is the All-Merciful, the All-Compassionate, the Independent, the Generous, the One who is Kind to His believing servants.

If you are diligent in practising these two kinds of remembrance, that will lead you to conscious awareness of fear and hope in every situation.

[38] See p. 118 above.

Allāh (Exalted is He) is the Custodian of helpful guidance, through His grace and His favour.

Subsection

It is therefore incumbent upon you to surmount this hurdle with perfect caution and circumspection, and with the utmost care, for it is a hurdle precarious to tackle and hazardous to cross. That is because its path lies between two perilous and dangerous paths, one being the path of [false] security and the other the path of despair. The path of hope and fear is the just path between the two unjust paths. If hope prevails upon you, so that you lose fear altogether, you will slip onto the path of [false] security.

> No one feels secure from Allāh's devising,
> *fa-lā ya'manu makra 'llāhi*
> except those folk who are losers.
> *illa 'l-qawmu 'l-khāsirūn.* (7:99)

If fear prevails upon you, so that you lose hope altogether, you will slip onto the path of despair.

> No one despairs of Allāh's Spirit,
> *inna-hu lā yai'asu min Rawḥi 'llāhi*
> except the unbelieving folk.
> *illa 'l-qawmu 'l-kāfirūn.* (12:87)

If you ride between fear and hope, and cling to them both together, that is the just and straight path, the way of Allāh's saints and His chosen friends, whom Allāh (Exalted is He) has described in His saying:

> They used to vie with one another in good deeds,
> *inna-hum kānū yusāri'ūna fi 'l-khairāti*
> and they cried to Us in longing and in fear,
> *wa yad'ūna-nā raghaban wa rahabā:*
> and they were submissive unto Us.
> *wa kānū la-nā khāshi'īn.* (21:90)

If three paths become apparent to you in this hurdle: (1) the path of [false] security and boldness, (2) the path of despair and hopelessness, and (3) the path of fear and hope, stretched out between them, and if you take a step away from it [the middle path] to your right or your left, you will slip onto one of the two deadly paths, and perish with those who perish.

Futhermore, the fact is that the two unjust and deadly paths are wider and more spacious, more attractive and easier to tread than the just path. If you look from the side of [false] security, you will see the vast extent of Allāh's mercy (Exalted is He), the abundance of His grace and the profusion of His generosity, to the point where no fear remains with you. You will therefore put all your trust in that, immediately, and you will feel secure. If you look from the side of fear, you will see the might of Allāh's power and authority (Exalted is He), the greatness of His awesome dignity, the precision of His commandment and the meticulousness of His reckoning, in relation to His saints and His chosen friends, to the point where hope will scarcely remain with you, so you will promptly despair.

This means that you should not look only at the vastness of Allāh's mercy, to the point where you become completely trusting and feel secure, and that you should not look only at His awesome dignity and meticulous reckoning, to the point where you despair. You should rather look at the former and the latter together, and take something from each. Then you must ride a narrow path between them, and stick to that path, so that you will be truly safe. The path of absolute hope is easy, broad and wide, and its ultimate outcome will bring you to false security and loss. The path of absolute fear is also broad and wide, and its ultimate outcome will bring you to error. Between the two lies the just path, by which I mean the path of fear and hope. Even if it is a narrow and difficult path, it is a safe road and a clear route, leading to forgiveness and beneficence, then to the Gardens and Riḍwān [the keeper of Paradise], and to meeting the Sovereign All-Merciful (Glory be to Him). You have surely heard His saying (Exalted is He) about the sons of this road:

> They call on their Lord in fear and hope.
> *yadʿūna Rabba-hum khawfan wa ṭamaʿā.* (32:16)

He then went on to say (Exalted is He):

> So no soul knows what comfort
> *fa-lā taʿlamu nafsun mā ukhfiya*

is kept secretly in store for them,
la-hum min qurrati aʿyun:
as a reward for what they used to do.
jazāʾan bi-mā kānū yaʿmalūn. (32:17)

You must consider all this with very great care, make ready for action, and pay close attention to the task, for it will not come easily. Allāh is the Custodian of enabling grace!

You must also know that it will not be a simple matter for you to tread this path, to force this obstinate lower self, with its lazy attitude to goodness, to abstain from what it dearly loves, and to perform the acts of obedience that weigh so heavily upon it. Progress depends on the strict observance of three essentials, and on keeping them constantly in mind, without a break and without a moment of heedlessness: (1) Remembering the sayings of Allāh (Exalted is He and Glory be to Him) concerning encouragement and intimidation. (2) Remembering His actions (Glory be to Him) relating to punishment and pardon. (3) Remembering His recompense for His servants, in the form of reward and chastisement in the Hereafter.

Many pages are needed to explain each of these essential points in detail, so we have compiled a book devoted to them, entitled: "The Awakening of the Heedless [*Tanbīh al-Ghāfilīn*]." In this present book, we shall provide quotations to help you achieve the goal, if Allāh (Almighty and Glorious is He) so wills. Allāh is the Custodian of enabling grace!

The first essential:
The sayings of Allāh
(Glory be to Him and Exalted is He)

You must turn, O man, to the Glorious Book, and contemplate the verses [*āyāt*] concerning encouragement and intimidation, the inspiring of hope and the instilling of fear. The verses of hope include His saying (Exalted is He):

Do not despair of the mercy of Allāh;
lā taqnaṭū min raḥmati 'llāh:
surely Allāh forgives sins altogether.
inna 'llāha yaghfiru 'dh-dhunūba jamīʿā. (39:53)

Who forgives sins but Allāh,
wa man yaghfiru 'dh-dhunūba illa 'llāh: (3:135)

the Forgiver of sin, the Accepter of repentance?
Ghāfiri 'dh-dhanbi wa Qābili 't-tawb. (40:3)

And He is the One who accepts repentance
wa Huwa 'lladhī yaqbalu 't-tawbata
from His servants, and pardons evil deeds.
ʿan ʿibādi-hi wa yaʿfū ʿani 's-sayyiʾāt. (42:25)

Your Lord has prescribed for Himself mercy,
kataba Rabbu-kum ʿalā Nafsi-hi 'r-raḥmata (6:54)
and My mercy embraces all things,
wa raḥmatī wasiʿat kulla shaiʾ:
so I shall prescribe it for those who are truly devout.
fa-sa-aktubu-hā li'lladhīna yattaqūna. (7:156)

To human beings, Allāh is surely
inna 'llāha bi'n-nāsi
Ever-Gentle, All-Compassionate,
la-Raʾūfun Raḥīm. (22:65)
and to the believers He is All-Compassionate.
wa kāna bi'l-muʾminīna Raḥīmā. (33:43)

These, and others like them, are the verses of hope [*āyāt ar-rajāʾ*].

The verses of fear and stricture [*āyāt al-khawf wa 's-siyāsa*] include His saying (Exalted is He):

O My servants, so beware of Me!
yā ʿibādi fa-'ttaqūn. (39:16)

What, did you suppose that We had created you
a-fa-ḥasibtum anna-mā khalaqnā-kum
for idle sport, and that you
ʿabathan wa anna-kum
would not be returned to Us?
ilai-nā lā turjaʿūn. (23:115)

What, does the human being suppose
a-yaḥsabu 'l-insānu
that he will be left to wander aimlessly?
an yutraka sudā. (75:36)

It will not be in accordance with your desires,
laisa bi-amāniyyi-kum
nor the desires of the People of the Book.
wa lā amāniyyi ahli 'l-Kitāb:
He who does something wrong
man yaʿmal sūʾan
will have the recompense thereof,
yujza bi-hi wa lā yajid

and he will not find against Allāh
la-hu min dūni 'llāhi
any protecting friend or helper.
waliyyan wa lā naṣīrā. (4:123)

Yet they reckon that they do good work.
wa hum yaḥsabūna anna-hum yuḥsinūna ṣunʿā. (18:104)

And there will appear to them, from Allāh,
wa badā la-hum mina 'llāhi
that wherewith they never reckoned.
mā lam yakūnū yaḥtasibūn. (39:47)

And We shall advance upon the work they have done,
wa qadimnā ilā mā ʿamilū min ʿamalin
and make it into scattered particles of dust.
fa-jaʿalnā-hu habāʾan manthūrā. (25:23)

We beg Allāh (Exalted is He) to save us by His mercy!

The fine verses that combine both fear and hope include His saying (Exalted is He):

Announce to My servants that
nabbiʾ ʿibādī annī
I am the All-Forgiving, the All-Compassionate.
Ana 'l-Ghafūru 'r-Raḥīm. (15:49)

—which He followed immediately with:

And that My torment is the painful doom.
wa anna ʿadhābī huwa 'l-ʿadhābu 'l-alīm. (15:50)

—so that hope would not take charge of you completely. He described Himself (Exalted is He) as:

The Stern in punishment.
Shadīdi 'l-ʿiqābi. (40:3)

—then He added immediately:

The Bountiful. There is no god but He.
Dhi 'ṭ-Ṭawl: lā ilāha illā Hū. (40:3)

—so that fear would not take charge of you completely. Even more surprising is His saying (Glory be to Him and Exalted is He):

And Allāh warns you to beware of Himself.
wa yuḥadhdhiru-kumu 'llāhu Nafsah. (3:30)

—which He followed immediately with:

> And Allāh is Kind and Gentle with His servants.
> *wa 'llāhu Ra'ūfun bi-'l-'ibād.* (3:30)

More surprising than this is His saying (Glory be to Him and Exalted is He):

> If someone fears the All-Merciful in secret....
> *man khashiya 'r-Raḥmāna bi'l-ghaibi....* (50:33)

—for He has linked fear to the Name "the All-Merciful [*ar-Raḥmān*]," not to another of His Names, such as "the All-Compelling [*al-Jabbār*]," "the Avenger [*al-Muntaqim*]," or "the All-Sublime [*al-Mutakabbir*]." He has done so to connect fear with mercy, so that fear will not overwhelm your heart completely. The instilling of fear is thus accompanied by a reassuring and calming influence, as when you say: "You must surely be afraid of offending the tender-hearted mother!" "You must surely be afraid of offending the kind father!" "You must surely beware of offending the noble commander!" The purpose of that is to strike a fair balance, so that you do not swing towards false security or despair.

May Allāh include you, and us, among those who cultivate this wise remembrance, and who act upon it through His mercy! He is the Generous, the Noble One. There is no might nor any power except with Allāh, the All-High, the Almighty.

The second essential: The actions and dealings of Allāh (Almighty and Glorious is He)

As for the aspect of fear, you must know that Iblīs worshipped Allāh for eighty thousand years. It is said that he never stepped away from a spot, without first performing an act of prostration before Allāh (Exalted is He) in that place. Then he disobeyed one commandment [to prostrate himself before Adam], so Allāh expelled him from His door, wiped eighty thousand years of worship from his face, cursed him till the Day of Doom, and prepared for him a painful torment, lasting for all eternity.

According to traditional report, the truthful and trustworthy [Prophet Muḥammad] (Allāh's blessings and peace be upon him) once saw Gabriel (peace be upon him) clinging to the curtains of the Ka'ba, while screaming and shouting [in fear]: "My God and my Master! Do not change my name, and do not alter my body!"

As for Adam (Allāh bless him and give him peace), His chosen friend and His Prophet, whom He created with His hand, before whom He made the angels prostrate themselves, and whom He transported on their necks into His vicinity; he lived in comfort [in the Garden of Paradise], but then he ate a single morsel for which he had not been granted permission, so he heard the call: "If someone disobeys Me, he will surely not be My neighbour!" Allāh then summoned the angels who carried Adam's couch, and commanded them to hurl him down from heaven to heaven, until they dropped him on the earth. According to traditional report, Allāh did not accept Adam's repentance, so he wept over that [act of disobedience he had committed] for two hundred years. He suffered the humiliation and tribulation that he suffered, and his offspring were left with the dire consequences of that [sin of his] for all eternity.

As for Noah, the Shaikh of the Envoys (may Allāh's blessings and peace be upon him and upon them all), who endured what he endured for the sake of his religion, he spoke just a single word that was out of place, so he heard the call:

> So do not ask of Me
> *fa-lā tas'al-nī*
> that whereof you have no knowledge.
> *mā laisa la-ka bi-hi 'ilm:*
> I admonish you, lest you be among the ignorant.
> *innī a'iẓu-ka an takūna mina 'l-jāhilīn.* (11:46)

According to some of the traditional reports, he did not raise his head heavenwards for forty years, due to his sense of shame before Allāh.

As for Abraham, Allāh's Bosom Friend [*Khalīlu 'llāh*] (peace be upon him), he committed only one mistake. He felt terribly afraid, so he made the humble entreaty:

> And Who, I ardently hope, will forgive me
> *wa 'lladhī aṭma'u an yaghfira lī*
> my sin on the Day of Doom.
> *khaṭī'atī yawma 'd-dīn.* (26:82)

It is related that he wept from the intensity of fear, so Allāh (Exalted is He) sent him the trustworthy Gabriel (peace be upon him), who said to him: "O Abraham, have you ever seen a bosom friend torment his bosom friend with fire?" Abraham replied: "O Gabriel, if I remember my mistake, I shall forget His bosom friendship!"

As for Moses (Allāh bless him and give him peace), the son of ʿImrān, he was guilty of delivering one slap out of anger. He felt terribly afraid, so he humbled himself and sought forgiveness, saying:

> "My Lord, I have wronged myself,
> *Rabbi innī ẓalamtu nafsī*
> so forgive me!"
> *fa-'ghfir lī.* (28:16)

As for Baʿlām ibn Bāʿūrāʾ, who lived in the time of Moses (peace be upon him), he was remarkable in that, when he looked towards the sky, he would see the Heavenly Throne [*ʿArsh*]. He is the person referred to in Allāh's saying (Exalted is He):

> Recite to them the tale of him to whom
> *wa 'tlu ʿalai-him nabaʾa 'lladhī*
> We gave Our signs, but he sloughed them off.
> *ātainā-hu āyāti-nā fa-'nsalakha min-hā.* (7:175)

His only offence was that he showed a predilection for this world and its people, on one occasion, and omitted a single mark of respect for one of Allāh's saintly friends. Allāh therefore stripped him of his knowledge and understanding, and compared him to the dog that is chased away, for He said:

> His likeness is therefore as the likeness of the dog;
> *fa-mathalu-hu ka-māthali 'l-kalb:*
> if you attack him, he pants with his tongue out,
> *in taḥmil ʿalai-hi yalhath*
> and if you leave him, he pants with his tongue out.
> *aw tatruk-hu yalhath:*
> Such is the likeness of the people who deny Our signs.
> *dhālika mathalu 'l-qawmi 'lladhīna kadhdhabū bi-āyāti-nā*
> So narrate to them the story,
> *fa-'qṣuṣi 'l-qaṣaṣa*
> for then they may reflect.
> *laʿalla-hum yatafakkarūn.* (7:176)

Balʿām's offence thus plunged him into the sea of error and perdition, for all eternity. I have even heard one of the scholars say: "At the beginning of his career, he was so remarkable that twelve thousand inkwells were provided in his classroom, for the students who took notes from him. Then he became outstanding as the first to compile a book, in which he stated that the universe has no creator." We take refuge with Allāh [from that blasphemy]! Then we take refuge with Allāh from His displeasure, from His painful torment, and from His disappointment, which we have no strength to endure. Consider the wickedness of this world and its evil, especially in its impact on the scholars, wake up and take heed, for the matter is perilous, life is short, too little work is done, and the Critic is Perceptive. If He sets the seal of goodness on our deeds, and pardons our mistakes, that is not difficult for Him.

As for David (peace be upon him), Allāh's deputy [*khalīfa*] on His earth, he committed one sin, so he wept over that, until his tears caused grass to sprout on the ground. He said: "My God, will You not have mercy on my weeping and my humble entreaty?" He received the reply: "O David, you have forgotten your sin, but you have remembered your weeping!" Allāh did not accept his repentance for forty days, or, some say, for forty years.

As for Allāh's Prophet Jonah (peace be upon him), he was guilty of one inappropriate burst of anger, so Allāh imprisoned him in the belly of the whale, beneath the depth of the oceans for forty days, while he cried:

> "There is no god but You. Glory be to You!
> *an lā ilāha illā Anta subḥāna-ka*
> I have been one of the evildoers."
> *innī kuntu mina 'ẓ-ẓālimīn.* (21:87)

The angels heard his voice, so they said: "Our God and our Master, a familiar voice from a place unknown!" Allāh (Exalted is He) said: "That is the voice of My servant, Jonah," so the angels interceded on his behalf. Then, in spite of all that, He changed his name [to Dhu 'n-Nūn], for He said:

> And Dhu 'n-Nūn....
> *wa Dha 'n-Nūni....* (21:87)

—and thereby linked him to his prison [since Dhu 'n-Nūn means

"Occupant of the Whale"]. Then Allāh said (Exalted is He):

> And the big fish swallowed him
> *fa-'ltaqama-hu 'l-ḥūtu*
> while he was blameworthy.
> *wa huwa mulīm.*
> And had he not been
> *fa-law lā anna-hu kāna*
> one of those who glorify [the Lord],
> *mina 'l-musabbiḥīna*
> he would have tarried in its belly
> *la-labitha fī baṭni-hi*
> until the day when they are resurrected.
> *ilā yawmi yubʿathūn.* (37:142-44)

Then He mentioned His blessing and His gracious favour, for He said (Exalted is He):

> Had there not overtaken him a blessing
> *law lā an tadāraka-hu niʿmatun*
> from his Lord, he would have been cast
> *min Rabbi-hi la-nubidha*
> upon the wilderness, while he was reprobate.
> *bi'l-ʿarāʾi wa huwa madhmūm.* (68:49)

You must contemplate this stricture, O miserable wretch!

Let us now move forward in time to the Chief of the Envoys, the most noble of Allāh's creatures, to whom He said:

> So tread the straight path as you are commanded,
> *fa-'staqim ka-mā umirta*
> and those who turn [to Allāh] with you,
> *wa man tāba maʿa-ka*
> and do not transgress.
> *wa lā taṭghaw:*
> He is All-Seeing of what you do.
> *inna-hu bi-mā taʿmalūna Baṣīr.* (11:112)

The Prophet (Allāh bless him and give him peace) used to say:

> Hūd [the 11th Sūra of the Qurʾān] and its sisters have made my hair turn grey!

It is said that he was referring to this verse [*āya*] and others like it in the Qurʾān, for Allāh (Exalted is He) said:

> And ask forgiveness for your sin.
> *wa 'staghfir li-dhanbi-ka.* (40:55)

—until Allāh bestowed forgiveness upon him, and said:

> And We have relieved you of your burden,
> *wa waḍaʿnā ʿan-ka wizra-k:*
> that weighed down your back.
> *alladhī anqaḍa ẓahra-k.* (94:2,3)

He also said (Exalted is He):

> That Allāh may forgive you
> *li-yaghfira laka 'llāhu*
> your former and your latter sins.
> *mā taqaddama min dhanbi-ka wa mā taʾakhkhara.* (48:2)

After that, the Prophet (Allāh bless him and give him peace) used to pray throughout the night, until his feet became swollen, so they would ask him: "Why do you still do this, O Messenger of Allāh, when Allāh has already forgiven you your former and your latter sins?" He would reply: "Am I not a grateful servant?" He would also say (peace be upon him):

> If Jesus and I were taken to task for what these two [lower selves of ours] have earned, we would suffer a torment suffered by no other creature.

He used to pray throughout the night, and he would weep and say:

> I take refuge with Your pardon from Your punishment, and with Your good pleasure from Your displeasure! I take refuge with You from You! I cannot praise You as well as You have praised Yourself!

As for the Companions, the best of a generation and the best of a community, they used to indulge in a certain amount of frivolity, so this saying of Allāh (Exalted is He) was sent down:

> Is not the time now ripe for the hearts
> *a-lam yaʾni li'lladhīna āmanū*
> of those who believe to be humbled
> *an takhshaʿa qulūbu-hum*
> to the Remembrance of Allāh
> *li-dhikri 'llāhi*
> and to the Truth which He has sent down,
> *wa mā nazala mina 'l-Ḥaqqi*
> and that they do not become like those
> *wa lā yakūna ka-'lladhīna*
> who received the Book of old,
> *ūtu 'l-Kitāba min qablu*
> but the term was prolonged for them,
> *fa-ṭālaʿalai-himu 'l-amadu*

> and so their hearts were hardened,
> *fa-qasat qulūbu-hum*
> and many of them are profligates.
> *wa kathīrun min-hum fāsiqūn*. (57:16)

Allāh (Exalted is He) then imposed strict rules and regulations and proprieties on this [Islāmic] Community, despite the fact that it is blessed with merciful compassion, so that Yūnus ibn ʿUbaid used to say: "Since He has prescribed the amputation of a member of your body [your hand], as the penalty for stealing five silver coins, you cannot be sure that His torment tomorrow [in the Hereafter] will not be similar!" We beseech Allāh (Exalted is He), the Compassionate, the Generous (Glory be to Him), imploring Him not to treat us with anything but His pure generosity. He is the Most Merciful of the merciful.

As for the aspect of hope, you must speak freely about Allāh's abundant mercy. Who knows its full extent? Who knows its true quality and its utmost limit? He is the One who pardons seventy years of unbelief in exchange for an hour of belief. Allāh (Exalted is He) has said:

> Tell those who disbelieve that, if they desist,
> *qul li'lladhīna kafarū in yantahū*
> that which is past will be forgiven them.
> *yughfar la-hum mā qad salaf*. (8:38)

Consider the case of Pharaoh's sorcerers, who came to fight Moses (peace be upon him), and who swore by the might of Pharoah, his enemy. What actually happened was that they witnessed the miraculous sign of Moses (peace be upon him), so they acknowledged the Truth and they cried:

> "We believe in the Lord of All the Worlds!"
> *āmannā bi-Rabbi 'l-ʿālamīn*. (26:47)

There is no mention of their having adopted any practice in addition to this [affirmation of belief], but notice how often Allāh has mentioned them in glowing terms in His Glorious Book. Notice how many major and minor sins He forgave them, in exchange for an hour—or an instant—of belief. They did nothing but say, from the sincerity of their hearts:

> "We believe in the Lord of All the Worlds!"
> *āmannā bi-Rabbi 'l-ʿālamīn*. (26:47)

—but see how He accepted them and pardoned all their previous sins, and how He made them the chief witnesses [to the Truth] in the Garden of Paradise, for all eternity. Such is the condition of those who acknowledged Allāh and affirmed His Oneness for a moment, after all that sorcery, unbelief, error and corruption, so what is the condition of someone who devotes all his life to the affirmation of His Oneness, and sees no one as worthy of that in the two abodes, apart from Him?

Consider the Companions of the Cave [*Aṣḥāb al-Kahf*], and how they had spent all their lives in the state of unbelief:

> When they stood forth and said:
> *idh qāmū fa-qālū*
> "Our Lord is the Lord of the heavens and the earth.
> *Rabbu-nā Rabbu 's-samāwāti wa 'l-arḍi*
> We shall cry to no god beside Him."
> *lan nad'uwa min dūni-hi ilāhan.* (18:14)

—and they took refuge with Him. Notice how He accepted them and pardoned them, then extolled them and honoured them, for He said:

> And We turned them over to the right,
> *wa nuqallibu-hum dhāta 'l-yamīni*
> then over to the left.
> *wa dhāta 'sh-shimāl.* (18:18)

Notice how He treated them with great respect, and clothed them with awesome dignity, to the point where He said to the noblest of creatures in His sight:

> If you had observed them closely,
> *lawi 'ṭṭala'ta 'alai-him*
> you would surely have turned away from them in flight,
> *la-wallaita min-hum firāran*
> and would have been filled with awe of them.
> *wa la-muli'ta min-hum ru'bā.* (18:18)

Notice, indeed, how He honoured a dog that followed them, to the point of mentioning it several times in His Glorious Book. He assigned it to their custody in this world, and He will cause it to enter the Garden of Paradise in the Hereafter, honoured and revered. Such is His gracious treatment of a dog, which accompanied a group of people who acknowledged Him and affirmed His Oneness for a number of days, without performing any act of worship or service. What does this tell us, then, about His grace in dealing with His believing servant, who has served

Him, affirmed His Oneness and worshipped Him for seventy years? What if he lived for seventy thousand years? He would surely be a candidate for servanthood!

Notice how Allāh censured Abraham (peace be upon him) for invoking destruction upon the sinners, and how He censured Moses (peace be upon him) in the matter of Qārūn, for He said: "Qārūn appealed to you for help, but you did not help him. By My Might and Glory, if he asked Me for help, I would help him and pardon him!"

Notice how Allāh censured Jonah (peace be upon him) in the matter of his people, for He said: "You feel sorry for a gourd-tree, which I caused to grow for a while, then caused it to wither, but you do not feel sorry for a hundred thousand people or more!" Then notice how He accepted their excuse, and deflected the terrible torment from them, after they had gone astray.

Notice how Allāh censured the Chief of the Envoys (may Allāh bless him and all his family) in connection with the following incident: It is related that the Prophet (Allāh bless him and give him peace) entered [the Sanctuary] through the Banī Shaiba Gate, where he saw some people laughing. He said: "Why are you laughing? Let me not see you laughing!" Then, when he was beside the Black Stone [in the Ka'ba], their previous despondency returned to them. He said:

> Gabriel came to me and said: "O Muḥammad, Allāh (Exalted is He) is saying to you: 'Why do you make My servants despair of My mercy?
>
> Announce to My servants
> *nabbi' 'ibādī*
> that I am the All-Forgiving, the All-Compassionate.'"
> *annī Ana 'l-Ghafūru 'r-Raḥīm.* (15:49)

This Messenger of Allāh (Allāh bless him and give him peace) says:

> Allāh (Exalted is He) is More Compassionate with His servant than the tender mother with her child.

According to the well-known traditional report, the Prophet (Allāh bless him and give him peace) also said:

> Allāh (Exalted is He) has more than a hundred mercies. He has divided one of them among the jinn, the human race and the animals, so it helps them to feel affection and sympathy for one another. He has kept ninety-nine of them in store for Himself, so that He may use them to treat His servants mercifully on the Day of Resurrection.

Since Allāh (Exalted is He) has given you a share of one mercy, all of these noble and splendid gifts are available to you, including knowledge of Him (Glory be to Him), membership in this mercifully blessed Community, and knowledge of the Sunna [the exemplary custom of the Prophet (Allāh bless him and give him peace)], as well as all the other external and internal blessings you enjoy. It is therefore reasonable to hope, from His tremendous grace, that He will perfect all that, for if someone embarks on good work completion is incumbent upon him. It is reasonable to hope that He will grant you an abundant portion from those other ninety-nine mercies. We therefore beseech Allāh (Glory be to Him), invoking His grace and imploring Him not to dash our hopes for His tremendous favour. He is the Generous Master, the Munificent, the All-Compassionate.

The third essential:
Remembering what Allāh (Exalted is He)
has promised and threatened with regard to the Hereafter

In this connection, we must remember five situations: (1) death, (2) the grave, (3) the Resurrection, (4) the Garden of Paradise, and (5) the Fire of Hell. We must also remember the enormous peril that each of them contains, for the obedient and the disobedient, the negligent and the diligent.

1. As for death, the thought of it reminds me of two men:

—Ibn Shubruma, who is reported as having said: "Along with ash-Sha'bī, I paid a visit to an invalid who was lying sick in bed. Another man was by his side, instructing him to say: 'There is no god but Allāh, Alone without any partner [*lā ilāha illa 'llāhu Waḥdah; lā sharīka la-h*],' so ash-Sha'bī said to the man: 'Be gentle with him!' Then the invalid spoke up, saying: 'Whether you instruct me or do not instruct me, I shall not fail to make that affirmation.' Then he recited:

> And He imposed on them
> *wa alzama-hum*
> the statement of true devotion,
> *kalimata 't-taqwā*
> for they were worthy of it and deserving of it.
> *wa kānū aḥaqqa bi-hā wa ahla-hā.* (48:26)

"Then ash-Sha'bī said: 'Praise be to Allāh, who has saved our companion!'"

—It is related that a pupil of al-Fuḍail ibn 'Iyās was close to death, so al-Fuḍail entered his presence, sat by his head, and recited the Sūra entitled *Yā-Sīn*. "O teacher," he said, "do not recite this Sūra," so al-Fuḍail fell silent for a while. Then he instructed him to say: "There is no god but Allāh [*lā ilāha illa 'llāh*]," but the pupil said: "I shall not say it, because I am exempt from it!" He died there and then, so al-Fuḍail went home and spent forty days weeping, without leaving his house.

Then, in a dream, he saw his pupil being dragged towards Hell, so he said: "Why did Allāh deprive you of knowledge and understanding, when you were the most knowledgeable of my pupils?" The pupil replied: "For three reasons: First of all, I was guilty of calumny, for I told my companions the opposite of what I told you. Second, I was guilty of envy. I was envious of my companions. Third, I had a disease, so I went to the physician and asked him about it, and he said: 'You must drink a bottle of wine each year, for, unless you do so, the disease will stay with you.' I acted on his advice."

We take refuge with Allāh from His displeasure, which we lack the strength to endure.

I also remember the condition of two other men:

—'Abdu'llāh ibn al-Mubārak (may Allāh the Exalted bestow His mercy upon him). It is related that when he was close to death, he looked up towards Heaven, laughed, and said:

> For the like of this, let the workers work.
> *li-mithli hādhā fa-l'-ya'mali 'l-'āmilūn.* (37:61)

[This Qur'ānic verse reminds me that] I also heard [my Shaikh] Imām al-Ḥaramain (may Allāh be well pleased with him) relate that Professor Abū Bakr (may Allāh bestow His mercy upon him) once said: "I had a companion in the days of teaching. He was a novice devoted to learning, righteous and committed to worshipful service. Despite his dedicated striving, however, he was acquiring only a little knowledge, so we found his condition surprising. Then he fell ill, so he stayed in his place among the saintly friends in the convent [*ribāṭ*], and did not enter the hospital. He continued to exert himself, despite his illness, so his condition deteriorated while I was at his side. While he was like that, he raised his eyes towards Heaven, then said to me: 'O Ibn Fūrak:

> For the like of this, let the workers work.
> *li-mithli hādhā fa-l'-ya'mali 'l-'āmilūn.* (37:61)'

"He died at that very moment (may Allāh bestow His mercy upon him)."

—Mālik ibn Dīnār (may Allāh bestow His mercy upon him). It is related that he entered the presence of a neighbour of his, who was close to death. "O Mālik," he said, "two mountains of fire are in front of me, and I am obliged to climb them." Mālik said: "I asked his family about him, and they told me: 'He used to have two measures, one for measuring what he dispensed, and the other for measuring what he received.' I sent for the two measures, and struck one of them against the other till I smashed them both to pieces. Then I asked the man how he was, and he said: 'The matter has only become more serious for me!'"

2. As for the grave and the situation after death, this subject also reminds me of the condition of two men:

—According to one of the righteous: "I saw Sufyān ath-Thawrī in a dream, after his death, so I asked: 'How is your condition, O Abū 'Abdi'llāh [Father of 'Abdu'llāh]?' He turned away from me and said: 'This is not the time for agnomens,' so I rephrased my question and asked: 'How is your condition, O Sufyān?' He responded in poetry, saying:

> 'I looked at my Lord directly and He said to me:
> "Welcome! Enjoy My good pleasure, O Ibn Sa'īd!
>
> You used to keep vigil when the night turned dark,
> with many an ardent tear and a steady heart,
>
> so draw near and choose any palace you wish,
> and visit Me, for I am not far away from you."'"

—It is related that someone was seen in a dream, looking very pale, with his hands fettered to his neck. He was asked: "What has Allāh done with you?" so he gave the poetic reply:

> Gone is a time with which we used to play,
> and this is a time that plays with us.

I am also reminded of the condition of two other men:

—It is related that one of the righteous said: "I had a son who was martyred, and I did not see him in a dream until the night when ʿUmar ibn ʿAbd al-ʿAzīz died (may Allāh be well pleased with him). I saw him that night, so I said: 'O my son, have you not become a corpse?' He said: 'No, but I have been martyred, so I am alive, sustained in the presence of Allāh (Exalted is He).' I said: 'What has brought you here?' He replied: 'The proclamation was made to the people of Heaven: "Let no Prophet, no champion of Truth, and no martyr stay away from the funeral service of ʿUmar ibn ʿAbd al-ʿAzīz!" I therefore came to attend his funeral service, and now I have come to you, to greet you with the salutation of peace.'"

—It is related that Hishām ibn Ḥassān once said: "A young son of mine died, and I saw him in a dream. He appeared as a grey-haired old man, so I said: 'O my son, what is this grey-haired condition?' He replied: 'When so-and-so approached us, Hell emitted a sizzling groan at his approach, so we all turned grey, without exception.'" We take refuge with Allāh, the All-Compassionate, from the painful torment!

3. As for the Resurrection [*Qiyāma*], you must contemplate the saying of Allāh (Exalted is He):

> On the day when We shall muster the truly devout
> *yawma naḥshuru 'l-muttaqīna*
> unto the All-Merciful, in fine style,
> *ila 'r-Raḥmāni wafdā:*
> and We shall drive the guilty culprits
> *wa nasūqu 'l-mujrimīna*
> into Hell, like a herd of beasts.
> *ilā jahannama wirdā.* (19:85,86)

One person will emerge from his grave, to find [the heavenly steed] Buraq at its head, as well as the crown and fine garments prepared for him, so he will dress and ride to the Gardens of Bliss. On account of his dignity, he will not be left to walk to the Garden of Paradise on his own two feet. Another will emerge from his grave, to encounter the stokers of Hell [*zabāniya*], along with the shackles and chains that will bind him. They will not let the poor wretch walk to the Fire on his own two feet. He will be dragged to the Inferno on his face. We take refuge with Allāh from His displeasure!

I have also heard one of the scholars relate that the Prophet (Allāh bless him and give him peace) once said:

> When the Day of Resurrection has arrived, one set of people will emerge from their graves with dromedaries for them to ride. Those dromedaries will have green wings, so they will fly with them over the plains of the Resurrection, until they alight on the walls of the Garden of Paradise. Then, when the angels see them, they will say to one another: "Who are these?" The only response will be: "We do not know. Perhaps they are members of the Community of Muḥammad (Allāh bless him and give him peace)." Then one of the angels will come to them and say: "Who are you?" To which of the communities do you belong?" They will reply: "We belong to the Community of Muḥammad (Allāh bless him and give him peace)," so the angels will say to them: "Have you been subject to the reckoning?" They will say: "No," so the angels will say: "Have you been weighed?" They will again say: "No," so the angels will say: "Have you read your records?" They will again say: "No," so the angels will say: "Go back, for all of that is behind you." They will say: "Have you given us something for which we may be called to account?"

According to another version of this traditional report:

> [They will say to the angels]: "We have not been guilty of anything that would make us deviate or go astray, but we worshipped our Lord until He summoned us, so we have answered Him." A crier will then proclaim [on behalf of the Lord]: "My servants have told the truth. There is no case to be made against those who do good."

Allāh is All-Forgiving, Compassionate. You have surely heard His saying (Exalted is He):

> Is he who is hurled into the Fire better,
> *a-fa-man yulqā fi 'n-nāri khairun*
> or he who comes secure on the Day of Resurrection?
> *am man ya᾿tī āminan Yawm al-Qiyāma.* (41:40)

How splendid is a man who witnesses those terrors, earthquakes and catastrophes, yet is so secure that no alarm disturbs his heart, and no heaviness weighs it down! We beseech Allāh the Almighty, imploring Him to include you, and us, among His blessed friends. That is not difficult for Allāh (Magnificent is His Majesty)!

4 & 5. As for the Garden of Paradise and the Fire of Hell, you must reflect on the relevant verses [*āyāt*] in the Book of Allāh (Exalted is He). These include His saying (Exalted is He):

> And their Lord will slake their thirst
> *wa saqā-hum Rabbu-hum*

with a pure drink.
sharāban ṭahūrā.
[And it will be said unto them]:
"Behold, this is a reward for you.
inna hādhā kāna la-kum jazā'an
Your endeavour has found acceptance."
wa kāna sa'yu-kum mashkūrā. (76:21,22)

He has also said (Exalted is He), referring to the others [the unbelievers]:

[They will say]:
"Our Lord, bring us forth out of it!
Rabba-nā akhrij-nā min-hā
Then, if we revert, we shall be evildoers indeed."
fa-in 'udnā fa-innā ẓālimūn.

He will say: "Slink away into it,
qāla 'khsa'ū fī-hā
and do not speak to Me."
wa lā tukallimūn. (23:107,108)

It is also related that they will turn into dogs, barking at one another in the Fire of Hell. We take refuge with Allāh, the Gentle, the All-Compassionate, from the painful torment!

According to Yaḥyā ibn Mu'ādh ar-Rāzī (may Allāh bestow His mercy upon him): "We do not know which of the two disasters is more terrible: losing the Gardens of Paradise, or entering the Fires of Hell. As for the Garden, its loss is intolerable. As for the Fire, its torment is insufferable. In any case, however, the loss of the bliss [of Paradise] is easier to bear than the torment of the Inferno. The greatest calamity and the most terrible disaster is the infinite duration [of the loss and the suffering]. If only the situation had an expiration date, it would at least be easier to contemplate! In fact, however, it will last for all eternity without end, so what heart can bear that prospect? What temperament can endure that with patience? That is why Jesus (peace be upon him) said: 'The hearts of the fearful are stopped by remembering the everlasting state of those who are everlastingly doomed.'"

It was mentioned in the presence of al-Ḥasan [al-Baṣrī] that the last of those who emerge from the Fire will be a man called Hannād. He will have been tormented for a thousand years, while crying: "O Tender One [*Ḥannān*], O Beneficent One [*Mannān*]!" This made al-Ḥasan weep, and he said: "If only I were Hannād!" His listeners were astonished, so he said: "Woe unto you! Will there not be a day when he comes out [at the end of a thousand years in the Fire]?"

The whole matter hinges, therefore, on one basic point, and that is the point that shatters backs, turns faces pale, make livers dissolve, stops hearts from beating, and causes the servants' eyes to bleed. That is the fear of being deprived of true knowledge [*maʿrifa*], for this is the ultimate fear of the fearful, over which the eyes of the weepers weep. According to one of the righteous: "Anxieties are three in number: (1) Anxiety about worshipful obedience, in that it may not be accepted. (2) Anxiety about sinful disobedience, in that it may not be forgiven. (3) Anxiety about true knowledge, in that it may be stripped away." According to one of the sincerely devout: "In reality, all anxiety is one, and that is anxiety about the deprival of true knowledge. Every other anxiety is insignificant by comparison, since it has a solution."

We are told that Yūsuf ibn Asbāṭ (may Allāh the Exalted bestow His mercy upon him) once said: "I entered the presence of Sufyān (may Allāh the Exalted bestow His mercy upon him), who wept throughout every night. I asked him: 'Is this weeping of yours over sins?' He waved a straw, and said: 'Sins are less important to Allāh than this! My only dread is that Allāh may deprive me of Islām."

We beseech Allāh, our Beneficent Lord (Glory be to Him), imploring Him not to try us with an affliction, to grant us much of His bounty, through His gracious favour, and to let us die in the religion of Islām. He is the Most Merciful of the merciful!

We have discussed the cause of the ultimate evil, and its significance, in the book entitled: "Revival of the Religious Sciences [*Iḥyāʾ ʿUlūm ad-Dīn*]," so you should study it there. The introduction to it here [in the present work] is concise, so try to understand this summary correctly, for the detailed account is more than can be imagined and described. Perhaps you will succeed, with Allāh's help and the blessing of His enabling grace!

You may ask: "Which of the two paths is more practicable, the path of fear or the path of hope?"

The answer will be: Neither by itself, but rather the combination of the two. According to one of the scholars: "If hope prevails over someone, he becomes a Murji'[39] because of it, and he may be in danger of becoming a Khurramī.[40] If fear prevails over someone, he becomes a Ḥarūrī."[41] The point is that the servant should not experience either of the two exclusively, for, in reality, genuine hope is inseparable from genuine fear, and genuine fear is inseparable from genuine hope. That is why, as someone said: "All hope belongs to the people of fear, not of security, and all fear belongs to the people of hope, not of despair."

You may ask: "Is one of the two preferable or more important in any particular situation?"

You should therefore know that if the servant is healthy and strong, fear is more appropriate for him. If he is sick and weak, on the other hand, especially if he is close to the Hereafter, hope is more appropriate. That is what I have heard the scholars say. According to traditional report, Allāh (Glory be to Him and Exalted is He) says:

> I am with those whose hearts are broken from fear of Me.[42]

Hope becomes more appropriate for the servant at that moment [of death], because of his heart being broken, while his fear takes precedence in the time of health, strength and capability. That is why they [whose hearts are broken] are told:

> Do not fear and do not grieve!
> *lā takhāfū wa lā taḥzanū.* (41:30)

You may say: "Are there are not many traditional reports concerning the need to think well of Allāh, and encouraging that attitude?"

You should therefore know that thinking well of Allāh (Exalted is He) involves being wary of disobeying Him, being afraid of His chastisement, and striving hard in His service.

[39] That is to say, he becomes a member of the sect called the Murji'a ["Postponers"], who probably acquired that name because of their great emphasis on the doctrine of *irjā'* [postponement], according to which the judgement of sinful believers must be deferred until the Resurrection.

[40] The Khurramiyya sect are said to have espoused a doctrine based on *ibāḥa* [permissibility], according to which everything that is "agreeable" [*khurram* in Persian] is lawful.

[41] That is to say, he becomes a member of the Ḥarūriyya sect, more commonly known as the Khawārij ["Seceders" or "Rebels"]. They withdrew to the village of Ḥarūrā' after they had deserted the army of 'Alī (may Allāh be well pleased with him), in protest against his appointment of a human tribunal—instead of relying on the Word of Allāh in the Qur'ān—to settle the violent dispute over the rightful leadership of the Islāmic community.

[42] This is a Sacred Tradition [*Ḥadīth Qudsī*], not a Qur'ānic verse [*āya*].

You should also know that there is a basic principle here, and an important concept, which many people fail to understand correctly. That principle is the difference between hope [*rajāʾ*] and desire [*umniyya*]. Hope is based on a foundation, whereas desire is not based on a foundation. For instance, if a farmer sows seeds, works hard, and gathers a harvest for threshing, then says: "I hope this will provide me with a hundred *qafīz* [large measures of flour]," that is a valid hope on his part. If another person sows no seeds, and does not work for a single day, but goes off and sleeps for much of the year, then says, when the time of threshing arrives: "I hope I will get a hundred measures of flour out of this," he will be asked: "From where do you get this hope?" That is a desire without foundation.

Likewise in the case of the servant, if he works hard in the service of Allāh, refrains from disobedience to Allāh (Exalted is He), then says: "I hope that Allāh will accept this slight effort from me, perfect this shortcoming, magnify this reward, and pardon the mistakes," and if he thinks well [of Allāh], this is a valid hope on his part. On the other hand, if he neglects all that, refrains from acts of worshipful obedience, commits acts of sinful disobedience, and is indifferent to Allāh's displeasure (Exalted is He) and His approval, to His promise and His threat, then dares to say: "I hope Allāh will grant me the Garden of Paradise and salvation from the Fire of Hell," that is a desire on his part, with no substance to underpin it. He calls it a hope and a good opinion [of Allāh], but that is a mistake and an error on his part. As the poet said:

You hope for salvation,
but you have not followed its courses.
The ship does not sail on dry land!

This principle is further explained by the saying attributed to the Prophet (Allāh bless him and give him peace):

> The shrewd and skilful person is one who subjugates his lower self, and works for what is after death. The incompetent is one who follows his lower self and his passion, and foists his desires on Allāh (Almighty and Glorious is He).

In this context, al-Ḥasan al-Baṣrī (may Allāh be well pleased with him) once said: "Some people are so preoccupied with desires for forgiveness, that they leave this world bankrupt, with no good work to their credit. One of them says: 'I think well of my Lord.' He is lying.

If he really thought well of his Lord, he would do good work for His sake." Then al-Ḥasan recited the saying of Allāh (Exalted is He):

> So whoever hopes for the meeting with his Lord,
> *fa-man kāna yarjū liqāʾa Rabbi-hi*
> let him do righteous work,
> *fa-'l-yaʿmal ʿamalan ṣāliḥan*
> and let him give no one any share at all
> *wa lā yushrik*
> in the worship due unto his Lord.
> *bi-ʿibādati Rabbi-hi aḥadā.* (18:110)

> And that, your thought that you did think
> *wa dhālikum ẓannu-kumu 'lladhī ẓanantum*
> about your Lord, has ruined you,
> *bi-Rabbi-kum ardā-kum*
> and you find yourselves among the lost.
> *fa-aṣbaḥtum mina 'l-khāsirīn.* (41:23)

According to Jaʿfar aḍ-Ḍabuʿī (may Allāh bestow His mercy upon him): "I saw Abū Maisara, the worshipful servant, and I noticed that his ribs were visible, because he worked so hard. I said: 'May Allāh bestow His mercy upon you! Allāh's mercy is vast indeed!' He was angry at this, and he said: 'Have you seen me show any sign of despair? Allāh's mercy is near to those who do good work!' His words made me weep."

Since all the Messengers, all the Abdāl[43] and all the saints were committed, with all this dedicated effort, to worshipful obedience and the avoidance of sinful disobedience, what do you say? Did they not have a good opinion of Allāh? Of course they did, for they were very well aware of the vast extent of His mercy, and they had an excellent opinion of His generosity, but they knew that all that, without dedicated effort, was merely desire and delusion. You must therefore consider this important point, reflect on their condition, and wake up from your slumber. Allāh (Exalted is He) is the Custodian of enabling grace!

Subsection

The gist of the matter is this: You must remember the vast extent of Allāh's mercy (Exalted is He), which has outstripped His wrath and encompassed everything, then remember that you belong to this

[43] See n. 14 on p. 48 above.

Community, which is mercifully blessed and noble in the sight of Allāh (Exalted is He), then remember the abundance of His splendid favour and the perfection of His noble generosity, and that He has addressed His Book to you with the heading:

> In the Name of Allāh, the All-Merciful, the All-Compassionate.
> *Bismi'llāhi 'r-Raḥmāni 'r-Raḥīm.*

You must also remember the multiplicity of His favours to you, and the blessing He has bestowed upon you, both outwardly and inwardly, without any intercessor or mediator on your behalf.

From another aspect, you must remember the perfection of His majesty and His might, and the magnificence of His authority and His dignity. You must remember the violence of His wrath, which the heavens and the earth cannot withstand. You must remember the enormity of your heedlessness, and the multiplicity of your sins, as well as your coarseness in contrast with the subtlety of His way of working, and the momentousness of His dealing with the all-embracing extent of His knowledge and His awareness of faults [*'uyūb*] and mysteries [*ghuyūb*].

Then you must remember the beauty of His promise and His reward, the essence of which no imagination can fathom, as well as the violence of His threat and the agony of His punishment, the recollection of which no heart can bear. Sometimes you must contemplate His gracious favour. Sometimes you must contemplate His torment. Sometimes you must contemplate His kindness and His mercy. Sometimes you must contemplate your lower self, observing its coarse and offensive behaviour.

If you do all this, it will lead you to fear and hope. You will have travelled the central thoroughfare, and avoided the two perilous sides—false security and despair—instead of wandering in them with those who go astray, and perishing with those who perish. You will have drunk the mixed drink of moderation, so you will not perish from the coldness of unadulterated hope, nor from the heat of unadulterated fear. It seems to me that you have reached the goal successfully, and been cured of the two diseases safely. You have found the lower self motivated to practise worshipful obedience, and committed to service by night and by day, without any pause or absent-mindedness, avoiding sinful acts of disobedience and atrocities, so you have finally been relieved of it [as a troublemaker].

As Nawf al-Bikālī said: "When Nawf remembers the Garden of Paradise, his ardent yearning is prolonged, and when he remembers the Fire of Hell, his sleep flies away."

You have now become one of the chosen few, the worshipful élite, whom Allāh (Exalted is He) has described in His saying:

> They used to compete with one another
> *inna-hum kānū yusāri'ūna*
> in good deeds, and they cried to Us
> *fi 'l-khairāti wa yad'ūna-nā*
> in longing and in fear,
> *raghaban wa rahabā:*
> and they were submissive unto Us.
> *wa kānū la-nā khāshi'īn.* (21:90)

You have left this dangerous hurdle behind you, with Allāh's consent (Exalted is He) and the blessing of His enabling grace. You will enjoy so much sweetness and serenity in this world, and so much noble treasure and splendid recompense awaits you in the Hereafter. We beseech Allāh (Exalted is He) to assist you, and us, with the blessing of His enabling grace and His guidance. He is the Most Merciful of the merciful and the Most Generous of the most generous. There is no might nor any power except with Allāh, the All-High, the Almighty.

The Sixth Hurdle
The hurdle of the impairments [*qawādiḥ*]

O my brother, may Allāh support you, and us, with the blessing of His enabling grace! Now that the way is clear to you, and the journey lies straight before you, your next duty is to separate your virtuous endeavour from everything that corrupts it and causes you to lose it. That can only be achieved by the practice of sincere devotion and gratitude, and by avoiding the opposite thereof, for two reasons:

1. The benefit contained in that practice, which is the blessing of acceptance from Allāh (Exalted is He) and the attainment of the reward. Without that acceptance and attainment, you will be rejected and deprived of the reward, in whole or in part. As related in the well-known tradition [*ḥadīth*], the Prophet (Allāh bless him and give him peace) once said:

> Allāh (Glory be to Him and Exalted is He) says: I am the Most Independent of those who are independent of partnership [*shirk*]. If a person does a job of work, and makes someone other than Me a partner in it, My share belongs to him [the partner], for I accept nothing but that which is purely for Me.

It is reported that Allāh (Exalted is He) will say to His servant on the Day of Resurrection, when he seeks the reward for his work:

> Were you not given space at the meetings? Were you not the head of the pack in the world? Did you not profit from your buying and selling? Were you not treated with honour?

The First Impairment [*qādiḥ*]
Hypocritical ostentation [*riyāʾ*]

These are examples of the danger and harm [that threaten your endeavour]. As for the danger of hypocritical ostentation [*riyāʾ*], it involves two ignominies and two disasters. The two ignominies are:

—First, ignominy in secret, in the form of blame in the presence of the angels, as related in the traditional report:

> The angels will raise the servant's work aloft, rejoicing in it, but Allāh (Exalted is He) will say: "Cast him into the Pit [*Sijjīn*], for he did not intend it for My sake!"

That servant and his work will thus be disgraced in the presence of the angels.

—Second, the ignominy of public exposure on the Day of Resurrection, in the presence of all creatures. It is related that the Prophet (Allāh bless him and give him peace) once said:

> The ostentatious hypocrite [*murā'ī*] will be addressed on the Day of Resurrection with four names: "O unbeliever [*yā kāfir*], O profligate [*yā fājir*], O traitor [*yā ghādir*] and O loser [*yā khāsir*]! Your endeavour has gone astray, and your recompense has been annulled, so there is no portion for you today. You must seek the recompense from those for whom you used to work, O swindler!"

According to another traditional report:

> A crier will proclaim on the Day of Resurrection, making all creatures hear: "Where are those who used to serve human beings? Stand up and receive your wages from those for whom you used to work, for I accept no work that anything has adulterated!

As for the two disasters, they are:

—First, the loss of the Garden of Paradise. The Prophet (Allāh bless him and give him peace) is reported as having said:

> The Garden of Paradise spoke, saying: "I am unlawful for every miser and ostentatious hypocrite!"

This report conveys two meanings: (1) The miser referred to is someone who is niggardly with the best of speech, that being the declaration: "There is no god but Allāh. Muḥammad is Allāh's Messenger (Allāh bless him and give him peace)." As for the ostentatious hypocrite, he is someone who is guilty of the most flagrant ostentation, for he is the hypocrite who makes a show of his faith [*īmān*] and his affirmation of Divine Oneness [*Tawḥīd*]. This interpretation leaves room for hope [of repentance]. (2) If someone does not desist from niggardliness and ostentation, and does not guard against them, he runs two risks: One is that the wickedness thereof may stick to him, so that he falls into unbelief and forfeits the Garden of Paradise absolutely. The only refuge is with Allāh! The other risk is deprival of faith, which will doom him to the Fire of Hell. We take refuge with Allāh from His displeasure and the violence of His wrath!

—The second disaster is entering the Fire of Hell. According to Abū Huraira (may Allāh be well pleased with him), the Prophet (Allāh bless him and give him peace) once said:

> The first to be summoned on the Day of Resurrection will be [three men]: a man who compiled the Qur'ān, a man who fought in the cause of Allāh, and a man who possessed much wealth.
>
> Allāh (Exalted is He) will say to the Qur'an-reader: "Did I not teach you what I sent down to My Messenger?" He will reply: "Yes indeed, O my Lord!" Allāh will then say: "What action did you take in accordance with what you learned?" To this he will reply: "I acted on it through the watches of the night and the ends of the day." Allāh will say: "You have told a lie," and the angels will say: "You have told a lie." Allāh (Glory be to Him) will go on to say: "You wished to have people say about you: 'So-and-so is a Qur'ān-reciter,' and that is what they said."
>
> The owner of wealth will be brought forward, and Allāh (Exalted is He) will say: "Did I not bestow abundance upon you, so that I did not leave you in need of anyone?" He will reply: "Yes indeed, O my Lord!" Allāh will then say: "What did you do with what I gave you?" To this he will reply: "I used to provide for my family and make charitable donations." Allāh will say: "You have told a lie," and the angels will say: "You have told a lie." Allāh (Glory be to Him) will go on to say: "You wished to have people say: 'You are very generous,' and that is what they said."
>
> The man who was slain in the cause of Allāh will then be brought forward, and Allāh will say: "What did you do?" He will reply: "I was commanded to wage the sacred struggle in Your cause, so I fought until I was killed." Allāh (Exalted is He) will say: ""You have told a lie," and the angels will say: "You have told a lie." Allāh will go on to say: "You wished to have people say about you: 'So-and-so is a brave and courageous man,' and that is what they said."

Allāh's Messenger (Allāh bless him and give him peace) then slapped his hand on his knees, and said:

> O Abū Huraira, those will be the first of Allāh's creatures to fuel the Fire of Hell!

Ibn 'Abbās (may Allāh be well pleased with him and his father) is reported as having said: "I heard Allāh's Messenger (Allāh bless him and give him peace) say:

> The Fire of Hell and its inhabitants will scream for refuge from the people guilty of hypocritical display.

"His listeners asked: 'O Messenger of Allāh, how will the Fire of Hell scream for refuge?' He replied:

> With [the noise of] the fierce heat by which they will be tormented."

In these ignominies [and disasters] there is an admonition for those endowed with faculties of perception. Allāh (Glory be to Him) is the Custodian of guidance, through His gracious favour.

You may say: "Tell me about the real meaning of sincerity [*ikhlāṣ*] and ostentation [*riyā᾽*], their legal status, and their effect on work."

You must therefore know that sincerity [*ikhlāṣ*], according to our scholars, is twofold: (1) sincerity in work, and (2) sincerity in seeking recompense.

As for sincerity in work, it is the intention to draw near to Allāh (Almighty and Glorious is He), to venerate His commandment and to answer His call. The incentive thereto is genuine belief. The opposite of this sincerity is hypocrisy [*nifāq*], which is drawing close to anything other than Allāh (Glory be to Him). According to our own Shaikh (may Allāh bestow His mercy upon him): "Hypocrisy is the corrupt belief held by the hyprocrite [*munāfiq*] about Allāh (Almighty and Glorious is He)."

As for sincerity in seeking recompense, it is the intention to obtain the benefit of the Hereafter by doing good work. Our own Shaikh (may Allāh bestow His mercy upon him) used to say: "It is the intention to obtain the benefit of the Hereafter by means of something irrefutably good, the best that the servant can possibly do, inasmuch as it is done in the hope of obtaining that benefit."

The Disciples [*Ḥawāriyyūn*] said to Mary's son Jesus (peace be upon him): "Who is sincere in his actions?" He replied: "Someone who works for the sake of Allāh, without needing to have anyone praise him for his work." This is an allusion to abstinence from ostentation, and he mentioned it specifically because ostentation is the strongest of all the causes that confound sincerity.

According to al-Junaid: "Sincerity is the purification of deeds from pollutants." According to al-Fuḍail: "Sincerity is constant vigilance and forgetting all worldly pleasures." This is the perfect explanation.

Sayings about this subject are numerous, but there is no point in quoting many more, now that the true facts have been disclosed.

When the Chief of the first and the last (Allāh bless him and give him peace) was asked about sincerity, he said:

> You say: "My Lord is Allāh (Exalted is He)," then you act correctly, as you have been commanded.

In other words: "You must not serve your passion and your lower self. You must serve none but your Lord, and act correctly in His worshipful service, as you have been commanded." This is an instruction to put everything apart from Allāh completely outside the scope of consideration. That is sincerity in the true sense.

The opposite of sincerity is ostentation, which is the intention to acquire the benefit of this world by doing the work of the Hereafter. There are two kinds of ostentation: (1) unmitigated ostentation and (2) mitigated ostentation. In its unmitigated form, what you intend by it is to gain the benefit of this world, and nothing else. In its mitigated form, it means that you intend to combine both the benefit of this world and the benefit of the Hereafter.

Such is the definition of the two [sincerity and ostentation]. As for their effect, sincerity in work causes you to perform the work as a virtuous deed [*qurba*], while sincerity in seeking recompense causes you to make it worthy of acceptance, abundant recompense and great respect. Hypocrisy [*nifāq*] invalidates the work, and prevents it from being a virtuous deed, worthy of the reward described in Allāh's promise (Exalted is He).

Unmitigated ostentation does not arise from one who knows the Truth, according to some of the scholars, and if it did, it would cancel half of the reward. Others maintain that unmitigated ostentation does sometimes arise from one who knows the Truth, and that it takes away half of the portions [of the reward], while mitigated ostentation takes away a quarter of the portions. The correct opinion, according to our own Shaikh (may Allāh bestow His mercy upon him), is that unmitigated ostentation does not arise from one who knows the Truth, so long as he remembers the Hereafter, but only during absent-mindedness. According to the preferred opinion, the effect of ostentation is the withholding of acceptance and reduction in the reward, though it [the reduction] cannot be quantified as one half or one quarter.

The full explanation of these questions is a very lengthy matter, and we have discussed them exhaustively in the book entitled: "Revival of the Religious Sciences [*Iḥyā' 'Ulūm ad-Dīn*]." We have also provided extensive treatment of the subject in "Secrets of Religious Practices [*Asrār Mu'āmalāt ad-Dīn*]."

You may ask: "Where is sincerity appropriate, and in which acts of worshipful obedience is it necessary?"

You must therefore know that actions, according to some of the scholars, are divided into three parts: (1) One part involves the two kinds of sincerity in combination, and that is essential outer worship [like the ritual prayer]. (2) One part involves nothing of either, and that is essential inner worship [like faith and trust]. (3) One part involves sincerity in seeking recompense, without sincerity in work, and that is the use of permissible concessions in preparation [for worshipful service]. According to our own Shaikh (may Allāh bestow His mercy upon him): "Sincerity in work is involved in every action, among the essential acts of worship, that may conceivably deviate towards anything other than Allāh (Exalted is He), so most of the internal acts of worship involve sincerity in work."

As for sincerity in seeking recompense, according to the Shaikhs of the Karramiyya sect: "It is not involved in the internal acts of worship, since no one witnesses them except Allāh (Glory be to Him), so the motives of ostentation are precluded from them. Sincerity in seeking recompense is therefore unnecessary." Our own Shaikh (may Allāh bestow His mercy upon him) used to say: "If the servant who is drawn close to Allāh performs internal acts of worship, but does so with the intention of obtaining the benefit of this world, that is also a form of ostentation."

In my own opinion, it is not unlikely, therefore, that the two kinds of sincerity are involved in many of the internal acts of worship. By the same token, the two kinds of sincerity are also necessary, in combination, when supererogatory acts of worship are undertaken. As for the use of permissible concessions in preparation [for worshipful service], this involves sincerity in seeking recompense, but not sincerity in work, since these concessions are not adequate in themselves to constitute virtuous conduct, but only as a means of preparation for such conduct.

You may say: "So much for where the two kinds of sincerity are appropriate. Now explain their timing in relation to the action."

You should therefore know that sincerity in work must accompany the action, without a doubt, and it may not be postponed till later. As for sincerity in seeking recompense, it may be postponed until after the action. According to some of the scholars: "The significant point is the time when the work has been concluded. Once the servant has finished his work, in a state of sincerity or ostentation, the matter is settled and he cannot go back and change it." According to the Shaikhs of the Karrāmiyya sect: "So long as the servant has not obtained the benefit sought by means of ostentation, it is possible for him to apply sincerity to his work, but if he has obtained that benefit, the opportunity is lost."

According to one of the scholars: "In the case of an obligatory religious duty [*farīḍa*], the possibility of applying sincerity to it lasts until death. As for supererogatory devotions [*nawāfil*], there is no such possibility, The difference between them is that Allāh (Exalted is He) has imposed the obligatory religious duty on the servant, so His gracious favour and facilitation are hoped for in its performance. As for the supererogatory duty, the servant has imposed it on himself, and made it his own responsibility, so he is accountable in accordance with the responsibility he has assumed."

There is a useful lesson in this discussion of the subject. That is to say, if someone has been guilty of ostentation in an act of work, or of omitting sincerity, it is possible for him to amend that situation and correct it, in one of the ways we have previously described. In reporting the doctrines of the scholars in such detail, our purpose is based on our knowledge of the present scarcity of active practitioners [of good work], and the lack of interest in the pursuit of this path. Our purpose is also to assist the novice in worshipful service, for if he does not find a cure for his illness in one opinion, he will find it in another, due to the diversity of diseases and symptoms, the defects of actions and their dire consequences. You must understand correctly, if Allāh (Exalted is He) so wills.

You may ask: "Does every act of work need a separate affirmation of sincerity?"

You should therefore know that the scholars have differed about that. Some maintain that every act of work needs a separate affirmation of sincerity. Others maintain the permissibility of a single affirmation of sincerity for a number of acts of worship. As for those acts of which the basic elements are prescribed, like the ritual prayer [*ṣalāt*] and ablution [*wuḍū'*], a single affirmation of sincerity is sufficient, because one of them is linked to another in rightness or wrongness, so they are like a single item.

You may ask: "If the servant performs his good work with the intention of obtaining a worldly favour from Allāh (Exalted is He), and not with the intention of gaining anything from people, such as praise or fame or benefit, does that constitute ostentation?"

You should recognize that as unmitigated ostentation. According to our scholars (may Allāh bestow His mercy upon them): "The crucial factor in ostentation is the intended object, regardless of whom you intend to impress. If a worldly favour is your intended object in performing good work, that amounts to ostentation, whether you seek to obtain the favour from Allāh or from people." Allāh (Exalted is He) has said:

> If someone desires the harvest of the Hereafter,
> *man kān yurīdu ḥartha al-ākhirati*
> We shall give him an increase in his harvest,
> *nazid la-hu fī ḥarthi-hi*
> and whoever desires the harvest of this world,
> *wa man kāna yurīdu ḥartha 'd-dunyā*
> We shall give him some of it,
> *nu'ti-hi min-hā*
> but in the Hereafter he will have no share.
> *wa mā la-hu fi 'l-ākhirati min naṣīb.* (42:20)[44]

You may ask: "What if the worldly benefit sought from Allāh is sympathy from people and preparation for Allāh's service? Is that a case of ostentation?"

You must therefore know that sympathy does not consist of material wealth, prestige and worldly vanities. It consists of contentment and reliance on the sufficient provision of Allāh (Glory be to Him).

As for preparation for the worshipful service of Allāh (Exalted is He), if that is the servant's intended object, it is not a case of

[44] ***Author's note:*** The term *riyā'* [ostentation] does not occur in this Qur'ānic verse. It is derived from the same root as the term *ru'ya* [seeing; taking notice], and it is commonly applied to this corrupt desire [in every context], though its linguistic reference is to people and their taking notice. This should be clearly understood.

ostentation. That preparation is connected with the business of the Hereafter and its means of attainment, and that becomes his purpose, absolutely. If this kind of object is intended by the performance of good work, the intention does not constitute a form of ostentation. That is because these matters become good by virtue of that intention, or come to be classed as deeds of the Hereafter, and the intention to do good work is not a form of ostentation.

The same is true if your intention is to gain respect in the sight of the general public, or affectionate regard from the Shaikhs and the Imāms, provided that your purpose therein is to be in a position to support the doctrine [*madhhab*] of the upholders of the Truth, or to refute the advocates of heretical innovations, or to disseminate knowledge, or to urge people to engage in worshipful service. Your purpose must be along these lines, not to gain personal honour for its own sake, nor to promote your worldly interest. All of this constitutes rightly guided aspiration and praiseworthy intentions, so no part of it comes under the heading of ostentation, since the purpose of it is, in reality, the business of the Hereafter.

You should also know that I asked one of our Shaikhs about the custom of our saints, regarding the recitation of the Sūra of the Event [*al-Wāqiʿa*] on the days of hardship. I said: "Surely the intended purpose is that Allāh may dispel that hardship from them, and grant them some worldly bounty, in keeping with the normal state of affairs. So how can it be correct to seek the bounty of this world, in exchange for the work of the Hereafter?"

In his reply, the Shaikh (may Allāh bestow His mercy upon him) said, in effect: "Their intended purpose is that Allāh may supply them with sufficient sustenance, or basic nourishment, to prepare them for the worshipful service of Allāh, and to give them strength for the study of knowledge. Such intentions are good, not worldly."

You should also know that this customary practice, meaning the recitation of this Sūra in time of hardship, for the sake of sustenance and the satisfaction of need, has been transmitted in reports concerning the Prophet (Allāh bless him and give him peace) and the Companions (may Allāh be well pleased with them all). For instance, when Abū Maʿsūd was blamed for leaving his children with nothing from this world, he said: "I have left them the Sūra of the Event [*al-Wāqiʿa*]!"

From that root in the Sunna, this custom has branched into the practices of our scholars (may Allāh bestow His mercy upon them). Had it not [been rooted in the Sunna], they would not have recognized the value of praising Allāh (Exalted is He) for hardship in this world, or for comfort therein.

As it is, our scholars take full advantage of the narrowness and hardship of this world, and vie with one another in the process. They count it as a tremendous favour from Allāh (Exalted is He). On the other hand, if they see a worldly benefit coming to them from Allāh, something that most people would simply regard as a gracious gift and blessing, they are afraid that it may be a temptation from Allāh (Exalted is He) and an affliction. That is because they are happily accustomed to travelling and going hungry in most situations, and their leaders say: "Hunger is the capital of our wealth!"

This is the basic doctrine of the masters of Ṣūfism, and it is my doctrine and the doctrine of my Shaikhs. That was also the guiding principle of our righteous forebears. As for the shortcoming of some more recent types, it is unworthy of consideration. We mention this distinction only to spare them [our righteous forebears] from being blamed by a critical outsider, ignorant of the goals of the people [of the Spiritual Path], or in case a sound-hearted novice misunderstands them and fails to learn the truth.

You may ask: "How can this [recitation of the Sūra in times of hardship] be consistent with the state of the people of knowledge, exclusive dedication [to worship] and abstinence, and the masters of patience and spiritual training?"

You should therefore know that this practice is taken from the Sunna [of the Prophet (Allāh bless him and give him peace)]. Furthermore, the goal is the attainment of contentment and preparation [for worshipful service], not the pursuit of greed, carnal desire, and weakness in the face of difficulty and hardship. Most of what you see in the wake of that [recitation of the Sūra] is contentment of the heart [*qalb*], loss of the dog [*kalb*] of hunger, and detachment from the gluttonous appetite for food. That is known by those who put it to the test of experience. You must understand all this successfully, if Allāh (Exalted is He) so wills.

The Second Impairment [*qādiḥ*]
Vain conceit [*'ujb*]

The avoidance of vain conceit is incumbent upon you for two reasons:

1. It presents a barrier to enabling grace and assistance from Allāh (Exalted is He), so he who is vainly conceited is left in the lurch. If the servant is cut off from enabling grace and assistance from Allāh (Exalted is He), he perishes so quickly! That is why the Prophet (Allāh bless him and give him peace) once said:

> There are three causes of perdition: a greed obeyed, a passion pursued, and a man's vain conceit in himself.

2. It corrupts righteous work. That is why the Messiah (blessing and peace be upon him) once said: "O company of the Disciples, how many a lamp has been blown out by the wind, and how many a worshipful servant has been corrupted by vain conceit!" Worshipful service is the purpose and the benefit [of righteous work], and this vice deprives the servant so that he obtains nothing good. Even if he does obtain something good, a little of that [vain conceit] is enough to corrupt it, so he is left with nothing at all. He is therefore obliged to be on his guard against that, and to exercise great caution. Allāh is the Custodian of enabling grace and protection!

You may ask: "So what is the real meaning of vain conceit? What is its significance, its effect and its legal status? Explain that to us!"

You must therefore know that the real meaning of vain conceit is the aggrandizement of righteous work. As defined in detail by our scholars (may Allāh bestow His mercy upon them), it is the servant's attribution of the honour obtained by righteous work to something other than Allāh (Almighty and Glorious is He), or to people, or to the lower self. They have said: "Vain conceit may be threefold, inasmuch as it may be attributed to all of these three together: the lower self, fellow creatures, and the thing [that is other than Allāh]. It may also be twofold, inasmuch as it may be attributed to two of these, or singlefold, inasmuch as it may be attributed to only one of them."

The opposite of vain conceit is gratitude, which means remembering that it [the honour obtained by righteous work] is due to the enabling grace of Allāh (Glory be to Him), and that He is the One who has honoured the servant and magnified his reward and his worth. This remembrance is an obligatory duty in the presence of the causes of vain conceit, and a supererogatory duty at other times.

As for the effect of vain conceit on the servant's work, one of our scholars has said: "If someone is vainly conceited, he is waiting for annulment [*iḥbāṭ*]. If he repents before his death, he will be safe; otherwise he will suffer annulment." This opinion was also held by Muḥammad ibn Ṣābir, one of the Shaikhs of the Karrāmiyya sect. According to him, annulment means that the servant's work is stripped of all good names, so that he is entitled to no reward and no praise, none whatsoever. According to another, *iḥbāṭ* means removal of the multiplication [of the reward], and nothing else.

You may ask: "For the servant who knows the Truth, how can there be any doubt that Allāh (Exalted is He) is the One who has enabled his righteous work, magnified his worth and multiplied his reward, through His grace and favour?"

You must therefore know that here we have a subtle hint and a noble treasure, indicating that, when it comes to vain conceit, people are of three types:

1. Those who are vainly conceited in every situation. They are [the sects known as] the Muʿtazila[45] and the Qadariyya,[46] who do not believe that Allāh grants them any favour in their actions, and who disavow His special help and enabling grace. That is because of a doubt that has prevailed upon them.

2. Those who gratefully acknowledge their indebtedness to Allāh in every situation. They are the rightly guided, who are not vainly conceited about any of their works. That is because they have been

[45] The Muʿtazila ["the Separatists"] played a major rôle in the development of Islāmic philosophy and theology. In the long run, their methods proved too speculative and rationalistic to win favour with the majority of the scholars in the Muslim community. For a certain period, however, the doctrines of the Muʿtazila were not merely accepted by the rulers in Baghdād, but were actively imposed as the official dogma of the Islāmic State.

[46] The Qadariyya were so called because of their refusal to accept the doctrine of absolute Divine predestination [*qadar*], and their belief in the power [*qudra*] of human beings to create their own actions. They played a significant rôle in the early period of Islāmic theological debate, prior to the emergence of the Muʿtazila.

endowed with a perceptive faculty of understanding, and singled out for special assistance.

3. The mixers, who constitute the majority of the people of the Sunna. They sometimes come to their senses, so they gratefully acknowledge Allāh's favour. Sometimes they are heedless, so they become vainly conceited in that regard, due to the influence of heedlessness, the gap in earnest endeavour, and the deficiency in perceptive understanding.

You may ask: "What is the state of the Qadariyya and the Muʿtazila with regard to their actions?"

You must therefore know that there are differences of opinion about that. Some say that their work is annulled on account of their belief. Others say: "In general, work is not annulled on account of a belief held by one the sects of Islām, unless every act of work is specifically viewed with vain conceit, just as the belief of the people of the Sunna does not automatically prevent vain conceit about every act of work, unless it is specifically accompanied by grateful acknowledgement [of Allāh's favour]."

Someone may ask: "Apart from vain conceit and ostentation, is work threatened by any other impairment [*qādiḥ*]?"

The answer will be: "Yes indeed, those two are not the only impairments, but we have singled them out because they are the central point, around which many related topics revolve." According to one of the Shaikhs: "In his work, the servant has a duty to guard against ten things: (1) hypocrisy [*nifāq*] (2) ostentation [*riyāʾ*], (3) mixing, (4) boasting, (5) harm, (6) regret, (7) vain conceit, (8) sorrow, (9) disdain, and (10) fear of people's criticism."

As our own Shaikh (may Allāh bestow His mercy upon him) has mentioned, each of these ten must be actively countered by its opposite: (1) The opposite of hypocrisy [*nifāq*] is sincerity [*ikhlāṣ*] in work. (2) The opposite of ostentation [*riyāʾ*] is sincerity in seeking recompense. (3) The opposite of mixing is singular devotion. (4) The opposite of boasting is submitting the work to Allāh. (5) The opposite of harm is keeping the work safe. (6) The opposite of regret is commitment of the lower self [to good work]. (7) The opposite of vain conceit is grateful acknowledgement [of Allāh's favour]. (8) The opposite of sorrow is taking full advantage of the benefit. (9) The opposite of disdain is respectful recognition of the enabling grace [of Allāh]. (10) The opposite of fear of people's criticism is the dread [of offending Allāh].

You should also know that hypocrisy [*nifāq*] annuls the work, that ostentation [*riyāʾ*] causes its rejection, and that boasting and harm annul [the reward of] charitable giving absolutely and immediately. According to some of the Shaikhs (may Allāh bestow His mercy upon him), they only annul its multiplications.

As for regret, it annuls the work, according to all the scholars, while vain conceit removes the multiplications of [the reward of] the work, and sorrow, disdain and fear of criticism diminish the gravity [*razāna*] of the work.

This means that acceptance and rejection, in the view of those who seek knowledge, depend on various kinds of respect and belittlement, and annulment is the cancellation of benefits acquired by the deed. Annulment sometimes takes the form of cancellation of the reward itself, and sometimes of cancellation of its multiplication. The reward is a benefit determined by the deed itself, as well as its contextual value and significance, while its multiplication is an addition to this. The gravity [*razāna*] of the work is also an addition, resulting from other associated factors, such as benefit provided to one of the people of goodness, then to parents, then to one of the Prophets. There may be instances where gravity is added, but there is no multiplication [of the reward].

This is an exposition of what I have ascertained about these concepts, so try to understand that. Allāh is the Source of enabling grace!

Subsection

You must surmount this perilous hurdle in the utmost state of wariness, for it is fraught with hazardous intersections and stretches of desert. The owner of the merchandise of acts of worshipful obedience has surmounted all those previous hurdles, and endured all those hardships, and he has thus amassed a noble and splendid store of worshipful service. He is not afraid for that merchandise of his, except on this hurdle, for it contains hazardous intersections where he risks being robbed of his merchandise, and stretches of desert where evils may lurk, threatening to corrupt his worshipful obedience. The most dangerous of all these perils, and those most likely to strike, are these two highway robbers: ostentation [*riyā'*] and vain conceit [*'ujb*]. Let us therefore describe each one of them in sufficient detail, so that you may recognize their essential features, with Allāh's consent and if Allāh (Exalted is He) so wills.

As for ostentation, you must observe these four essentials:

1. First of all, you must remember the saying of Allāh (Glory be to Him):

> It is Allāh who has created seven heavens,
> *Allāhu 'lladhī khalaqa sab'a samāwātin*
> and of the earth their like.
> *wa mina 'l-arḍi mithla-hunn:*
> The Command comes down between them gradually,
> *yatanazzalu 'l-amru baina-hunna*
> so that you may know
> *li-ta'lamū*
> that Allāh is Powerful over all things,
> *anna 'llāha 'alā kulli shai'in Qadīr:*
> and that Allāh has encompassed
> *wa anna 'llāha qad aḥāṭa*
> everything in knowledge.
> *bi-kulli shai'in 'ilmā.* (65:12)

It is as if Allāh (Glory be to Him) is saying: "I have created the heavens and the earth and all that is between them, in the form of all these works and wonders of creation, and I have paid you enough attention for you to realize that I am All-Powerful, All-Knowing. In spite of all that, you perform two cycles of ritual prayer [*rak'atain*] with so many faults and shortcomings, and you attach so little importance to My watching over you, My knowledge of you, My commendation of you and My appreciation of you, that you love to have your fellow creatures praise you for that [performance of ritual prayer]. Is that a sign of loyalty? Is that a sign of intelligence, the kind of intelligence that anyone would be pleased to possess? Woe unto you, for you surely do not comprehend!"

2. The second essential is this: Suppose that someone had a precious jewel, for which he could have set the price at a million gold coins, yet he sold it for a penny. Would that not be a tremendous loss, an atrocious stupidity, and a clear sign of low ambition, lack of knowledge, weakness

of vision and feebleness of intellect? As for what the servant gains by his work, in the form of praise and worldly vanities from his fellow creatures, in relation to the good pleasure of the Lord of All the Worlds, His appreciation, His commendation and His reward, it is less than a penny beside a million gold coins, and many times that, or even beside this whole world, and even more and greater still. It is surely part of the manifest loss [*al-khusrān al-mubīn*],[47] that you should forfeit those noble and glorious blessings in exchange for these despicable worldly things!

In order to escape from this low ambition, you must aim for the Hereafter and let this world follow after you. Better still, you must seek the Lord, and Him Alone, for He will grant you the two abodes, since He is the Owner of them both. As He has said (Exalted is He):

> Whoever desires the reward of this world,
> *man kāna yurīdu thawāba 'd-dunyā*
> with Allāh is the reward of this world
> *fa-ʿinda 'llāhi thawābu 'd-dunyā*
> and the Hereafter.
> *wa 'l-ākhira.* (4:134)

The Prophet (Allāh bless him and give him peace) once said:

> Allāh (Exalted is He) will surely grant this world in exchange for the work of the Hereafter, but He will not grant the Hereafter in exchange for the work of this world.

If you are sincere in your intention, and your ambition is solely for the Hereafter, you will therefore gain the Hereafter and this world together. If you seek this world, the Hereafter will immediately depart from you, and you may not obtain what you seek in this world. Even if you do obtain it, you will not keep it for long, so you will soon have lost both this world and the Hereafter. You must therefore consider this with care, O intelligent one!

3. The third essential is this: If the creature for whose sake you work, and whose approval you seek, knew that you were working for his sake, he would hate you, despise you, scorn you and belittle you. So how can the intelligent man work for the sake of someone who, if he knew that he was seeking his approval, would despise him and scorn him? You must therefore work, O miserable wretch, for the sake of the One who, if you work for His sake, make Him the goal of your effort, and seek His

[47] An allusion to Q. 22:11.

approval thereby, will love you, give to you and honour you, until He is well pleased with you, makes you independent of everything, and satisfies you completely. You must understand this well, if you are intelligent.

4. The fourth essential is this: If someone is capable of the effort that will earn him the approval of the mightiest king in this world, but he uses that effort to seek the approval of a wretched street sweeper, that will be a sign of foolishness and stupidity on his part, and it will bring misfortune upon him. He will be asked: "Why do you need the approval of this street sweeper, when it is possible for you to win the approval of the king? Suppose the street sweeper is displeased with you, because of the king's displeasure? You will then lose everything!" This is the condition of the ostentatious hyprocrite.

Why do you need to please a weak and despicable creature, when you are capable of obtaining the good pleasure of Allāh, the Lord of All the Worlds, the All-Sufficing? If your aspiration has been feeble, and your perception blurred, so that you have inevitably sought the approval of a creature, your way out is to dedicate your intention and devote your effort solely to Allāh (Glory be to Him). The hearts and the forelocks [of His creatures] are in His hand, so He will incline their hearts towards you, attach their feelings to you, and fill their breasts with love for you. From that you will gain what you cannot gain by your exertion and your endeavour. If you do not follow this advice, but work with the intention of pleasing creatures, instead of Allāh (Glory be to Him and Exalted is He), He will turn hearts away from you, cause feelings to recoil from you, and make creatures displeased with you. You will thus obtain the displeasure of Allāh and the displeasure of creatures combined. What a dreadful loss and deprivation!

According to al-Ḥasan [al-Baṣrī]: "A man used to say: 'By Allāh, I shall worship Allāh with a worship for which I shall be remembered!' He was always the first to enter the mosque, and the last to leave it. No one ever saw him, unless he was praying at the time of prayer, fasting without breaking fast, or sitting in the circle of remembrance [*dhikr*]. He kept that up for seven months, so he never passed by a group of people without their saying: 'May Allāh deal with this ostentatious hypocrite!' He therefore reproached his lower self, telling it: 'I see that I am getting nowhere. Let me devote all my work to Allāh!' He added nothing to the work he had been doing before that, except that his intention changed for the better. From then on, whenever he passed by people, they would say: 'Allāh has bestowed His mercy on so-and-so. He has now moved in the right direction.'" Then al-Ḥasan recited the Qur'ānic verse:

> As for those who believe and do righteous deeds,
> *inna 'lladhīna āmanū wa ʿamilu 'ṣ-ṣāliḥāti*
> the All-Merciful will surely grant them love.
> *sa-yajʿalu la-humu 'r-Raḥmānu wuddā.* (19:96)

The poet spoke the truth when he said:

> O you who desire praise and reward
> for a deed, your desire is to no avail.
>
> Allāh has thwarted the ostentatious hypocrite,
> and annulled the effort and the labour.
>
> If someone hopes to meet a Lord,
> he must act sincerely from fear of offending Him.
>
> Eternal life and the Fire are in His hands,
> so show Him [your deeds] and He will give you the benefit.
>
> People have nothing in their possession,
> so why do you show them an error?

As for vain conceit [*ʿujb*], let us mention the following essential points:

1. No real value accrues to the servant's work, except through the approval and acceptance conferred by Allāh. Otherwise, you see the hired workman toiling all day for a couple of dirhams [silver coins], and the watchman staying awake all night for a couple of dāniqs [each worth one sixth of a dirham]. The same applies to craftsmen and professionals, each of whom works by night and day, so the value of that work is a number of silver coins. If you dedicate your work to Allāh (Exalted is He), and spend one day fasting for the sake of Allāh (Exalted is He), your fasting on that day will be priceless, if He is well pleased with it and accepts it. Allāh (Exalted is He) has said:

> Surely those who endure with patience
> *innamā yuwaffa 'ṣ-ṣābirūna*
> will be paid their wages in full without reckoning.
> *ajra-hum bi-ghairi ḥisāb.* (39:10)

According to the traditional report, [the Prophet (Allāh bless him and give him peace) once said]:

> [Allāh says]: "I have prepared for My fasting servants that which no eye has ever seen, of which no ear has ever heard, and which has never occurred to the heart of a human being."

Well, this day of yours, the material value of which is two silver coins, along with the toil and trouble you endure, has acquired all this spiritual value through the postponement of breakfast till the evening! If you spent the night in vigil for the sake of Allāh (Exalted is He), and devoted it sincerely to Him, your vigil would be priceless in nobility and preciousness. Allāh (Exalted is He) has said:

> So no soul knows what comfort
> *fa-lā taʿlamu nafsun mā ukhfiya*
> is kept secretly in store for them,
> *la-hum min qurrati aʿyun:*
> as a reward for what they used to do.
> *jazāʾan bi-mā kānū yaʿmalūn.* (32:17)

This night of yours, the material value of which is two dāniqs or two dirhams, would thus acquire all this spiritual worth and value. Indeed, [you would obtain this enormous benefit] if you devoted a short time to Allāh, and performed two light cycles of ritual prayer in that time, or even a single breath, in which you said: "There is no god but Allāh [*lā ilāha illa 'llāh*]!" Allāh (Exalted is He) has said:

> And whoever does right, whether male or female,
> *wa man ʿamila ṣāliḥan min dhakarin aw unthā*
> and is a believer,
> *wa huwa muʾminun*
> such will enter the Garden,
> *fa-ulāʾika yadkhulūna 'l-jannata*
> where they will be nourished without stint.
> *yurzaqūna fī-hā bi-ghairi ḥisāb.* (40:40)

This is one of those breaths of yours that have no value in the sight of the people of this world, nor in your own sight, so how many like it do you waste for nothing, and how much time passes by you with no benefit? Yet that breath could acquire this tremendous worth, if it happened to be pleasing to Allāh (Exalted is He), for He would magnify its worth, and its value would be multiplied by His gracious favour.

It is therefore incumbent on the intelligent person to recognize the insignificance of his work, and the paucity of its worth as such. He must acknowledge only the gracious favour of Allāh (Exalted is He), which He has conferred upon him by ennobling the value of his work and magnifying its reward. He must beware of acting in a way that is not appropriate for Allāh, and that does not gain His approval, so that his work loses the value it has acquired, and reverts to its trivial price in dirhams or dāniqs, or even less than that.

For the sake of comparison, consider the case of a bunch of grapes or a sheaf of sweet basil, the market value of which is a dāniq. If someone presents it to a king, in spite of its triviality, and it meets with approval, the king may give him a thousand gold coins for it, on account of the good pleasure it has evoked. Something priced at a pip has thus become worth a thousand gold coins. If the king is not pleased with it, however, and hands it back to him, it reverts to its trifling value of a pip or a dāniq. The same applies to the case that interests us, so wake up, recognize the gracious favour of Allāh, and preserve your work from that which mars it in the sight of Allāh (Almighty and Glorious is He)!

2. The second essential point is this: As you know, the king in this world provides someone with rations, in the form of food, or drink, or clothes, or a few gold or silver coins that are soon spent. In exchange, that person serves him through the watches of the night and the day, with all the abasement and humiliation that entails. He stands before the king until his legs turn numb, and he runs in front of him when he goes riding. He sometimes needs to be on guard at his door throughout the night. An enemy may appear, so he will need to fight the foe, sacrificing his irreplaceable spirit for the king's sake. He endures all this service, inconvenience, danger and harm, for the sake of that pitiful and trifling benefit, although it is really from Allāh (Exalted is He), and the king is merely in the position of an instrument. It is your Lord who created you, when you were nothing. Then He brought you up and trained you well. Then He blessed you with outer and inner blessings in your religion, your person and your worldly life, to an extent unfathomable by your understanding and your imagination. He said (More Glorious is He than any other sayer):

> And if you try to reckon the bounty of Allāh,
> *wa in taʿuddū niʿmata 'llāhi*
> you will never count it.
> *lā tuḥṣū-hā.*
> The human being is indeed a wrongdoer, an ingrate.
> *inna 'l-insāna la-ẓalūmun kaffār.* (14:34)

You perform two cycles of ritual prayer, with all the faults and vices you include in them, and knowing what He has promised for them in the future, in the form of excellent reward and various gifts of grace, so you should treat that [performance of prayer] with great respect, yet you are vainly conceited about it. That is not the mark of an intelligent person, if you take notice!

3. The third essential point is this: The king is the one who is served by the governors and the commanders, the one before whom the leaders and the dignitaries stand at attention, whose service is conducted by the clever and the wise, whose praise is sought by the intelligent and the scholars, and in front of whom walk the elders and the chiefs. Suppose the king permits a plebeian or a villager to enter his door, as an act of kindness and care for him, so that he rubs shoulders with those governors, leaders and elders, and with those who are distinguished in his service and his commendation, and suppose he assigns him a known station in his presence, and views his acts of service with the eye of approval, even though they are flawed and faulty. People will surely say about that commoner: "This miserable wretch has received great favour and splendid attention from the king!" Then, if this miserable wretch expects the king to show gratitude for that faulty service, if he takes great pride in it, and is vainly conceited about it, people will surely say: "That is a very stupid fool, or a lunatic, who understands nothing at all!"

Once this point has been established, we may go on to say that our God [*Ilāh*] (Glory be to Him) is the King who is glorified by the seven heavens and the earth, and by all that they contain. There is nothing that does not glorify His praise. He who is Worthy of worship is the One to whom those in the heavens and on earth bow down in prostration, willingly or unwillingly. The servants at His door include Gabriel the Trustworthy, Michael, Isrāfīl and ʿIzrāʾīl, the Bearers of the Heavenly Throne, the Cherubs and the Spiritual Beings, and all the Angels

Brought Near, whose number is counted only by Allāh, the Lord of All the Worlds. They are present in their lofty stations, in their visible forms, and in their splendid acts of worshipful service.

The following are also included among those who are servants at His door: Adam, Noah, Abraham, Moses, Jesus and Muḥammad, the best of all creatures, as well as all the other Prophets and Messengers (may Allāh's blessings and peace be upon them all), in their exalted degrees, their honourable and glorious virtues, their noble stations, and their majestic and splendid customs.

Then come the scholars, the religious leaders, the righteous and the ascetics, in their magnificent degrees, their clean and pure bodies, and their many sincere and manifest acts of worshipful service.

The lowliest of the servants at His door are the kings and tyrants of this world, who prostrate themselves humbly before Him with their chins on the ground, rub their faces in the dust, and present their needs to Him, weeping, wailing and moaning. They acknowledge their servitude to Him, and confess their own deficiency, bowing down in humble prostration, so He sometimes casts a glance at them and fulfils a need for them, by His gracious favour, or pardons a mistake for them, by His noble generosity.

Regardless of this Might, Majesty, Sovereignty and Perfection of His, Allāh has granted you permission [to enter His service] in spite of your wretchedness, your faults and your impurities. You are the kind of person who might not receive permission from the chief of your town, if you applied to him for permission. If you speak to the governor of your district, he may not speak to you. If you bow down to the ground before the ruler of your country, he may not pay attention to you. Nevertheless, Allāh (Magnificent is His Majesty) has granted you permission to worship Him, to extol Him, and to address Him in speech. You may even direct a request to Him, and express it to Him frankly, asking Him to fulfil your need and satisfy your concerns. He will be pleased with your two cycles of ritual prayer, with all their faults. Indeed, He will prepare for you a reward that would never occur to the human heart, yet you are vainly conceited about these two cycles of ritual prayer! You think you have done a great deal of work, and you are very proud of your performance. You do not acknowledge the gracious favour that Allāh has bestowed upon you. What a bad servant you are, and what an ignorant person!

Allāh (Exalted is He) is the One from whom we seek help. To Him we complain of this ignorant lower self, and in Him we put all our trust.

Subsection

Let us now consider the following scenario: The mighty king grants permission for gifts to be presented to him, so into his presence come the commanders, the elders, the chiefs, the noblemen and the rich, bearing all kinds of gifts, such as valuable jewels, precious treasures and magnificent properties. Then a greengrocer comes with a bunch of vegetables, or a villager brings a basket of grapes, equal in value to a dāniq or a pip, so he enters the king's presence and rubs shoulders with those elders and rich men, with their many noble gifts. The king accepts that poor man's gift with obvious approval and good pleasure, and awards him a precious cloak of honour. That surely represents the utmost favour and noble generosity on the king's part!

Suppose this poor man expects the king to grovel in gratitude for his gift. Suppose he is vainly conceited about it, takes great pride in it, and forgets to acknowledge the king's gracious favour. People will surely say: "This is a lunatic, mentally deranged, or a stupid fool with bad manners, extremely ignorant!"

What is now required of you, therefore, when you keep vigil at night for the sake of Allāh, and perform two cycles of ritual prayer for His sake? It is that you must think of the many servants who are keeping vigil this night for the sake of Allāh (Glory be to Him), in all the regions of the earth, on land and at sea, on the mountains and in the towns, from the ranks of the rightly guided, the champions of Truth, the fearful, the ardent, the dedicated and the humbly submissive. You must consider how much is being presented at this very moment, at the door of Allāh (Glory be to Him), in the form of pure worship and genuine service, performed in fear of offending Him, with clean tongues, weeping eyes, devout hearts, immaculate breasts and unstained limbs.

As for your ritual prayers, even if you have spared no effort in refining them and observing their rules, and in performing them with sincerity, they will hardly be suitable for the presence of this Almighty King. They will hardly compare with those acts of worship that are being offered there [at the door of Allāh (Glory be to Him)]. How can they compare, when you have acted with a negligent heart, mixed with all kinds of faults, a body defiled by the filth of sins, and a tongue stained by all kinds of disobedience and transgression? How can this be fit to be conveyed into that presence? How can it be worthy of being offered to the Lord of Might and Glory?

Our Shaikh (may Allāh bestow His mercy upon him) once said: "Look hard, O intelligent one! Have you ever directed one of your ritual prayers towards Heaven, like a table of food that you sent to the homes of the rich?" Abū Bakr al-Warrāq used to say: "I have never concluded a ritual prayer without feeling ashamed of it. My sense of shame was always greater than that felt by a woman after unlawful sexual intercourse!"

The Noble and Generous Lord (Glory be to Him) has magnified the worth of these two cycles of ritual prayer, by His sheer generosity and gracious favour, and He has promised for them the abundant reward that He has promised. You are His servant and you are in His employ. You have done what you have done through His enabling grace and His facilitation. In spite of all that, however, you are vainly conceited about your work, and you forget Allāh's gracious favour. This, by Allāh, is utterly astonishing! The like of it could hardly emanate from anyone but a thoughtless ignoramus, a mindlessly negligent person, or a dead and empty heart. We beseech Allāh to grant us sufficient provision, through His grace and favour!

Subsection

After all that has been said above, you must wake up from your slumber, O man, on this hurdle! If not, you will be among the losers, for this is the toughest, hardest, harshest and most bruising hurdle that has confronted you on this path. It is the culmination of all the previous hurdles, so, if you surmount it safely, you will gain great benefit and profit. If the opposite is the case, all effort has been to no avail, hope has been dashed, and life has been wasted.

Everything hinges on the fact that three things are combined in this hurdle: (1) the problem is a very subtle matter, (2) the risk of error is serious, and (3) the danger is enormous.

1. As for the subtle nature of the problem, the channels through which deeds are infiltrated by ostentation and vain conceit are extremely subtle and concealed. Hardly anyone is alert to that process, except those who are adept in the sphere of religion, keenly perceptive, wakeful at heart, and prudently cautious. How can it be detected by the stupid ignoramus and the heedless addict of sleep?

In Nishāpūr, I heard the following account from one of our scholars (may Allāh bestow His mercy upon them): "ʿAṭāʾ as-Sulamī (may Allāh bestow His mercy and His good pleasure upon him) wove a garment, tailored it to perfection and made it very beautiful. Then he took it to the market and put it on display, but the draper offered a cheap price, saying: 'It has so many flaws. Look here, and here....' ʿAṭāʾ took it back and sat weeping bitterly. The man felt sorry, became apologetic and offered him the price he wanted, so ʿAṭāʾ said to him: 'The problem is not as you suppose. I work at this craft [of weaving], and I tried hard to perfect this garment, to improve it and make it beautiful, so that it would be flawless. Then, when it was displayed to someone able to detect its faults, he showed me flaws that I had failed to notice.'"

What does that say about these deeds of ours, when they are displayed tomorrow [at the Resurrection] to Allāh? How many flaws and defects, of which we are heedless today, will become apparent in them then?

We are told that one of the righteous said: "One night at the time before dawn, I was in a room next to a main street, reciting the Qurʾānic Sūra entitled *Ṭā-Hā*. As soon as I had concluded the recitation, I fell into a doze, and I saw a figure descend from the sky, holding a copy of the Qurʾān in his hand. He spread it out in front of me, and there was the Sūra *Ṭā-Hā*! Ten merits were recorded under each word of the text, with the exception of one word. A blank space had been substituted for that word, and I saw nothing underneath it. I said: 'By Allāh, I recited this word, but I see no reward for it, and I do not see it inscribed.' The figure said: 'You have told the truth. You did recite it, and we inscribed it, but then we heard a crier calling from the direction of the Heavenly Throne: "Erase it, and drop its reward," so we erased it.' I wept in my sleep, and I said: 'Why did you do that?' He replied: 'A man passed by [during your recitation], so you raised your voice to impress him, and away went the reward [for reciting that word].'"

2. As for the seriousness of the risk of error, ostentation and vain conceit are a terrible affliction, which can strike in the twinkling of an eye, and may ruin your worship of seventy years.

It is related that a man once entertained Sufyān at-Thawrī (may Allāh bestow His mercy upon him) and his companions, so he said to his family: "Fetch the platter—not the one I brought on the first Pilgrimage, but the one I brought on the second Pilgrimage." Sufyān looked at him and said: "Poor wretch! He has spoiled his Pilgrimage by saying this!"

This is another aspect of the risk of error: To the slightest obedience that is immune to ostentation and vain conceit, Allāh (Almighty and Glorious is He) assigns a value that has no end. On the other hand, the greatest amount of obedience remains without value, if this affliction strikes it, unless Allāh (Exalted is He) sets it right.

It is reported that ʿAlī (may Allāh be well pleased with him) once said: "An accepted deed is absolutely not of little value. How can an accepted deed be of little value?"

Someone asked an-Nakhaʿī about the reward for a certain kind of good work. He replied: "If it is accepted, its reward is incalculable."

According to Wahb: "Among those before your time, there was a man who worshipped Allāh for seventy years, fasting without breaking fast from Saturday to Saturday. Then he asked Allāh to satisfy a need, but it was not satisfied, so he reproached his lower self, saying: 'I have been ruined by you. Had there been any goodness to your credit, your need would have been fulfilled.' Allāh (Exalted is He) then sent down an angel, who said: 'O son of Adam! The moment when you rebuked your lower self is worth more than your previous worship [of seventy years]!'"

The intelligent person should reflect on this saying. It is surely a sign of the risk of error, that one person labours and toils for seventy years, while another takes thought for a single moment, and a moment's thought is worth more in Allāh's sight than the worship of seventy years! Yet you lose that opportunity unnecessarily! By Allāh, that is the greatest risk of error! To neglect it is surely the most serious loss. If a mode of conduct is so worthless and so fraught with danger, you must guard against it and avoid it.

Because of this kind of consideration, those worshipful servants who are endowed with faculties of discernment have investigated these kinds of subtleties. They have concerned themselves with these kinds of secrets, in order to become familiar with them, first of all, then to monitor them and take precautions against them, in second place. They have not been satisfied with the multiplicity of good deeds in the realm of external appearance, and they have said: "It is a matter of pure intent, not of multiplicity." They have also said: "A single jewel is better than a pearl."

As for those who have little knowledge, and whose interest in this topic is slight, they are ignorant of the deeper meanings, and heedless of the faults within their hearts. They are preoccupied with compelling their lower selves to bow and make prostration [in the ritual prayer], to abstain from food and drink, and so on. They are deluded by the number and frequency [of their acts of worship], and do not consider the spiritual benefits and purity of heart involved. The number of walnuts is not sufficient, if they contain no kernels. The erection of roofs is useless, if their underlying structures are not firmly established. No one understands these realities, except those who manifest true knowledge of Allāh. Allāh (Exalted is He) is the Custodian of right guidance, by His gracious favour.

3. As for the enormity of the danger, there are several aspects to consider:

—First, the One who is Worthy of worship is a Sovereign of endless Majesty and Might, and you are indebted to Him for countless and innumerable blessings. You have a body that is flawed by hidden faults, afflicted by many afflictions, and your situation is perilous, since your lower self is rushing towards a mishap that may befall you. The servant therefore needs to produce work that is pure and sound, from a body that is flawed and a lower self that is always inclined to wickedness, always instigating evil. He must produce that work in a manner befitting the Lord of All the Worlds, in keeping with His Majesty, His Might, and the abundance of His blessings and His gracious favour. Your work must be worthy of His approval and acceptance, otherwise you will forfeit the enormous profit, which the lower self cannot bear to lose, and you may even be afflicted by a disaster that you simply cannot endure. This, by Allāh, is a dreadful and terrible prospect.

—As for the Majesty and Might of the Sovereign, the righteous angels-brought-near are active in His service through the watches of the night and the day. Some of them have been in an upright posture [*qiyām*] since Allāh (Exalted is He) created them. Some have been in a bowing posture [*rukūʿ*] and some in prostration [*sujūd*], while some have been engaged in glorification [*tasbīḥ*] and *tahlīl* [proclaiming: "There is no god but Allāh (*lā ilāha illa 'llāh*)"]. The one who is standing upright does not conclude his standing, nor the one who is bowing his bowing, nor the one in prostration his prostration, nor the glorifier his glorification, nor the *muhallil* [proclaimer of Allāh's Uniqueness] his *tahlīl*, extending the sound of it till the blowing of the trumpets. Then, when they have finished this tremendous service, they all cry out together: "Glory be to You! We have not served You as You truly deserve!"

The Chief of the Messengers, the best of all creatures, the most knowledgeable and most excellent of all human beings, Muḥammad (Allāh bless him and give him peace), says [to his Lord]:

> I do not count any praise as worthy of You. You are as You have praised Yourself.

He is saying, in effect: "I cannot praise You with any praise that You deserve, let alone worship You as You deserve! It is also he who said:

> No one will enter the Garden of Paradise on account of his work.

They said: "Not even you, O Messenger of Allāh?" He replied:

> Not even I, unless Allāh covers me with His mercy!

—As for the abundance of His gracious favours and blessings, it is as He has said (Exalted is He):

> And if you try to reckon the bounty of Allāh,
> *wa in taʿuddū niʿmata 'llāhi*
> you will never count it.
> *lā tuḥṣū-hā*. (14:34)

According to traditional report, He will gather people [at the Resurrection] on the basis of three lists: the list of good deeds, the list of bad deeds, and the list of gracious favours. The good deeds will be collated with the gracious favours, so that no good deed is noted without a gracious favour being noted, until the gracious favours cover and overflow the good deeds. The bad deeds and sins will remain, so what is to be done about them depends on Allāh's will.

—As for the faults and vices of the lower self, we have discussed them in their own chapter. The danger to be feared is that the servant may toil in worshipful service and persist for seventy years, heedless of his faults and his vices, so that not one of his acts of worship is accepted. He may labour for years, only to have his work corrupted by a single moment. Even worse than all that is the danger that Allāh (Exalted is He) may look at the servant while he is making a display of his worship and his service, seeking to impress his fellow human beings. In other words, he has presented his external appearance to Allāh, and his inner being to creatures, so Allāh will drive him into an exile from which there is no return. The only refuge is with Allāh!

I have heard from one of the scholars that al-Ḥasan al-Baṣrī (may Allāh bestow His mercy upon him) was seen in a dream after his death, so he was asked about his condition, and he said: "Allāh made me stand in His presence, and He said: 'O Ḥasan, do you remember the day when you were praying in the mosque, and people kept staring at you, so you improved the performance of your prayer? If the first part of your prayer had not been sincerely devoted to Me, I would have banished you today from My door. I would have cut you off from Me once and for all.'"

Since the matter as a whole is extremely precarious and difficult, those endowed with perceptive faculties have examined it meticulously, fearing for themselves. Some of them have gone so far as to disregard everything that makes people notice their deeds. It is related that Rābiʿa [bint Ismāʾīl al-ʿAdawiyya (may Allāh bestow His mercy upon her)] once said: "Whatever is noticeable to me among my deeds, I count it as nothing." Someone else said: "Conceal your good deeds, just as you conceal your bad deeds." Another says: "If it is possible for you to keep a good deed in hiding, you must do so." It is also related that Rābiʿa was asked: "By what means do you hope to achieve what you hope for the most?" She said: "By despairing of the bulk of my work!"

We are told that Muḥammad ibn Wāsiʿ and Mālik ibn Dīnār once met together, and Mālik said: "Either obedience to Allāh, or the Fire of Hell!" Muḥammad ibn Wāsiʿ said: "Either Allāh's mercy, or the Fire of Hell!" Mālik then said: "How great is my need for a teacher like you!"

According to Abū Yazīd al-Bisṭāmī (may Allāh bestow His mercy upon him): "I laboured at worshipful service for thirty years, then I noticed someone saying to me: 'O Abū Yazīd, His treasuries are filled with worshipful service, so, if you wish to attain to Him, you must practise humble submissiveness and feel in need of Him.'"

I heard Professor Abu'l-Ḥasan relate that Professor Abu'l-Faḍl (may Allāh bestow His mercy upon them both) used to say: "I know that the acts of obedience I perform are not accepted in the sight of Allāh (Exalted is He)." He was questioned about that, so he replied: "I know what is necessary for work to be accepted, and I know that I do not meet that requirement, so I know that my deeds are not accepted." He was asked: "So why do you do them?" He replied: "Perhaps Allāh (Exalted is He) will improve me one day, so my lower self will become accustomed to good work. I do not need to make it accustomed to that from the outset."

Such is the state of these luminaries, and of those who are dedicated to striving and making spiritual progress, so you must be as the poet said:

> Seek friendship for yourself with Someone other than people,
> so that despair befalls and hopes [of them] are dashed.
>
> You will never catch up, at a sluggish pace, with leaders
> who have wearied themselves and succeeded in making progress.

At this point, I have decided to quote a traditional report from the truthful and trustworthy [Prophet Muḥammad] (may Allāh's blessings and peace be upon him and his family), though we have already quoted it in more than one book. It reads as follows:

It is related on the authority of Ibn al-Mubārak (may Allāh bestow His mercy upon him), that a man called Khālid ibn Maʿdān said to Muʿādh: "Tell me a story [*ḥadīth*] that you heard from Allāh's Messenger (Allāh bless him and give him peace), one that you have learned by heart and remembered every day, because of its forcefulness and its subtlety." Muʿādh agreed, then he spent a long time weeping, then he said: "How I yearn for Allāh's Messenger (Allāh bless him and give him peace) and the meeting with him!" Then he said: "While I was with Allāh's Messenger (Allāh bless him and give him peace), he mounted a riding beast and mounted me behind him. Then we travelled, and he raised his eyes towards the sky, then he said:

> Praise be to Allāh, who decrees for His creatures whatever He wills, O Muʿādh!

"I said: 'Doubly at your service [*labbaik*], O Chief of the Messengers!' He said:

> I shall tell you a story that will benefit you if you learn it by heart. If you waste it, however, the evidence in your favour will be dismissed [on the Day of Resurrection] in the presence of Allāh (Almighty and Glorious is He). O Muʿādh, Allāh (Blessed and Exalted is He) created seven domains before He created the heavens and the earth. To each heaven He assigned an angel as a gate-keeper and treasurer. At each of the gates of the heavens He appointed an angel as a keeper, in accordance with the status of the gate and its majesty.
>
> The guardian angels ascend with the servant's work, which has a light and radiant beams like the sun, until, when it reaches the heaven of this world, the guardians augment his work and increase it. Then, when it reaches the gate, the angel [in charge of that heaven] says to the guardians: "Take this work and use it to strike its owner in the face! I am the overseer of backbiting. If someone is guilty of backbiting people, my Lord has commanded me not to allow his work to pass beyond me to another [gate-keeper]."
>
> The guardian angels then ascend, the next day, bearing a righteous work that has a shining light. The guardians augment it and increase it, until, when they finally bring it to the second heaven, the angel in charge says: "Stop! Take this work and use it to strike its owner in the face! He performed it for the sake of worldly gain. My Lord has commanded me not to allow his work to pass beyond me to another [gate-keeper]." The angels then curse him [the servant] until the evening arrives.
>
> The guardian angels then ascend with the work of the servant who takes great delight therein. It includes charitable giving, fasting and much piety, so the guardians augment it and increase it. Then, when they finally bring it to the third heaven, the angel on duty at the gate says: "Stop! Take this work and use it to strike its owner in the face! I am the angel in charge of arrogant pride [*kibr*]. My Lord has commanded me not to allow his work to pass beyond me to another [gate-keeper], for he used to treat people with arrogant pride at their meetings.
>
> The guardian angels then ascend with another servant's work, while it shines with the radiance of the stars and the brilliant planet. It includes a gentle murmur, a glorification [of the Lord], a fast, a ritual prayer, a Pilgrimage and a Visitation [*ʿUmra*]. Then, when they finally bring it to the fourth heaven, the angel assigned to it says: "Stop! Take this work and use it to strike its owner in the face! I am the angel in charge of vain conceit. My Lord has commanded

me not to allow his work to pass beyond me to another [gate-keeper], for, when he performed an act of work, he used to infect it with vain conceit."

The guardian angels then ascend with another servant's work, which is paraded as the bride is carried in procession to her bridegroom. Then, when they finally reach the fifth heaven, bearing that good work consisting of sacred combat [*jihād*], a Pilgrimage and a Visitation [*ʿUmra*], and shining like the sun, the angel on duty says: "I am the angel in charge of envy. He used to envy people for what Allāh had given them from His gracious favour. He was displeased with that which pleased Allāh. My Lord has commanded me not to allow his work to pass beyond me to another [gate-keeper]."

The guardian angels then ascend with another servant's work, consisting of a perfect ablution, much prayer, fasting, a Pilgrimage and a Visitation [*ʿUmra*], Then, when they finally pass on with it to the sixth heaven, the angel on duty at the gate says: "I am the angel in charge of mercy. Take this work and use it to strike its owner in the face! He never treated any human being with mercy, and if a servant was afflicted, he would gloat over his misfortune. My Lord has commanded me not to allow his work to pass beyond me to another [gate-keeper]."

The guardian angels then ascend with another servant's work, consisting of much charitable expenditure, fasting, ritual prayer, sacred combat, and pious caution. It has a sound like the sound of thunder, and a light like the flash of lightning. Then, when they finally bring it to the seventh heaven, the angel assigned to that heaven says: "I am the overseer of reputation, meaning celebrity and fame among the people. The owner of this work performed it with the intention of being talked about at public meetings, being highly esteemed by his fellows, and acquiring prestige in the sight of the elders. My Lord has commanded me not to allow his work to pass beyond me to another [gate-keeper]. If any work is not devoted sincerely to Allāh (Exalted is He), it is an act of ostentation, and Allāh (Almighty and Glorious is He) does not accept the ostentatious hypocrite."

The guardian angels then ascend with another servant's work, consisting of ritual prayer, alms-giving, fasting, Pilgrimage, Visitation [*ʿUmra*], good ethics and morality, taciturnity, and remembrance of Allāh (Exalted is He). The angels of the seven heavens collaborate in removing all the obstacles to Allāh (Glory be to Him), so they stand in the presence of the Lord (Magnificent is His Majesty) and bear witness to Him that the servant's work is righteous, devoted sincerely to Allāh (Glory be to Him).

Allāh (Exalted is He) then says: "You are the guardians of My servant's work, and I am the Observer of what his inner being contains. He did not intend this work for My sake. He intended it for someone other than Me, and he did not devote it sincerely to Me. I know best what he intended by his work. My curse be upon him! He has deceived his fellow human beings, and he has deceived you, but he has not deceived Me, for I am the Knower of things unseen, the Overseer of what the hearts contain. No secret is hidden from Me, and nothing absent is absent from Me. My knowledge of what has been is like My knowledge

> of what will be. My knowledge of what has passed is like My knowledge of what remains. My knowledge of the first is like My knowledge of the last. I know the secret and what is more deeply hidden still, so how can My servant deceive Me with his work? He only deceives those creatures who do not work, and I am the Knower of things unseen. My curse be upon him!"
>
> The seven angels and the three thousand collaborators then say: "O our Lord, upon him be Your curse and our curse!" The people of the heavens say: "Upon him be Allāh's curse and the curse of all those who curse!"

Muʿādh (may Allāh bestow His mercy upon him) wept at this point, sobbed bitterly, and said: "O Messenger of Allāh, how can I obtain salvation from what you have described?" He replied: "O Muʿādh, you must follow your Prophet in certitude." Muʿādh said: "You are Allāh's Messenger and I am Muʿādh ibn Jabal. Can I somehow obtain salvation and deliverance?" He said:

> Yes, O Muʿādh. If your work contains a shortcoming, you must restrain your tongue from insulting people, especially your brethren who know the Qurʾān by heart. Your knowledge of your own fault must dissuade you from insulting other people. You must not flatter yourself by blaming your brethren, nor exalt yourself by putting your brethren down. You must not put your work on display, to make yourself known among people. You must not become so involved in this world that it makes you forget the business of the Hereafter. You must not whisper to a man while another is in your presence. You must not treat people haughtily, for if you do, you will be deprived of the benefits of this world and the Hereafter. You must not speak or act obscenely at your meeting, so that people shun you because of your bad morality. You must not taunt people, and you must not rip them apart with your tongue, for if you do, the hounds of Hell will rip you apart. This is referred to in His saying (Exalted is He):
>
> By the rippers ripping....
> *wa 'n-nāshiṭāti nashṭā....* (79:2)
>
> In other words, they are tearing the flesh from the bones.

Muʿādh said: "O Messenger of Allāh, who is capable of these virtues?" He replied:

> O Muʿādh, what I have described to you is easy for someone, if Allāh (Exalted is He) makes it easy for him. All that you need is to like for other people what you like for yourself, and to dislike for them what you dislike for yourself, for then you will have been saved and delivered.

According to Khālid ibn Maʿdān: "Muʿādh did not recite the Qurʾān as often as he recited this Prophetic tradition [*ḥadīth*] and mentioned it at his public meeting."

All of you have now heard this glorious Prophetic tradition, the impact of which is so great that hearts are disturbed by it, minds are bewildered by it, breasts are too narrow to bear it, and lower selves are alarmed by it. You must therefore take refuge with your Master, the God [*Ilāh*] of all the Worlds, and cling to His door with humble submission, entreaty and weeping, through the watches of the night and the ends of the day, in the company of those who are humbly submissive and imploring.

There is no escape from this situation except through His mercy, and no safety from this ocean except through His favour, His enabling grace and His providential care. You must therefore wake up from the slumber of the heedless, give the matter its rightful due, and struggle with your lower self on this perilous hurdle, so that you may not perish with those who perish. Allāh is the One whose help is sought in every case, for He is an Excellent Helper, and He (Exalted is He) is the Most Merciful of the merciful. There is no might nor any power except with Allāh, the All-High, the Almighty.

Subsection

The gist of the matter is this: If you pay careful attention, you will see the value of obedience to Allāh (Exalted is He). You will see the inadequacy of creatures, their weakness and their ignorance, so you must attach no importance to them with your heart. You must be indifferent to their praise, their commendation and their high esteem, in which there is no benefit. You must not seek any of that in exchange for your worshipful obedience. Since you notice the mean and trivial nature of this world, and the speed at which it passes away, you must also not seek it from Allāh in exchange for your obedience.

You must say: "O lower self, the praise of the Lord of All the Worlds, and His appreciation, is better than the praise of incompetent and ignorant creatures, who do not recognize the true value of your work, and what you have endured in its performance. Far from acknowledging what you really deserve for your work and your endurance, they may well think more highly of someone who is inferior to you by a thousand degrees. They may desert you and forget you at the times of greatest need. Even if they do not do that, what do they have at their disposal, and of what are they capable? Besides, they are in the grip of Allāh (Exalted is He), who handles them as He wills, and uses them for whatever purpose He wills. You must therefore be intelligent, O lower self, so that you do not waste your honourable obedience on them, and do not forfeit the praise of Him whose praise is every glory, and the gift of Him whose gift is every treasure."

The poet spoke the truth when he said:

> Insomnia of the eyes for other than Your sake is futile,
> and their weeping for other than Your loss is wasteful.

You must also say: "O lower self, which is better, the Garden of eternity or a glimpse of this world's unlawful bounty and its wretched, fleeting rubbish? You are capable of obtaining that permanent blessing in exchange for your worshipful obedience, so do not be mean in your aspiration, vile in your intention, and base in your deeds. Look at the doves when they fly aloft, and see how their worth ascends and their value increases! You must therefore raise all your aspiration heavenwards. You must devote your heart entirely to Allāh (Exalted is He), the One in whose Hand the whole matter is held. You must not waste what you have gained by your worshipful obedience. If you contemplate with care, you will see in this obedience the enormous benefits and favours bestowed upon you by Allāh (Exalted is He):

"First of all, He made it possible for you and gave you the means [to practise obedience]. Secondly, He removed the impediments from you, leaving you free to practise this obedience. Thirdly, He singled you out for enabling grace and assistance, and made obedience easy for you and beautified it in your heart, so that you put it into practice. Fourthly, regardless of His Majesty and His Might, His independence of you and of your obedience, and the abundance of His gracious favour unto you, He prepared for you, in exchange for this easy work, the bountiful praise and the vast reward that you do not deserve. Fifthly, He showed you grateful appreciation for that, praised you with bountiful praise for this easy work, and loved you for doing it.

"All of this is due to His stupendous favour, nothing else. Were it not so, what entitlement would you have, and what would be the value of your mean and faulty work? You must therefore remember, O lower self, the gracious favour of your Lord, the All-Generous, the All-Compassionate (Glory be to Him), in granting you the blessing of this worshipful service. You must be ashamed of attaching importance to the work, and attribute the grace and favour to Allāh (Exalted is He) in every case. Your sole preoccupation, after achieving this worshipful obedience, must be humble entreaty and supplication to Allāh (Glory be to Him), imploring Him to accept your obedience. You have surely heard the saying of His Bosom Friend [*Khalīl*], Abraham (peace be upon him), when he had concluded his service in building His house [the Ka'ba], and how he implored Allāh to bless him with acceptance. He said:

> "Our Lord, accept from us!
> *Rabba-nā taqabbal min-nā*
> You are the All-Hearing, the All-Knowing."
> *inna-ka Anta 's-Samī'u 'l-'Alīm.* (2:127)

"Then, when he had finished his supplication, he said:

> "Our Lord, and accept the prayer of supplication!"
> *Rabba-nā wa taqabbal du'ā'.* (14:40)

"If he now favours you with acceptance of this paltry merchandise, He has perfected the blessing and magnified the gracious favour, conferring so much happiness, power, glory and exaltation. He has adorned you with so many robes of honour, bounties, treasures and tokens of esteem. If the opposite is the case, however, you will suffer so much loss, forfeiture and deprivation. You must therefore attend to this matter with care, and make it your sole preoccupation.

"If you are diligent in this, repeat it to your heart in the wake of your act of obedience, and seek help from Allāh (Almighty and Glorious is He), He will divert you from paying attention to creatures and the lower self. He will distract you from ostentation and vain conceit, and direct you towards utterly sincere devotion to Allāh (Exalted is He) in acts of obedience and constant remembrance of Allāh's gracious favour (Exalted is He), in all situations. You will achieve the best acts of obedience you could hope for, pure and containing no fault, sincere good deeds containing no blemish, and accepted acts of worship containing no deficiency.

"Even if you achieve the like of this only once in your lifetime, it really amounts to very much indeed. By my life, even if it is little in number, its significance is great, its value is tremendous, its benefits are many, and its consequence is excellent. Enablement to succeed in the like thereof is glorious, and great is the servant's debt to Allāh (Exalted is He) for the benefit conferred. What gift is more magnificent than a gift that is accepted by the Lord of All the Worlds? What merchandise is more splendid than merchandise that is chosen and approved by the Lord of All the Worlds?"

You must therefore pay close attention, O miserable wretch, and beware of being among the deprived. If the matter proceeds in accordance with all of this advice, you will be among those who are sincerely devoted to Allāh (Glory be to Him), afraid of offending Him, mindful of His gracious favours, and well pleasing [to Him]. You will have left this perilous hurdle behind you and been saved from its disasters. You will have gained its benefits and its fruits, acquiring its noble gifts and its bountiful blessings for all eternity.

Allāh (Glory be to Him) is the Custodian of enablement and protection, by His gracious favour and His noble generosity. There is no might nor any power except with Allāh, the All-High, the Almighty.

The Seventh Hurdle
The hurdle of praise [*ḥamd*] and thankfulness [*shukr*]

Your next duty—may Allāh assist you, and us, with His enabling grace!—after surmounting these hurdles, and achieving the goal of this worshipful service safe from disasters, is to give praise and thanks to Allāh (Glory be to Him) for this enormous blessing and generous favour. That is incumbent upon you for two simple reasons: (1) to ensure that the enormous blessing will last, and (2) in order to obtain still more.

1. As for the permanence of the blessing, thankfulness is the means of securing blessings. With it they continue and persist, and without it they disappear and pass away. Allāh (Glory be to Him) has said:

> Allāh does not change what is in a people,
> *inna 'llāha lā yughayyiru mā bi-qawmin*
> until they change what is in themselves.
> *ḥattā yughayyirū mā bi-anfusi-him.* (13:11)

He has also said (More Glorious is He than any other sayer):

> But it was ungrateful for Allāh's blessings,
> *fa-kafarat bi-an'umi 'llāhi*
> so Allāh made it experience
> *fa-adhāqa-ha 'llāhu*
> the garb of starvation and fear
> *libāsa 'l-jū'i wa 'l-khawfi*
> because of what they used to do.
> *bi-mā kānū yaṣna'ūn.* (16:112)

—and He has said (Glory be to Him):

> What concern has Allāh for your punishment,
> *mā yaf'alu 'llāhu bi-'adhābi-kum*
> if you are thankful and truly believe?
> *in shakartum wa āmantum.* (4:147)

The Prophet (Allāh bless him and give him peace) once said:

> Blessings are untamed beasts, like the beasts of the wild, so tie them with thankfulness!

2. As for obtaining more, just as thankfulness is the means of securing the blessing, it is also the cause of increase. Allāh (Glory be to Him) has said:

> If you are thankful, I will surely give you more.
> *la-in shakartum la-azīdanna-kum.* (14:7)
>
> And those who are guided aright,
> *wa 'lladhīna 'htadaw*
> them He increases in guidance.
> *zāda-hum hudan.* (47:17)
>
> And as for those who strive in Our cause,
> *wa 'lladhīna jāhadū fī-nā*
> surely We shall guide them in Our ways.
> *la-nahdiyanna-hum subula-nā.* (29:69)

If a wise master sees that his servant treats a favour with proper respect, he will grant him another, and consider him worthy of it. Otherwise, he will withhold that [extra favour] from him.

Blessings are of two kinds: (1) worldly and (2) religious. The worldly kind is of two types: (1) the blessing of benefit [*naf*ʿ] and (2) the blessing of protection [*daf*ʿ].

The blessing of benefit is conferred on you in the form of things that are in your interest and to your advantage. Advantages are of two sorts: (1) a nature that is sound in its health and well-being, and (2) carnal pleasures like food, drink, clothing, women, and similar benefits.

The blessing of protection is conferred by shielding you from causes of corruption and harm. It takes two forms: (1) It protects your physical body, by keeping you safe from its diseases, afflictions and illnesses. (2) It protects you from harmful influences, such as impediments of various kinds, or the evil intention of a human being, a jinnī, a savage beast, a pest, or some other creature.

As for religious blessings, they are of two types: (1) the blessing of enabling grace [*tawfīq*] and (2) the blessing of immunity [ʿ*iṣma*].

The blessing of enabling grace [*tawfīq*] means that Allāh enables you, first of all, to accept Islām, then to follow the Sunna [exemplary custom of the Prophet (Allāh bless him and give him peace)], then to practise worshipful obedience.

The blessing of immunity [*ʿiṣma*] means that He makes you immune, first of all, to unbelief [*kufr*] and polytheism [*shirk*], then to other sinful acts of disobedience. The detailed account of that can be reckoned by none but the All-Knowing Master, who has bestowed His blessing upon you. As He has said (Glorious and Exalted is He):

> And if you try to reckon Allāh's blessing,
> *wa in taʿuddū niʿmata 'llāhi*
> you will never count it.
> *lā tuḥṣū-hā.* (14:34)

As for the permanence of all these blessings, after He has bestowed them upon you, and what is added to every part of them, that is beyond the calculating power of your imagination. They all depend on one thing, and that is thankfulness and praise for Allāh. When a virtue has such value, and contains all this benefit, it deserves to be adhered to without the slightest neglect, for it is a precious jewel and a marvellous alchemy [*kīmiyāʾ*]. Allāh is the Custodian of enabling grace.

You may ask: "What is the real meaning of praise and thankfulness? What is their spiritual significance and their legal status?"

You should therefore know that the scholars have drawn a distinction between praise and thankfulness. According to their interpretation, praise [*ḥamd*] is one of the forms of glorification [*tasbīḥ*] and *tahlīl* [proclaiming: "There is no god but Allāh (*lā ilāha illa 'llāh*)"], so it is one of the external acts of worship. Thankfulness, on the other hand, is one of the forms of patience and delegation [*tafwīḍ*], so it is one of the internal acts of worship. Thankfulness is contrary to ingratitude, while praise is contrary to blame. Praise is more common and more frequent, while thankfulness is less frequent and more special. Allāh (Exalted is He) has said:

> And few of My servants are very thankful.
> *wa qalīlun min ʿibādiya 'sh-shakūr.* (34:13)

It is thus established that praise and thankfulness are two distinct concepts. Furthermore, praise means commending someone for good behaviour. This point is stressed by our own Shaikh (may Allāh bestow His mercy upon him).

As for thankfulness, the experts have had much to say about its meaning. According to Ibn ʿAbbās (may Allāh be well pleased with him and his father): "Thankfulness is worshipful obedience, with all the limbs and organs, to the Lord of all creatures, in secret and in public." One of our own Shaikhs held a similar view, for he said: "Thankfulness is the performance of acts of worshipful obedience, both outwardly and inwardly." He then reconsidered and said: "It is the avoidance of sinful acts of disobedience, both outwardly and inwardly."

Another said: "Thankfulness is guarding against the voluntary commission of sinful acts of disobedience against Allāh. You must stand guard over your heart, your tongue and your limbs, so that you do not disobey Allāh (Almighty and Glorious is He) with any of these three, in any way at all." The difference between his opinion and that of the first Shaikh is that he [this second Shaikh] (may Allāh the Exalted be well pleased with him) has assigned a definite significance to being on guard, in addition to avoiding sinful acts of disobedience. As for avoidance of the sinful act of disobedience, it is simply a matter of not committing that act in the presence of its stimulants. It is not in itself an acquired virtue, with which the servant is preoccupied and immunized against ingratitude.

According to our own Shaikh (may Allāh the Exalted be well pleased with him): "Thankfulness means extolling the Benefactor for His benefaction, in a manner that precludes disrespect for the Benefactor and ingratitude towards Him."

You may say: "If thankfulness means extolling someone who does good work, in recognition of that good work of his, it is surely correct to maintain that thankfulness flows from Allāh to the servant."

That is a good point, and we have discussed its detailed implications in the book entitled: "Revival of the Religious Sciences [*Iḥyāʾ ʿUlūm ad-Dīn*]," as well as in other books. The crux of the matter, however, is that thankfulness from the servant is a reverence that precludes disrespect for One who treats him well, and it signifies remembering the Benefactor's benefaction, the virtue of the thankful in his thankfulness, and the vice of the ingrate in his ingratitude.

The least that is due to the Benefactor for His benefaction is that it should not be used as an instrument of disobedience. How vile is the condition of someone who uses the Benefactor's benefaction as a weapon with which to disobey Him! It is therefore incumbent on the servant, if he is to fulfil the duty of thankfulness in its true sense, to have a reverence for Allāh (Glory be to Him) that forms a barrier between him and his sinful acts of disobedience, based on the remembrance of His blessings. If he meets this fundamental requirement, then matches it with serious effort in obedience and dedicated commitment to the performance of service, the benefaction has been treated with all due respect, for guarding against sinful disobedience is absolutely essential. Allāh is the Source of enabling grace!

You may ask: "In what context is thankfulness appropriate?"

You should therefore know that it is appropriate in the context of both worldly and religious blessings, in accordance with their respective values. As for hardships and misfortunes in this world, affecting yourself, your family or your property, the scholars have discussed the question: "Is thankfulness for them incumbent on the servant?" Some of them have said: "Thankfulness for them, as such, is not incumbent on the servant. The only necessary response to them is patient endurance. As for thankfulness, it is for blessings, not for anything else." They have also said: "There is no hardship that is not accompanied by Allāh's blessings (Exalted is He), so thankfulness is required for the blessings associated with the hardship, but not for the hardship itself."

Ibn ʿUmar (may Allāh be well pleased with him and his father) was referring to those blessings [associated with hardship] when he said: "I have never been afflicted with an affliction, unless it contained four blessings bestowed on me by Allāh (Exalted is He): (1) It did not affect my religion. (2) It was not greater than the blessings. (3) I was not deprived of contentment with it. (4) I hoped for the reward for suffering it."

It has also been said: "Those blessings include the fact that hardship is transitory, not permanent, and that it comes from Allāh (Exalted is He), not from anyone other than Him. If it is caused indirectly by a creature, it is to your credit against him, not to his credit against you. The servant is therefore obliged to be thankful for blessings associated with hardship."

Others have said, expressing the preferred opinion of our own Shaikh (may Allāh the Exalted bestow His mercy upon him): "The hardships of this world are among those things for which the servant must be thankful, because those hardships are blessings in reality, since they expose the servant to enormous benefits, abundant rewards and generous compensations in the Hereafter. The pain of these hardships seems like nothing beside them, and what blessing is greater than this?

"For the sake of comparison, consider the situation where someone makes you drink a nasty, bitter medicine to remedy an ailment, or subjects you to phlebotomy or blood-cupping to cure a serious and dangerous disease. That treatment restores you to psychological health, physical well-being and a comfortable way of life, in spite of the pain it makes you suffer from the bitterness of the medicine, or the wound inflicted in the blood-letting operation. In reality, it is a tremendous blessing and an obvious favour, even if its outer form is so disgusting that human nature recoils from it, and the lower self is repelled by it. You will not only praise the physician who provided you with this treatment, but do all you possibly can for his benefit."

As you are surely aware, the Prophet (Allāh bless him and give him peace) praised Allāh and thanked Him for adversities, just as he thanked Him for occasions of delight, when he said:

> Praise be to Allāh for what causes grief and what causes happiness!

You must also recall His saying (Magnificent is His Majesty):

> It may happen that you hate a thing
> *fa-ʿasā an takrahū shaiʾan*
> in which Allāh has placed much good.
> *wa yajʿala ʾllāhu fī-hi khairan kathīrā.* (4:19)

What Allāh calls good is more than your imagination can conceive!

This view is corroborated by the fact that blessings are not good because of pleasure and what the lower self desires by its instinctive nature. A blessing [*niʿma*] is that which causes increase in the exaltation of spiritual degrees. That is why it is called *niʿma,* in the sense of increase [*ziyāda*]. If hardships become a cause of increase in the servant's nobility and the exaltation of his spiritual degree, they are blessings in reality, even if they are counted as adversities and trials because of their external appearance. You must understand that successfully!

You may ask: "Is the thankful servant more virtuous, or the one who is patiently enduring?"

You must therefore know that someone said: "The thankful servant is more virtuous, on the strength of Allāh's saying (Exalted is He):

> And few of My servants are very thankful.
> *wa qalīlun min ʿibādiya 'sh-shakūr.* (34:13)"

He has thus included them among the most special of the special few. He has also said, in praise of Noah (peace be upon him):

> He was a very thankful servant.
> *inna-hu kāna ʿabdan shakūrā.* (17:3)

He has described Abrahām (peace be upon him) as:

> Thankful for His bounties.
> *shākiran li-anʿumi-h.* (16:121)

—and He has also commended him because he was at the spiritual station of benefaction and well-being.

That is why someone said: "To be blessed and to be thankful [for the blessing] is dearer to me than being afflicted and enduring [the affliction] with patience." According to someone else, however: "He who endures with patience is actually more virtuous, because his suffering is greater, so he is entitled to greater reward and higher spiritual station." Allāh (Exalted is He) has said [of the Prophet Job (peace be upon him)]:

> We found him patient,
> *innā wajadnā-hu ṣābirā:*
> an excellent servant indeed!
> *niʿma 'l-ʿabd.* (38:44)

He has also said (Exalted is He):

> Surely those who are patient will be paid
> *innamā yuwaffa 'ṣ-ṣābirūna*
> their wages in full without reckoning.
> *ajra-hum bi-ghairi ḥisāb.* (39:10)

—and He has said (Exalted is He):

> Allāh loves those who are patient.
> *wa 'llāhu yuḥibbu 'ṣ-ṣābirīn.* (3:146)

In reality, someone who is thankful [*shākir*] cannot be other than patient [*ṣābir*], and someone who is patient cannot be other than thankful. That is because, if someone is thankful in the abode of trial and tribulation, he is undoubtedly bound to experience a trial that he endures with patience. He cannot be impatient, since thankfulness means reverence for the Benefactor, to an extent that precludes disobeying Him, and impatience is a form of disobedience.

If someone is patient, he is bound to receive a blessing, for, as we have mentioned, hardships are a blessing in reality, in the primary sense. His patience is therefore thankfulness, in reality, if he is patient in enduring hardships, because he restrains himself from impatience as a mark of reverence for Allāh (Exalted is He). This is thankfulness itself, since it is a reverence that precludes disobedience.

Furthermore, in the case of someone who is thankful, he precludes himself from ingratitude, if he patiently refrains from disobedience, moves himself to thankfulness, and is patient in obedience. He thus becomes patient in reality. In the case of someone who is patient, he extols Allāh (Exalted is He) to the point where his reverence for Him precludes him from impatience with what afflicts him, and that reverence moves him to patience. He has thus given thanks to Allāh (Exalted is He), and so become thankful in reality.

Moreover, restraining the lower self from ingratitude, despite its inclination thereto, is a hardship that is endured with patience by the thankful servant. As for the enabling grace and immunity bestowed upon the patient servant, they constitute a blessing for which he gives thanks, so neither of the two [patience and thankfulness] can be separated from the other. Their inseparability is also due to the fact that they are inspired by a single perception, and that is the perception of rectitude, according to some of our scholars.

For all these reasons, we maintain that neither of the two [patience and thankfulness] can be separated from the other. You must therefore understand all this correctly. Allāh is the Source of enabling grace!

Subsection

It is therefore incumbent upon you, O man, to spare no effort in surmounting this relatively easy hurdle, for the benefit is great, glorious in essence and tremendous in worth. You must also consider two fundamental points:

1. The blessing is only conferred on someone who truly understands its value, and the only one who truly understands its value is the thankful servant. The proof of our assertion is the saying of Allāh (Glory be to Him) in the story about the ingrates and the response they received:

> "Are these the ones whom Allāh favours among us?"
> *a-hā'ulā'i manna 'llāhu 'alai-him min baini-nā*
> Is not Allāh Best Aware of those who are thankful?
> *a-laisa 'llāhu bi-A'lama bi'sh-shākirīn.* (6:53)

Those ignoramuses supposed that the mighty blessing and the generous favour would only be granted to people wealthier than the believers, and more noble in lineage and descent. They said: "Of all the slaves and the free, why should these paupers get what they claim? They have been given this mighty blessing because of their claim, instead of us!" Then they asked, in an arrogant and derisive manner:

> "Are these the ones whom Allāh favours among us?"
> *a-hā'ulā'i manna 'llāhu 'alai-him min baini-nā.* (6:53)

Allāh (Exalted is He) responded to them with this brilliant remark:

> Is not Allāh Best Aware of those who are thankful?
> *a-laisa 'llāhu bi-A'lama bi'sh-shākirīn.* (6:53)

He was saying by implication: "The Noble and Generous Master bestows His blessing only on those who truly understand its worth, and none truly understand its worth except those who accept it with heart and soul, prefer it to anything else, do not worry about the trouble they went through in the process of obtaining it, and then stand constantly at the door, giving thanks for the blessing.

"It was in Our sempiternal knowledge that these weaklings would truly understand the value of this blessing, and would be thankful for it. They were therefore more deserving of this blessing than you, regardless of your wealth and your riches, your prestige in this world and your entourage, your lineage and your pedigree. The only blessing that interests you is this world and its vanities, pedigree and lineage, not religion, knowledge and understanding of the truth. You revere and take pride in nothing but that. You would hardly accept this religion, knowledge and truth, except as a favour to the one who brought it to you, because you consider it so trivial and care so little about it.

"As for these weaklings, they sacrifice themselves for that, and expend their spirit for its sake. They are not worried about what they lose, or what enemies they face. You must therefore know that they are the ones who truly understand the value of this blessing, and that reverence for it is firmly rooted in their hearts. The loss of everything else is unimportant to them, and they gladly endure every hardship for its sake, so they immerse their whole lives in thankfulness for it. That is why they are entitled to this noble favour and mighty blessing, in Our sempiternal knowledge, and We have singled them out for it, instead of you."

The same applies to every group of people whom Allāh (Exalted is He) has singled out for one of the blessings of religion, in the form of knowledge or of practice, so you will find them to be, in reality, the people most aware of its value, those with the most intense reverence for it, those most vigorous in its acquisition, those who honour it most highly, and those who are most persistently thankful for it.

As for those whom Allāh has deprived of that [blessing of religion], He has deprived them because of their scant concern and lack of reverence for its true worth, after the sempiternal foreordainment. If reverence for knowledge and worship, in the hearts of the common folk and the marketers, had been like the reverence in the hearts of the scholars and those devoted to worship, they would not have preferred their market and would have thought nothing of forsaking it.

Suppose a jurist [*faqīh*] succeeded in solving a difficult and complex problem. His heart would be so relieved, and he would feel so happy! That solution would occupy a such a glorious place in his heart, that even if he happened to find a thousand gold coins, their discovery would not match it. He may be so interested in a problem in the sphere of religion, that he ponders it for a year, or ten or twenty years, or even longer, without finding that too much and without becoming bored. Allāh (Exalted is He) may then provide him with understanding of the problem, so he will count that as a most enormous favour and a most superb blessing. He will see it as making him richer than any rich man, and nobler than any noble.

A similar problem may be explained to a common man, or to lazy student, who regards himself as equal [to the jurist] in the desire for knowledge and the love of it, but he will not listen with proper attention. If the explanation is very lengthy, he may become bored or fall asleep. Even if the solution becomes clear to him, he will not consider that to be of any great importance.

Comparable to the jurist is the penitent returning to Allāh (Exalted is He). He strives so hard, and tirelessly persists in spiritual exercise, restraining the lower self from carnal desires and pleasures, and bridling the members of the body in all situations of movement and of rest. Allāh may then enable him to complete two cycles of ritual prayer [*rakʿatain*] with due propriety and in a state of purity. For so much humble submission to Allāh (Exalted is He), He may grant him an hour of intimate converse in a state of serenity and sweetness. If he achieves that once in a month, or once in a year, or even once in his whole life, he will consider it a most superb favour and a most enormous blessing. It will make him so happy, and he will be so thankful to Allāh (Exalted is He). He will think nothing of the hardships he has undergone, the weariness of those nights of vigil, and the pleasures that have escaped him.

Now consider those who claim to be fond of acts of worship, keen to obtain something from them. If what they need, in order to obtain the like of this pure worship, is to go without a morsel of their supper, or to refrain from talk that does not concern them, or to make their eyes lose an hour of sleep, their lower selves will find that intolerable, and their hearts will not be pleased. Even in the rare case where they happen to experience an act of worship in a state of serenity, they do not count that as a matter of importance, and they do not accord it many thanks. The only occasions when their happiness blooms, and they express their praise prolifically, are when they obtain a silver coin, or when they receive a piece of bread with some tasty broth, or when they enjoy a long slumber in a good state of physical health. On those occasions they say: "Praise be to Allāh! This is from Allāh's gracious favour."

How can these heedless and incompetent types be on a par with those fortunate ones who exert themself with serious and dedicated effort? These miserable wretches have come to be deprived of all this benefit, while those enabled to obtain it are triumphantly successful. That is how the matter has been determined by the Wisest of judges

(Glory be to Him), for He is the Best Aware of those who are aware. This is the import of His saying (Exalted is He):

> Is not Allāh Best Aware of those who are thankful?
> *a-laisa 'llāhu bi-Aʿlama bi'sh-shākirīn.* (6:53)

You must therefore understand this well, and give it the attention it deserves. You should also know that you are never deprived of something good that you desire, except because of your own lower self. You must therefore spare no effort in order to comprehend the value of Allāh's blessing (Exalted is He). You must revere it with the reverence it deserves, so that you may be worthy of it and of its bestowal. Allāh will then grant you its continuance, as He has granted it to you initially, in accordance with what we have mentioned in the second fundamental point. He is indeed the Kind One, the All-Compassionate.

2. The second fundamental point is that the blessing is only removed from someone who does not truly understand its value. He who does not truly understand its value is the ingrate who is ungrateful for it, and who does not give thanks for it. The proof of that is His saying (Exalted is He):

> Recite to them the tale of him to whom
> *wa 'tlu ʿalai-him nabaʾa 'lladhī*
> We gave Our signs, but he sloughed them off,
> *ātainā-hu āyāti-nā fa-'nsalakha min-hā*
> so Satan overtook him
> *fa-atbaʿa-hu 'sh-shaiṭānu*
> and he became one of those who are led astray.
> *fa-kāna mina 'l-ghāwīn.*
>
> And had We so willed,
> *wa law shiʾnā*
> We could have raised him thereby,
> *la-rafʿnā-hu bi-hā*
> but he clung to the earth
> *wa lākinna-hu akhlada ila 'l-arḍi*
> and followed his own passion.
> *wa 'ttabaʿa hawā-h:*
> His likeness is therefore as the likeness of the dog;
> *fa-mathalu-hu ka-mathali 'l-kalb:*
> if you attack him, he pants with his tongue out,
> *in taḥmil ʿalai-hi yalhath*
> and if you leave him, he pants with his tongue out.
> *aw tatruk-hu yalhath:*

> Such is the likeness of the people who deny Our signs.
> *dhālika mathalu 'l-qawmi 'lladhīna*
> *kadhdhabū bi-āyāti-nā*
> So narrate to them the story,
> *fa-'qṣuṣi 'l-qaṣaṣa*
> for then they may reflect.
> *la'alla-hum yatafakkarūn.* (7:175,176)

Allāh (Exalted is He) is saying by implication: "We blessed this servant with enormous blessings and momentous favours in the sphere of religion. We thereby enabled him to acquire the supreme rank and the lofty station at Our door, so that he could become exalted in Our sight, mighty in worth and great in prestige. But he was ignorant of the value of Our blessing, so he inclined towards this mean and despicable world, and preferred the base and vile desire of his lower self. He did not know that this world, in its entirety, weighs less in Allāh's sight than one of the blessings of religion, and is not equal in His sight to the wing of a gnat.

"He was thus in the position of the dog, which cannot distinguish honour and comfort from disparagement and hardship, nor exaltation and nobility from wretchedness and meanness. Just like the dog, he pants with his tongue out in both situations. Generous favour, as he sees it, consists entirely of a piece of bread to eat, or the bones that are tossed to him from a table. It makes no difference whether you seat him on a couch beside you, or make him stand in the dust and dirt in front of you. As far as he is concerned, his favour and blessing amount to no more than that [bread or bones].

"This is the bad servant, since he is ignorant of the value of Our blessing, and does not recognize the true worth of the generous favour We have bestowed upon him. His perceptive faculty is weak, and his behaviour in the station of nearness is bad, because of the attention he pays to others apart from Us, and his preoccupation with this vile world and trivial pleasure. We have therefore brought him under strict control, placed him in the court of justice, and subjected him to the rule of Omnipotence [*Jabarūt*]. We have stripped him of all Our robes of honour and Our noble gifts, and removed familiarity with Us from his heart. He has thus been stripped naked of all that We had bestowed upon him from Our gracious favour. He has become a banished dog and an accursed rebellious devil."

We take refuge with Allāh, then again we take refuge with Allāh from His displeasure and the pain of His chastisement! He is indeed Kind and Compassionate with us.

You should be content with the analogy of a king who honours a servant of his, by conferring his own fine robe upon him, drawing him close to his royal presence, placing him above his other servants and chamberlains, and commanding him to cling to his door. Then he commands the construction of palaces for that servant's use, in another place, as well as the erection of couches and tables for his sake. He also provides him with beautiful maidservants and appoints menservants to work for him. When the servant returns [to his own palace] from the king's service, his royal master seats him there as a king who is served and honoured. Between his situation of service and that of his kingship and authority, the space is no more than an hour of the day, or even less.

If this servant looks to the side of this king's door, and takes notice of a stableman who is eating a loaf of bread, or a dog that is chewing a bone, he will be distracted from the service of the king. He will fail to pay attention to the robes of honour and the gracious favour he has received, so he will rush over to that stableman, stretch out his hand and ask him for a piece of the loaf, or compete with the dog for a bone, for he will envy them both and think highly of what they have at their disposal.

If the king sees him in this condition, he will surely say: "This is a stupid, unambitious fool, who does not realize the value of our noble generosity. He does not recognize the worth of the dignity we have bestowed upon him, by clothing him with robes of honour and drawing him close to our presence, as well as granting him our caring attention and commanding that he should be given treasures and all kinds of favours. This is nothing but a dropout, an ignoramus of little discernment. Strip him of his robes of honour and drive him away from our door!"

This is the state of the scholar, if he inclines towards this world, and of the worshipful servant if he follows passionate desire, after Allāh has honoured him with His worshipful service and intimate knowledge of His favours, His Sacred Law [*Sharīʿa*] and His judgements. Since he has failed to recognize the value of that honour, he will end up with the meanest thing in the sight of Allāh (Almighty and Glorious is He) and the most contemptible in His sight, for he will desire it and seek it greedily. It will loom larger in his heart and be dearer to him than all those splendid blessings he has received, in the form of knowledge, worshipful service, wise insights and real experiences.

The same applies in the case of someone whom Allāh specially favoured with various kinds of His enabling grace and His protection, whom He adorned with the lights of His service and His worship, whom He regarded with compassion in most of his moments, whom He extolled to His angels, to whom He granted leadership and dignity at His door, on whom He conferred the right of intercession, and whom He appointed to the station of the mighty. It came to the point where, if he appealed to Allāh, He would answer him and declare Himself at his service, and if he asked Him for something, He would give to him and enrich him. If he interceded on behalf of some creatures, He would accept his intercession on their behalf, and make him well pleased. If he swore an oath by Him, He would endorse it and fulfil it. If something occurred to his mind, He would grant it to him before he asked for it with his tongue.

Suppose this were someone's condition, but he did not truly understand the value of these blessings, or did not recognize the worth of this position, so he turned away from all that towards a wicked selfish passion, with no sense of shame, or a piece of worldly rubbish with no permanence to it. Suppose he paid no attention to those generous favours, robes of honour, presents, benefits and gifts, nor to what he had been promised and prepared for him in the Hereafter, in the form of tremendous reward and abundant and lasting bounty. How vile that person would be! What a bad servant he would be! How great would be his peril, if he did but know, and how atrocious his conduct, if he did but understand!

We beseech Allāh, the Gentle, the Compassionate, to improve us with the splendour of His grace and the abundance of His mercy. He is indeed the Most Merciful of the merciful.

It is therefore incumbent upon you, O man, to spare no effort in order to understand the true value of the blessings you receive from Allāh (Exalted is He). When He blesses you with the blessing of religion, you must beware of paying attention to this world and its vanities, for that would be nothing but a kind of disdain, on your part, for the blessings of religion entrusted to you by your Lord. You have surely heard His saying (Exalted is He) to the Chief of the Messengers:

> We have given you seven of the oft-repeated [verses]
> *wa la-qad ātainā-ka sabʿan mina 'l-mathānī*
> and the Mighty Qur'ān.
> *wa 'l-Qur'āna 'l-ʿaẓīm.*
>
> Strain not your eyes toward that which
> *lā tamuddanna ʿainai-ka ilā mā*
> We cause some wedded pairs among them to enjoy,
> *mattaʿnā bi-hi azwājan min-hum*
> and be not grieved on their account,
> *wa lā taḥzan ʿalai-him wa 'khfiḍ*
> and lower your wing for the believers.
> *janāḥa-ka li'l-mu'minīn.* (15:87,88)

Allāh (Exalted is He) is saying by implication: "For everyone who has been given the Mighty Qur'ān, it becomes a duty never to regard this vile world with a look of delight and approval, in addition to having no desire for it." He must be constantly thankful to Allāh for that [gift of the Mighty Qur'ān], for it is the gracious favour eagerly sought by His Bosom Friend [*Khalīl*] Abraham (may Allāh's blessings and peace be upon him), who wished that He would confer it upon his father, but He did not do so. Then His Chosen Friend [*al-Muṣṭafā*] (Allāh bless him and give him peace) longed for Him to confer it upon his paternal uncle, Abū Ṭālib, but He did not do so.

As for the vanities of this world, they are the rubbish that He dumps on every unbeliever, Pharaoh, apostate, atheist, ignoramus and profligate, they being the most despicable of His creatures in His sight, until they drown in those vanities. He keeps the rubbish of this world away from every Prophet, special friend, champion of the Truth, scholar and worshipful servant, they being the dearest to Him of all His creatures, so they hardly acquire a piece of bread to eat and a tattered cloak to wear. He favours them with that which does not stain them with its filth. Speaking to Moses and Aaron (peace be upon them), He said (More Glorious is He than any other sayer):

> If I wished to adorn you with an adornment [of this world], so that Pharaoh would know, when he saw it, that his power was incapable of producing it, I would do so, but I am withholding this world from you and making you averse

> to it. I do likewise with My saintly friends. I drive them away from its bounty, as the caring shepherd drives his camels away from the pools of dung. I surely keep them from enjoying its comfort and its pleasant life, and that is not because of their unimportance to Me, but in order to perfect their share of My gracious favour.

He has also said (Exalted is He):

> And were it not that mankind would have become
> *wa law lā an yakūna 'n-nāsu*
> one community, We might well have appointed
> *ummatan wāḥidatan la-ja'alnā*
> for those who disbelieve in the All-Merciful,
> *li-man yakfuru bi'r-Raḥmāni*
> roofs of silver for their houses
> *li-buyūti-him suqufan min fiḍḍatin*
> and stairs [of silver] for them to mount,
> *wa ma'ārija 'alai-hā yaẓharūn.*
> and, for their houses, doors
> *wa li-buyūti-him abwāban*
> and couches [of silver] on which to recline,
> *wa sururan 'alai-hā yattaki'ūn.*
> and ornaments of gold.
> *wa zukhrufā:*
> Yet all that would have been
> *wa in kullu dhālika*
> but a provision of the life of this world,
> *lammā matā'u 'l-ḥayāti 'd-dunyā*
> and the Hereafter with your Lord
> *wa 'l-ākhiratu 'inda Rabbi-ka*
> would have been for the truly devout.
> *li'l-muttaqīn.* (43:33–35)

Notice the difference between the two situations, if you are perceptive, and say: "Praise be to Allāh, who has favoured us with the favours of His saints and His special friends, and has dispelled from us the trial of His enemies, so that we may be happy and experience the most abundant thankfulness, the greatest praise, the most copious benefit and the mightiest blessing, which is Islām." That [blessing of Islām] is the most excellent of all, so you must not abate your thankfulness for it throughout your night and your day. If you are incapable of recognizing its true worth, you should know for a fact that, even if you were created at the beginning of this world, and engaged in thankfulness for the blessing of Islām from the very first moment till eternity, you would not complete that [thankfulness]. You would leave some of the duty unfulfilled, because the gracious favour of that blessing is so tremendous.

You should also know that the space [available in this book] does not allow me to discuss the full extent of my knowledge concerning the value of this blessing. Even if I dictated a million sheets of paper on the subject, the extent of my knowledge would reach beyond that. I must confess, however, that what I know, beside what I do not know, is like a drop in all the oceans of this world. You have surely heard—woe unto you!—His saying (Exalted is He) to the Chief of the Messengers (Allāh bless him and give him peace):

> You did not know what the Book was,
> *mā kunta tadrī ma 'l-Kitābu*
> nor what the faith.
> *wa la 'l-īmānu.* (42:52)

—until He said to him:

> And [Allāh] taught you what you did not know.
> *wa ʿallama-ka mā lam takun taʿlam:*
> Allāh's grace towards you has been tremendous.
> *wa kāna faḍlu 'llāhi ʿalaika ʿaẓīmā.* (4:113)

Allāh (Exalted is He) said to a group of people:

> It is rather that Allāh is treating you with gracious favour,
> *bali 'llāhu yamunnu ʿalai-kum*
> inasmuch as He has guided you to faith,
> *an hadā-kum li'l-īmāni*
> if you are honest.
> *in kuntum ṣādiqīn.* (49:17)

You have surely heard the saying of the Prophet (Allāh bless him and give him peace), when he heard a man say: "Praise be to Allāh for Islām!" He said to him:

> You are praising Allāh for a tremendous blessing!

When the bringer of glad tidings [about Joseph] came to Jacob (peace be upon him), he said: "In what religion did you leave him?" The man replied: "In the religion of Islām." Jacob then said: "The blessing is now complete!"

Someone said: "No statement is dearer to Allāh (Exalted is He), or more expressive of thankfulness in His sight, than for the servant to say:

'Praise be to Allāh, who has blessed us and guided us to the religion of Islām!'"

Beware of neglecting thankfulness for Islām, and of being mistaken about your present condition with regard to Islām, true knowledge, enabling grace and immunity. Where that is concerned, there is no room for false security and heedlessness, for matters depend on the ultimate consequences. Sufyān ath-Thawrī (may Allāh the Exalted bestow His mercy upon him) used to say: "Whenever someone feels too secure about his religion, he will be dispossessed."

Our own Shaikh (may Allāh the Exalted bestow His mercy upon him) used to say: "When you hear about the state of the unbelievers and their everlasting sojourn in the Fire of Hell, do not feel secure about yourself, for the matter is at risk. You cannot tell what the outcome will be, nor what has been predestined for you in the decree of the Unseen, so do not be deceived by the clarity of the times, for beneath it lie the obscurities of misfortunes."

One of the Shaikhs used to say: "O you who are deceived by immunities, beneath them lie all kinds of adversities. Allāh graced Iblīs with various forms of His immunity, though he was doomed in His sight to the realities of His curse. He also graced Bal'ām with the lights of His friendship, though he was doomed in His sight to the realities of His hostility."

'Alī (may Allāh be well pleased with him) is reported as having said: "Many a one is misled by the good treatment he receives. Many a one is deceived by the good things that are said about him. Many a one is deluded by the fact that he is granted pardon." Dhu'n-Nūn was asked: "By what is the servant most likely to be deceived?" He said: "By gracious favours and generous gifts." That is why Allāh (Glory be to Him) has said:

> We shall lead them on
> *sa-nastadriju-hum*
> by steps from whence they do not know.
> *min ḥaithu lā ya'lamūn.* (68:44)

According to the masters of intimate knowledge [this means]: "We shall grant them abundant blessings, and make them forget to be thankful." As the poet said:

You have thought well of the days, since they have been good,
and you have not feared the evil of what destiny may bring.

Your nights have been peaceful, so you have been deceived by them,
for it is during the calm of the nights that trouble occurs.

You must also know that, whenever you come to be closer [to the Lord], your situation is more perilous and more difficult, performance of the task [of worhsip] is harder and more delicate, and the danger to you is greater. The higher something rises, the harder will be the fall, if it topples down. As someone said in poetic verse:

Birds do not fly and rise aloft [indefinitely];
as they fly up, so do they fall to earth.

There is therefore no justification whatsoever for overconfidence, neglect of thankfulness, and failure to appeal for protection. Ibrāhīm ibn Ad'ham used to say: "How can you feel secure, when Abraham, the Bosom Friend [*al-Khalīl*] (may Allāh's blessings and peace be upon him), used to say:

'My Lord, make this territory safe,
Rabbi 'j'al hādha 'l-balada āminan
and preserve me and my sons
wa 'jnub-nī wa baniyya
from serving idols.'
an na'buda 'l-aṣnām. (14:35)

—"and Joseph, the Champion of the Truth [*aṣ-Ṣiddīq*] (peace be upon him) used to say:

'Let me die as one
who is truly submissive [to You].'"
tawaffa-nī musliman. (12:101)

Sufyān ath-Thawrī never ceased saying: "O Allāh, save, save!"—as if he were aboard a ship and afraid of drowning. I have heard that Muḥammad ibn Yūsuf (may Allāh bestow His mercy upon him) once said: "I observed Sufyān ath-Thawrī one night, and he wept the whole night through, so I said to him: 'Is this weeping of yours on account of sins?' He waved a straw, and said: 'Sin is less important to Allāh than this. All that I dread is that Allāh may strip me of Islām and refuge with Allāh.'"

I also heard one of those who know by experience say: "One of the Prophets (peace be upon them) asked Allāh (Exalted is He) about the case of Bal'ām and his banishment after those signs and noble favours, so Allāh (Exalted is He) explained:

> He was not thankful to Me for what I gave him, not for a single day. Had he been thankful to Me for that, just once, I would not have dispossessed him."

You must come to your senses, O man, and observe with very great care the principle of thankfulness and praise to Allāh for His blessings in the sphere of religion. The loftiest of those blessings are Islām and true knowledge, while the lowliest of them are, for example, the successful utterance of a glorification [*tasbīḥ*], or an immunity from talk that does not concern you. Perhaps He will complete His blessings upon you, and not test you with the bitterness of their removal. The bitterest of things, and the hardest to endure, are abasement after honour, banishment after being drawn close, and separation after communion. Allāh (Exalted is He) is the Noble One, the Generous, the Kind, the Compassionate.

Subsection

The gist of the matter is this: You have taken a good close look at the tremendous favours Allāh (Exalted is He) has bestowed upon you, and His stupendously generous and noble gifts, which your heart cannot count and your imagination cannot encompass, and you have finally left these difficult hurdles behind you. You have found the treasures of knowledge and perceptive understanding, and been cleansed of sins and serious offences. You have overtaken the impediments, repelled the hindrances, conquered the incentives, and been saved from the impairments.

You have acquired many a noble virtue in the process, and many a lofty and dignified rank, the first of them being perspicacity and enlightenment, and the last of them being proximity and ennoblement. You have contemplated these blessings to the full extent of your intelligence and the enabling grace you have received. You have been thankful to Allāh to the extent of your ability, so that He would keep your tongue busy with praising and extolling Him, fill your heart with His Might and His Majesty, bring you to a point where you are barred from disobeying Him, and stimulate you to serve Him, as well as you can, or to the extent of your ability, while admitting the shortfall in recognition of the true value of His gracious favour and His benefaction.

Whenever you have been negligent in thankfulness to Him, or slackened off, or made a slip, you have recovered, worked hard, turned to Him in humble submission and entreaty, and appealed to Him by saying: "O Allāh, O my Master! As you began by blessing me with Your gracious favour, to which I had no entitlement, complete Your blessing now, again without entitlement!"

You must call out to him with the call of His saints, who have discovered the crown of His guidance, tasted the sweetness of His intimate knowledge, and feared for themselves the scorching heat of banishment and degradation, the desolation of distance and wandering astray, and the bitterness of isolation and removal. They submitted themselves humbly at the door [of His mercy], pleading for help. They stretched the palms of their hands towards Him, and cried out loud in lonely places:

> Our Lord! Do not cause our hearts to stray
> *Rabba-nā lā tuzigh qulūba-nā*
> after You have guided us aright,
> *baʿda idh hadaita-nā.*
> and bestow on us mercy from Your Presence
> *wa hab la-nā min ladun-ka raḥma:*
> You, only You are the Bestower.
> *inna-ka Anta 'l-Wahhāb.* (3:8)

As I understand it—Allāh knows best, of course!—this conveys the meaning: "We have received from You a blessing, so we are eager for another. You are the Generous Bestower, so, as You have granted us the grace of blessing at the outset, grant us the mercy of completion at the end!"

You have surely heard—woe unto you!—the first supplication [*duʿāʾ*] taught by the Lord of All the Worlds to His Muslim servants, whom He selected from among all His creatures. This supplication is expressed in His saying (Exalted is He):

> Guide us in the straight path.
> *ihdina 'ṣ-ṣirāṭa 'l-mustaqīm.* (1:5)

That is to say: "Set us firmly upon it and make it permanently ours." This is how you must humbly entreat Him, for the matter is tremendously important!

It has been said: "As for the wise, they have examined the misfortunes of creatures and all their trials, and they have reduced them to five: (1) Illness during absence from home. (2) Poverty in old age. (3) Death in youth. (4) Blindness after sight. (5) Unbelief after true knowledge."

Even better than that is the saying of the poet:

> For everything, when you part with it, there is a substitute,
> but for Allāh, if you part with Him, there is no substitute.

Another poet said:

> If this world lets a man keep his religion,
> what he misses from it is not a harmful loss.

[You must entreat Him] likewise in the case of every blessing that He has bestowed upon you, and every assistance with which He has supported you in the surmounting of any of the hurdles, so that He may establish for you what He has given, and may grant you even more than you wish and desire. If you do that, you will have left this dangerous hurdle behind you, and you will have gained the two mighty and noble treasures that are right conduct and the quest for extra blessing. You will keep the existing blessings that He has granted you, so do not fear their loss, and, of the missing blessings that have not yet been granted, He will give you more than you see fit to ask for and desire, so do not fear their loss.

You will then be included among the truly knowledgeable, the scholars who act in accordance with the religion, the penitents, the pure, those who abstain from this world, those who are dedicated to service, those who conquer the devil, those who practise true devotion with the heart and the members of the body, those who curtail their expectation, those who show good will, those who are humbly submissive, those who put all their trust [in the Lord], those who delegate [their affairs to Him], those who are content, those who are patient, those who are afraid [of offending Him], those who are hopeful [of His mercy], those who are sincere, those who remember the gracious favour, and those who are thankful for the blessings of their Master, the Lord of All the Worlds.

Then, after that, you will come to be among the righteous, the ennobled, the champions of the Truth. You must therefore consider all that has been said. Allāh (Exalted is He) is the Custodian of enabling grace.

You may say: "If the matter is as you have described it, rare indeed is the worshipful servant of this Master, and few can ever reach this goal! Who has the strength to cope with these burdens, to meet these stringent conditions and observe these customary practices [*sunan*]?"

You must therefore know that Allāh (Exalted is He) says likewise:

> And few of My servants are very thankful.
> *wa qalīlun min ʿibādiya 'sh-shakūr.* (34:13)

> But most human beings do not give thanks.
> *wa lākinna akthara 'n-nāsi lā yashkurūn.* (2:243)

> And most of them do not understand.
> *wa aktharu-hum lā yaʿqilūn.* (5:103)

> But most of them do not know.
> *wa lākinna akthara-hum lā yaʿlamūn.* (6:37)

Yet that is easy for someone for whom Allāh (Exalted is He) makes it easy. The servant is responsible for dedicated effort, and right guidance is Allāh's responsibility (Glory be to Him). Allāh (Exalted is He) has said:

> And as for those who strive in Our cause,
> *wa 'lladhīna jāhadū fī-nā*
> surely We shall guide them in Our ways.
> *la-nahdiyanna-hum subula-nā.* (29:69)

If the weak servant fulfils what is incumbent upon him, what do you think about the Lord All-Powerful, Independent, Generous and Compassionate?

You may say: "Life is short, and these hurdles are long and difficult, so how can life last until these stipulations are completely fulfilled, and these hurdles are surmounted?"

By my life, these hurdles are indeed long and the stipulations concerning them are difficult indeed. Nevertheless, if Allāh (Exalted is He) wishes to grant His servant special favour, He will shorten their length for him, and ease their difficulty for him, so that he will say, after surmounting them: "How close is this path [to its destination], and how short it is! What a simple matter this is, and how easy!" As I said in my own poetic verses, when I achieved this aim:

> The signpost of the highway is plain to him who seeks it,
> but I see the hearts in blindness to the highway.
>
> I was amazed to see someone perish, when his salvation
> was at hand, and I was amazed to see someone escape.

There are some who take seventy years to surmount this hurdle, some who take twenty years, some who take ten years, some who achieve it in one year, and some who surmount it in a month, or even in a week, or even in an hour. There are even some who achieve it in a split second, with special enabling grace and sempiternal providence from Allāh (Glory be to Him).

You surely remember the Companions of the Cave [*Aṣḥāb al-Kahf*], and how short their survival threatened to be, when they saw the change in the face of their king, Diqyānūs, so they said:

> "Our Lord is the Lord of the heavens and the earth.
> *Rabbu-nā Rabbu 's-samāwāti wa 'l-arḍi*
> We cry to no god beside Him,
> *lan nadʿuwa min dūni-hi ilāhan*
> for then we would utter an enormity."
> *la-qad qulnā idhan shaṭaṭā.* (18:14)

True knowledge came to them, and they perceived the realities contained within this path. They traversed this path, so they became delegators, trusting entirely [in Allāh] and rightly guided. They said:

> "Then seek refuge in the Cave;
> *fa-'wū ila 'l-kahfi*
> your Lord will spread for you of His mercy
> *yanshur la-kum Rabbu-kum min raḥmati-hi*
> and will prepare for you a pillow in your plight."
> *wa yuhayyiʾ la-kum min amri-kum mirfaqā.* (18:16)

All of that happened to them in the space of an hour or an instant. You surely remember the sorcerers of Pharaoh, and how barely an instant passed, when they witnessed the miracle of Moses (peace be upon him), before they said:

"We believe in the Lord of All the Worlds,
āmannā bi-Rabbi 'l-ʿālamīn:
the Lord of Moses and Aaron."
Rabbi Mūsā wa Hārūn. (26:47,48)

They perceived the path and traversed it, so, in a few moments or even less, they came to be among those who truly know Allāh (Exalted is He), who are content with Allāh's decree (Exalted is He), who patiently endure His trial, who are thankful for His blessings, and who yearn for the meeting with Him. They cried:

"It is no hurt, for to our Lord we shall return."
lā ḍaira innā ilā Rabbi-nā munqalibūn. (26:50)

We have related that Ibrāhīm ibn Ad'ham (may Allāh bestow His mercy upon him) was engaged in his worldly business, whatever that was, but then he turned away from it and set out to embark on this path. He had travelled no farther than the distance from Balkh to Marwarūdh, when he saw a man falling from the bridge into deep water, so he signalled to him: "Stop!" The man stopped at his place in the air, and so he was saved [from falling into the water and drowning].

We have also related that Rābiʿa al-Baṣriyya, as a very old slave woman, was conducted around the market of Baṣra, but nobody was interested in her because of her old age. Then one of the merchants took pity on her, purchased her for about a hundred silver coins, and emancipated her. She then chose this path and embarked on worshipful service. Barely a year had passed, before she was visited by the ascetics of Baṣra, its Qurʾān-reciters and its scholars, because of the grandeur of her spiritual station.

As for someone for whom providential care has not been foreordained, he will not be treated with gracious favour and guidance, so he must rely on his own devices. He may remain in a rift of one hurdle for seventy years, without surmounting it. He will scream and yell so very often: "How dark is this path and how difficult! How hard is this business and how perplexing!" That is because the whole matter hinges on one basic point, and that is the foreordainment of the Almighty, the All-Knowing, the Just, the Wise.

You may ask: "Why is one person singled out for special enabling grace, and another deprived of it, when both of them share the noose of servitude?"

In response to this question, a voice cries out from the awnings of Majesty: "To enjoin proper conduct, and to make known the secret of Lordship and the reality of servitude, for:

> He will not be questioned as to what He does,
> *lā yusʾalu ʿammā yafʿalu*
> but they will be questioned.
> *wa hum yusʾalūn.* (21:23)"

The likeness of this path in this world is the Narrow Bridge [*Ṣirāṭ*] in the Hereafter, with its hurdles, its distances and its intersections, and the differing conditions of the people traversing it. One of them passes over it like flashing lightning, one of them passes over it like the stormy wind, another like the race horse, another like the bird, while another walks on foot, another crawls so that he becomes as black as coal, another listens to the sizzling sound [of Hell], and another is seized with iron hooks and thrown into Hell.

Such is the condition of this path with its travellers in this world, for there two narrow bridges: the narrow bridge of this world and the Narrow Bridge of the Hereafter. The Narrow Bridge of the Hereafter is for the lower selves to cross, and its terrors are visible to those endowed with faculties of perception. The narrow bridge of this world is for the hearts, and its terrors are visible to those endowed with faculties of perception and intelligence. The differing conditions of those travelling in the Hereafter are due to the difference of their conditions in this world. You must consider that well and truly. Allāh is the Source of enabling grace!

Subsection

What you must realize is that this path of ours, in both its length and its shortness, is not like the physical distances travelled by the lower selves. They traverse them on foot, so their traversing them depends on the physical strength and weakness of the lower selves. This is a spiritual path, travelled by the hearts, so you traverse it with thoughts in accordance with beliefs and perceptions. Its origin is a heavenly light and a Divine glance, which penetrates the servant's heart, so by it he sees the state of the two abodes in reality.

The servant may sometimes seek this light for a hundred years, without finding it or any trace of it. That is due to his error in the search, his shortcoming in dedicated effort, and his ignorance of the method thereof. Another may find it in fifty years, another may find it in ten, another in a day, and another in an hour or an instant, through the providential care of the Lord of Might and Glory. He (Exalted is He) is the Custodian of guidance, but the servant is commanded to strive with dedicated effort, so it is incumbent upon him to do as he has been commanded, and the commandment is predestined, foreordained. The Lord is a Just Judge, who does whatever He wills and decrees whatever He wishes.

You may say: "How great is this peril, and how difficult is this business! This weak servant is in need of so much! What is the purpose of all this work and effort, and the fulfilment of these stipulations?"

By my life, you are telling the truth when you say that the business is difficult and the peril is great. That is why He has said (Exalted is He):

> Indeed, We created the human being in trouble.
> *la-qad khalaqna 'l-insāna fī kabad.* (90:4)

—and He has said (Exalted is He):

> We offered the trust to the heavens and the earth
> *innā ʿaraḍna 'l-amānata ʿala 's-samāwāti wa 'l-arḍi*
> and the hills, but they shrank from bearing it
> *wa 'l-jibāli fa-abaina an yaḥmilna-hā*
> and they were afraid of it.
> *wa ashfaqna min-hā*
> And man assumed it.
> *wa ḥamala-ha 'l-insān:*
> Surely he is sinful, very foolish.
> *inna-hu kāna ẓalūman jahūlā.* (33:72)

That is why the Chief of the Messengers (may Allāh's blessings and peace be upon him and upon them) once said:

> If you knew what I know, you would weep a great deal and laugh very little.

It is related that the crier cries from the direction of Heaven: "Would that creatures had not been created! Since they have been created, would that they knew why they have been created! Once they do know, if only they would act in accordance with what they know!" The righteous predecessors (may Allāh be well pleased with them) say likewise. Abū Bakr aṣ-Ṣiddīq [the Champion of Truth] (may Allāh be well pleased with him) is reported as having said: "I dearly wish that I were green grass, so that animals would eat me, on account of my fear of the torment [in the Hereafter]." ʿUmar (may Allāh be well pleased with him) is said to have heard a man recite:

> Has there ever come upon the human being
> *hal atā ʿala 'l-insāni*
> a while of time
> *ḥīnun mina 'd-dahri*
> when he was a thing unremembered?
> *lam yakun shaiʾun madhkūrā.* (76:1)

He said: "If only that time would last forever!"

According to Abū ʿUbaida ibn al-Jarrāḥ (may Allāh be well pleased with him): "I dearly wish that I were a sheep for my family, so that my flesh would be divided, my broth would be drunk, and I would not have been created!"

According to Wahb ibn Munabbih: "The human being was created stupid. Were it not for his stupidity, he would not enjoy life."

According to al-Faḍl ibn ʿIyāḍ (may Allāh bestow His mercy upon him): "I do not envy an angel brought near [to the Lord], nor a Prophet sent as a Messenger, nor a righteous servant. Will not these be censured on the Day of Resurrection? I envy only those who have not been created."

According to ʿAṭāʾ as-Sulamī (may Allāh bestow His mercy upon him): "If a fire was ignited, and I was told: 'If someone throws himself into it, he will become nothing,' I am afraid I would die of joy before reaching the fire!"

Well then, O man, the business is difficult, as you say. It is actually more difficult and more serious than you think and imagine, but it is a matter predestined in the knowledge of the Sempiternal, and managed by the Almighty, the All-Knowing, so the servant has no option but to spare no effort in servitude, cling to the lifeline of Allāh, and engage in constant supplication to Allāh (Glory be to Him). Perhaps He will bestow His mercy upon him, so he will be saved by His gracious favour.

As for your asking about the purpose of all this, the question indicates a great heedlessness on your part. Your proper question should be: "What does all this mean in relation to what the weak servant is seeking?"

Do you know what the weak servant is seeking? The least of what he is seeking amounts to two things: (1) safety in the two abodes [this world and the Hereafter], and (2) dominion in the two abodes.

1. As for safety in the two abodes, this world, its disasters, its corruption and its calamities are such that even the angels brought near [to the Lord] are not safe from them. I have heard it related, in the story of Hārūt and Mārūt, that when the servant's spirit is transported into the sky, the angels of the heavens will say, in their astonisment: "How has this one escaped from an abode in which the best of us were corrupted?" As for the Hereafter, its terrors and its hardships are such that the Prophets and Messengers (peace be upon them) will scream there: "My own self, my own self! I beg You today for my own self alone!" According to one account: "Even if a man did the work of seventy Prophets, he would think that he would never be saved."

If someone wishes to be saved from the troubles of this world, let him leave them by means of Islām, for then he will be safe [*sālim*] and no affliction will befall him. If he wishes to be saved from the terrors of the Hereafter, let him enter the Garden of Paradise, for then he will be safe and no disaster will befall him. Will this be an easy matter?

2. As for dominion and noble dignity, dominion is the effective exercise of dispensation and volition. In this world, that really belongs to the saints of Allāh (Almighty and Glorious is He) and His special friends, who are well pleased with His decree. The whole earth, both land and sea, is but one step for them. The desert and the town are gold and silver for them. The jinn and humankind, the animals and the birds are subject to them. They do not wish for anything without it becoming theirs, for they do not wish for anything except what Allāh wills, and whatever Allāh wills comes to be. They are not in awe of any of their fellow creatures, but all their fellow creatures are in awe of them. They serve no one except Allāh (Almighty and Glorious is He), and everyone but Allāh serves them. Where do the kings of this world have one percent of this rank? They are insignificant and inferior by comparison!

As for the dominion of the Hereafter, Allāh (Exalted is He) says:

> And when you see, there you will see
> *wa idhā raʾaita thamma*

a state of bliss and a grand dominion.
ra'aita na'īman wa mulkan kabīrā. (76:20)

How splendidly the Lord of Might and Glory describes it, when He calls it "a grand dominion"!

You know that this world in its entirety amounts to very little, and that its duration from first to last is very little. The share of any one of us in this little is very little. One of us may expend his material wealth and his spirit, so that he may obtain a little amount of this little for a little while. If he does achieve that, he will be excused or even envied, and he will not begrudge the expense of his material wealth and personal effort. In the words of the poet Imru'l-Qais:

My companion wept when he saw the road ahead of him,
for he was sure that we would be overtaking Caesar.

So I told him: "Your eye must not weep! We shall either
gain a dominion or die, and so we shall be excused."

What can be said, therefore, about the condition of someone who seeks the grand dominion in the abode of permanent and everlasting bliss? Would he consider it too much to perform two cycles of prayer for the sake of Allāh (Exalted is He), or to spend a couple of silver coins, or to stay awake for two nights? By no means! Even if he had a million selves, a million spirits and a million lives, every life greater and longer than the life of this world, he would expend all that for the sake of this mighty goal. That expense would be little indeed, and, if he finally achieved success, that would be a tremendous booty and a gracious favour from the One who gave him so much. You must therefore wake up, O miserable wretch, from the slumber of the heedless!

I also considered what Allāh (Glory be to Him) gives the servant if he obeys Him, clings to His service, and travels this path all his life. I found that these gifts add up to forty noble awards and robes of honour, twenty in this world and twenty in the Hereafter:

1. Of the gifts bestowed in this world, the first is that Allāh (Glory be to Him) remembers him and praises him. How great an honour for a servant, that Allāh, the Lord of All the Worlds, should favour him with His remembrance and His praise!

2. Allāh (Magnificent is His Majesty) thanks him and treats him with respect. If a feeble creature, like yourself, were to thank you and

treat you with respect, you would be honoured by that, so consider the honour bestowed by the God of the first and the last!

3. He loves the servant. If you were loved by the chief of a tribal encampment, or the governor of a city, you would glory in that, and benefit by it in important situations, so consider what it means to be loved by the Lord of All the Worlds!

4. He becomes a trustee for the servant, managing all his affairs.

5. He becomes for the servant a guarantor of sustenance, which He provides for him from situation to situation, without imposing any trouble or burden.

6. He becomes a defender for the servant, protecting him from every foe and shielding him from everyone with bad intent.

7. He becomes an intimate friend for the servant, who is therefore never lonely and fears no change or alteration.

8. The servant is blessed with personal esteem, so he is not degraded by the service of this world and its people. Indeed, it would not please him to be served by the kings of this world and its tyrants.

9. The servant is blessed with lofty aspiration, so he rises above being stained by the filth of this world and its people. He takes no interest in its vanities and its amusements. Like sensible men, he rises above the playgrounds of boys and women.

10. The servant acquires richness of the heart, so he becomes richer than every rich man in this world. He always feels happy and spacious in the breast. No mishap alarms him and no deprivation worries him.

11. The servant receives the light of the heart, so he is guided by that light to many kinds of knowledge, secrets and wisdom, to some of which others are not guided, except with tremendous effort and over a long span of life.

12. The servant enjoys expansiveness of the breast, so he does not feel constricted by any of this world's trials and misfortunes, nor by people's vexations and machinations.

13. The servant acquires dignity and respect in people's hearts, so the best and the worst of them revere him, and every Pharaoh and tyrant is in awe of him.

14. The servant enjoys loving affection in people's hearts. The All-Merciful instils affection for him, so you see all their hearts disposed to

love him, and all their instincts moved to treat him with reverence and honour.

15. The servant derives blessing from everything in general, be it a word, a deed, an article of clothing, or a place. He derives benefit even from a speck of dust on which he treads, a place where he rests for a day, and a person who befriends him and sees him for a while.

16. The servant has the earth at his disposal, both on land and at sea, so he may travel through the air, if he wishes, or walk on the water, or cross the face of the earth in less than an hour.

17. The servant has the animals at his disposal, be they predators and savage beasts, or reptiles and the like, so the wild beasts love him and the lions wag their tails for him.

18. The servant has the keys of the earth in his possession. If he wishes for two treasures, he has only to strike with his hand, and if he needs a spring of water, he has only to stamp with his foot. Wherever he alights, a table is set before him, if he wishes to dine.

19. The servant is endowed with leadership and prestige at the door of the Lord of Might and Glory, so people depend on his service to gain access to Allāh (Exalted is He), and on his prestige and his grace to obtain satisfaction of their needs from Allāh (Exalted is He).

20. The servant is guaranteed a response from Allāh (Exalted is He) to his supplication, so he never asks Allāh (Exalted is He) for anything without His giving it to him, and he never intercedes on anyone's behalf without his intercession being accepted. If he swore a solemn oath by Allāh (Exalted is He), He would grant him what he wished. It could even happen that, if such a servant pointed to a mountain, it would disappear, for he does not need to ask with the tongue. If something occurred to him, it would be realized, so he would not even need to gesture with his hand.

These [first twenty] are gracious gifts of honour in this world. The following are granted in the Hereafter:

21. First of all, Allāh eases for the servant the agonies of death, of which the hearts of the Prophets (blessings and peace be upon them all) were afraid, so they asked Allāh to make them easy for them. For some, death may be like a drink of cool water for the thirsty. Allāh (Almighty and Glorious is He) has said:

Those whom the angels cause to die when good.
alladhīna tatawaffā-humu 'l-malā'ikatu ṭayyibīna. (16:32)

22. Confirmation in true knowledge and faith, the prospect of losing which is the cause of all fear and alarm, of all weeping and anguish. Allāh has said (More Glorious is He than any other sayer):

Allāh confirms those who believe,
yuthabbitu 'llāhu 'lladhīna āmanū
with the Word that stands firm,
bi'l-qawli 'th-thābiti
in the life of this world
fi 'l-ḥayāti 'd-dunyā
and in the Hereafter.
wa fi 'l-ākhira. (14:27)

23. The delivery of spiritual comfort, fragrant perfume, good tidings, good pleasure and reassurance. As He has said (Glory be to Him and Exalted is He):

The angels keep coming down to say:
tatanazzalu ʿalai-himu 'l-malā'ikatu allā takhāfū
"Do not fear and do not grieve, but hear
wa lā taḥzanū wa abshirū
good tidings of the Garden [of Paradise]
bi'l-jannati 'llatī
that you have been promised."
kuntum tūʿadūn. (41:30)

The servant is therefore not afraid of what awaits him in the Hereafter, not does he grieve for what he has left behind in this world.

24. Everlasting life in the Gardens of Paradise and the proximity of the All-Merciful.

25. There is splendour in the secret realm for the servant's spirit, which ascends above the angels of the heavens and the earth in honour, grace and blessing. There is also splendour in the external realm for his physical body, through the celebration of its funeral procession, the thronging of the congregation at the funeral prayer held over it, and prompt attention to its preparation for burial, by which people hope to gain abundant reward, and which they count as an enormous bounty.

26. Immunity from the torment of the interrogation in the grave, and instruction in how to answer correctly. The servant is thereby kept safe from that terror.

27. The widening and illumination of the grave, so that the servant will be in one of the meadows of the Garden of Paradise until the Day of Resurrection.

28. The entertainment and honourable reception of the servant's spirit and its breath of life, for it will be installed in the abdomens of green birds, together with the righteous brethren, rejoicing and welcoming the gracious favour that Allāh has brought them.

29. Resurrection in glory and honour, wearing fine garments and a crown, and riding a heavenly steed [*burāq*].

30. Fairness of the face and its radiant light. Allāh (Exalted is He) has said:

> That day will faces be resplendent,
> *wujūhun yawma'idhin nāḍira:*
> looking towards their Lord.
> *ilā Rabbi-hā nāẓira.* (75:22,23)
>
> Some faces on that day will shine,
> *wujūhun yawma'idhin musfira:*
> laughing, joyous.
> *ḍāḥikatun mustabshira.* (80:38,39)

31. Security from the terrors of the Day of Resurrection. Allāh (Exalted is He) has said:

> Or he who comes secure on the Day of Resurrection?
> *am man ya'tī āminan Yawm al-Qiyāma.* (41:40)

32. Receiving the record with the right hand. Some of them will be spared the record altogether.

33. Facilitation of the reckoning. Some of them will not be subjected to any reckoning at all.

34. Weighing in the Balance. Some of them will not be weighed at all.

35. Delivery of the Basin [*Ḥawḍ*] to the Prophet (Allāh bless him and give him peace). The servant will drink a drink after which he will never be thirsty again.

36. Crossing the Narrow Bridge [*Ṣirāṭ*] and salvation from the Fire of Hell. Some of them will not even hear its sizzling sound. They will be everlastingly in what their souls desired, and the Fire will abate for them.

37. Intercession on the fields of the Resurrection, like the intercession of the Prophets and the Messengers.

38. The estate of eternity in the Garden of Paradise.
39. The greatest satisfaction.
40. Meeting the Lord of All the Worlds, the God of the first and the last, without qualification [*bi-lā kaif*] (Magnificent is His Majesty).

I have recounted all that to the best of my understanding and the full extent of my knowledge, with all its shortcoming and deficiency. I have nevertheless summarized and abridged the subject matter, and mentioned only the essentials and the main points. If I had treated some of that in detail, the book would not have contained it. For instance, you will notice that I have listed the estate of eternity [#38 above] as one single mark of honour. If I described it in detail, it would amount to forty marks of honour, including the radiance of the houries [*ḥūr*], the palaces, the fine garments, and so on. Every item includes many details that are comprehended by none but the Knower of the unseen and the visible, the One who is their Creator and their Owner. How can we desire to know all that, when our Lord (Glory be to Him) tells us:

> So no soul knows what comfort is kept
> *fa-lā taʿlamu nafsun mā ukhfiya*
> secretly in store for them,
> *la-hum min qurrati aʿyun:*
> as a reward for what they used to do.
> *jazāʾan bi-mā kānū yaʿmalūn.* (32:17)?

Allāh's Messenger (Allāh bless him and give him peace) has said:

> He has created in it [the Garden of Paradise] that which no eye has ever seen, of which no ear has heard, and which has never occurred to any human heart.

Concerning His saying (Exalted is He):

> The sea would be used up before
> *la-nafida 'l-baḥru qabla*
> the words of my Lord were exhausted.
> *an tanfada kalimāti Rabbī.* (18:109)

—the commentators have said: "These are the words that Allāh (Exalted is He) will say to the people of the Garden, within the Garden, with gracious kindness and honour."

Such is the condition of the estate of eternity, so how can we grasp even one out of a million parts of it, when we are merely human, or how can the knowledge of a creature comprehend it? No indeed, our aspirations wane, and our minds fall short of it, and it is right and proper that it should be that way. The estate of eternity is the gift of the Almighty, the All-Knowing, in accordance with His tremendous favour and His sempiternal generosity.

However hard the workers work and the strivers strive for the sake of this momentous goal, they must know that all their effort is the least of the least beside what they need, what they seek and what they undertake. They must know that four things are indispensable to the servant: (1) knowledge, (2) work, (3) sincerity, (4) fear.

1. First of all, he must know the path; otherwise he is blind.
2. He must put his knowledge into practice; otherwise he is blocked.
3. He must be sincere in his work; otherwise he is misled.
4. He must not cease to be afraid and on guard against disasters, until he finds safety; otherwise he is deluded.

Dhu'n-Nūn spoke the truth when he said: "All creatures are dead, except the scholars. All the scholars are asleep, except those who put their knowledge into practice. All those who put their knowledge into practice are deluded, except those who are sincere. All those who are sincere are in tremendous danger."

Four people really make me wonder about them:

1. An intelligent person who is not a scholar. Has he no interest in knowing and understanding what lies in front of him? Why does he not investigate what he will experience after death, by studying these signs and admonitions, listening to these Qur᾽ānic verses [*āyāt*] and warnings, and checking these notions and suggestions in the lower self? Allāh (Exalted is He) has said:

> Have they not considered
> *a-wa lam yanẓurū*
> the dominion of the heavens and the earth,
> *fī malakūti 's-samāwāti wa 'l-arḍi*
> and what things Allāh has created?
> *wa mā khalaqa 'llāhu min shai᾽in.* (7:185)

> Do they not think that they shall be raised up
> *a-lā yaẓunnu ulā᾽ika anna-hum mab῾ūthūna*
> one awful day?
> *li-yawmin ῾aẓīm.* (83:4,5)

2. A scholar who does not put his knowledge into practice. Does he not consider what he knows for certain about what lies in front of him, in the form of stupendous terrors and difficult hurdles? This is the important information that you are discarding!

3. Someone who works, but is not sincere. Does he not heed the saying of Allāh (Exalted is He):

> So whoever hopes for the meeting with his Lord,
> *fa-man kāna yarjū liqā'a Rabbi-hi*
> let him do righteous work,
> *fa-'l-ya'mal 'amalan ṣāliḥan*
> and let him give no one any share at all
> *wa lā yushrik*
> in the worship due unto his Lord.
> *bi-'ibādati Rabbi-hi aḥadā.* (18:110)?

4. Someone who is sincere, but not afraid. Does he not notice how Allāh (Magnificent is His Majesty) treats His special friends, His saints and His servants, who show the way between Him and His creatures? As He says to [the Prophet (Allāh bless him and give him peace)] the noblest of creatures in His sight:

> It has been revealed to you
> *wa la-qad ūḥiya ilai-ka*
> as to those before you:
> *wa ila 'lladhīna min qabli-k:*
> If you ascribe a partner to Allāh your work will fail
> *la-in ashrakta la-yaḥbaṭanna 'amalu-ka*
> and you will be among the losers.
> *wa la-takūnanna mina 'l-khāsirīn.*
> Oh no! Allāh you must serve,
> *bali 'llāha fa-''bud*
> and be among the thankful.
> *wa kun mina 'sh-shākirīn.* (39:65,66)

It is related that the Prophet (Allāh bless him and give him peace) used to say:

> [The Sūra entitled] Hūd and its sisters have turned my hair grey!

The gist of the matter, as well as its detailed explanation, is contained in what the Lord of All the Worlds has said in four verses [*āyāt*] of the Mighty Book:

1. His saying (Almighty and Glorious is He):

What, did you suppose
a-fa-ḥasibtum
that We had created you for idle sport,
anna-mā khalaqnā-kum ʿabathan
and that you would not be returned to Us?
wa anna-kum ilai-nā lā turjaʿūn. (23:115)

2. His saying (Glorious is His Name):

And let every soul consider
wa 'l-tanẓur nafsun
what it has forwarded for the day ahead.
mā qaddamat li-ghad:
And practise true devotion to Allāh.
wa 'ttaqu 'llāh:
Allāh is indeed Aware of what you do.
inna 'llāha Khabīrun bi-mā taʿmalūn. (59:18)

3. His saying (More Glorious is He than any other sayer):

And as for those who strive in Our cause,
wa 'lladhīna jāhadū fī-nā
surely We shall guide them in Our ways.
la-nahdiyanna-hum subula-nā. (29:69)

4. He summed it all up when He said (He is the Most Truthful of sayers):

And whoever strives, strives only for himself,
wa man jāhada fa-inna-mā yujāhidu li-nafsi-h:
for Allāh is altogether Independent of creatures.
inna 'llāha la-Ghaniyyun ʿani 'l-ʿalamīn. (29:6)

We seek forgiveness from Allāh (Exalted is He) for every slip of the foot, or transgression of the pen. We seek His forgiveness for all our sayings that do not match our deeds. We seek His forgiveness for all that we have claimed and pretended to understand about the knowledge of Allāh's religion (Exalted is He), despite our shortcoming therein. We seek His forgiveness for every notion that has made us guilty of affectation and pretence in a book we have written, or a speech we have composed, or a teaching we have taught. We beg Him to cause us, and you, O brethren, to put what we know into practice, with the sole intention of pleasing Him. We beg Him not to weigh that as a heavy load against us, but to set it in the scale of righteous deeds, when our deeds are returned to Him. He is indeed Munificent, All-Generous!

The Shaikh [Imām al-Ghazālī] (may Allāh be well pleased with him) concluded this work by saying:

"This is what we intended to mention, in explaining the nature of the journey on the path of the Hereafter, and we have been enabled to achieve the goal. Praise be to Allāh, for by His favour good works are accomplished, and blessings descend by His grace. May Allāh bless the best of those born into this world, who summoned his fellow human beings to the Most Excellent Master; that is to say, may He bless the Prophet Muḥammad and his family, and grant them much good and blessed peace in every situation."

About the Translator

Muhtar Holland was born in 1935, in the ancient city of Durham in the North East of England. This statement may be considered anachronistic, however, since he did not bear the name Muhtar until 1969, when he was moved—by powerful experiences in the *latihan kejiwaan* of Subud—to embrace the religion of Islām.*

At the age of four, according to an entry in his father's diary, he said to a man who asked his name: "I'm a stranger to myself." During his years at school, he was drawn most strongly to the study of languages, which seemed to offer signposts to guide the stranger on his "Journey Home," apart from their practical usefulness to one who loved to spend his vacations traveling—at first on a bicycle—through foreign lands. Serious courses in Latin, Greek, French, Spanish and Danish, with additional smatterings of Anglo-Saxon, Italian, German and Dutch. Travels in France, Germany, Belgium, Holland and Denmark. Then a State Scholarship and up to Balliol College, Oxford, for a degree course centered on the study of Arabic and Turkish. Travels in Turkey and Syria. Then National Service in the Royal Navy, with most of the two years spent on an intensive course in the Russian language.

In the years since graduation from Oxford and Her Majesty's Senior Service, Mr. Holland has held academic posts at the University of Toronto, Canada; at the School of Oriental and African Studies in the University of London, England (with a five-month leave to study Islamic Law in Cairo, Egypt); and at the Universiti Kebangsaan in Kuala Lumpur, Malaysia (followed by a six-month sojourn in Indonesia). He also worked as Senior Research Fellow at the Islamic Foundation in Leicester, England, and as Director of the Nūr al-Islām Translation Center in Valley Cottage, New York.

* The name Muhtar was received at that time from Bapak Muhammad Subuh Sumohadiwidjojo, of Wisma Subud, Jakarta, in response to a request for a suitable Muslim name. In strict academic transliteration from the Arabic, the spelling would be *Mukhtār*. The form *Muchtar* is probably more common in Indonesia than *Muhtar*, which happens to coincide with the modern Turkish spelling of the name.

His freelance activities have mostly been devoted to writing and translating in various parts of the world, including Scotland and California. He made his Pilgrimage *[Ḥajj]* to Mecca in 1980.

Published works include the following:

Al-Ghazālī. *On the Duties of Brotherhood*. Translated from the Classical Arabic by Muhtar Holland. London: Latimer New Dimensions, 1975. New York: Overlook Press, 1977. Repr. 1980 and 1993.

Sheikh Muzaffer Ozak al-Jerrahi. *The Unveiling of Love*. Translated from the Turkish by Muhtar Holland. New York: Inner Traditions, 1981. Westport, Ct.: Pir Publications, 1990.

Ibn Taymīya. *Public Duties in Islām*. Translated from the Arabic by Muhtar Holland. Leicester, England: Islamic Foundation, 1982.

Hasan Shushud. *Masters of Wisdom of Central Asia*. Translated from the Turkish by Muhtar Holland. Ellingstring, England: Coombe Springs Press, 1983.

Al-Ghazālī. *Inner Dimensions of Islamic Worship*. Translated from the Arabic by Muhtar Holland. Leicester, England: Islamic Foundation, 1983.

Sheikh Muzaffer Ozak al-Jerrahi. *Irshād*. Translated [from the Turkish] with an Introduction by Muhtar Holland. Warwick, New York: Amity House, 1988. Westport, Ct.: Pir Publications, 1990.

Sheikh Muzaffer Ozak al-Jerrahi. *Blessed Virgin Mary*. Translation from the original Turkish by Muhtar Holland. Westport, Ct.: Pir Publications, 1991.

Sheikh Muzaffer Ozak al-Jerrahi. *The Garden of Dervishes*. Translation from the original Turkish by Muhtar Holland. Westport, Ct.: Pir Publications, 1991.

Sheikh Muzaffer Ozak al-Jerrahi. *Adornment of Hearts*. Translation from the original Turkish by Muhtar Holland and Sixtina Friedrich. Westport, Ct.: Pir Publications, 1991.

Sheikh Muzaffer Ozak al-Jerrahi. *Ashki's Divan*. Translation from the Original Turkish by Muhtar Holland and Sixtina Friedrich. Westport, Ct.: Pir Publications, 1991.

Shaikh ʿAbd al-Qādir al-Jīlānī. *Revelations of the Unseen (Futūḥ al-Ghaib)*. Translated from the Arabic by Muhtar Holland. Houston, Texas: Al-Baz Publishing, Inc., 1992. Second edition, Fort Lauderdale, Florida: Al-Baz Publishing, Inc., 1998.

Shaikh ʿAbd al-Qādir al-Jīlānī. *The Sublime Revelation (al-Fatḥ ar-Rabbānī)*. Translated from the Arabic by Muhtar Holland. Houston, Texas: Al-Baz Publishing, Inc., 1992. Second edition, Fort Lauderdale, Florida: Al-Baz Publishing, Inc., 1998.

Shaikh ʿAbd al-Qādir al-Jīlānī. *Utterances (Malfūẓāt)*. Translated from the Arabic by Muhtar Holland. Houston, Texas: Al-Baz Publishing, Inc., 1992. Second edition, Fort Lauderdale, Florida: Al-Baz Publishing, Inc., 1998.

Shaikh ʿAbd al-Qādir al-Jīlānī. *The Removal of Cares (Jalāʾ al-Khawāṭir)*. Translated from the Arabic by Muhtar Holland. Ft. Lauderdale, Florida: Al-Baz Publishing, Inc., 1997.

Shaikh ʿAbd al-Qādir al-Jīlānī. *Sufficient Provision for Seekers of the Path of Truth (Al-Ghunya li-Ṭālibī Ṭarīq al-Ḥaqq)*. Translated from the Arabic (in 5 vols.) by Muhtar Holland. Hollywood, Florida: Al-Baz Publishing, Inc., 1997.

Shaikh ʿAbd al-Qādir al-Jīlānī. *Fifteen Letters* (*Khamsata ʿAshara Maktūban*). Translated from the Arabic by Muhtar Holland. Hollywood, Florida: Al-Baz Publishing, Inc., 1997.

Shaikh Walī Raslān ad-Dimashqī. *Concerning the Affirmation of Divine Oneness (Risāla fi't-Tawḥīd)*. Translated from the Arabic by Muhtar Holland. Hollywood, Florida: Al-Baz Publishing, Inc., 1997.

Al-Ghazālī. *The Proper Conduct of Marriage in Islām* (*Ādāb an-Nikāḥ*). (Book twelve of *Iḥyāʾ ʿUlūm ad-Dīn*). Translated from the Arabic by Muhtar Holland. Hollywood, Florida: Al-Baz Publishing, Inc., 1998.

Shaikh Muḥammad ibn Yaḥyā at-Tādifī. *Necklaces of Gems (Qalāʾid al-Jawāhir)*. Translated from the Arabic by Muhtar Holland. Fort Lauderdale, Florida: Al-Baz Publishing, Inc., 1998.

Shaikh Aḥmad Fatḥu'llāh Jāmī. *The Call to the Believers in the Clear Qurʾān (Nidāʾ al-Muʾminīn fi 'l-Qurʾān al-Mubīn)*. Translated from the Arabic by Muhtar Holland. Fort Lauderdale, Florida: Al-Baz Publishing, Inc., 2000.

Ismāʿīl Muḥammad Saʿīd al-Qādirī. *Emanations of Lordly Grace (Al-Fuyūḍāt ar-Rabbāniyya)*. Translated from the Arabic by Muhtar Holland. Fort Lauderdale, Florida: Al-Baz Publishing, Inc., 2000.

Shaikh ʿAbd al-Qādir al-Jīlānī. *The Book of the Secret of Secrets and the Manifestation of Lights* (*Kitāb Sirr al-Asrār wa Maẓhar al-Anwār*). Translated from the Arabic by Muhtar Holland. Fort Lauderdale, Florida: Al-Baz Publishing, Inc., 2000.

Al-Ghazālī. *The Path of the Worshipful Servants to the Garden of the Lord of All the Worlds* (*Minhāj al-Ābidīn ilā Jannati Rabbi 'l-ʿĀlamīn*). Translated from the Arabic by Muhtar Holland. Fort Lauderdale, Florida: Al-Baz Publishing, Inc., 2000.

BOOKS PUBLISHED BY AL-BAZ PUBLISHING INCLUDE:

1. **Revelations of the Unseen** (*Futūḥ al-Ghaib*) $20.00
   78 Discourses by Shaikh ʿAbd al-Qādir al-Jīlānī
2. **The Sublime Revelation** (*Al-Fatḥ ar-Rabbānī*) $29.00
   62 Discourses by Shaikh ʿAbd al-Qādir al-Jīlānī
3. **Utterances of Shaikh ʿAbd al-Qādir** (*Malfūẓāt*) $18.00
4. **The Removal of Cares** (*Jalāʾ al-Khawāṭir*) $24.95
   45 Discourses by Shaikh ʿAbd al-Qādir al-Jīlānī
5. **Sufficient Provision for Seekers of the Path of Truth**
   (*Al-Ghunya li-Ṭālibī Ṭarīq al-Ḥaqq*) $125.00 Set
   by Shaikh ʿAbd al-Qādir al-Jīlānī (may Allāh be well pleased with him)
   This encyclopedic work is a complete resource on the inner and outer aspects of Islām. The translation has been published in 5 volumes. Translated by Muhtar Holland and over five and a half years in the translating, this work is undoubtedly the publishing event of this century and a treasure of unimaginable value to the believers. 1738 pages.
6. **Fifteen Letters** $12.00
   (*Khamsata ʿAshara Maktūban* otherwise known as *Maktūbāt*)
   Fifteen letters by Shaikh ʿAbd al-Qādir al-Jīlānī to one of his disciples. Originally written in Persian, they were translated into Arabic by ʿAlī Ḥusāmu'd-dīn al-Muttaqī (the Devout), who said of them, "... these letters comprise nuggets of wisdom and spiritual counsel, couched in various forms of allegory, metaphor, paraphrase and quotation, including approximately two hundred and seventy-five Qurʾānic verses. They also contain allusions to the experiences *[adhwāq]* and spiritual states *[ḥālāt]* of the Ṣūfis (may Allāh's good pleasure be conferred upon them all). Translated by Muhtar Holland.
7. **Concerning the Affirmation of Divine Oneness** $15.00
   (*Risāla fi't-Tawḥīd*)
   by Shaikh Walī Raslān ad-Dimashqī (d. A.H. 540)
   This is a Risāla on *shirk khafī* (hidden *shirk*). *Shirk* is associating partners with Allāh. Also in the book is a commentary by Shaikh Zakariyyāʾ al-Anṣārī (d. A.H. 926) called *Kitāb Fatḥ ar-Raḥmān*. Also in the book is a commentary by Shaikh ʿAlī ibn ʿAṭiyya ʿAlawān al-Ḥamawī (d. A.H. 936) called *Sharḥ Fatḥ ar-Raḥmān*. This is a very important book. Translated by Muhtar Holland.

8. **The Proper Conduct of Marriage in Islām** $18.00
(Ādāb an-Nikāḥ)
by Imām al-Ghazālī
This is Book 12 of *Iḥyā' 'Ulūm ad-Dīn*. Translated by Muhtar Holland.

9. **The Most Beautiful Names of God** $11.00/12.50
(Al-Asmā' al-Ḥusnā)
by Jamā'a Majhūla
A chanted recital of the 99 Names of Allāh. Vocals only; men and boys
Track 2: The Boundless Grace of al-Qur'ān
Audio tape and CD.

10. **Necklaces of Gems** $29.95
(Qalā'id al-Jawāhir)
by Shaikh Muḥammad ibn Yaḥyā at-Tādifī (d. A.H. 963)
A Biography of Shaikh 'Abd al-Qādir al-Jīlānī (may Allāh be well pleased with him), on the Marvelous Exploits of the Crown of the Saints, the Treasure-trove of the Pure, the Sulṭān of the *Awliyā'*, the Sublime *Quṭb*, Shaikh Muḥyi'd-dīn 'Abd al-Qādir al-Jīlānī. Translated by Muhtar Holland.

11. **Emanations of Lordly Grace** $29.00
(al-Fuyūḍāt ar-Rabbāniyya)
by Ismā'īl Muḥammad Sa'īd al-Qādirī
A collection of the work and explanations of Shaikh 'Abd al-Qādir al-Jīlānī (may Allāh be well pleased with him), that includes definition and attributes of the seven selves *[nafs]*, an explanation of the names of the seven stations *[maqāmāt]*, the creed *['aqīda]* of the Supreme Helper (may Allāh be well pleased with him), the meaning of the names of the Qādiriyya order, the remarkable virtues of al-Jīlānī the *Quṭb*, the names of our master, 'Abd al-Qādir, litanies *[awrād]* for the taming of hearts and for emergency situations; how to offer the greeting of peace *[salām]*to the men of the unseen *[Ghaib]* and much much more. Translated by Muhtar Holland.

12. **The Call to the Believers in the Clear Qur'ān** $35.00/39.00
(Nidā' al-Mu'minīn fi 'l-Qur'ān al-Mubīn)
by Shaikh Aḥmad Fatḥu'llāh Jāmī
Shaikh Aḥmad Fatḥu'llāh Jāmī is the Shaikh of the Shādhilī Order, the native of Mush [in Eastern Turkey], the Khālidī by descent, the Shāfi'ī by school of Islāmic Law, the resident of Marash. In the clear and Glorious Qur'ān, eighty-nine verses [*āyāt*] bear the explicit address: "O you who believe..." [*yā ayyuha 'lladhīna āmanū*]. The author provides a thorough and enlightening commentary [*tafsīr*] for each and every one of these. This is the first book in our "Living Shaikh Series." 968 pages, translated by Muhtar Holland.

13. The Book of the Secret of Secrets and the Manifestation of Lights $17.00

(Kitāb Sirr al-Asrār wa Maẓhar al-Anwār)

by Shaikh ʿAbd al-Qādir al-Jīlānī

The Muhtar Holland English translation of this precious work. Although there has been previously published an English interpretation by respected Shaikh Tosun Bayrak, this is the first actual translation into the English language and includes transliteration of all Arabic key words. The contents are too diverse to describe here, but include: The shops of the spirit in the body; Division of knowledge into knowledge on the tongue and knowledge in the inner core; The number of the sciences; Explanation of the Sacred Law [*Sharīʿa*], the Spiritual Path [*Ṭarīqa*], Direct Knowledge [*Maʿrifa*] and Reality [*Ḥaqīqa*]; Concerning the people of spiritual culture [*taṣawwuf*]; The difference between the ascetics and the people of intimate knowledge; Meanings of the term *taṣawwuf*; The five tokens of bliss; The tokens of misery; The four domains, the spirits, the manifestations, the intellects and so on. This is a most important book for anyone traveling the spiritual path. Twenty-four sections.

14 Beads of Dew from the Source of Life **$25.00**

(*Rashāḥat ʿAin al-Ḥayāt*)

by Mawlāna ʿAlī Ibn Ḥusain Ṣafī.

ʿAlī ibn Ḥusain Ṣafī, the author of the Rashaḥāt, lived in the beginning of the 10th Century AH. He was brother-in-law of the famous mystic and poet Jāmī who gave him the name 'Ṣafī'. In the Rashaḥāt ʿAin al-Ḥayāt, Ṣafī gives an account of the lives and teachings of a group of Ṣūfī mystics known as the Khwājagān – the Masters of Wisdom. The Khwājagān lived in Central Asia between the 4th and the 9th centuries Hijri. The ranks of the Khwājagān include the great sufis ʿAbd al-Khāliq al-Ghujdawānī and Bahaʾ ad-Dīn Naqshband, who gave his name to the Naqshbandi order, though he did not found it. The many branches of the Naqshbandiyya survive to this day. This book is the first translation of the Rashaḥāt into English and provides the present generation with clear and precise biographies of the great and genuine Ṣūfīs who emerged in Turkestan at a most significant period.

For further titles, check our web site at www.albaz.com. Orders or enquiries, or to be placed on our mailing list, contact:

Al-Baz Publishing, Inc.
1516 NE 38th Street
Oakland Park, Florida 33303-0348

Phone: (425) 891-5444
E-mail: albaz@bellsouth.net